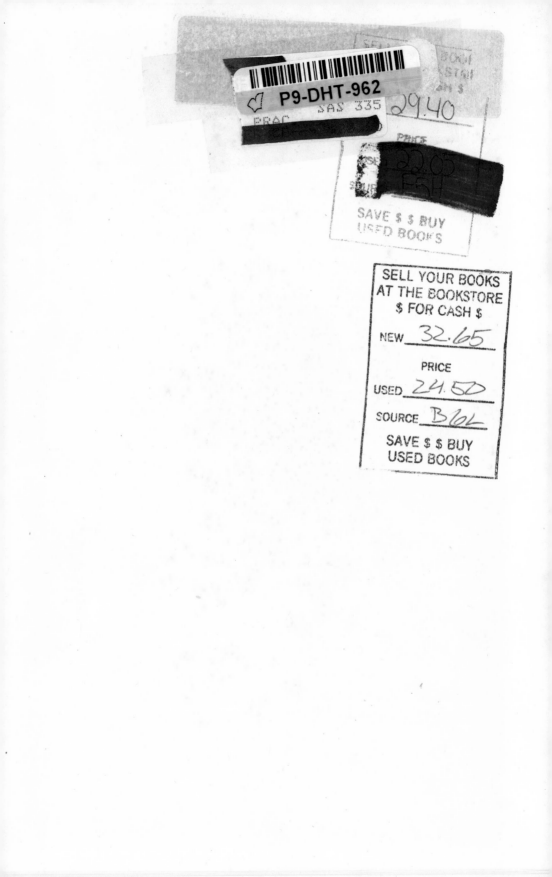

P9-DHT-962

PRAC     SAS 335     29.40

PRICE

SAVE $ $ BUY
USED BOOKS

# An Introduction to Group Work Practice

**RONALD W. TOSELAND**
*State University of New York at Albany*

**ROBERT F. RIVAS**
*Siena College*

*MACMILLAN PUBLISHING COMPANY*
*New York*

*COLLIER MACMILLAN PUBLISHERS*
*London*

*To our parents,*
*Stella and Ed,*
*Marg and Al*

Macmillan Publishing Company
866 Third Avenue, New York, New York 10022

Collier Macmillan Canada, Inc.


**Library of Congress Cataloging in Publication Data**

Toseland, Ronald W.
   An introduction to group work practice.

   Bibliography: p.
   1. Social group work. 2. Leadership. I. Rivas,
Robert F. II. Title.
HV45.T68 1984          361.4          83-14850
ISBN 0-02-421130-3

Printing: 1 2 3 4 5 6 7 8     Year: 4 5 6 7 8 9 0 1 2

ISBN   0-02-421130-3

# Foreword

*by Max Siporin*

This book expresses a major paradigmatic shift that is taking place in the human service professions, particularly in social work, with regard to helping people through the use of groups.

For several decades, work with groups has been a neglected child. Such work has almost been lost in the focus on psychotherapy of the individual person, including family therapy, as well as in the development of "generic" social work. Although groups have been widely used in many service settings, their primary function has been to serve as a context, rather than as a medium or instrument, of the helping process.

More recently, there have been increasing expressions of sentiment and need for a re-emphasis of group processes in group work practice, and a recommitment to such basic values as social interdependence, reciprocity, altruism, and solidarity. The authors have chosen to use the term *group work* as a way of making such work stand out as a mode and instrument of helping practice in which group processes are used for the realization of these basic values and the attainment of helping goals. They thus have placed their work within the historical mainstream of group work in social work, with its dual concern for social cause and technical function.

Today there is a rediscovery of the major importance of group membership, group roles, identities, and relationships for the optimal psychosocial functioning of all·human beings. The current social scene of economic depression, frightening world-wide violence, technological and sociocultural change, and what appears to be extensive societal and family breakdown— these trends have accentuated the need for and advantages of group membership and solidarity.

From this perspective, Ronald W. Toseland and Robert F. Rivas have formulated an approach to the helping process with a three-fold, interrelated focus: on individuals as group members, on groups as social units, and on individuals and groups in relation to their social situations. Such an orientation constitutes a traditional person-in-situation perspective within social work, what is now termed an "ecological systems" approach. It also expresses and helps to realize the social work value system, with its emphasis on human worth and dignity and on acceptance of diversity and collaborative interdependence.

This systems framework facilitates a theoretical eclecticism and a fruitful use of psychodynamic, behavioral, and other orientations and procedures. It emphasizes the principles and procedures of situational interventions with groups. These group/situational interventions are pursued and accomplished in the interests of individual members, as well as for the benefit of their groups,organizations, communities, and welfare service systems. At the same time, this framework is open to the further development of theory and procedures based, hopefully, both on practice experience and on research.

In addition, the authors have given much more attention than others have done to describing helping practice using task as well as treatment groups, and using natural as well as formed helping groups. This book's typology of treatment and task groups, and its discussions of how these group characteristics influence change and leadership activities are a very helpful contribution. The authors also have situated group work in the context of the institutional social welfare service systems, in which it has its essential existence and its characteristic social purposes.

These considerations are important because of the fact that most social work helping activity takes place in organizational groups, with the social worker as a group member and/or group leader. The content of this book thus serves not only to aid the student and practitioner in learning and improving group leadership skills with clients directly, but also serves to aid in learning and improving both their membership and leadership skills within interventive groups and networks of many kinds.

The conception of group work presented here is further noteworthy in its theoretical integration of socioemotional and task purposes and of technical concerns. There are detailed, practical, and clear discussions of varied helping stage processes, of principles, skills, and interventive procedures. This material is presented with live illustrations of how these are to be used by the group leader, generically and differentially, with treatment and task groups. As much as possible, these discussions are grounded in a wide-ranging and impressive recourse to the literature and to scientific research findings.

The innovative presentation of procedures for assessment, for monitoring and evaluation, and for generalizing and maintaining the effects of change are fine examples of their abilities to combine and apply their considerable theoretical knowledge and the lessons of their solid empirical research and clinical practice experience. These chapters are a welcome aid for meeting the current demand for accountability and the emphasis on outcome measures. They offer a way of demonstrating practice effectiveness, but with a concern for what clients themselves feel and say in self-reports about their expectations and helping experience.

This book is a timely and outstanding contribution to the theory and practice of group work. It stands within a rich tradition of social work with groups, and also moves us forward to new fruitful perspectives on helping effectiveness in group services to clients.

# Preface

We decided to write this book because we believed that there was a need for an introductory text that would synthesize and integrate existing knowledge about the practice of group work. In order to present a coherent and organized overview of the field, we have developed a typology of treatment and task group practice. To integrate the diverse models of practice with treatment and task groups, we have developed an interactional model of group leadership which takes into account the many factors that influence how a group is conducted. In addition, we indicate that workers should attend to three focal areas when practicing with any type of treatment or task group: (1) the individual group member, (2) the group as a whole, and (3) the environment in which the group functions. The text suggests how workers can assess, intervene, and evaluate in each of these focal areas. This model of leadership is intended to build a bridge between the group-centered, process-oriented approaches and the individual member, structure-oriented approaches to group work practice.

Because we are keenly aware that students and practitioners want practical suggestions about how to proceed when leading and staffing groups, much of this book is devoted to explicating practical steps that can be taken at each phase of the group work process. This is most apparent in the chapters on the middle phase of treatment and task groups, where many specific intervention methods are described, but it is not lacking in our discussion of the other phases of group work practice. We have sought to provide a book that examines the knowledge base of group work practice and integrates and explicates the methods, skills, and techniques that are useful in leading different types of groups.

The ideas expressed in this book have evolved over many years of study and practice. Some of the earliest and most powerful influences that have shaped this effort have come about through our contact with Sheldon Rose, Alan Klein, and Bernard Hill. Their contribution to the development of our thoughts is evident throughout this book. Perhaps even more important, however, was their support and encouragement in the early years of our professional development and their belief in our ability to make a contribution to knowledge about group work practice.

The ideas expressed in this book were also greatly influenced by Margaret Hartford, Catherine Papell, Norma Lang, and Max Siporin, who spent a considerable amount of time reading a draft of the entire manuscript. Their detailed comments and incisive suggestions were invaluable.

Other colleagues took the time to read draft chapters of the text or to share pertinent material with us. Among these were Lester Brown, Bonnie Carlson, Mary Coppola, Liane Davis, Jeff Edleson, Roland Etcheverry, Burton Gummer, William Reid, Aaron Rosenblatt, Ed Sherman, and Barry Sherman. Their comments, reactions, and suggestions were also helpful in improving the quality of the book.

We are indebted to the many practitioners and students with whom we have worked over the years. Sharing practice experiences, discussing successes and failures, and giving and receiving constructive feedback helped us to improve our practice and to clarify the ideas presented in this text.

We would also like to acknowledge the material support and the encouragement given to us by our respective educational institutions. The administrative and supportive staff of both the School of Social Welfare of the State University of Albany and Siena College have played important roles in helping us accomplish this project. In particular we would like to acknowledge the editorial assistance of Dennis Chapman and the secretarial assistance of Joan Gorzynski, Jackie Jones, Marcia Masterson, Barbara Rogers, Cheryl Savini, Gail Texter, Margaret Venezia, and Mary Weseman in preparing the text for publication.

More than anyone else, we are especially grateful to our spouses, Sheryl Holland and Donna Allingham Rivas. Their insights have done much to enrich this book. Without their continuous support and encouragement, we would not have been able to complete this work.

R. W. T.<br>R. F. R.

# Contents

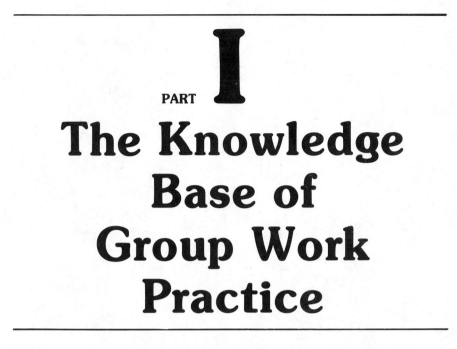

PART **I**

# The Knowledge Base of Group Work Practice

# 1

# Introduction

This text is concerned with the practice of group work by professional social workers. Group work entails the deliberate use of intervention strategies and group processes to accomplish individual and group goals utilizing the value base and ethical practice principles of the social work profession. As we prepare to become effective social work practitioners, it is important for us to realize the impact that groups have on our lives. It is not possible to be a member of society without becoming a member of numerous groups and becoming familiar with others. Although it is possible to live in an isolated manner on the fringes of groups, our social nature makes this neither desirable nor healthy.

Groups provide the structure on which communities and the larger society are built. They provide both formal and informal structure in the workplace. But more important, they provide a means through which relationships with significant others are carried out. Participation in family groups, peer groups, and classroom groups helps members to learn acceptable norms of social behavior, to engage in satisfying social relationships, to identify personal goals, and to derive a variety of other benefits that result from participating in closely knit social systems. Experiences with social groups, church groups, scouting, sports teams, and work groups are also important in the development and maintenance of people and society.

## THE FOCUS OF GROUP WORK PRACTICE

Social work practitioners use group work skills to help members meet their personal needs and to help groups accomplish their goals. In this text, group work is conceptualized from a broad perspective. Group work involves:

1. Practice with a wide variety of treatment and task groups.
2. Work in three focal areas, that is, with individual group members, the group as a whole, and the group's environment.
3. Utilization of generic skills for leading all types of treatment and task groups.
4. Integration and utilization of specialized skills from differing approaches to practice for leading specific groups in particular situations.

Viewing group work from a narrow focus is not conducive to developing a broad base of knowledge and skills that can be used when leading a variety of different groups. In many group work texts, little effort is made to examine the broad range of groups that may be used for helping purposes. Most texts make scant mention of task groups such as committees and teams, although these are common in practice settings. This text will examine the broad range of treatment and task groups with which workers may practice.

Some prominent group workers (Hartford, 1971; Shulman, 1979; Klein, 1972) focus on the group as a whole as the unit of intervention and place less emphasis on work with individuals in the group. Others place their emphasis on changing individual group members within the group context (Rose, 1977; Glasser, Sarri, and Vinter, 1974; Garvin, 1981). We believe both of these perspectives are useful. When leading any group, workers should direct their attention to individual group members, the group as a whole, and the environment in which the group functions. The worker focuses on individual members to assist them in accomplishing their goals. The worker intervenes with the group as a whole to achieve an optimum level of group functioning and to assure that the group accomplishes its purposes. The worker should also assess a group's environment and decide whether to help the group adapt to it or change it.

We believe that the purpose of the group helps to determine the emphasis that each of these focal areas should receive. For example, in a support group for recently separated persons, the worker may wish to focus on the development of mutual aid among members of the group as a whole. In an assertion training group, the worker may wish to focus on assessing members' specific skills and deficits and developing individualized treatment plans. In both cases, however, other focal areas should not be neglected. For example, in the support group it is necessary to help individual members develop plans for dealing with specific problems they are facing. In the assertion training group, it is important to enhance group cohesion, mutual sharing, and mutual aid in the group as a whole. In both groups, attention must also be given to the environment in which the group functions. Later in this text, we will examine in detail these three focal areas.

Another aspect of our conceptualization of group work practice is that workers should have a generic base of knowledge and skills that they can apply in a wide variety of treatment and task groups. Although generic skills are identified for both treatment and task groups throughout the text, there are other, more specialized skills that are appropriate for particular types of groups. These specialized skills, which have been selected from a variety of approaches to group work, are also explicated throughout this text.

Most experienced practitioners continue to learn by exposure to a variety of approaches to group work. Although some approaches to group work are not easily integrated with one another (behavioral and humanistic approaches), even widely divergent approaches have many commonalities. An eclectic use of specialized approaches can be helpful in deciding on the most effective methods to use when intervening in a particular group. Exclusive adherence to one approach may work very well for a particular group in a particular situation, but it may not always work well when leading other groups in different situations. Rigid adherence to one approach tends to make a worker blind to other potentially useful methods of working with groups. Rigidity can also distort a worker's assessment of a situation. A worker may mistakenly attempt to fit data from a situation to a particular practice approach, rather than choosing the practice approach to fit the situation. For these reasons, we believe that group workers can be most effective when they are familiar with a number of different approaches to group work, and when they apply specialized knowledge and skills differentially depending on the particular group work endeavor.

Our approach also recognizes the interactional nature of the helping process (Maluccio, 1979). The interactional model of group leadership presented in Chapter 4 suggests some of the factors that workers should consider when making decisions about how to proceed when leading a group.

## Values in Group Work Practice

In social work, the focus of group work practice is also influenced by a system of values. These values affect workers' styles of intervention and the skills they use in working with clients. They also affect clients' reactions to the worker's efforts.

Values are beliefs that delineate preferences about how one ought or ought not to behave. They refer to some goal that is worth or not worth attaining (Rokeach, 1968). There is no such thing as value-free group work practice. All group workers operate on the basis of certain specific assumptions and values regarding the nature of man, the role of members, and the role of the group leader. Values influence the methods that are used to accomplish group and individual goals. Even when a leader is completely permissive and nondirective, the worker's actions reveal values which are embodied in that type of stance.

A worker's actions in the group are affected by contextual values, client value systems, and the worker's personal value system (Morales and Sheafor, 1977). The context in which the group functions affects the values exhibited in the group. Contextual sources of values include the values of society, values of the agency sponsoring the group, and values of the social work profession. Brill (1973, p. 1) has mentioned four dominant values of American society. These include:

1. Judeo-Christian doctrine with its emphasis on the dignity and worth of people and people's responsibility for their neighbor.

2. Democratic values that emphasize equality and participation, including men's and women's rights to life, liberty, and the pursuit of happiness.
3. The Puritan ethic, which emphasizes men's and women's responsibility for themselves, and the central role of work in a moral life.
4. Social Darwinism, which emphasizes the survival of the strongest and the fittest in a long-term evolutionary process.

The agency or institution that is sponsoring the group is also a part of the contextual value system which can influence a worker's stance toward the group. Agencies have a history and a tradition with regard to the services they provide. Before proposing to begin a group, the worker should become familiar with the agency's formal and informal values, which are embodied in the agency's policies, procedures, and practices. Are treatment groups a preferred method of delivering therapeutic services? Are decisions often made in task groups consisting of staff members, or are decisions imposed on staff by the agency's administrators? Becoming aware of the policies, procedures, and practices regarding the use of groups in a particular agency can help the worker to prepare for possible resistance and to evaluate and utilize sources of support within the agency.

The worker and the group are also affected by professional values. The National Association of Social Workers has developed a code of ethics to guide members of the association in their functioning. The code of ethics is an operational statement of the central values of the social work profession. Some of the major social work values have been summarized by Max Siporin (1975) in his writings about ethical practice principles. These include respecting the worth and dignity of the individual, respecting a person's autonomy and self-direction, facilitating a person's participation in the helping process, maintaining a nonjudgmental attitude, assuring equal access to services and social provisions, and affirming the interdepencence of the individual and society.

Beyond the values held by all professional social work practitioners, group workers share a special concern and interest in certain values that are basic to group work practice. Some of the key values of group work have been stated by Gisela Konopka (1963, pp. 69–78). She suggests that all group workers should agree on the importance of:

1. Participation and positive relations among people of different color, creed, age, national origin, and social class in the group.
2. The value of cooperation and mutual decision making embodied in the principles of a participatory democracy.
3. The importance of individual initiative within the group.
4. The importance of freedom to participate, including expressing thoughts and feelings about matters of concern to individual members or the group as a whole, and having the right to be involved in the decision-making process of the group.
5. The value of high individualization in the group so that each member's unique concerns are addressed.

These values are not absent in other aspects of social work practice, but in group work they are of central importance. The group is uniquely suited for the exercise of these values, and all group workers should give them their careful attention.

In addition to values that are derived from the context of practice, members bring their own values to the group. Each individual has a unique value system, and it is not possible to identify a general or common value system for all group members. Often, members are not clear about their own values or they have not given their own values careful consideration. Part of the worker's task is to help members clarify their values and to identify and resolve value conflicts between individual members and within the group as a whole.

Although it is not possible to identify a common set of values for all group members, the worker should be especially sensitive to the effects that culture, race, and ethnicity can have on values. For example, Lewis and Ho (1977) point out that in the Native American culture, although cooperation is an important value, it is considered impolite to offer advice, help, or opinion to someone unless it is solicited. Giordano (1973) suggests that group members with Irish ethnic backgrounds often prefer not to express their feelings openly, whereas Italian Americans are more likely to express their feelings freely.

Workers' personal value systems also affect how they practice. If workers are uncomfortable discussing certain value-laden topics, or if they impose their own values on the group, their work will be seriously impaired. Similarly, if they are not aware of the implications of their values, they are likely to come into conflict with members who may have different values.

Workers who are not aware of their own values will also have difficulty when faced with ambiguous and value-laden situations. Sometimes, the goals of the worker, the agency, the community, and the group members differ. This is often so with involuntary clients who may be receiving the service of a worker at the request of law enforcement officials or others in the community who find the client's behavior unacceptable. The more clear workers are about their own values and their own purposes and stances in relation to working with the group, the easier it will be for them to sort through conflicting goals and make their own purposes known to group members.

One of the best ways for workers to become aware of their own values and their own stance in working with a group is to obtain supervision and consultation on their work. Although a worker will never become value-free, seeking out and utilizing supervision and consultation can help workers become aware of the values they bring to the group. Supervision can help workers to modify or change values that are not consistent with those of the social work profession or helpful to their practice. Value clarification exercises can also be helpful for identifying personal and professional values of workers that may influence their work with a group (see, for example, Smith, 1977).

## THE PRACTICE OF GROUP WORK

The practice principles presented in this text are based on social work practice theory. However, as a method of practice, group work is used by a wide variety of helping professionals. Nurses, psychologists, counselors, psychiatrists, teachers, clergy, and other helping professionals regularly employ treatment group methods in working with their clients. Managers, supervisors, administrators, staff development specialists, politicians, community organizers and other professionals employ task group methods to carry out the mandates of their organization and the functions of their jobs.

Although group work is utilized extensively in service delivery and agency functioning, it is infrequently identified as an important part of professional education and training. Nurses and physicians study medicine, teachers learn educational methods, managers and administrators concentrate on organizational theory; yet, when these professionals begin to carry out the functions of their jobs, they frequently rely on group work as a method of practice. Therefore, although this text is focused on group work in the context of social work practice, the study of groups and group work can be useful for practice in many different professions.

### Group Versus Individual Efforts

*Advantages and Disadvantages of Treatment Groups.* There are a number of advantages and disadvantages in using a group rather than an individual effort to help clients meet their needs and to help organizations accomplish their tasks. In relation to meeting client needs, Levine (1979, p. 11) suggests that "group therapy can help with most anything that individual therapy can, providing an appropriate group is available and the individual will accept the group as the mode of treatment." A number of writers have suggested that group treatment has advantages over individual treatment (see, for example, Northen, 1982; Yalom, 1975; Shulman, 1979; Lieberman and Borman, 1979). Groups help members to realize that they are not alone with their problems. They allow members to share their concerns and to hear that others have similar concerns (Yalom, 1975; Shulman, 1979). They also give members the opportunity to help others by being supportive, giving feedback, making helpful suggestions, and providing useful information. Liberman and Borman (1979) have noted the therapeutic benefit of the "helper-therapy principle" for members of groups that develop on a mutual aid basis. As members give and get help, they observe others achieving their goals. This process provides what Yalom (1975) refers to as an "installation of hope" which is absent in individual treatment.

Treatment groups provide other benefits that cannot be replicated in individual treatment. According to Northen (1982), group treatment is the preferred modality when the main problem of a client concerns relationships with others. The presence of others gives members a chance to receive feedback that can assist them in their change efforts. Peer feedback can be particularly beneficial for adolescents and involuntary adult clients who may resist the suggestions of the worker, because he or she is viewed as an authority figure (Northen, 1982). It can also be beneficial for those who face problems of social isolation, such as older persons who have lost peers and social roles, persons who have been removed from their families, and those in hospitals and other institutions.

Groups can be valuable because they allow members to engage in reality testing (Klein, 1972; Rose, 1977; Gilbert, Miller, and Specht, 1980). Groups can develop into "social microcosms" (Yalom, 1975) in which members recreate problems they have experienced in the outside world. This can enable members to work through previously unsatisfying relationships with family members, peers, or friends (Levine, 1979; Konopka, 1963).

Groups can provide members with multiple opportunities to engage in role playing, testing new skills and rehearsing new behaviors in the "safe" environment of the group (Rose, 1977). Members of groups also have an opportunity to learn about themselves through the experiences of others, which they see enacted in the group (Corey and Corey, 1977). Opportunities for vicarious learning are limited in individual treatment.

Although these advantages provide justification for utilizing group work in treatment, a number of potential disadvantages to group treatment should be considered. Groups can encourage member conformity (Corey and Corey, 1977) and member dependency (Klein, 1972). When members open themselves up to other members through self-disclosure, they are vulnerable to harmful or unsupportive responses from them (Corey and Corey, 1977). Groups can scapegoat individual members (Konopka, 1963). Groups sometimes focus on a few particularly assertive or talkative members, creating a danger that these members' problems receive attention whereas other, less assertive or less talkative members receive little help (Yalom, 1975; Shulman, 1979).

In general, members can benefit from treatment groups when they have some ability to communicate with others, and when their common concerns or problems lend themselves to group discussion. To the extent that certain group members, such as autistic children or schizophrenic adults, cannot communicate effectively, group work must be modified to include nonverbal program activities and, where appropriate, simple, brief verbal activities that are consistent with those members' skill level. People who have an extreme need for privacy or confidentiality may also be unable to take part in group treatment without considerable support or reassurance. Groups are contraindicated for people whose behavior is so alien to others that it results in negative rather than positive interactions, or when it leads to the failure of others to continue with the group.

***Advantages and Disadvantages of Task Groups.*** There are also advantages to a group as compared to an individual effort in helping agencies and organizations accomplish tasks. In working with people in organizational task groups, democratic participation is often ideologically desirable. Participation through group interaction helps members of organizations feel that they have a stake in the organization. Resistance to change can be minimized when those who are to be affected by change are given the opportunity to participate in the change through group discussion. (See Resnick and Patti, 1980, and Bennis, Benne, and Chin, 1969.)

Group discussion and group deliberation have other benefits. The increased quantity of information available in groups is often beneficial for generating alternative action plans, for problem solving, and for making decisions. Certain tasks are complex, requiring the pooling of talents, expertise, or opinions in order to be completed in a satisfactory manner (Kiesler, 1978). The division of labor that occurs in well-run groups can also assist members in completing tasks in a timely and efficient manner.

Some disadvantages should be kept in mind when considering selecting group rather than individual efforts for accomplishing tasks. For example, it has been suggested that group problem solving takes more time than individual problem solving (Hartford, 1971). Napier and Gershenfeld (1981) note that groups that are poorly run can make members feel frustrated, bored, or unappreciated. For example, groups that suffer from poor leadership often get little accomplished (Edson, 1977). Groups are also sometimes used to make simple decisions or solve simple problems that could be solved more quickly and efficiently by individuals. Under these conditions, group meetings can be costly to an organization and can be frustrating and unnecessary for group members.

In general, the advantages and disadvantages of group work should be evaluated in relation to a particular situation when deciding on whether or not it is the most appropriate method to use. The needs of the group members and the requirements of the task should be given paramount consideration when deciding whether or not to use group work. Although this text suggests that group work methods have a fairly wide applicability for many different types of client and organizational problems, these problems are sometimes best approached by using a number of different practice methods. Thus, although group work is a valuable method by itself, it is also valuable as part of larger planned change efforts that may use additional methods such as community organization or social casework to achieve particular goals. (See, for example, Siporin, 1975; Pincus and Minahan, 1973; Anderson, 1981; Germain and Gitterman, 1980; Hartford, 1978.)

## The Phases of Group Work

Group work can be conceptualized as a series of generic skills and activities carried out by the worker over the life of the group. Many writers use phase theory and suggest any number of phases for the practice of group work. We have found that it is helpful to conceptualize the practice of group work as consisting of four phases: (1) planning, (2) beginning, (3) middle, and (4) ending. These phases of group work correspond to predictable stages of group development; that is, groups exhibit certain properties and processes during the beginning, middle, and ending stages of their development. It is possible for the worker to use many of the same skills and activities throughout the life of the group (see, for instance, Shulman, 1979), but certain skills are more appropriately used during particular stages of a group's development (see, for instance, Shulman, 1981; Rivas and Toseland, 1981). Because group workers use stage-specific skills and activities, group work can be conceptualized as an orderly, sequential process. This occurs whether or not the worker is placed in a short-term or a long-term group or a group with open or closed membership.

This text is organized, in part, around the four phases of group work mentioned previously. Prior to discussing each phase, Part I of this text covers the knowledge base of group work practice. Chapter 1 introduces basic group work concepts and outlines the many types of groups that practitioners may work with in practice settings. Chapter 2 provides a basis for group work practice by examining the history and traditions of group work and by reviewing social science findings related to group processes. Chapter 3 provides a framework for examining group processes and group dynamics. Chapter 4 focuses on the processes and skills used in group leadership.

Part II examines the planning phase of group work practice. Chapter 5 explains the worker's activities in planning for the group. During the planning phase, the worker assesses the need for a group, considers potential group membership and sponsorship, and identifies the group's purpose. Additionally, the worker composes the group, recruits and orients members, and prepares for the first meeting by locating a suitable room and making other necessary arrangements.

Part III examines the beginning phase of group work practice. Chapter 6 explains the skills necessary for beginning a group. The beginning phase of group work occurs during the first few meetings of the group. As members begin face-to-face interaction, the worker helps to build relationships by clarifying the group's purpose. During the beginning phase, the worker helps members to get to know each other. Together, the worker and the members identify individual and group goals, and contracts are developed for work that will be accomplished during the middle phase of group work.

Part IV examines the middle phase of group work. Chapter 7 focuses on the process of assessment. Assessment is conceptualized as a process that occurs at three levels: the individual group member, the group as a whole, and the group's environment. Chapter 7 discusses each of the foci of assessment and describes appropriate assessment methods that can be utilized at each of these levels. Chapter 8 deals with the skills and activities that the worker employs during the middle phase of work with treatment groups, and Chapter 9 focuses on middle-phase skills with task groups. During the middle phase, the worker helps members achieve their individual goals and helps the group accomplish its tasks. The worker helps structure the group's work and helps to build group dynamics that are conducive to achieving the expressive and instrumental goals of the groups. Chapters 8 and 9 describe a variety of specific methods and techniques for intervening in task and treatment groups.

Part V examines the ending phase of group work. Chapter 10 describes how to evaluate group work practice. Chapter 11 explains the skills that can be used in ending the group. The worker helps the group make the most of the time remaining so as to accomplish the group's tasks. The worker helps members to generalize and maintain changes that have already been made and helps them to end their association.

## DEFINITION OF GROUP WORK

Because many professions have contributed to the knowledge base of group work, it is difficult to sort out each profession's contributions and viewpoints. It has been suggested that although group work has emerged as a conscious professional activity, there is little reason to believe that "there is conceptual agreement or even clarity regarding its definition, purposes, practice methods and techniques" (Alissi, 1980, p. 3). Although approaches to group work are quite different, there is general agreement that each approach has its merits and particular practice applications. Therefore, a functional definition of group work should focus on the generic aspects of practice as well as allowing for specialized approaches. The broad definition offered in this chapter allows beginning practitioners to understand the boundaries of group work as well as its many practice applications. It includes both treatment and task group practice. Group work can be defined as:

> Goal-directed activity with small groups of people aimed at meeting socioemotional needs and accomplishing tasks. This activity is directed to individual members of a group and to the group as a whole within a system of service delivery.

This definition describes group work as goal directed activity, which refers to planned, orderly, worker activities carried out in the context of professional practice with people. Goal-directed activity has many purposes. For example, group workers may aim to rehabilitate members, to educate them, to help them socialize, or to help them grow. Workers may also help members of a group develop leadership skills so that they can take increasing responsibility for the group's development. At the same time, workers should enable their groups to change the social environment. This includes helping members gain greater control over the organizational and environmental systems that affect their lives. This idea is not new. Several writers advocate a person-in-system view of practice (Siporin, 1975; Pincus and Minahan, 1973; Klein, 1972; Schwartz and Zalba, 1971). Other writers focus on techniques of individual change within small groups (Vinter, 1974a; Rose, 1980; Sarri, 1974). Both approaches are valuable, and attention should be given to both when groups set their goals.

The next component of the definition of group work refers to working with small groups of people. A large group may not allow for face-to-face interaction. It is difficult to compose a large group around common purposes and common goals. The members of a large group sometimes think of themselves as an audience rather than as group members. Thus, the term *small group* implies the ability of members to identify themselves as members, to engage in face-to-face interaction, and to exchange thoughts and feelings among themselves through verbal and nonverbal communication processes.

The definition of group work also indicates that workers practice with both treatment and task groups. Most workers are called upon both to help clients meet their personal needs and to help their agency or organization accomplish its tasks. For example, most direct service workers have many opportunities to work with task groups as well as with groups that help members meet their personal needs. Similarly, administrators and supervisors are often expected to lead educational groups for staff members in addition to leading numerous task groups such as committees, staff meetings, or treatment conferences.

Our definition of group work also emphasizes that the worker should have a dual focus within any group: goal-directed activities with individual members and with the group as a whole. The literature on group work is not particularly clear on this point. Some writers favor working with the goals of individual group members (see, for example, Sarri, 1974; Garvin and Glasser, 1971; Vinter, 1974a). Others emphasize working with the group as the primary focus of attention (see, for example, Schwartz and Zalba, 1971; Klein, 1972). Few hold views that are mutually exclusive. Writers who emphasize the individual member as the primary client system usually note the importance of the group as a whole. Those who focus on the group as the primary client system frequently note the importance of the individual member's needs, concerns, and goals. Both the individual member and the group as a whole have life experiences, developmental patterns, needs, goals, and characteristic patterns of behavior that should be of concern to the worker. Therefore, both the group as a whole and individual group members should receive the attention of the worker.

The final portion of the definition of group work emphasizes that a group does not exist in a vacuum. It exists in relation to many systems, particularly the system of service delivery that sponsors, legitimizes, and influences its purposes. Even self-help groups and groups conducted in private practice are influenced by service delivery arrangements under which they are offered. Usually, there is an exchange of influence between a group and its sponsoring agency. A group is often influenced by the limits of agency resources or agency policies. At the same time, a group may be the catalyst for a needed change in agency policies or procedures. For example, in a support group for young parents sponsored by a family service agency, the worker limits the group's membership to the geographic area served by the agency. Because of the need for child care during meetings, the group serves to highlight the need for the agency to expand its day care services for children of working parents. In this example, the group is influenced by and influences the agency that sponsors it.

## CLASSIFYING GROUPS

In order to understand the breadth of group work practice, it is helpful to become familiar with the wide variety of groups that can be led in practice settings. Because there are so many different kinds of groups that workers may be called upon to lead, it is also helpful to distinguish among them. In the following two sections, distinctions are made among groups on the basis of whether they are formed or occur naturally and whether they are treatment- or task-oriented.

## Formed and Natural Groups

Formed groups are those that come together through some outside influence or intervention. They do not usually exist without some sponsorship or affiliation. They are literally convened for a particular purpose. Some examples of formed groups are therapy groups, classroom groups, committees, clubs, and teams. Natural groups are those that come together in a spontaneous fashion on the basis of naturally occurring events, interpersonal attraction, or the mutually perceived needs of members. They often lack formal sponsorship. Natural groups include family groups, peer groups, friendship networks, street gangs, and cliques.

This text is primarily concerned with formed groups. Natural groups are not given extensive coverage because of major differences between formed and natural groups. For example, natural groups such as families are neither planned nor constructed by a group worker. They have a long developmental history, which has unique implications for the relationships established among members and hence for the interventions that are used by workers. For these reasons, a separate body of knowledge has been developed for work with natural groups. For example, work with families is a rather separate and distinct field of practice, utilizing a separate body of knowledge and research, as well as distinct intervention techniques.

Despite the differences that exist between formed and naturally occurring groups, many of the generic skills examined in this text are readily applicable to work with natural groups. We encourage group work practitioners to use the knowledge and skills presented in this text in their work with natural groups. Some efforts have already been made in this regard, such as attempts to utilize group work skills in working with the family unit as a group (see, for example, Bell, 1975; 1981), to apply group work skills to work with gangs (see, for example, Spergel, 1969; 1966), and a relatively recent and growing interest in using group work skills to enhance or establish social networks for those who are socially isolated (see, for example, Toseland, Decker, and Bliesner, 1979; Toseland, Sherman, and Bliven, 1981; Collins and Pancoast, 1970).

## Purpose and Group Work

Formed groups can be classified according to the purposes for which they are organized. The term *purpose* can be defined as the general aims of a group. The importance of purpose in group work cannot be overemphasized. According to Wilson (1976, p. 41), "the nature of the framework for the practice of group work depends on the purpose of the group [which is] served." A group's purpose identifies the reasons for bringing members together. As Klein (1972, p. 35) notes, "purpose guides group composition."

It also helps to guide the group's selection of goal-directed activities and to define the broad parameters of the services to be delivered.

In this text, the term *treatment group* is used to signify a group whose major purpose is to meet members' socioemotional needs. The purposes for forming treatment groups include meeting members' needs for education, growth, behavior change, or socialization. In contrast, the term *task group* is used to signify any group in which the major purpose is neither intrinsically nor immediately linked to the needs of the members of the group. In task groups, the overriding purpose is to accomplish a mandate and complete the work for which the group was convened.

The concept of purpose in groups is sometimes difficult to understand because few groups exist for only one purpose. Most groups involve both meeting members' personal needs and accomplishing one or more group tasks. For example, in some approaches used in treatment groups, personal needs are met through a problem-solving approach or a task-centered approach (Toseland, 1980; Somers, 1976; Garvin, Reid, and Epstein, 1976). Treatment is conceptualized as a series of tasks to be accomplished. Completing these tasks is associated with a favorable outcome. A socialization group might, for example, plan and carry out a series of structured role plays to increase members' social skills. A growth group might engage in a series of exercises to increase members' self-awareness. In both cases, members have met their personal needs by participating in a group task. Thus, it is common for treatment groups to accomplish tasks as well as to serve members' socioemotional needs.

## Treatment and Task Groups

In classifying groups as either treatment- or task-oriented, it is important to consider how the two types differ. Table 1–1 points out some of the major differences between treatment and task groups on selected characteristics. Table 1 is, in part, based on comparisons made by Klein (1972) and earlier by Jennings (1950). The bond that is present in a group is usually based on the purpose for which it is convened. Members of treatment groups are bonded together by their common needs and their common situations. Task groups create a common bond among members by having them work together to accomplish a task, produce a product, or carry out a mandate.

In treatment groups, roles are not set before the group forms, but develop through interaction among members. In task groups, members take on roles through a process of interaction and also are frequently assigned roles by the group. Roles that may be assigned include team leader, secretary, and fact finder.

Communication patterns in treatment groups are open. Members are usually encouraged to interact with one another. Task group members are more likely to address their communications to the worker and to keep their communication focused on a particular group task. In some task groups, the amount that members communicate on a particular agenda item may be limited by the worker. In other task groups, members may limit their own

*Table 1–1*

## A COMPARISON OF
## TASK AND TREATMENT GROUPS

| Selected Characteristics | Type of Groups | |
| --- | --- | --- |
| | **Treatment Group** | **Task Group** |
| Bond | Members' personal needs | Task to be completed |
| Roles | Develop through inter-action | Develop through inter-action or are assigned |
| Communication Patterns | Open | Focused on the discussion of a particular task |
| Procedures | Flexible or formal, depending on the group | Formal agenda and rules |
| Composition | Based on common concerns, problems, or characteristics | Based on needed talents, expertise, or division of labor |
| Self-disclosure | Expected to be high | Expected to be low |
| Confidentiality | Proceedings usually private and kept within the group | Proceedings may be private but are sometimes open to the public |
| Evaluation | Success based on members meeting treatment goals | Success based on members accomplishing task, mandate, or producing a product |

communication because they believe they will not be well received by the group.

Treatment groups usually have somewhat flexible procedures for meetings, such as a warm-up period, a period for working on member concerns, and a period for summarizing the group's work. Task groups usually proceed from an agenda. They are more likely than treatment groups to have formalized rules that govern how members discuss the business of the group.

Although a similar set of procedures can be used for composing both treatment and task groups, the actual composition of these types of groups may differ. For example, treatment groups are composed so that members have common concerns, problems, or abilities. Task groups are composed in order to provide the group with the necessary human resources it needs to do its job.

In treatment groups, members are expected to disclose their own concerns and problems. Therefore, self-disclosures often occur regarding emotionally charged, personal concerns. In task groups, member self-disclosure

is relatively low. It is generally expected that members will confine themselves to discussions about accomplishing the group's task and will not share
intimate, personal concerns.

The members of treatment groups often decide that the proceedings of
their groups should be confidential. The meetings of some task groups, such
as treatment conferences, may be private, but the meetings of other task
groups, such as task forces and delegate councils, are usually open to the
public. These groups circulate the proceedings of their meetings to interested persons and organizations.

The criteria for evaluating success also differ for treatment and task
groups. Treatment groups are successful to the extent that they help members meet their individual treatment goals. Task groups are successful when
they accomplish group goals, such as generating solutions to problems,
planning strategies, making correct decisions; or when they develop group
products, such as a report, a new set of regulations, or a series of recommendations concerning a particular issue.

An example in which a worker is responsible for leading both types of
groups may help to illustrate the differences between treatment and task
groups.

In the first group, the worker meets with adults who have recently
become parents for the first time. The purpose of the group is to provide a
forum for discussion about their adjustment to life as parents.

In the second group, the worker brings together a number of community
representatives to study day-care resources in order to make recommendations to a government agency regarding changes in government support
for day-care services. In this group, the focus is task-oriented, and the
purpose is external to the personal needs of the members.

The parents' group is classified as a treatment group because it is convened to meet the personal needs of its members. The parents' group is
bonded together by its common purpose and the common needs and concerns of its members. It is expected that friendships may develop among
group members and that members will act as resources in helping each other
in their adjustment to parenthood. It is also expected that the feeling level
and the level of self-disclosure will be high because of the similar characteristics of the members and the problems they face. Because members may
self-disclose about personal issues, the proceedings of the group are confidential. Roles develop based on how members assist in accomplishing the
purpose of the group and on how members meet each other's needs. Because parenting is a developmental phenomenon involving constant discov-
ery and change, the procedures of the group are flexible, allowing members
to share their immediate weekly concerns. The parents group was composed
around the similarity of parent concerns. Patterns of communication focus
on the needs of members, such as adjusting to parenthood and becoming
effective parents. In order to evaluate the success of the parents' group, the
worker focuses on members' satisfaction with the group experience and
whether or not the group has met their needs.

In the second group, members are bonded together by a common cause or concern to improve day care service. They are expected to contribute their personal viewpoints only to the extent that these contribute to the group's task. Personal feelings are shared, but not to any great extent. Observations are contributed on an objective, impersonal level rather than on a subjective, personal level. The group is publicized and seeks outside, expert testimony to contribute to its deliberations. Confidentiality is impractical because it would hinder the accomplishment of the group's task. Roles are assigned by the worker. For example, members are appointed to subcommittees to collect needed data. Roles also develop on the basis of how each member contributes to the task of the group. To facilitate an organized approach to task accomplishment, the group works from an agenda, which is published in advance to give participants time to prepare for the proceedings. The group was composed by selecting members who had some knowledge of day care programs and by selecting those who had different areas of expertise in order to facilitate a division of labor and encourage different perspectives. Patterns of communication focus on the task rather than on members' personal concerns. In evaluating the effectiveness of the group at accomplishing its task, the worker examines the group's decisions, actions, or written report and recommendations for clarity, thoroughness, and feasibility.

## A TYPOLOGY OF TREATMENT AND TASK GROUPS

The broad distinctions between formed and natural groups and treatment and task groups can be further refined and developed into a classification system of treatment and task groups. One way to develop a classification system is to categorize treatment and task groups according to their primary purpose. Many writers have attempted to identify the primary purposes of the groups that workers may lead in practice settings. For example, Hartford (1964, p. 14) suggests that groups may focus on "the social functioning, growth or change or rehabilitation of the group members." Schwartz (1974, p. 218) suggests that groups are "an enterprise in mutual aid," and Murphy (1959, p. 34–35) suggests that groups enhance members "social functioning through a purposeful group experience."

Other writers have attempted more ambitious classifications of group purposes. For example, Douglas (1979) suggests that group purposes may include (1) individual growth and adjustment, (2) group development toward specific needs, and (3) social action, social change, and changing society through the group experience. Klein's (1972) "objectives for group workers" define a wide range of purposes for treatment and task groups. According to Klein (1972), group purposes can include (1) rehabilitation—restoring members to their former level of functioning; (2) habilitation—helping members grow and develop; (3) correction—helping members who are having problems with social laws or mores; (4) socialization—helping members learn how to do what to get along with others and to do what is socially acceptable; (5) prevention—helping members to develop and function at an optimum level and helping members to prepare for events that are likely to occur; (6) social action—helping members to change their environment; (7) problem solving—helping members to resolve complex issues and concerns; and (8) developing social values—helping members to develop a humanistic approach to living.

In the following pages, a typology of treatment groups and a typology of task groups have been developed. These typologies are based on the primary purposes of treatment and task groups. Although groups with only one purpose rarely exist in practice, developing "pure" categories, that is, groups with a single purpose, has a useful function in illustrating differences between groups and in demonstrating the many ways that groups can be utilized in practice settings.

## TREATMENT GROUPS

Four primary purposes for treatment groups are (1) education, (2) growth, (3) remediation, and (4) socialization. Although other purposes such as support and mutual aid could have been included, these latter purposes are basic to all types of treatment groups and therefore have not been identified as separate and distinct purposes in the typology.

In practice settings, there are innumerable variations of treatment groups that combine the four primary purposes. For example, a group for parents of Down's Syndrome children may be oriented toward both education and growth. A group for alcoholics may have all four of the primary purposes. However, in order to show clearly the similarities and differences among different types of groups, we have drawn up the treatment group typology shown in Table 1–2, which sets forth selected characteristics of a typical treatment group with only one of each of the four primary purposes. Table 1–2 can be used as a guide by workers who are planning to lead groups with only one purpose or groups that combine several purposes.

### Educational Groups

Educational groups are those whose primary purpose is to help members learn about themselves and their society. Educational groups are used in a wide variety of settings, including treatment agencies, schools, nursing homes, correctional agencies, and hospitals. Some examples of educational groups are:

1. An adolescent sexuality group sponsored by a family planning agency.
2. A preparation-for-parenthood group sponsored by a family service agency.
3. A group for prospective foster parents sponsored by a child welfare agency.
4. A board member training group sponsored by the United Way.

All educational groups are aimed at increasing members' information or skills. Most routinely involve presentations of information and knowledge

*Table 1–2*
## TYPOLOGY OF
## TREATMENT GROUPS

| Selected Characteristics | Purpose of the Group | |
|---|---|---|
| | Education | Growth |
| Purpose | To educate<br>Learning through didactic presentations, discussion and experience | To develop member's potentials<br>Awareness, insight, and development through discussion and growth-producing experiences |
| Leadership | Leader as teacher and provider of structure for group discussion | Leader as facilitator and role model |
| Focus | Individual learning focus<br>Structuring of group for learning | Either member or group focus, depending on the approach<br>Individual grows through the group experience |
| Bond | Common interest in learning, skills development | Common goals among members<br>Contract to use group to grow |
| Composition | Similarity of educational or skill level | Can be quite diverse<br>Based on members' ability to work toward growth and development |
| Communication | Frequently leader to member, didactic<br>Sometimes member to member during discussions<br>Self-disclosure low | Highly interactive<br>Members often take responsibility for communication in the group<br>Self-disclosure moderate to high |

***Table 1–2 (cont'd.)***

**Purpose of the Group** *(cont'd.)*

| Remediation | Socialization |
|---|---|
| To change behavior<br>Correction, rehabilitation, coping and problem solving through behavior change interventions | To increase communication and social skills<br>Improved interpersonal relationships through program activities, structured exercises, role plays, etc. |
| Leader as expert, authority figure, or facilitator, depending on approach | Leader as director of the group's actions or programs |
| Focus on individual members' problems, concerns, or goals | Focus on the group as a medium for activity, participation, and involvement |
| Common purpose with separate member goals<br>Relationship of member with worker, group, or other members | A common activity, enterprise, or situation |
| Can be diverse or can be composed of people with similar problems or concerns | Depending on location of group and purpose, can be diverse or homogeneous |
| Leader to member or member to member depending on approach<br>Self-disclosure moderate to high | Often represented in activity or non-verbal behavior<br>Self-disclosure low to moderate and often nonverbal |

by experts. They also often include opportunities for group discussion to foster learning. When leading educational groups, workers concentrate on both the individual learner and on the group as a whole, as a medium for learning, reinforcement, and discussion.

Members of educational groups are bonded together by a common interest in the material to be learned as well as by common characteristics, such as being adolescents, expectant parents, welfare recipients, or board members. In composing educational groups, workers consider each member's knowledge of the subject matter and level of skills and experience, so that all members are able to get the most they can out of the learning process. Some educational groups seek members who have different levels of exposure to the subject matter so that beginners can learn from advanced members. When the educational group is small, there are generally opportunities for member-to-member communication and group discussion. Depending on the norms of the group and the subject matter under consideration, member self-disclosure varies from low to moderate. In general, a relatively low level of self-disclosure is expected in an educational group because the group is often structured around a presentation of material by the worker, a guest speaker, or a member. Usually, the material to be learned is seen as more important than the needs of members to self-disclose.

Although the widespread use of educational groups in classrooms has led to a societal expectation that educational groups should focus on the content to be learned rather than on the individual learning needs of group members, some workers utilize a personalized approach to learning that emphasizes the developmental learning needs of individual group members. Other approaches to leading educational groups emphasize learning as a social experience. Workers who use this approach focus on group discussion and group activities rather than on didactic methods.

## Growth Groups

Growth-oriented groups are also commonly found in a wide variety of settings. A growth orientation in group work implies opportunities for members to become aware of, to expand, and to change their thoughts, feelings, and behaviors regarding self and others. The group is used as a vehicle to develop members' capabilities to the fullest extent possible. Growth groups focus on promoting socioemotional health rather than remediating socioemotional illness. Some examples of growth groups include:

1. An encounter group for married couples.
2. A values clarification group for adolescents.
3. A consciousness-raising group sponsored by a women's community center.
4. A group at a senior citizens service center that focuses on how to make the most of retirement.

Growth groups generally stress self-improvement and the potential of human beings to live a full and rewarding life, especially through improved relationships with others. They provide a supportive atmosphere for individual members to gain insights, experiment with new behaviors, get feedback, and grow as human beings. The bond in growth groups stems from members' commitment to use the group to help one another develop their potential. When composing growth groups, workers often select a diverse membership so that exposure to members with different characteristics will enhance growth. However, some growth groups are composed of members with similar characteristics in order to enhance inter-member empathy and increase the supportive element of the group. In most growth-oriented groups, self-disclosure is moderate to high.

In this text, the term *growth* is used in its broadest sense. In the late 1960s and early 1970s, a number of new group work techniques for personal growth emerged during what has been referred to as the Human Potential Movement (Schutz, 1967). Several writers describe these types of groups and the techniques that were employed to increase self-awareness and improve personal functioning (Schutz, 1967; Howard, 1970). Our broad interpretation of the term *growth* in group work stresses members coming together to develop their potential and increase their socioemotional health, regardless of the techniques used to lead the group.

## Remedial Groups

Remedial groups are the most easily identifiable and the most frequently cited type of group in the literature. Remedial groups help members change their behavior, cope with or ameliorate their personal problems, or rehabilitate themselves after a social or health trauma.

In group work practice, a particular importance is often attached to the remedial group, even to the exclusion of other types of group work. This may be because of the importance attributed to the "medical model" which stresses therapy and treatment to bring "sick" or dysfunctional persons back to health. As Konopka (1963, p. 33) has noted, "the high status of psychiatry on the North American continent" helped to make the *therapy* more precious and more important than the terms *casework* or *group work* which are used by the social work profession. Thus, remedial groups are often associated with the professionalism of group work as a method of practice. They are also frequently associated with a process of study, diagnosis, and treatment that is used in order to help group members achieve their individual goals (Vinter, 1974a). Some examples of remedial groups include:

1. A psychotherapy group for outpatients at a community mental health center.
2. A group for people who want to stop smoking sponsored by a voluntary health association.
3. A first offenders group in a juvenile diversion program sponsored by a probation department.
4. A group for those who are addicted to drugs that is sponsored by a hospital.

In remedial groups, members come together to solve their problems. The group leader is often viewed as an expert, an authority figure, and a change agent who helps members solve their problems. Members' problems are assessed and treatment goals are developed with the help of the worker. Although there is usually a common purpose for the group, each member may have a different problem with different symptoms. In addition, the etiology and development of each member's problem is unique. Because members' problems are unique, in order to achieve individual goals, the worker often focuses on one member at a time. This approximates a one-to-one treatment relationship in a group. Depending on the approach or stance of the worker, the members of remedial groups may be expected to help each other work on their problems. The level of member self-disclosure is usually quite high but can depend somewhat on the type of problems experienced by group members.

Members of remedial groups are often personally involved in the group because they have much to gain: symptom relief, loss of emotional pain, or problem resolution. A good deal of planning usually takes place before beginning a remedial group. Therapeutic interventions are selected after a careful assessment of individual members has been made, and the group is composed in relation to the problems that members experience. Often, members participate in an intake procedure so that the worker can test members' interest, determine suitability for group treatment, and begin to explain the purpose of the group to each prospective member. Although these procedures are also used in working with other types of groups, they are often emphasized when working with remedial groups.

## Socialization Groups

The final type of group in the treatment group typology is the socialization group. Socialization groups are frequently referred to in the group work literature (see, for instance, Klein, 1972; Garvin, 1981; Boyd, 1938). Socialization groups help members to learn social skills and socially accepted behavior patterns so they can function effectively while living in the community. Socialization groups frequently use program activities such as games, role plays, or outings to help members accomplish individual goals (Whittaker, 1974; Middleman, 1968). The personal needs of members and the goals of the group are often met through program activities rather than exclusively through group discussion. Thus, socialization groups feature a "learning through doing" approach in which members improve their interpersonal skills by participating in program activities.

Some examples of socialization groups include:

1. An activity group for children who act out in school.
2. A social club for ex-mental patients.
3. A weekly cottage meeting in a residential treatment center for children.
4. A Parents Without Partners group, which includes picnics, dances, and other social activities.

Leadership in socialization groups can be directive or nondirective depending on the complexity of program activities and the competencies of group members. Member participation is the key to successful individual and group outcomes. The group is a medium for activity, participation, and involvement, and members are bonded to each other through these activities. The composition of socialization groups can be based on the similar interests and needs of members or on the common experiences offered by a particular program activity. There are at least three common forms of socialization groups: (1) social skills groups, (2) governance groups, and (3) recreation groups.

Some social skills groups, such as assertiveness training groups, are formed for "normal" adults who wish to improve their existing skills. Unlike the other types of groups in our typology, socialization groups can be particularly useful for individuals who are unable or unwilling to communicate effectively and for those who have difficulty engaging in satisfying social relationships. Young children, shy adolescents and mildly retarded adults are examples of client populations that can benefit from social skills groups. Program activities can aid in drawing out these types of group members. They help members to form meaningful relationships and assist them in learning social skills. They provide the basis for interaction and communication without the requirement of direct, verbal communication. Thus, by using program activities, group work can take place through nonverbal means. In other cases, role plays, psychodrama, and other program activities requiring verbal as well as nonverbal communications can be used to increase members' skills and promote socialization. The behavior displayed during these activities can also help a worker assess members' problems and plan effective interventions.

Another type of socialization group that is often found in residential settings, such as nursing homes, psychiatric hospitals, correctional facilities, and the residential treatment centers, is the governance group. The purpose of these groups is to involve residents (of the unit, ward, floor, or cottage) in the daily governance of an institution. Although governance groups are closely related to task groups because they solve problems and make decisions, they have been classified as treatment groups because of their primary focus on the needs of members. Through their participation in the governance process, members learn communication and conflict resolution skills. They also learn to share with others, to take responsibility for their actions, and to participate in decision-making processes.

The concept of a governance group is borrowed, in part, from the concept of the therapeutic community, where members have input into the rules that govern their behavior. Examples of governance groups include cottage meetings, resident councils, "family" meetings, and patient rights meetings. Participation in governance groups is seen as valuable and therapeutic to group members. All members of the community are encouraged to attend each meeting so that everyone will have a voice in their own governance. In some settings, such as residential treatment centers, attendance may be required.

A third type of socialization group is focused on recreational activities. Much of the recent group work literature has tended to understate the importance of recreational groups in meeting members' personal needs. The roots of group work can be traced back to recreational groups such as scouting, camping, sports, and club groups (Boyd, 1935; Smith, 1935; Wilson, 1976;

Slavson, 1945; 1946). Recreation can be both an end and a means to an end. As an end, recreation can be a desirable leisure time activity. As a means, recreation can be a way of helping a particular population to be involved in an activity that has therapeutic benefits, such as increasing social skills.

Recreational groups are particularly important for working with children, youth, and adults in neighborhood centers. Because they are enjoyable, recreational groups are often helpful when attempting to engage resistant clients such as pre-delinquent, latency-age children, and gang members. They can help members to understand community values and accepted norms of behavior, to develop interpersonal skills, and to feel a sense of belonging. In addition, they help members to develop confidence in their ability to function as a part of a group and to function in other social situations. In order to carry out these important purposes, recreation groups require the leadership of workers who are skilled in both group work and the recreational mode or program activity that is utilized.

## TASK GROUPS

Task groups are commonplace in most agencies and organizations. They are used to find solutions to organizational problems, to generate new ideas, and to make decisions regarding many different issues. There are two primary purposes for task groups: (1) serving organizational needs, and (2) serving the needs of clients. Task groups whose primary purpose is serving organizational needs include (1) committees, (2) administrative groups, and (3) delegate councils. Task groups whose primary purpose is serving client needs include (1) teams, (2) treatment conferences, and (3) social action groups. Selected characteristics of each type of group are presented in Table 1–3, and additional readings about each type of task group are listed in Appendix A. As with the treatment group typology, there is often some overlap between different types of task groups in actual practice situations. Thus, the typology should act as a heuristic guide for workers who may be called upon to lead different types of task groups, rather than a rigid classification system to which practitioners must adhere.

### Committees

The most common type of task group is the committee. It is almost impossible to be associated with an agency or organization without having some contacts with committees. Committees are used to accomplish a wide variety of tasks. Although they are most often used to meet organizational needs, in human service fields organizational needs often overlap with client needs. For example, a committee may meet to respond to a request by the United Way to improve service. The results of the committee's work is beneficial to both the agency and its clients.

A committee is a group of people who come together through a process of appointment or election. Their task is to "accomplish a charge" (Pincus and Minahan, 1973. p. 61), which is delegated to the committee members from a higher source of authority, such as an agency executive or organizational by-laws. Committees may be a temporary creation (ad hoc committees) or may be more permanent parts of the structure of an organization (standing committees). Some examples of committees include:

1. A group of young people who are responsible for recommending activities for the local community center.
2. A group of employees who are assigned the task of studying and recommending changes in the agency's personnel policy.
3. A group of social workers who meet to consider ways to improve service delivery to pregnant teenagers.
4. A group of staff members who meet to develop recommendations for an employee assistance program.

In these examples of committees, members are concerned with producing reports, accomplishing tasks, making recommendations, or making decisions. In each example, the committee's work requires the collective wisdom of a number of people with varied viewpoints, expertise, and abilities.

Although members are expected to share their personal views during deliberations, the level of self-disclosure in committees is frequently low. In some cases, however, there are variations in the level of self-disclosure, depending on the norms that have developed in the committee and on the nature of the issues being discussed. For example, when the subject matter is of a sensitive nature, discussing personal viewpoints may require a high level of member self-disclosure.

Most committees tend to follow a standard set of procedures in carrying out their work. Sometimes committees rely on procedures found in *Roberts Rules of Order* to conduct their meetings. In other cases, committees develop their own rules and regulations that control how members bring up issues, how issues are discussed, and how decisions about them are reached.

It is useful for an agenda to be specified for each meeting so that committee members are able to follow the activity of the group and to know what to anticipate. The agenda provides a structure, focus, and direction for the group. The person responsible for seeing that the agenda and the formalized procedures are carried out is the chairperson. The chairperson may be appointed by the authority that has given the committee its mandate or may be elected by committee members.

Committees frequently deal with issues that are complex, requiring the group to divide large tasks into a series of smaller subtasks. Committees tend to assign roles to members in order to divide labor. When large committees deal with multiple issues or complex tasks, they frequently do much of their work through subcommittees, using the entire committee as a coordinating body or as a mechanism of approval for the recommendations of the subcommittees. Subcommittees divide labor and expedite the completion of complex tasks. The larger committee authorizes the formation of one or more subcommittees from its membership to consider parts of a larger task or to research important questions relative to the overall task. Subcommittees report back to the larger committee on the outcome of their work.

*Table 1–3*
## TYPOLOGY OF TASK GROUPS

| Selected Characteristics | Organizational Needs | | |
| --- | --- | --- | --- |
| | Committees | Administrative Groups | Delegate Councils |
| Purpose | A group product, report, or task | Policy making, organizational change, or system maintenance | Representation of different units Collective action and input |
| Leadership | Appointed or elected | Provided by legitimized authority, i.e. agency director | Representatives elected or appointed by the units, agencies, or systems represented |
| Focus | Low member focus High product focus | High agency focus High or low member focus, depending on style of administration | Equality of representation Focus on larger issues and concerns |
| Bond | Committee task, or mandate | Organizational goals | Larger purpose or community concern rather than individual or agency's concern |
| Composition | Diversity to aid decision making and division of labor | Depends on agency staffing patterns | Diverse by definition: represents different subsystems, organizations, interests |
| Communication | Relative to task Low member self-disclosure | Provides basis for formal organizational communication Low member self-disclosure | Provides a forum for communication between large systems Member is communication link between council and the agency as represented unit Low member self-disclosure |

*Table 1–3 (cont'd.)*

| | Client Needs | |
| Teams | Treatment Conferences | Social Action Groups |
| --- | --- | --- |
| Mutual involvement with a client system | Decision making regarding a client's treatment plan | Individual or social change |
| Appointed by sponsoring agency | Neutral chair or chaired by member with most responsibility | Change agent is the coordinator-enabler <br> Case manager |
| Build team to function smoothly <br> High member focus | Decision-oriented <br> Low member focus <br> High Client focus | Action-oriented <br> High client focus |
| Team spirit <br> Needs of organization and client | Client system <br> Treatment plan <br> Inter- or intra-agency agreement | Helping the client system achieve particular goals |
| Often heterogeneous <br> Diversity by function | Diversity by function, speciality, expertise | Diversity of self-interests <br> Sameness of purpose (client system) <br> depends on goals of the social action group |
| Theoretically close, sometimes artificial or inspirational <br><br> Low to moderate self-disclosure | Attempts to consider all points of view about the client system <br> High disclosure regarding client contact | Depends on characteristics of the social action group |

The composition of subcommittees is the responsibility of the chairperson. The chairperson considers the special qualifications and abilities of committee members and selects subcommittee members on the basis of their ability to complete a particular task. In some cases, the chairperson may ask for volunteers rather than appoint members. This is particularly true when the subcommittee will deal with a particularly onerous task and highly motivated members are needed.

A committee is generally held accountable to a higher authority for its actions. The power vested in a committee by a higher authority depends on the committee's mandate and on the extent to which the committee's actions are binding. It is a common practice for committees to be given the power to make recommendations rather than to make decisions that are binding.

The importance of the committee as a type of task group cannot be overemphasized. Most of the other types of task groups mentioned in our typology utilize elements of committee structure to complete their tasks. It can be argued that other forms of task groups such as delegate councils, treatment conferences, and administrative groups are special forms of committees.

### Administrative Groups

The second type of group in the task group typology is the administrative group. They help agencies to carry out organizational goals. Organizational policies and procedures are frequently formulated in administrative groups. Administrative groups also serve to enable formal communications within the organization. Agencies rely on administrative groups to share important information and to provide a forum for discussing agency functioning. Some examples of administrative groups include:

1. A board of directors meeting at a private social service agency.
2. A weekly meeting of social work staff and the director of social services in a large municipal hospital.
3. A meeting of United Way representatives with agency representatives to discuss funding proposals.
4. A meeting of department heads in a county social services department.

Whereas committees frequently recommend to a higher authority, administrative groups are more often delegated the authority to make decisions and to act to achieve them. This varies, of course, depending on the administrative structure of the agency. It is not uncommon, however, for organizations to utilize administrative staff groups to make important organizational decisions.

One common type of administrative group is the board of directors, which is legally responsible for the agency or organization under its articles of incorporation. The board is the body of authority to whom the agency executive is responsible. All important policy decisions must be approved by this group in keeping with the by-laws or charter of the agency. The board of directors may be divided into smaller subgroups or committees to work on special functions such as budgeting, hiring personnel, or fund raising, with each subgroup reporting back to the board for approval of its recommendations.

Working with a board of directors requires patience, diplomacy, and organizational skills. Boards are composed of members who may not be experts in the services delivered by the human service agency, but who are chosen for their influence in the community or for their ability to assist in fund raising. Frequently, board members have connections that can be used to provide credibility, resources, and power to the agency. Some boards attempt to include direct service workers or service consumers to help educate board members who have little knowledge about the services offered by the agency. The resultant diversity in board membership can sometimes be a problem for those who must relate to a board of directors as a source of authority. However, it can also be a tremendous asset for the well-being of the agency and the agency's overall status in the community.

Another common type of administrative group is composed of supervisors, department heads, or other administrative personnel of an agency. Frequently, agencies utilize administrative staff groups to exchange information and engage in planning, policy deliberations, and evaluation of services. The composition of administrative staff groups depends largely on the organizational chart of the agency and agency staffing patterns. However, these groups are usually composed of people who are designated as administrators, supervisors, or department heads.

The size of an administrative staff and the authority and power it possesses depends upon the size and structure of the organization. A large, bureaucratic agency may use several administrative staff groups to conduct its business. In these agencies, the authority and power vested in a staff group depends on its place on the organizational chart and on the authority delegated to it by top-level administrators. In smaller organizations, administrative staff groups tend to have more authority and power than in larger organizations, because they are often composed of top-level administrators who have a great deal of influence on agency policy.

Authority and power are important issues in administrative groups. Members of administrative groups are motivated to be productive, on the basis of their perceptions of how much authority and power they have to influence policy and produce organizational change. In this text, *authority* is defined as the official right or sanction to lead and to command obedience from others. *Power* is the ability to influence, irrespective of whether the person has an official sanction to lead. Power will be discussed in greater detail in Chapter 4 in connection with group leadership.

## Delegate Councils

A third type of task group is the delegate council. A variation of the delegate council is the delegate assembly, which is distinguished by its larger size. In this type of task group, individuals are appointed or elected to the council by a sponsoring unit. Members usually represent the interests of their sponsoring unit during council meetings. Delegate councils are often composed for the purposes of eliciting interagency communication and cooperation, studying large social issues or social problems, engaging in collective social action, or for purposes of governance. Some examples of delegate councils include:

1. A number of agency representatives who meet monthly to improve interagency communication.
2. A group of elected representatives from local chapters of a professional organization who meet to approve the organization's budget.
3. A task force to study family violence composed of members appointed from each county in a state.
4. A yearly meeting of representatives from family service agencies throughout the county.

Representation is an important issue in delegate councils. A member represents a group of people, an agency, or another system, to the delegate council. The member is often given authority to speak on behalf of a represented unit. Because the unit has agreed to participate by sending a representative, the represented unit generally agrees to abide by decisions made by the delegate council.

There are differing ways to achieve representation. The number of representatives for each sponsoring unit can vary with the size or importance of the unit. For example, legislative bodies frequently determine the number of representatives by considering the population of each voting district, county, or state, and apportioning an appropriate number of representatives for each district. Other councils' representation may be dictated by a sanctioning authority to ensure control over policy decisions. For example, a consumer council for a large department of social service may have more employees than clients to ensure department control over the decisions made by the group.

Delegate councils provide an effective communications link between groups of people who might otherwise not be able to communicate in a formal way. For example, delegate councils frequently serve as a forum for communication among human service agencies or among departments within a large human service organization. Such agencies or departments might not otherwise communicate effectively with each other.

Delegate councils are usually concerned with broad issues that affect a number of agencies, a large segment of a population, or a group of people in a wide geographic area. They sometimes serve large numbers of people who hold common interests and membership in unions or professional organizations. Delegate councils can be either discussion-oriented or action-oriented, or they may have components of both orientations. The White House Conference on Aging, for example, involved a series of delegate councils that discussed issues of concern to older Americans and made recommendations for government action.

Delegate councils are formed in a number of ways. Some councils are the product of ad hoc task forces or small groups of people who have been meeting for some time on an informal basis. Other councils begin through sponsorship from a particular agency until the council can decide on its rules and procedures, obtain membership, and establish its own identity. Representatives to delegate councils are either elected or appointed, and leadership is usually determined through an election.

Because council members are responsible for representing the views, interests, and positions of their sponsors to the delegate council, members of delegate councils often act formally on behalf of their constituency. Delegates communicate with their sponsors regarding the proceedings of the council. The effectiveness of the delegate council depends on the ability of each delegate to achieve two-way communication between the council and the represented unit. The individual delegates are not expected to engage in a high level of personal self-disclosure because they are bound by a mandate to represent the collective views of a group of people.

## Teams

A fourth type of task group is the team. A team can be defined as:

> a number of individual staff members, each of whom possesses particular knowledge and skills, who come together to share their expertise with one another for a particular purpose.[1]

Team members coordinate their efforts and work together on behalf of a particular client group. Some examples of teams include:

1. An interdisciplinary group of professionals who are working on discharge planning with burn patients in a hospital.
2. A group of professionals who deliver home-based hospice care.
3. A number of researchers who are working together to conduct a statewide welfare study.
4. A group of professionals and aides who work with inpatients in a psychiatric hospital.

The functioning of the team is the responsibility of a team leader. Team leaders are frequently appointed by the team's sponsoring agency or are elected by team members. The team leader is responsible for conducting meetings, motivating team members, and seeing that individual helping efforts are coordinated as a team effort. The team leader is a facilitator and coordinator for the group and is accountable to the agency for the actions of the team.

In most, if not all cases, an agency sanctions the mutual involvement of team members on behalf of a particular client population. Often, the team is composed of members with several different professional orientations, such as social work, nursing, physical and occupational therapy, and medicine. The team may also be composed of paraprofessionals such as mental health therapy aides. The agency and the team leader pay particular attention to

[1]Toseland, Palmer-Ganeles and Chapman, 1983.

how the team members work together as a group, which is frequently referred to as team building. Members are bonded together by a team spirit that assists them in their work as a group rather than as a collection of individuals representing disparate concerns and professional issues regarding their clients. At the same time, when building and maintaining an effective team, the worker should attend to members' unique personal and professional needs.

Considerable effort is spent by the team leader in team building and maintenance. Ideally, team members meet regularly to discuss their efforts as a group. Communication among team members varies according to the working situation of the team. Sometimes team members work independently of each other. For example, child care workers may be considered team members although they work different shifts. In such situations, frequent meetings are held to promote adequate communication and a coordinated team effort.

## Treatment Conferences

A fifth type of task group is the treatment conference, a group of people who meet for the purpose of discussing a particular client or client system. Its task is to consider the client's situation and decide on a plan of action that each member will pursue as individuals working with the client. Sometimes the plan of action is carried out by only one member who is entirely responsible for the client's care. Some examples of treatment conferences include:

1. An interdisciplinary group of professionals who meet to plan for the deinstitutionalization of an inpatient in a mental hospital.
2. A group of child care workers, social workers, nurses, and a psychiatrist who meet to determine a treatment plan for a child in residential treatment.
3. A parole board that meets to consider testimony regarding the release of an inmate in a correctional facility.
4. A group of community mental health professionals who meet to consider treatment methods for an anorexic young woman.

Treatment conferences are specialized forms of task groups. Participants focus on one client at a time. Members who are familiar with the client contribute information that may be helpful in developing or improving a treatment plan for the client. Other members, who may not be familiar with the client, can also contribute their expertise about how to most effectively treat the type of problem the client is experiencing. On the basis of this information, the group discusses the overall circumstances of the client and considers alternative treatment plans. The group decides on one plan of action that they all agree will be the most helpful for the client.

Treatment conferences are oriented to decision making, problem solving, and coordinating the actions of members. The group focuses its attention on the needs of a client rather than on the needs of the members of the treatment conference group. The bond that group members feel toward the group is based on their concern for a client and their commitment to an agreed-upon treatment plan.

Treatment conferences usually include all helping professionals who are working with a client. The group can also include consultants or experts who do not work directly with a client but who can contribute to the treatment plan by offering insights, resources, or advice. Treatment conference membership is as diverse as possible so as to include as many viewpoints and insights as possible. In some agencies, it is common practice for the client to be a participant in the proceedings of the treatment conference. If sensitive or speculative material is discussed, the client may be invited to the treatment conference after the group has had a preliminary discussion. There is no empirical data about when, or even if, it is best to invite the client to the proceedings of a treatment conference. However, because clients' rights to self-determination are an important part of the value base of social work practice (Siporin, 1975), we believe that clients should be given an opportunity to have input into the treatment plans that will affect their lives.

Treatment conference leadership can occur in a variety of ways. In some, a neutral chairperson is appointed. This person does not work directly with the client and therefore can lend objectivity to the proceedings. The designated leader can also be the person who has the most responsibility for the treatment of the client or the most involvement with the client.

Although treatment conferences are similar to team meetings, the treatment conference differs from the team in four respects. First, members of a treatment conference may not all work together as members of a team. Second, treatment conferences may not have the closeness or spirit that is essential in teamwork. Third, treatment conference groups often meet less frequently than teams. Finally, the composition of the treatment conference group can vary considerably, depending on the client under consideration. In team meetings, the composition is relatively stable.

## Social Action Groups

The social action group is the sixth type in the task group typology. In the social action group, the worker helps members to engage in a planned change effort in order to alter some aspect of the social or physical environment in which they live. While the goals of a planned change effort are frequently linked to the needs of the members of the social action group, in the latter there may be a more generalized goal that benefits others outside of the group. Thus, social action groups serve the "common good" of both members and non-members. Examples of social action groups include:

1. A citizens group advocating increased police protection on behalf of the elderly population in a neighborhood.
2. A group of social workers lobbying for increased funding for social services.
3. A tenants group seeking support for establishing a playground area in their housing complex.
4. A group of staff members working to eliminate an unethical agency practice.

Workers involved in social action groups can assume a number of leadership roles, depending on the nature of the change effort and the needs of the group. A worker can assume an enabler role, helping the group to acquire needed information or resources, to determine its priorities and procedures, and to plan a strategy for action. In working with a tenants' group, for example, the worker may help the group to organize itself so that it can pursue its goals. Alternatively, workers may take a directive role because of their expertise regarding the change effort. In a lobbying effort, for example, a worker might be particularly knowledgeable about techniques for influencing legislators. In this instance, the worker may be asked to speak for the social action group or may encourage the group to examine particular issues or use particular strategies, such as bargaining or collaborating.

Although directive approaches to leading social action groups are sometimes useful and appropriate, the worker should be guided by the purpose of the group and the preferences of group members. The worker should make sure that a directive approach does not inhibit indigenous leadership from developing among members. Abels (1980) suggests that the worker should assume the role of an "instructed" advocate for the group. Using this approach, the worker's role is defined and limited by the social action group and includes four major goals: "(1) to help the group achieve its purpose, (2) to help the group remain together as a unit long enough to achieve these purposes, (3) to enable members to function in an autonomous manner, and (4) to help the group to come to terms with its community (environment)" (Abels, 1980, p. 327).

The composition of the social action group can vary depending on the nature and circumstances of the change effort. Sometimes workers take a leadership role in composing a social action group, while in other cases the group may form as a result of a "grass roots" effort. In the latter case, the worker is often asked to be a consultant, lending his or her expertise to the change effort without necessarily influencing the composition of the group. When the worker does have a role in composing the group, consideration should be given to the level of support generated for the change effort by key community leaders. In some instances, the worker may seek members who can exert influence in the environment, or who have the diverse skills and resources needed to empower the group.

Communication patterns in social action groups also vary with the circumstances of the group. The worker helps the group develop open communication patterns so that all members have a chance to become actively involved. The worker also helps the group to establish communication linkages with its environment. Good communication linkages help to avoid misunderstandings and promote a cooperative effort among all those who may have some stake in the change effort.

A more broadly conceived form of the social action group is what Pincus and Minahan (1973) describe as the "action system". An action system can be defined as "those with whom the worker deals in his efforts to accomplish the tasks and achieve the goals of the change effort" (Pincus and Minahan, 1973, p. 61). The action system is similar to the social action group in that it is usually a group formed to engage in a planned change effort in the environment on behalf of a client system. However, it may vary significantly from the social action group in terms of the worker's role, the bond that unites the group and the group's composition and communication. A worker usually forms an action system and directs it on behalf of a client system. In an action system, the worker frequently assumes the role of a change agent and a case manager as well as an enabler.

There may be other differences as well. Members of action systems may have little or no interaction with each other, and may rely on the worker to coordinate communication. This is rarely the case in social action groups. Members of action systems may be acting on behalf of a particular client rather than on behalf of other clients, or for the common good. Despite these differences, action systems are related to social action groups and workers need to know group work skills in order to work with both action systems and social action groups.

## SUMMARY

This introductory chapter provides a framework for studying and working with groups. Group work is a broad field of practice carried out by a variety of professionals. A definition of group work is offered that encompasses the breadth of group work practice and is sufficiently flexible to allow for specialized approaches and objectives.

In order to understand the types of groups that exist in practice, a distinction is made between treatment and task groups. Although some of the functions and objectives of task and treatment groups overlap, treatment and task groups are distinguished by a variety of characteristics, which are discussed in this chapter. Despite these differences, group workers should understand that there are generic practice principles and generic stages of group development that exist in all forms of group work practice.

This chapter also assists in clarifying the kind of task and treatment groups commonly encountered in practice and illustrates the commonalities and differences among these groups. The typology of treatment groups distinguishes between those with four different primary purposes: (1) education, (2) growth, (3) remediation, and (4) socialization. The typology of task groups distinguishes between six task groups with two primary purposes: (1) groups whose primary purpose is to serve organizational needs, and (2) groups whose primary purpose is to serve client needs. Types of task groups that serve organizational needs include (1) committees, (2) administrative groups, and (3) delegate councils. Types of task groups that serve client needs include (4) teams, (5) treatment conferences, and (6) social action groups.

# 2
# Historical Developments

In order to develop a broad perspective concerning the potential uses of groups in practice settings, it is helpful to understand the developments that have occurred in the study of groups and in the practice of group work over the years. This historical perspective also gives the group worker a firm foundation upon which to build a knowledge base for effective group work practice.

Two general types of inquiries have enhanced our understanding of groups. One type of inquiry has come from social scientists who have studied groups by experimenting with them in laboratories. This inquiry has led to social science findings about basic properties of groups. The other type has come from group work practitioners who have examined how groups function in practice settings. The results of both inquiries have led to improved methods for working with a variety of different types of groups.

Practitioners often criticize the findings of social scientists as not being generalizable to "real world" practice settings. This is because social scientists frequently conduct their research in artificial laboratory settings, using short-term groups with participants who are not well motivated. Despite criticisms, the results of laboratory studies have proven to be helpful to practitioners in their attempts to understand the forces that operate in small groups. In addition, some social scientists have utilized naturalistic observations to study the functioning of community groups, thereby overcoming the deficiencies of laboratory methods. For example, Lewin (1947, 1948), Bales (1955), Whyte (1943), Thrasher (1927), and Roethlisberger and Dickson (1939) have developed their theories based on observations of groups' functioning in community settings. Thus, studies undertaken by both practitioners and social scientists have been helpful in developing a knowledge base for group work practice.

   In the following pages, historical developments within group work practice are examined and the influence of these developments on current practice trends is explored. Following this, there is a brief review of major social science findings that have implications for understanding group processes. The chapter concludes with a review of some major theories that currently influence group work practice.

## KNOWLEDGE FROM GROUP WORK PRACTICE

Developments in the understanding of groups by practitioners have come from a variety of fields. Social work, psychology, education and recreation all have contributed to our knowledge base about working with groups. Today group work still remains a practice method that is used by members of many professional disciplines. Although there have been developments within education, recreation, counseling, and psychology this text will concentrate its historical review on social work, the profession which has contributed most extensively to theory and practice about group work.

   Casework began in England and the United States in charity organizations in the late nineteenth century, and group work grew up largely in English and American settlement houses. There were some exceptions to this general trend. For example, as early as 1895, there was a realization on the part of some in the charity organization movement that there was a need to organize the poor for social change as well as to work with them on a one-to-one basis (Brackett, 1895). Group work was also used for therapeutic purposes in state mental institutions (Boyd, 1935) but much of the interest in group work stemmed from those who had led socialization groups, adult education groups, and recreation groups in settlement houses and youth service agencies (McCaskill, 1930).

   It is often believed that group work is considerably younger than casework, but group work agencies actually started only a few years after casework agencies. There were courses for group workers in schools of social work in the early 1900s (Maloney, 1963), and both casework and group work were used by social workers in the early part of the twentieth century. However, as Schwartz (1981) points out, the real historical difference between the two movements is that casework soon became identified with the social work profession whereas group work did not begin to become formally linked with the social work profession until much later during the National Conference of Social Work in 1935. The identification of group work with the social work profession increased during the 1940s (American Association of Group Workers, 1947) although group workers continued to maintain loose ties with recreation, adult education, and mental hygiene until the 1950s when group workers joined together with six other professional groups to form the National Association of Social Workers in 1955.

   The use of group work in settlement houses and casework in charity organizations was not an accident. Group work, and the settlement houses where it was practiced, offered citizens the opportunity for education, recreation, socialization, and community involvement. Unlike the charity organizations that primarily focused on the diagnosis and treatment of the problems of the poor, settlement houses offered groups as an opportunity for citizens to join together to share their views, to gain mutual support, and to exercise the power derived from their association for social change.

The focus on innovative educational techniques and social change led to action. As compared to caseworkers who relied on insight developed from psychodynamic approaches and on the provision of concrete resources, group workers relied on program activities to spur members to action. Program activities of all types were the medium through which groups attained their goals (see, for example, Addams, 1909, 1926; Boyd, 1935, 1938; Smith, 1935). Activities such as camping, singing, group discussion, games, and arts and crafts were used for recreation, socialization, education, support, and rehabilitation. Unlike casework, which was largely focused on problem solving and rehabilitation, group work activities were used for enjoyment as well as to solve problems. Thus, the group work methods that developed from settlement house work had a different focus and a different goal than casework methods.

Differences between casework and group work can also be clearly seen in the helping relationship. Caseworkers sought out the most underprivileged victims of industrialization, treating "worthy" clients by providing them with resources, and acting as good examples of virtuous, hardworking citizens. Although they also worked with those who were impaired and those who were poor, group workers did not focus solely on the poorest cases nor on those with the most problems. They preferred the word *members* to *clients* (Bowman, 1935). They emphasized working with members' strengths rather than their weaknesses. Helping was seen as a shared relationship in which the group worker and the group members worked together for mutual understanding and action regarding their common concerns for the community in which they lived. As concerns were identified, group members acted to support and to help one another, and the worker acted as a mediator between the demands of society and the needs of group members (Schwartz, 1981).

Shared interaction, shared power, and shared decision making placed demands on the group worker that were not experienced by caseworkers. Group workers frequently had to act quickly during complex and often fast-paced group interactions while remaining aware of the welfare of all group members. The number of group members, the fact that they could turn to one another for help, and the democratic decision-making processes that were encouraged in groups meant that group workers had to develop skills that were different from those of caseworkers. William Schwartz has summed up the feelings engendered by the new group work method very well in the statement "there are so many of them and only one of me" (Schwartz, 1966, p. 572).

Between 1910 and 1920, those who were concerned with adult education, recreation, and community work began to realize the full potentials of group work. They began to understand that groups could be used to help people participate in their communities, to enrich people's lives, and to support those persons whose primary relationships were not satisfying.

They became aware of the potential that groups had for helping people learn social skills and problem-solving skills. They began to use groups to prevent delinquency and to rehabilitate those who were maladjusted (Addams, 1909, 1926).

It was during this time that some leaders of this movement began to write about the groups they saw operating in their own communities. Often, they drew upon their own practice experiences. Siporin (1980b), for example, describes the history of "The Inquiry," an organization dedicated to the advancement of adult education that began in 1923. Among the members of "The Inquiry" were Edward Lindeman, "the father" of adult education. In 1921, he published a book about community groups, entitled *The Community*. Other members included Alfred Sheffield, who published several books about group discussion; Mary Follett, whose book *The New State*, published in 1918, described the organization of small community groups for political action, which she viewed as vital to the democratic process; Harrison Elliott, whose book, *The Process of Group Thinking* (1928), examined interpersonal communication and interaction in small, problem-solving discussion groups; and Grace Coyle, who was developing her research on social processes in groups for her doctoral dissertation. The work of those early writers suggests that group work was used for problem solving, discussion, and debate about social issues, as well as for social action, recreation, socialization, education, and for promoting harmony between different cultural and social groups.

Unlike the early writing of caseworkers, which emphasized improving practice outcomes by careful study, diagnosis, and treatment (Richmond, 1917), the early writings of group workers (Coyle, 1930; 1935) emphasized the processes that occurred during group meetings. For example, Grace Coyle (1930), one of the first social workers to publish a text on groups, entitled her work *Social Process in Organized Groups*, whereas the first text on casework by Mary Richmond (1917) was called *Social Diagnosis*. The emphasis on process has remained throughout the history of the group work. Group workers have always been concerned with how to best use the unique possibilities offered by the interaction of different people in a group. Thus, the group as a whole as well as the individual members are the focus of the worker's attention.

During the 1940s and 1950s, group workers began to use groups more frequently to provide therapy and remediation in mental health settings. In 1942, Fritz Redl started a group program for emotionally disturbed children in the Detroit area. These groups provided specialized diagnostic services unavailable at that time in child guidance centers (Reid, 1981). In the late 1940s, spurred on by the work of Gisela Konopka, group services became an integral part of child guidance programs. In general, therapy groups were insight-oriented in character relying less on program activities and more on diagnosis and treatment of members' problems (see for example, Konopka, 1949, 1954; Redl, 1944; Trecker, 1956).

The emphasis on the use of groups for therapy and remediation was the result, in part, of the influence of Freudian psychoanalysis and ego psychology and partly of World War II, which created a severe shortage of trained workers to deal with mentally disabled war veterans. It was spurred on by the continued interest in the use of groups in psychiatric settings during the 1950s, as can be seen in the proceedings of a national institute on this topic in 1955 (see Trecker, 1956).

The increased emphasis on diagnosis and treatment of the individual in the group could also be seen in the definition of group work accepted by the Commission of Social Work Practice of the newly formed National Association of Social Workers (Wilson, 1956). Other definitions of the social group work method were, however, somewhat broader. One widely accepted definition, for example, emphasized maintaining or improving the personal and social functioning of group members within a broad range of purposes, including (1) corrective, (2) preventive, (3) normal social growth, (4) personal enhancement, and (5) citizenship responsibility and participation (Hartford, 1964).

Although there was an increased emphasis in the 1940s and 1950s on utilizing groups to improve the functioning of individual group members, interest remained in using groups for recreational and educational purposes, especially in Jewish community centers and in youth organizations such as the Girl Scouts and the YWCA. During the 1940s and 1950s, groups were also used for purposes of community development and social action in many different neighborhood centers and community agencies. At the same time, there was an accompanying increase in the study of small groups as a social phenomenon. According to Hare (1976), the 1950s was the golden age of the study of groups.

During the decade of the 1960s the popularity of group services declined. This can be seen in accounts of well-known projects such as the Mobilization For Youth experiment (Weissman, 1969). Weissman for example, (1969, p. 180), stated "the planners of Mobilization For Youth did not accord group work services a major role in the fight against delinquency." Work training programs and educational opportunities were viewed as being more significant than group work services except in the area of community organization, where the skill of group workers played an important role in organizing youths and adults around important social concerns. Also, during the 1960s, the push toward a generic view of practice and the movement away from specializations in casework, group work, and community organization, tended to weaken group work specializations in professional schools and to reduce the number of professionals who were trained in group work as their primary mode of practice. Taken together, these factors contributed to the decline of group work during the decade of the 1960s.

During the 1970s interest in group work continued to wane. Fewer professional schools offered advanced courses in group work and fewer practitioners used group work as a practice method. In order to increase practitioners' awareness about the potential benefits of groups, group workers throughout the United States and Canada came together and held the First Annual Symposium for the Advancement of Group Work in 1979. Each year since then, annual symposia about group work have been convened.

This brief review of historical trends in group work practice is intended to enable the reader to understand current trends in group work practice from a broad perspective. Today, a remedial approach focusing on improving the functioning of individual group members continues as the preferred method of practice by group work educators in social work (Cowger, 1980). Recent writers such as Vinter (1967), Garvin (1981), Rose (1977), and Henry (1981) stress the use of groups for remedial purposes. Their models of practice are based on problem identification, assessment, and treatment. Other writers, however, carry on other group work traditions. For example, Schwartz (1976), Klein (1972) and Shulman (1979) emphasize the mutual aid characteristics of group work. For these writers, the worker's role is to mediate between the needs of group members and society. Ruth Middleman (1968) has written about the use of program activities and nonverbal action methods in achieving goals that are mutually agreed on by all group members. These activities are reminiscent of the social, recreational, and therapeutic activities used in settlement houses and youth organizations during the early 1900s.

The differing focuses of current practice models are equally valid, depending on the purposes, practice situations, and tasks facing the group. As mentioned in Chapter 1, groups can have many purposes. A remedial purpose, for example, may be appropriate for some populations and in some settings, such as outpatient community mental health clinics and mental hospitals.

Mutual aid and shared, reciprocal responsibility are also quite appropriate purposes for certain types of groups. This is especially true in such settings as group homes that are designed for helping members to live together, to support each other, and to cope with distressing life events. It is also true in community groups where reciprocal sharing of mutual concerns and the giving and receiving of support are central purposes. Professional social workers are frequently involved as consultants or as leaders of self-help groups that emphasize the mutual aid characteristics of a group (Toseland and Hacker, in press). For example, in Make Today Count, a medical self-help group for cancer patients, members are encouraged to share their concerns, their experiences, and the reactions of their family members in order to help each other cope with their illness. In other groups, such as Parents Without Partners, program activities such as dances, dinners, and guest speakers who present material of interest to single parents are used to enhance the enjoyment of members and to increase the beneficial effects of the group.

The usefulness and the appropriateness of different practice models suggest that group workers should make differential use of group work methods, depending on the purposes, objectives, and goals of the group they are leading. This view is shared by Kenneth Reid (1981). In a comprehensive review of the history of group work, he concludes that there has always been more than one model of group work operating in the United States and that there will continue to be several models in use to meet the many purposes and goals of group work. Group work practice has an eclectic base, which developed as a response to diverse needs for educational, recreational, mental health, and social services. For additional information, some recent writings, such as those of Alissi (1980), Papell and Rothman (1980a), Roberts and

Northen (1976), Lang (1979a, 1979b, 1972), and Papell and Rothman (1980b), review in more detail the historical trends that have resulted in the eclectic base of group work practice.

With the exception of Trecker (1946, 1980) there has been scant mention of task groups in texts about group work practice. Those who mention task groups spend only a brief portion of their texts on these groups (Henry, 1981, Klein, 1972). Earlier in the history of group work, the journals *The Group*, published between 1939 and 1955, and *Adult Leadership*, published from 1952 to 1977, devoted much of their space to articles about leading task groups. The distinction between task groups and treatment groups made today was not made in the earlier history of group work. Groups were used simultaneously for both task and treatment purposes (Siporin, 1980b). Recently, as can be seen in the bibliography in Appendix A, journals have devoted more attention to task groups.

Task groups have operated in social agencies since the settlement houses and charity organizations began more than 100 years ago. Task groups are essential for effective client service and for the smooth operation of social agencies. The current need for expertise about task groups is becoming critical as more agencies then ever before use team approaches for service delivery. Siporin (1980b, p. 19) states, "there is a need to give much more attention than we do at present in social work practice and in social work education to work with task groups."

## KNOWLEDGE FROM SOCIAL SCIENCE RESEARCH

According to Hare (1976), the scientific study of groups began at the turn of the century. A basic research question, which was asked at that time and continues to receive much attention today, concerns the extent to which being a part of a group influences the individual group member. Triplett (1898), for example, examined the effect that other cyclists had on individual cyclists during races and found that a racer's competitiveness appeared to depend on the activities of others on the track. Taylor (1903) found that productivity increased among workers who were freed from the pressure to conform to the standards of other workers. Those early findings suggest that the presence of others has a significant influence on an individual group member. The presence of others tends to generate forces to conform to the standards of behavior that are expected of those who belong to the group.

Other early social scientists also recognized the influence of groups on an individual behavior. Le Bon (1910) referred to the forces that were generated by group interaction as "group contagion" and "group mind," recognizing that people in groups react differently from individuals. McDougall (1920) extended the concept of the "group mind." He noted the existence of groups as entities and pointed out a number of group as a whole properties that could be studied as separate and distinct phenomenon from properties affecting individuals working outside of a group.

The concept of a primary group was also an important contribution to the study of groups. Cooley (1909) defined a *primary group* as a small, informal group such as a family or a friendship group, which has a tremendous influence on members' values, moral standards, and normative behaviors. The primary group was therefore viewed as essential in understanding socialization and development.

Few studies of small group processes were published between 1905 and 1920, but activity in these areas increased after World War I (Hare, 1976). A number of experiments conducted during that time illustrated the powerful effects of group forces on the judgments and the behavior of group members. Allport (1924), for example, found that the presence of others improved task performance. Sherif (1936) placed subjects in a darkened room with a pinpoint of light at one end of it. Known as the autokinetic effect, a stable light in a darkened room appears to move slightly. After Sherif determined an average range of perceived movement based on the responses of individual subjects, he placed them together in groups in the darkened room. He found that subjects modified their estimates of the amount the light moved based on the opinions of others in the group. Further, the subjects continued to give these modified estimates after leaving the group.

Asch (1957), following up on Sherif's findings, placed confederates who had been instructed to give false estimates in a room with subjects who were asked to judge the length of a line in comparison to a standard line of a given length. Confederates were instructed to make incorrect responses in the presence of the subject. Would the subjects adhere to their correct judgments or alter their judgments based on the confederates' responses? The subjects altered their judgments to conform to those of the confederates 30 percent of the time even though the confederates' judgments were clearly incorrect.

After World War I, social scientists also began to study groups operating in the community. One of the earliest social scientists to study groups in their natural environments was Frederic Thrasher (1927). He studied gangs of delinquents in the Chicago area by becoming friendly with gang members and by observing the internal operations of gangs. Thrasher (1927) noted that every member of a gang had a status within the group that was attached to the functional role that the member played for the gang. Thrasher also drew attention to the culture that developed within a gang, suggesting there was a common code that all members followed. The code was enforced by group opinion, coercion, and physical punishment. Thrasher's work and the works of Clifford Shaw (1930) and William Whyte (1943) have influenced the ways that group work is practiced with youths in settlement houses, neighborhood centers, and youth organizations.

Later, Sherif and his collegues (1953, 1955, 1956) relied on naturalistic observations of groups of boys in a summer camp to demonstrate how cohesion and intergroup hostility develop. Groups of boys who spent time together and had common goals such as winning a tug-of-war became more cooperative, developed liking for one another, and felt solidarity with their teammates. As this occurred, antagonism between groups increased. Bringing boys from different groups together only served to increase tension until tasks were assigned that required the joint effort of boys from different groups.

Social scientists also learned more about people's behavior in groups from studies done in industry and in the United States Army. Perhaps the most famous of all industrial studies is the classic series of studies at Western Electric's Hawthorne Plant in Chicago (Roethlisberger, 1941; Roethlisberger and Dickson, 1939, 1975). These studies were designed to test whether piece-rate wage incentives were effective in increasing the output of workers who assembled telephone equipment. The incentives were designed in such a way that rate increases by one team member would also benefit other team members. Management believed such a system would encourage individual productivity and increase group spirit and morale because all team members would benefit from the increase in productivity.

It was found that an informal group had developed among team members. Despite the opportunity to improve individual and group wages, workers did not produce more under the new incentive system. Results from the studies suggest that informal norms of what constituted a fair day's work governed the workers' behavior. Members of a work group that produced too much were ridiculed as being "rate busters" and those that produced too little were called "chiselers." Occasionally, more severe sanctions called "binging" were applied by team members when a worker did not conform with the team's notion of a fair day's work. "Binging" consisted of striking a fellow worker as hard as possible on the upper arm while verbally asking the worker to comply with the group's norms.

Studies conducted on combat units during World War II have also illustrated the powerful effects that small groups can have on the behavior of their members. For example, in describing the fighting ability of combat soldiers, Stouffer (1949) and Shils (1950) have suggested that the courage of the average soldier was only partially sustained by hatred of the enemy and the patriotic ideas of a democratic society. Their studies revealed that soldiers' loyalty to their particular unit strengthened their morale and supported them during periods of particularly intense combat stress. Similarly, studies conducted in other settings by Lewin (1951) and by Cartwright and Lippitt (1961) found that individuals needed social supports to uphold their values and beliefs and that when members diverge too greatly from a group's norms and values they will be punished for their behavior or expelled from the group.

During the 1950s, an explosion of knowledge concerning small groups took place. Earlier experiments by Lewin, Lippitt, and White (1939), Jennings (1947, 1950), Moreno (1934), Jennings (1947, 1950), Moreno (1934), and Bales (1950) spurred interest in the study of both task and treatment groups during the 1950s. Some of the most important findings from this period are summarized in the work of Hare (1976), Cartwright and Zander (1968), Shaw (1976), Kiesler (1978), and Nixon (1979). Because they are reflected in a discussion of group dynamics and leadership in Chapters 3 and 4 of this text, they will not be repeated here. It is interesting to note, however, that the major themes of small group research that were initially developed in the first half of the twentieth century, that is, conformity, communication, and interaction patterns, leadership, interpersonal preference, and social perception continue to dominate the research efforts of social scientists investigating the dynamics of small groups today.

## INFLUENTIAL THEORIES

From knowledge about small groups accumulated over the years in laboratory and natural settings, investigators of group phenomenon began to develop comprehensive theories to explain group functioning. An enormous variety of these theories exist (see Douglas, 1979). This chapter will consider five major theories: (1) psychoanalytic theory, (2) learning theory, (3) field theory, (4) social exchange theory, and (5) systems theory. Although we believe that a thorough knowledge of systems theory is basic to all group work practice, we have included other theories in the following discussion because they have had an important influence on group work practice and we believe that group work practitioners should be familiar with them. When continuing to improve and refine practice skills, group workers may want to examine one or more of these theories in greater depth.

### Psychoanalytic Theory

Psychoanalytic theory has had an important influence on group work practice. In his work *Group Psychology and the Analysis of the Ego*, Freud (1922) set forth his theoretical formulations about groups and their influence on human behavior. Many of Freud's other works have also had an important influence on group work practice. For example, commonly used terms such as *insight*, *ego strength*, and *defense mechanisms* originated in Freud's work. Although psychoanalytic theory focuses primarily on the individual and Freud did not practice group psychotherapy, many of his followers, including Redl (1942, 1944), Bion (1959), Whitaker and Lieberman (1964), and Yalom (1975), have adapted psychoanalytic theory for working with groups. Psychoanalytic theory has also had an important influence on the founders of other practice theories used in groups. These include Eric Berne's transactional analysis, Fritz Perls's gestalt therapy, and Frank Moreno's psychodrama.

According to psychoanalytic theory, group members act out unresolved conflicts from early life experiences in the group. In many ways the group becomes a re-enactment of the family situation. Freud (1922), for example, describes the group leader as the all-powerful father figure who reigns supreme over group members. Group members identify with the group leader as the "ego ideal" (Wyss, 1973). Members form transference reactions to the group leader and to each other on the basis of their early life experiences. Thus, the interactions that occur in the group illustrate members' personality structure and defense mechanisms. The group leader uses transference reactions to help members work through unresolved conflicts by exploring past behavior patterns and by linking these patterns to current behaviors. The group leader might, for example, interpret the behavior of the two group members who were struggling for the leader's attention as unresolved sibling rivalry. When interpretations made by the group worker are timed appropriately, members gain insight into their own behavior. According to psychoanalytic theory, insight is the essential ingredient in modifying and changing behavior patterns inside and outside of the group.

More recent conceptions of psychoanalytic group treatment (see, for example, Polansky, 1982; Yalom, 1975) have adapted and modified classical psychoanalytic theory to include a greater emphasis on the here-and-now experiences of group interaction. Emphasis on the here-and-now experiences of group members are useful in ensuring that members deal with issues of immediate concern to them. From an analysis of here and now behavior patterns in the group, the leader can help members reconstruct unresolved childhood conflicts. Through direct, mutual, interpersonal communications, members build their interpersonal skill, their adaptive capacities, and their ego strength, as well as gain insight into their behavior. The cohesiveness of the group allows members to reveal intimate details about their personal lives and to act out their conflicts in a safe, supportive environment.

A thorough discussion of psychoanalytic theory of group functioning is beyond the scope of this book. For further explanation of modern adaptations of psychoanalytic theory to group work practice, see Yalom (1975) and the *International Journal of Group Psychotherapy*.

## Learning Theory

Learning theory has also had an important influence on current methods of group work practice and current concepts of group functioning, although, like psychoanalytic theory, it primarily focuses on the behavior of individuals rather than on the behavior of groups. According to social learning theory (Bandura, 1977b), the behavior of group members can be explained by one of three methods of learning. In the classical approach to learning theory, behavior becomes associated with a stimulus. For example, a worker responds by making a negative verbal comment each time a member turns and speaks to another member while the worker or other group members are speaking. After several times, the mere stimulus of the member turning, without speaking, will be enough to cue the worker to respond with a negative verbal comment.

A second and more common method of learning is called operant conditioning. In this paradigm, the behavior of the group members and the worker are governed by the consequences of their actions. Thus, if member A acts in a certain way and member B reacts in a positive fashion, member A would be likely to continue the behavior and repeat it in the future. Similarly, if a group worker receives negative feedback from group members about a particular behavior, the worker would be less likely to behave that way in the future.

A number of writers (see, for example, Rose 1974, 1977; Feldman and Wodarski, 1975; Feldman, Caplinger, and Wodarski, 1983) use operant learning theory principles in their approach to group work. For example, Rose (1977) suggests that tokens, praise, or other reinforcers can be used to increase desired behavior and decrease undesired behavior in the group or in the external environment. In the group, the worker might use praise to increase member to member communications and negative verbal comments to decrease member to leader communications. To help members with a problem they have experienced in the outside environment, such as being overweight, the group leader might ask the member to develop a plan that specifies self-imposed rewards for behavior that decreases caloric intake and self-imposed sanctions for behavior that increases caloric intake.

Bandura (1977b) has developed a third learning paradigm called social learning theory. If group members or the group worker were to wait for classical conditioning or operant conditioning to occur, behavior in groups would be learned very slowly. Bandura (1977b) proposes that the majority of learning takes place through observational learning and vicarious reinforcement or punishment. For example, when a particular group member is praised for a certain behavior, that group member and other group members reproduce the behavior at a later time hoping to receive similar praise. When a group member who performs a certain behavior is ignored or punished by social sanctions, other group members learn not to behave in that manner because such behavior results in a negative outcome.

In response to concerns that learning theory has not taken into consideration motivations, expectations, and other cognitive aspects of behavior, Mahoney (1974) and others have developed cognitive approaches to learning theory. Although learning theorists have not attempted to explain the functioning of groups as a whole, learning theory principles have been shown to be useful in helping members to make desired changes. All group workers should be familiar with the basic principles of learning theory and cognitive behavior modification. Because of its particular relevance for treatment groups, we will draw upon many principles of classical, operant, and social learning theory in our discussion of treatment groups in Chapter 8.

## Field Theory

Kurt Lewin, more than any other social scientist, has come to be associated with the study of group dynamics. He conducted numerous experiments on the forces that account for behavior in small groups. For example, in an early study investigating leadership, Lewin, Lippett, and White (1939) created three types of groups with authoritarian, democratic, and laissez-faire leadership. The results of this study are reported in Chapter 4. Lewin and his colleagues were the first to apply the scientific method in developing a theory of groups. In 1944, he and his colleagues set up laboratories and formed the Research Center for Group Dynamics at the Massachusetts Institute of Technology.

According to Lewin's field theory, "a group has a life space, it occupies a position relative to other objects in this life space, it is oriented toward goals, it locomotes in pursuit of these goals, and it may encounter barriers in the process of locomotion" (Shepard, 1964, p. 25). The unique contribution of field theory is that it views the group as a gestalt, that is, an entity of opposing forces that acts to hold members in the group and to move the group along in its quest for goal achievement. According to Lewin (1947), groups are constantly changing to cope with their social situation although there are times when a "quasi-stationary equilibrium" exists for all groups. In all cases, however, the behavior of individual group members and the group itself must be seen as a function of the total situation (Lewin, 1946).

In developing field theory, Lewin introduced a member of concepts to aid in understanding the forces at work in a group. Among these are (1) roles, which refer to the status, rights, and duties of group members; (2) norms, which are rules governing the behavior of group members; (3) power, which is the ability of members to control one another; (4) cohesion, which is the amount of attraction the members of the group feel for one another and for the group; (5) consensus, which is defined as the degree of agreement regarding goals and other group phenomena; and (6) valence, which is the potency of goals and objects in the life space of the group.

Lewin sought to understand the forces occurring in the group as a whole from the perspective of individual group members. He did this mathematically and topographically, using vectors to describe group forces. Emphasizing the importance of properties of the group as a whole on the individual member, most field theorists have focused their research efforts on *cohesion*, which they define as the totality of forces acting on individual members to keep them in the group. Studies by field theorists have shown that cohesion is related to agreement on goals and norms, shared understanding, and similar demographic backgrounds of members, as well as to productivity, satisfaction, and cooperative interaction patterns (Cartwright, 1951; Lippitt, 1957; Cartwright and Zander, 1968).

Along with his interest in formulating a theoretical model of group dynamics, Lewin was interested in the impact of groups on individuals' psychological makeup. Before his death in 1947, Lewin developed the t-group as a way to observe the effects of group processes on group members and as a means to help individual group members change their own behavior. Although he was not directly involved, he helped to find the first National Training Laboratory in Group Development in 1947. Since then, t-groups have been used extensively at the National Training Laboratories as an experiental means to train group facilitators, to teach individuals about the effects of group dynamics, and to help individuals examine and change their own behavior. Relying on a principle in Lewin's field theory which suggests that individuals will not change their own behavior unless they see their behavior and their attitudes as others see them, the t-group experience attempts to provide participants with extensive feedback about their own behavior. Members are confronted with the effects of their behavior on other group members and on the group's facilitator. Role plays, simulations, and other experimental program activities are often used to illustrate how group processes develop and how they affect members.

## Social Exchange Theory

Whereas field theory emphasizes the group as a whole, social exchange theory focuses on the behavior of individual group members. Thibaut and Kelley (1959); Blau (1964); and Homans (1961) are the principal developers of this approach to groups. Deriving their theory from animal psychology, economic analysis, and game theory, social exchange theorists suggest that when people interact in groups each will attempt to behave in a way that will maximize rewards and minimize punishments. Group members initiate interactions because these social exchanges provide them with something of value such as approval. According to social exchange theorists, because something is not ordinarily gained without giving something, there is an exchange implied in all human relationships.

In social exchange theory, group behavior is analyzed by observing the ways that individual members seek rewards while dealing with the sustained social interaction occurring in a group. For the individual in the group, the decision to express a given behavior is based on a comparison of the rewards and punishments that are expected to be derived from the behavior. Group members act to increase positive consequences and decrease negative consequences. Social exchange theory also focuses on the way members influence one another during social interactions. According to social exchange theorists, the result of any social exchange is based on the amount of social power and the amount of social dependence in a particular interaction.

Social exchange theory has been criticized as being mechanistic because it assumes that people are always rational beings who act according to their analysis of rewards and punishments (Shepard, 1964). For the most part, these criticisms are unfounded. Social exchange theorists are aware that cognitive processes affect how people behave in groups (see, for example, Kelley and Stakelski, 1970; Kelley and Thibaut, 1969). Group members' perceptions of rewards and punishments are influenced by cognitive processes such as intentions and expectations. Thus, the work of social exchange theorists in psychology and of symbolic interaction theorists in sociology have helped to account for the role of cognitive processes in the behavior of individuals in groups and other social interactions. The influence of symbolic interaction theory on group work practice can be seen in the work of Balgopal and Vassil (1983).

## Systems Theory

Systems theory attempts to understand the group as a system of elements that are interacting. Although psychodynamic, behavior, field, and social exchange theory are useful in understanding aspects of group functioning, systems theory is probably the most widely utilized and broadly applied theory of group functioning (Anderson, 1979; Olsen, 1968). A number of writers have applied systems theory to group functioning. Each has a somewhat different conception of groups as social systems. Some of the most important concepts used by several systems theorists will be described here to present a balanced view of systems theory from a variety of perspectives.

Talcott Parsons (1951) is a leading contributor to our understanding of groups as social systems. To Parsons, groups are social systems with a number of interdependent members attempting to maintain order and a stable equilibrium while they function as a unified whole. Groups are constantly facing changing demands in their quest to attain goals and to maintain a stable equilibrium. Groups must mobilize their resources and act to meet changing demands if they are to survive. According to Parsons, Bales, and Shils (1953), there are four major functional tasks for systems such as a group: (1) integration, which is ensuring that members of groups fit together;

(2) adaptation, which is ensuring that groups change to cope with the demands of their environment; (3) pattern maintenance, which is ensuring that groups define and sustain their basic purposes, identities, and procedures; and (4) goal attainment, which is ensuring that groups pursue and accomplish their tasks. According to Parsons (1951), in order for groups to be effective, they must successfully accomplish these four functional tasks to remain in equilibrium.

The work of successfully carrying out these four functional tasks is left to the group's leader and to its members. The group leader and the group members act to help their group survive so they can be gratified as the group reaches its goal (Mills, 1967). To do this, group members observe and assess the group's progress toward its goals and take action to avoid problems. The likelihood that a group will survive depends on the demands of the environment, the extent to which members identify with group goals, and the degree to which members believe goals are attainable. By overcoming obstacles and by successfully handling the functional tasks confronting them, groups strive to remain in a state of equilibrium.

Robert Bales, another important systems theorist, has a somewhat different conception of groups as social systems. Whereas Parsons was interested in developing a generalizable systems model to explain societal as well as group functioning, Bales has concentrated his efforts on observing and theorizing about small task groups in laboratory settings. According to Bales (1950), groups must solve two general types of problems to maintain themselves. These include (1) instrumental problems, such as the group reaching its goals, and (2) socioemotional problems, which include interpersonal difficulties, problems of coordination, and member satisfaction (Wilson, 1978). Instrumental problems are caused by demands placed on the group from the outside environment, and socioemotional problems arise from within the group.

The group worker should always be concerned about process and outcome, that is, about members' social and emotional needs and the task accomplishments expected of the group. However, the two types of problems must be balanced if the group is to survive. Attention to instrumental problems alone will lead to dissatisfaction and conflict within the group. Exclusive attention to socioemotional problems, however, leads to the group's failure to accomplish its objectives and goals. The worker, therefore, is placed in the precarious position of attending to both sets of problems to maintain the group's adequate functioning. Because instrumental and socioemotional needs are often in conflict, it is usually impossible to attend to both sets of problems simultaneously. Therefore, workers are forced to work on either instrumental or socioemotional problems at any one time.

In comparison to Parsons, Bales' systems model emphasizes tension and antagonism rather than harmony and equilibrium. Groups tend to vacillate between adaptation to the outside environment and attention to internal integration. Bales (1950) calls this the group's "dynamic equilibrium." Swings in attention are the result of the functional needs of the group in its struggle to maintain itself. In order to study this "dynamic equilibrium",

Bales observed interactions in a number of different kinds of task groups such as conferences, teams and delegate councils (Bales 1950, 1954, 1955). Bales found that, in order to deal with instrumental problems, group members asked for or gave opinions, asked for or gave information, and made or asked for suggestions. To handle socioemotional problems, group members expressed agreement and disagreement, showed tension or released tension, and showed solidarity or antagonism. Through these interactions group members dealt with problems of communication, evaluation, control, decision making, tension reduction, and integration.

Bales (1950) has developed a scheme for analyzing group interaction, based on his theory about how group members deal with instrumental and expressive tasks. This scheme is called Interaction Process Analysis. It classifies members interactions in twelve categories. Analysis of the distribution of interactions in each category in problem-solving groups suggests that typical task groups emphasize giving and receiving information early in group meetings, giving and asking for opinions in the middle phase, and giving and asking for suggestions in later phases (Shepard, 1964). Bales' (1954, 1955) research suggests that groups go through a natural process of evolution and development. It also indicates that in most groups about 25 percent of all members' behaviors are positive reactions, 56 percent are responses to questions, 12 percent are negative reactions, and 7 percent are asking questions. Therefore, about half of all communications in groups are responses to questions, and the other half are divided between positive reactions, negative reactions, and questions (Shepard, 1964). Bales, Cohen, and Williamson (1979) have continued to develop and refine this system of analyzing group interactions. The new system, known as SYMLOG, is explained in Chapters 5 and 8.

The final conception of systems theory relevant to our understanding of group dynamics has been presented in Homans' (1950) early work, *The Human Group*. It is also evident in the writings of Germain and Gitterman (1980 and Siporin (1980a) on ecological systems theory. According to these writers, groups are in constant interaction with their environments. They occupy an ecological niche. Homans (1950) suggests that groups have an external system and an internal system. The external system represents a group's way of handling the adaptive problems that result from its relationship with its social and physical environment. The internal system consists of the patterns of activities, interactions, and norms occurring within the group as it attempts to function. Like Bales, Homans notes that the relative dominance of the internal system as compared to the external system varies, depending on the demands of the external and the internal environment of the group. Homans, however, denies the homeostatic idea of equilibrium proposed by Parsons and Bales, preferring to conceive of groups as ever-changing entities in which change and the constant struggle for new equilibrium are commonplace.

Although they share many of their ideas with Homans (1950) and other system theorists, the model of practice developed by Germain and Gitterman (1980), and by Siporin (1980a), suggest that attention should be given to the dynamic, ever-changing equilibrium of task and treatment groups. They point out the constant exchange that all social systems have with their environment. They also emphasize the possibilities for growth and change, called *morphogenetic properties*, that are a part of all social systems.

The different conceptualizations of systems theory described here may at first appear somewhat confusing. However, when considering the vast array of groups in modern society and the differences in people's experiences in them, it becomes easier to understand how different conceptualizations of systems theory have developed. It is important to recognize that each conceptualization of systems theory represents a unique attempt to understand the processes which occur in all social systems. Concepts derived from these differing views of systems theory which are particularly relevant for group workers include

1. The existence of properties of the group as a whole that arise from the interactions of individual group members.
2. The powerful effects of group forces on members' behavior.
3. The struggle of groups to maintain themselves as entities when confronted with conflicts.
4. The awareness that groups must relate to an external environment as well as attend to their internal functioning.
5. The idea that groups are in a constant state of becoming, developing, and changing, which influences that equilibrium and continued existence.
6. The notion that groups have a developmental life cycle.

Workers can use these concepts to facilitate the development of group processes that help treatment and task groups achieve their goals and help members satisfy their socioemotional needs.

## SUMMARY

This chapter described historical developments in the practice of group work and in the social sciences. A historical perspective was presented to help workers develop a broad understanding of the uses of groups in practice settings and to develop a knowledge base they can use to practice effectively with many different types of groups.

The historical overview of group work practice presented in this chapter suggests that throughout the twentieth century groups have been used for a variety of different purposes including education, recreation, socialization, and remediation. The emphasis on the use of groups for education, recreation, and socialization has declined in recent years in favor of an increased interest in the use of groups for remediation. This trend parallels the gradual transition during the 1930s and 1940s away from group work's amorphous roots in adult education, recreation, and social work to its formal incorporation into the social work profession during the 1950s.

This chapter also briefly explored historical developments in social science research that have relevance for understanding group processes. Findings from these studies emphasize the powerful influence that the group as a whole has on individual group members. The chapter closed with a review of five theories: (1) psychoanalytic theory, (2) learning theory, (3) field theory, (4) social exchange theory, and (5) systems theory, all of which have had an important influence on group work practice.

# 3

# Understanding
# Group Dynamics

An understanding of group dynamics is useful for practicing effectively with both task and treatment groups. Although many theories describe group functioning, fundamental to all of them is an understanding of groups as social systems (Anderson, 1979). A system is made up of elements and their interactions. Task and treatment groups, as social systems, can be defined as people and their interactions. These interactions are often referred to as the *group process*. The group process generates unique forces that influence group members and the group as a whole. The forces generated by the group process are often referred to as *group dynamics*. These forces have been of interest to group workers for many years. (See, for example, Elliott, 1928; Coyle, 1930, 1937.) In this text, we use the term *group dynamics* to refer to the properties that result from the group process, such as norms, roles, and status hierarchies. When we discuss the functioning of the group as a whole, we are focusing on how group processes develop and on the group dynamics that result from this development.

One of the worker's most important tasks is to recognize and utilize the potent dynamics that are generated by a group as it develops. Helen Northen (1969) and others remind us that this is not an automatic process. Appropriate use of group dynamics can lead to positive outcomes for the group and its members. Inattention to these dynamics, however, can result in a lack of direction and focus, and inappropriate use can have detrimental effects. For example, in an in-depth examination of a variety of different encounter groups, Lieberman, Yalom, and Miles (1973) found that many of the groups they studied produced casualties, some of which resulted in severe mental disorders among group participants. Similar findings reported by Galinsky and Schopler (1977) and by Bednar and Kaul (1978) suggest that the forces exerted in groups can be powerful and therefore should be carefully monitored by the worker as the group develops. It is clear that groups can unleash harmful as well as helpful forces. The Hitler youth movement of the 1920s and 1930s, the Ku Klux Klan, and the tragedy at Jonestown are just three examples of the use of group dynamics for harmful purposes. This chapter seeks to help group workers recognize, understand, and use the dynamics that are generated through the group process so as to achieve goals that are consistent with the humanistic value base of the social work profession.

## GROUP DYNAMICS

Although there have been several attempts to develop comprehensive schemes for classifying group dynamics, none has proven to be totally satisfactory. Our discussion focuses on four areas of group dynamics that are of particular importance to group workers in understanding and working effectively with all types of task and treatment groups. These areas include (1) the communication and interaction patterns occurring in groups, (2) the attraction of groups for their members, (3) the social controls that are exerted in groups, and (4) the culture that develops in groups. A firm grasp of these areas is essential for understanding the social structure of groups and for developing beginning-level skills in group work practice.

### Communication and Interaction Patterns

According to Helen Northen (1969, p. 17), "social interaction is a term for the dynamic interplay of forces in which contact between persons results in a modification of the behavior and attitudes of the participants." Verbal and nonverbal communications are the components of social interaction. Communication is the process by which people use symbols to convey meanings to each other. Communication entails (1) encoding of a person's perceptions, thoughts, and feelings into language and other symbols, (2) the transmission of these symbols or language, and (3) the decoding of the transmission by another person. This process is shown in Figure 3–1. As members of a group

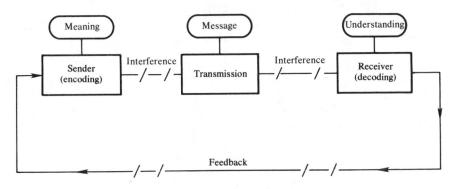

**Figure 3–1**   A Model of the Process of Communication

communicate to one another, a reciprocal pattern of interaction emerges. The interaction patterns that develop can be beneficial or harmful to the group. A group worker who is knowledgeable about helpful communications and interactions can intervene in the patterns that are established in order to help the group achieve desired goals and to assure the socioemotional satisfaction of members.

*Communication As a Process.*   The first step in understanding and intervening in interaction patterns is for the worker to be aware that whenever people are together in a group they are communicating. As shown in Figure 3–1, all communications intend to convey a message. Silence, for example, can communicate disinterest, sorrow, thoughtfulness, or anger. In addition, every group member communicates not only to transmit information but also for many other reasons. Kiesler (1978) has suggested that people communicate with such interpersonal concerns as (1) understanding other people and finding out where they stand in relation to other people, (2) persuading others, (3) gaining or maintaining power, (4) defending themselves, (5) provoking a reaction from others, (6) making an impression on others, (7) gaining or maintaining relationships, (8) presenting a unified image to the group. Many other important reasons for communication could be added to this list.

Workers who are aware that group members communicate for many reasons can observe and assess the communication and interaction patterns of each group member and of the group as a whole. Because patterns of communication are often consistent across different situations, group workers can use this information to work with individual group members and the group as a whole. For example, a worker observes that one member is consistently unassertive in the group. The worker may help the member to practice responding assertively to a situation in the group. Because the pattern of unassertiveness is likely to occur in situations outside the group, the worker might also suggest that the member practice being assertive in selected situations encountered between group meetings.

In addition to the meanings that are transmitted in every communication, the worker should also be aware that messages are often received selectively. *Selective perception* refers to the screening of messages so that they are congruent with one's belief system. As shown in Figure 3–1, messages are decoded and their meanings are received. Individual group members have a unique understanding of communications on the basis of their selective perception. Selected screening sometimes results in blocking of messages so that they are not decoded and received. Napier and Gershenfeld (1981) suggest that (1) life positions which result from experience in early childhood, (2) stereotypes, (3) the status and position of the communicator, (4) previous experiences, and (5) assumptions and values can all influence the perception of a communication. Thus, what might appear to a naive observer as a simple, straightforward, and objective social interaction might have a great deal of hidden meaning, for the sender and the receiver of a particular communication.

It is not possible, or even desirable, for workers to analyze each interpersonal communication that occurs in a group. However, with a little practice, workers can develop a "third ear," that is, workers can train themselves to be aware of the meanings behind messages and their impact on a particular group member and on the group as a whole. Using this skill, group workers are in a much better position to intervene in the group than if they remain naive to the meanings of messages being communicated and received by each member.

Communications can also be distorted in transmission. In Figure 3–1, distortion is represented as interference. Among the most common transmission problems are language barriers. Frequently, workers conduct groups with members from different cultural, racial, and ethnic backgrounds for whom English is a second language. In addition to problems of understanding accents and dialects, the meanings of many words are culturally defined and may not be interpreted in the way the communicator intended. Special care must be taken in these situations. Draper (1979), Kadushin (1972), and Gitterman and Schaeffer (1972) offer some helpful suggestions for becoming aware of how language barriers affect communication.

Similarly, problems in receiving messages may cause communication barriers for the aged and others who frequently experience hearing losses. Noise and other distortions inside or outside of the meeting room can cause transmission problems that interfere with effective communication. Approximately one third of all elderly men have some hearing impairment (Kart, Metress, and Metress, 1978). Thus, when working with groups of older persons, the practitioner should be alert to members' potential difficulties in hearing what other members are saying. Techniques for transmitting messages to the hearing impaired are suggested by Blazer (1978).

In order to prevent distortions in communications from causing misunderstandings and conflict, it is important to ensure that members receive feedback about their communications. Feedback is a way of checking to ensure that the meanings of the messages that are communicated are understood correctly. For feedback to be used appropriately it should (1) describe the content of the communication or the behavior as it is perceived by the group member, (2) be given to the member who sent the message as soon as the message has been received, and (3) be expressed in a tentative manner so that those who send messages understand that the feedback is designed to check for distortions rather than to confront or attack them. Examples of feedback are "John, I understood you to say . . ." or "Mary, if I understand you correctly, you are saying. . . ." When feedback is used correctly and frequently, it can prevent many distortions that arise from faulty encoding, transmission, or decoding of messages. For an extensive discussion about the effects of feedback on task group behavior, see Nadler (1979).

*Interaction Patterns.*    In addition to becoming aware of communication processes, the worker must also consider patterns of interaction that develop in a group. A variety of different interaction patterns have been identified in the social work literature (Middleman, 1978) including the (1) maypole, in which the leader is the central figure, and communication occurs from leader to member, or from member to leader, (2) round robin, in which each member takes a turn at talking, (3) hot seat, in which there is an extended back and forth exchange between the leader and a member as the other members watch, and (4) free floating, in which all members take responsibility for communicating according to what is being said and not said in the group. The first three patterns are leader-centered, because the leader structures these patterns. The fourth pattern is group-centered, because it emerges from the initiative of group members.

In most situations, workers should strive to facilitate the development of group-centered rather than leader-centered interaction patterns. In group-centered patterns, members freely interact with each other. Communication channels between members of the group are open. In leader-centered patterns, communications are directed from members to the worker, or from the worker to group members, thereby reducing members' opportunities to freely communicate with each other. Group-centered communication patterns tend to increase social interaction, increase group morale, and increase members' commitment to group goals. However, group-centered patterns can be less efficient than leader-centered patterns because communication by some group members may be superfluous or extraneous to group tasks (Shaw, 1964; Bavelas, 1950). Sorting out useful communications can take a tremendous amount of group time. Therefore, in task groups that are making routine decisions, when time constraints are important and when there is little need for creative problem solving, the worker may deliberately choose to encourage leader-centered rather than group-centered interaction patterns.

In order to establish and maintain appropriate interaction patterns, the worker should be familiar with the factors that influence them. Patterns of interaction are affected by (1) the cues and the reinforcements that members receive for specific interactional exchanges, (2) the emotional bonds that develop between group members, (3) the subgroups that develop in the group, (4) the size and physical arrangement of the group, and (5) power and status relationships in the group. Workers can change interaction patterns by modifying these important factors.

CUES AND REINFORCERS. After discussing changes in interaction patterns that may enhance the group's functioning, workers and members can decide to use verbal and non-verbal behaviors to facilitate modifications in established patterns. Cues such as words or gestures can act as signals to group members to talk more or less frequently to one another or to the worker. Workers and members can also use selective attention and other reinforcers to encourage beneficial interactions. As more appropriate interaction patterns are established, cues and reinforcers can be used intermittently and then be allowed to fade gradually to maintain newly developed patterns (Toseland, Krebs and Vahsen, 1978).

EMOTIONAL BONDS. Positive emotional bonds such as interpersonal liking and attraction serve to increase interpersonal interaction, and negative emotional bonds reduce solidarity between members and result in decreased interpersonal interaction. Attraction and interpersonal liking between two members may occur because they share common interests, similar values and ideologies, complementary personality characteristics, or similar demographic characteristics (Newcomb, 1956; Hare, 1976). Bonds may also form because of the emotional or social needs of members. From a social exchange theory perspective, Thibaut and Kelley (1959) propose that interpersonal attraction results from the rewards and satisfactions that are obtained when needs are met by fellow group members. Sometimes positive emotional bonds between particular group members form as a result of particular concerns or self-interests. Emotional bonds may also be based on mutual dislike of others in the group, mutual disatisfactions with the group process, or mutual apathy about the process. Hartford (1971) calls alignments based on emotional bonds "interest alliances." For example, two members of a planning council may vote the same way on certain issues and they may communicate similar thoughts and feelings to the other members of the council on the basis of their common interests in the needs of the business community. Similarly, members of a minority group may form an interest alliance based on their perception that they have similar concerns about the lack of community services for minority groups.

SUBGROUPS. Subgroups also affect the interaction patterns in a group. Subgroups form from emotional bonds and interest alliances among subsets of group members. They occur in all groups; without them there would be no dynamic tension in the group. However, subgroups become a problem when the attraction of members within a subgroup becomes greater than their attraction to the group as a whole. Hartford (1971) discusses a variety of different types of subgroups including dyads, triads, and cliques. Hartford (1971) also mentions special forms of the subgroup, such as the isolate and the scapegoat, both of whom stand alone in a group. Isolates do not interact with the group, whereas scapegoats receive negative attention and critical evaluative communications from the group.

In some situations the worker may actively encourage members to form subgroups. This is particularly true in groups that are too large and cumbersome for detailed work to be accomplished. For example, subgroup formation is often necessary and useful in large task groups such as committees, delegate councils, and some teams so that work can be accomplished in smaller units. Members are assigned to a particular subgroup in order to work on a specific task or subtask. The results of the subgroup's work is then brought back to the larger group for consideration and action.

Whether or not the worker actively encourages members to form subgroups, they occur naturally because not everyone in a group will interact with equal valence. The formation of intense subgroup attraction, however, can be problematic for the worker. Subgroup members may challenge the worker's authority. They may substitute their own goals and their own methods of attaining them for the goals of the larger group. Subgroup members can be disruptive by communicating among themselves while others are speaking and by failing to listen to group members who are not a part of the subgroup.

When intense subgroup attraction appears to be developing, the worker may want to intervene to prevent it from interfering with the group as a whole. This can be done by changing seating arrangements, asking for certain members to interact more frequently with other members, using program materials and exercises that separate subgroup members, or by assigning tasks for members to do outside of the group in subgroups that are composed of different groupings of members. If intense subgroup loyalties have already formed within a group, the worker should facilitate a discussion of the reasons for them and their impact on the group as a whole. A frank discussion of the reasons for subgroup formation can often benefit the entire group, because it can reveal problems in the group's goal setting, communication, interaction, and decision-making processes. After the discussion, the worker should try to increase the attraction of the group for its members and help them reach out to one another to reopen channels of communication.

In some cases, the worker may wish to utilize subgroups for therapeutic purposes. For example, Yalom (1975) suggests that the worker can use relationships between members to recapitulate the family group experience. Transference and countertransference reactions among members may be used to help members resolve issues and concerns that are the result of unresolved developmental issues in their early family life.

SIZE AND PHYSICAL ARRANGEMENTS. Other factors that influence interaction patterns in groups are the size and physical arrangement of the group. As the size of the group increases, the possibilities for potential relationships increase dramatically. For example, with three people there are six potential combinations of relationships, but in a group with seven people there are 966 possible relationships (Kephart, 1951). Thus, in large groups, each member has more social relationships to be aware of and to maintain but less opportunity to maintain them (Huff and Prantianida, 1968). With increased group size there are also fewer opportunities and less time for members to communicate. In some groups, the lack of opportunity to participate may not be much of a problem. It should not be automatically assumed that members who are not actively participating are uninvolved in the group, although this may be true. Commonly, some group members welcome a chance for active involvement and participate only when they have an important contribution that might otherwise be overlooked.

Often, however, a reduced chance to participate leads to dissatisfaction and a lack of commitment to decisions made by the group. Increased group size also tends to lead to subgroup formation, as members strive to get to know those who are in close physical proximity to where they are seated. In large groups, one or two members often do much of the talking, positioning themselves before the group and maintaining a leader-centered interaction pattern (Zimet and Schneider, 1969). In this way, these individuals attempt to maintain control over the group, reducing the chances for subgroup formation, and decreasing the possibilities for members to communicate with one another.

The physical arrangement or structure of the group also influences the interaction patterns. Most of the research on the physical arrangement of the group has been conducted by Bavelas (1950) and by Leavitt (1951). Figure 3–2 shows seven different structural arrangements that are possible in groups. The circular pattern is, of course, the pattern that is most often found in treatment groups. Bavelas (1950) and Leavitt (1951) found that the circle tended to be leaderless, unorganized, and erratic. However, members enjoyed this pattern of group structure. The wheel and the Y patterns have a

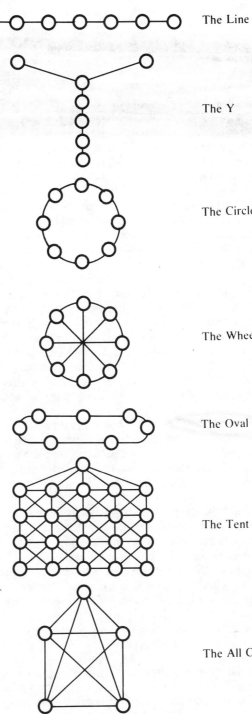

The Line

The Y

The Circle

The Wheel

The Oval

The Tent

The All Channel

**Figure 3–2** Selected Patterns of Communication

more centralized leader. Members at the outside of the chain pattern, the Y pattern, and the wheel pattern have less opportunity to communicate and they were less satisfied than those who were in the middle. Findings from investigations of the different patterns suggest that if the leader wants to maintain a dominant position and a leader-centered interaction pattern, the central positions of the Y or wheel pattern or a position facing members, such as the all channel or tent patterns shown in Figure 3–2 are best. Variations in the all channel and the tent patterns are often found in task groups with strong central leaders. For democratic, member-centered groups, the circular pattern shown in Figure 3–2 is preferred.

POWER AND STATUS.   Two other factors affecting communication and interaction patterns are members' relative power and status. Initially, members are accorded power and status on the basis of their position and prestige in the community, their physical attributes, and their position in the agency sponsoring the group. As a group develops, members' status and power change, depending on how important a member is in helping the group accomplish its tasks, or in helping other members meet their socioemotional needs. When members carry out roles that are important to the group their power and status increases. Thus, members' performances in the group affect their power and status either positively or negatively. When a member enjoys high status and power, other members are likely to direct their communications to that member (Napier and Gershenfeld, 1981). Members with high status feel free to talk to all group members, but low-status members may be reluctant to communicate with high-status members because they are fearful of being evaluated by those who have power (Kelley, 1951).

*Principles for Practice.*   With basic information about the nature of communication and interaction patterns in groups, workers can intervene in any group to modify or change the patterns that develop. When considering an intervention, workers may find the following principles about communication and interaction patterns helpful:

1. Members of the group are always communicating.
2. Members who communicate often have a purpose for communicating beyond merely conveying information.
3. There is meaning in all communications.
4. Messages are often perceived selectively by the receiver.
5. Messages may be distorted in transmission.
6. Feedback provides a means for communications to be understood effectively.
7. Open, group-centered communications are often but not always the preferred pattern of interaction.
8. Interaction patterns can be changed by reinforcing desired interaction patterns, by increasing or decreasing emotional bonds between members, by changing subgroups, by changing group size or group structure, and by altering the power or the status relationships in a group.

Following these principles, workers can intervene to help groups develop patterns of communication and interaction that meet members' socioemotional needs while accomplishing group purposes.

## Group Attraction

Group attraction, or group cohesion, as it is often called, can be defined as the result of all forces acting on members to remain in a group (Festinger, 1950). People are attracted to groups for a variety of reasons. According to Cartwright (1968), four interacting sets of variables determine members' attraction to a group, including (1) needs for affiliation, recognition, and security, (2) incentives and resources of the group such as the prestige of its members, the group's goals, its program activities, and style of operation, (3) the subjective expectations of members about the beneficial or detrimental consequences of the group, and (4) a comparison of the group to other group experiences. Groups that are attractive generally satisfy the needs which prompted members to join the group. Some members might have a need to socialize because their relationships outside of the group are unsatisfactory or nonexistent. For example, Toseland, Decker, and Bliesner (1979) have shown that group work can be effective in meeting the needs of socially isolated older persons. In other cases, groups provide members with a sense of security. Schachter (1959), for example, has shown that fear and anxiety increase people's needs for affiliation, presumably to reduce their fear and to help them determine the appropriate reactions to anxiety-provoking situations.

The attractiveness of a group can also be accounted for by incentives that are sometimes provided for group membership. Many people join groups because of the people they expect to meet and get to know. Opportunities for making new contacts and associating with high-status members are also incentives for joining a group. In some groups, the tasks to be performed are enjoyable. Other groups may help by enabling a member to accomplish tasks that could not be completed without the help of others. Prestige may be an incentive for some members. For example, being nominated to a delegate council or other task group may enhance a member's prestige and status in an organization or the community. Another inducement to group membership may be access to services or resources not otherwise available.

Expectations of gratification and favorable comparisons with previous group experiences are two other reasons that groups are attractive to members. For example, members who have high expectations for a group experience and little hope of attaining the same or similar satisfactions elsewhere will be attracted to a group. Thibaut and Kelley (1959) have found that members' continued attraction to a group depends on the "comparison level for alternatives", that is, the satisfaction derived from the current group experience as to that derived from other possible experiences.

Members' reasons for being attracted to a group may affect the group's functioning. Back (1951) found that members who were primarily attracted to a group because they perceived others as similar and as potential friends related on a personal level in the group, often engaging in conversations not focused on the group's task. Members attracted by the group's task wanted to complete it quickly and efficiently, doing so by maintaining task-relevant conversations. Members who were attracted by the prestige of group membership were cautious not to risk their status in the group. They initiated few controversial topics and focused on their own actions rather than those of other group members.

Attraction and cohesion also affect the functioning of groups in other ways. According to Cartwright (1968), cohesive groups tend to maintain their membership. They influence their members more than groups that are less cohesive. Members of cohesive groups are more likely to exert influence on each other and are more readily influenced by each other. Members of cohesive groups are more likely to continue to participate and more likely to persevere in attempts to accomplish the group's goals. In cohesive groups, attendance is higher (Sage, Olmsted, and Atlesk, 1955) and members accept more responsibility for group functioning (Back, 1951; Dion, Miller, and Magnan, 1970).

Cohesive groups also have positive effects on their members' satisfaction and personal adjustment. For example, Pepitone and Reichling (1955) found that members of cohesive groups felt more comfortable in engaging in hostile remarks and felt more secure when confronted with an "insult." Seashore (1954) found that members of an industrial work group were less likely to feel psychological distress when they participated in cohesive rather than noncohesive groups. In an extensive look at the effects of cohesiveness on members of therapy groups, Yalom (1975) found that cohesiveness leads to increased self-esteem, more willingness to listen to others, freer expression of feeling, better reality testing, greater self-confidence, and the effective use of other members' evaluations in enhancing a member's own development.

*Principles of Practice.*   Because attraction and cohesion have many beneficial effects, workers should strive to develop these forces in groups. In general, groups that have high levels of attraction and cohesiveness include:

1. Groups where there is plenty of interaction among all members.
2. Groups that are successful in achieving their goals.
3. Groups that have noncompetitive, intragroup relationships.
4. Groups that have competitive intergroup relationships.
5. Groups that are small enough so that all members can participate and have an impact on decision-making processes.
6. Groups that meet the needs of their membership.
7. Groups that fulfill the expectations of their membership.
8. Groups that increase the prestige and the relative status of their membership.
9. Groups that have access to rewards and resources that individual members alone could not obtain.

Overall, the benefits of participating in a group should exceed the costs of participation in the group or members may stop attending (Thibaut and

Kelley, 1954). Although workers cannot ensure that all factors mentioned here are present in every group, they should strive to make groups as cohesive and as attractive as possible.

## Social Control

Social control is the term used to describe the processes by which the group as a whole gains sufficient compliance and conformity from its members to enable it to function in an orderly manner. Social controls can be used by workers and members to gain compliance from deviant group members. Without a certain amount of conformity and compliance, a group cannot function. Social interaction would become chaotic and unpredictable. Social order and stability are prerequisites for the formation and maintenance of a cohesive group. Yet, social controls that are too stringent can reduce group attraction and lead to intragroup conflict and dissatisfaction.

Social control results from forces generated by several interrelated factors, including the norms that develop in the group and the roles and status of individual group members. The extent of social controls varies from group to group. In groups with strong social controls, members must give up a great deal of their freedom and individuality. In some groups this is necessary for effective functioning. For example, in a management team there is often little room for experimentation, individual preference, or interchangeability of assigned tasks. In other groups, however, members may have a great deal of freedom within some broad range of acceptable behavior.

*Norms.* Norms are shared expectations and beliefs about the proper and appropriate ways to act in a social situation such as a group. They refer to specific member behaviors and to the overall pattern of behavior that is acceptable in a group. Norms result from what is valued, preferred, and accepted behavior in the group. Certain members' opinions may be given greater consideration than other members' opinions in the development of group norms. For example, the designated leader or a high status member may be particularly influential in the development of norms. In most groups, however, all members share to a considerable extent in the development of the norms that emerge in the group.

Norms develop as the group develops. Members learn about group norms by watching each other behave. As members are rewarded for certain behaviors and punished for other behaviors, norms become clarified. Soon it becomes clear that sanctions and social disapproval result from certain behavior and that praise and social approval result from other behaviors. The emergence of norms reduces the need for personal power and control by the worker. Because norms are shared expectations about appropriate behaviors that are developed through the interactions of group members, they also help to avoid the capricious use of power by one group member or the need for excessive external controls imposed on the group from the outside environment.

Norms vary in some important ways. Rosenblatt (1962), for example, suggests that norms vary in the extent to which persons hold them to be binding. Some norms are strictly enforced while others are rarely enforced. Some norms are more elastic than others, that is, some norms permit a great deal of leeway in behavior while others prescribe narrow and specific behaviors. Norms also have various degrees of saliency for group members. For some members, a particular norm may be especially important, while for others it may have little meaning and little effect on their behavior.

Norms stabilize and regulate behavior in groups. By providing clear guidelines for what is acceptable and appropriate behavior, norms increase predictability and security for members. Norms aid groups in establishing procedures for coordinated action to reach goals. Overall, they are essential for a group's functioning.

*Roles.* Although norms are an important means of social control in groups, roles also influence members. Roles are closely related to norms. Whereas norms are shared expectations held, to some extent, by everyone in the group, roles are shared expectations about the functions of individuals in the group. Unlike norms, which define behavior in a wide range of situations, roles define behavior in relation to a specific function or task that the group member is expected to perform.

Roles are important for groups because they allow for division of labor and appropriate use of power. They ensure that someone will be designated to take care of vital group functions. Roles serve as a means of social control in groups by prescribing how members should behave in certain situations. Performing in a certain role capacity not only prescribes certain behavior but also limits members' freedom to deviate from the expected behavior of someone who performs that role. Thus, it would be viewed as inappropriate for a task leader to express feelings and emotional reactions about a personal issue that was not relevant to the group's task.

*Status.* Along with norms and role expectations, social controls are also exerted through members' status in a group. Status most often refers to an evaluation and ranking of each member's position in the group relative to all other members (Northern, 1969, Nixon, 1979). The method used to rank members' status varies from group to group. Therefore, the same person may have a different status in different groups. In one group, status may be determined by members' position in the agency sponsoring the group. In another group, members' status may be determined by how well they are liked by other group members, how much the group relies upon their expertise, or on how much responsibility they have in the group. A person's status within the group is determined, in part, by the person's prestige, position, and recognized expertise outside of the group. It is also determined by how a person acts once he or she becomes a member of a group. Since status is defined relative to other group members, a person's status in a group is also affected by the other members who compose the group.

Status serves a social control function in a rather complex manner. Low status members are the least likely to conform to group norms since they have little to lose by deviating. This is less likely if they have hopes of gaining a higher status. Medium-status group members tend to conform to group norms so that they can retain their status and perhaps gain a higher status. High-status members perform many valued services for the group and generally conform to valued group norms when they are establishing their position. However, because of their position, high-status members have more freedom to deviate from accepted norms. They are often expected to do something special and creative when the group is in a crisis situation (Nixon, 1979). If medium- or low-status members consistently deviate from group norms, they are threatened with severe sanctions or forced to leave the group. If high status members consistently deviate from group norms, their status in the group is diminished but they are rarely threatened with severe sanctions or forced to leave the group.

***Principles for Practice.*** Norms, roles, and status are interrelated concepts that affect the social controls exerted on individuals in the group. It is important for group workers to be familiar with the factors that influence social control in groups because of their powerful influence. Workers should be aware of the needs for individuality, freedom, independence, and autonomy that each group member experiences. At the same time, workers should recognize that social controls stabilize and regulate group processes, helping groups to function efficiently and effectively. In working with task and treatment groups, workers must balance the needs of individuals and of the group as a whole, managing conformity and deviation, and ensuring that social controls are working to benefit rather than hinder or limit individual members and the whole group.

Workers can expect that members will conform to norms, status, and role expectations under certain conditions but may deviate from them when these conditions are not present. Members are likely to conform when:

1. The group experience is attractive and cohesive.
2. The group's goals are recognized by members as being important and meaningful.
3. Members desire continued membership because of their own needs, or because of pressure from sources within or outside of the group.
4. Sanctions are available if members deviate from norms, status, and role expectations.
5. Rewards are available if members comply with norms, status, and role expectations.
6. There is sufficient freedom and independence within the range of acceptable behavior.

Deviation from group norms is not necessarily harmful to a group. Deviation from group norms can often help groups to move in new directions or to challenge old ways of accomplishing group tasks that are no longer functional. Despite the positive effects of group norms, norms may be dysfunctional or unethical, and it may be beneficial for members to deviate from them. For example, in a treatment group, norms may develop that make it difficult or impossible for members to express intense emotions. A member who deviates from this norm may help the group to re-examine its norms and may enable members to deepen their level of communication. Rather than immediately applying greater social controls when members deviate from established group norms, the worker should try to determine the reason for the deviation. Often, workers will find that changes or modifications in group norms, changes in the status hierarchy, or changes in role expectations will reduce members' needs to deviate and will improve the overall functioning of the group at the same time.

Changes or modifications of roles can best be undertaken by a discussion of members' roles, by clarifying the responsibilities and the privileges of existing roles, by changing members' roles, or by adding new roles according to preferences expressed during the group's discussion. Status hierarchies are most easily changed by the addition or removal of group members. If this is not possible, group discussion may help members to express their opinions and feelings about the effects of the current status hierarchy and to modify it.

Because they are so pervasive and so powerful, norms are somewhat more difficult to change than role expectations or status hierarchies. Therefore, whenever possible, workers should strive to ensure that the original norms that develop in a group are functional for the group. Recognizing the difficulty of changing norms, Lewin (1947) suggested three stages are necessary for changing the equilibrium and the status quo that hold norms constant. According to Lewin (1947), there must first be disequilibrium or unfreezing caused by a crisis or other tension-producing situation. During the disequilibrium period, group members re-examine the current group norms. Sometimes a crisis may be induced by the worker through a discussion or demonstration of how current norms will affect the group in the future. In other cases, dysfunctional norms will lead to a crisis.

In the second stage, members return to a new equilibrium with new norms replacing previous ones. According to Lewin (1947), the second stage is called freezing. In the third stage, called refreezing, a new equilibrium is stabilized. New norms become the recognized and accepted rules by which the group functions. Although changing group norms is difficult, Napier and Gershenfeld (1981) have suggested a number of ways this can be done, including:

1. Discussing, diagnosing, and modifying the group's norms.
2. Having the worker or other high-status member intervene in the group to change a norm.
3. Responding to influences on the group from the external environment.
4. Hiring a consultant to work with the group to change its norms.
5. Having the worker or group members deviate from the group's norms and then helping the group adapt to the new norms resulting from the change.

In these ways, workers can ensure that the norms, role expectations and the status hierarchy which develop in a group satisfy members' needs and accomplish goals established for individuals and the group as a whole.

## Group Culture

Although it has often been overlooked in discussions of group dynamics, group culture is an important force in the group as a whole. *Group culture* refers to values, beliefs, customs, and traditions that are held in common by group members (Olmstead, 1959).

Group culture emerges slowly as a group develops. Members contribute unique sets of values to a group that result from their backgrounds as well as from their ethnic, cultural, and racial heritages. These values are blended through the communications and interactions that take place in a group. In early meetings, members explore each other's unique value system and attempt to find a common ground on which they can relate to each other. By later meetings, members have had a chance to share and to understand each other's value systems. As a result, a common set of values develops that becomes the group's culture. The group's culture is carried forward from meeting to meeting but continues to evolve throughout the group's life.

Culture is also influenced by the environment in which a group functions. As part of the organizational structure of an agency, a community, and a society, groups share the values, traditions, and heritage of these larger social systems. The extent to which these systems influence the group depends on the degree of interaction that the group has with them. For example, on one end of the continuum, an administrative team's operational procedures are often greatly influenced by agency policies and practices. On the other end of the continuum, gangs tend to isolate themselves from the dominant values of society, the community, and local youth organizations. Group workers can learn a great deal about groups by examining how they interact with their environment.

*Principles for Practice.* The culture that a group develops has a powerful influence on its ability to achieve its goals while satisfying members' socioemotional needs. A culture that emphasizes values of self-determination, openness, fairness, and diversity of opinion can do much to facilitate the achievement of group and individual goals. Sometimes members bring ethnic, cultural or social stereotypes to the group that inhibit its development and its effective functioning. Through interaction and discussion, workers can help members confront stereotypes and arrive at a more accurate understanding and appreciation of group members who bring different values and different cultural heritages to the group.

In helping the group to build a positive culture the worker should enable members to:

1. Examine and compare the values they bring to the group.
2. Identify the values of the sponsoring agency, the community and the society in which the group functions.
3. Free themselves from stereotypes which interfere with their ability to interact with other group members.
4. Satisfy their socio-emotional needs as well as their needs to accomplish individual and group goals.

## STAGES OF GROUP DEVELOPMENT

Most of this text is organized around the skills that workers can use during each stage of a group's development. In this section, some of the different ways that group development has been conceptualized are reviewed. A group's entire social structure, its communication and interaction patterns, attraction, social controls, and culture change and evolve as the group develops. Many attempts have been made to classify these developmental changes into stages of group development. According to Northen (1969, p. 49), "a stage is a differentiable period or a discernible degree in the process of growth and development." Although "phases" and "stages" are often used interchangeably in the literature, in this text *phases* of group work refer to a worker's activities during the *stages* of a group's development.

Models of group development have been presented by many writers. Table 3–1 lists some of the models of group development that have appeared in the literature. Most of the models are based on descriptions of groups that the authors of each model have worked with or observed. Most models propose that all groups pass through similar stages of development (see, for example, Hartford, 1971, p. 63). As can be seen in Table 3–1, however, different writers have different ideas about the number and type of stages through which all groups pass. For example, Bales' (1950) model of group

*Table 3–1*
### STAGES OF GROUP DEVELOPMENT

| Development Stage | Bales (1950) | Tuckman (1963) | Northen (1969) | Hartford (1971) |
|---|---|---|---|---|
| *Beginning* | Orientation | Forming | Planning & Intake Process | Pre-Group Planning |
| | | | Orientation | Convening |
| | | | | Group Formation |
| *Middle* | Evaluation | Storming | Exploring & Testing | Disintegration & Conflict |
| | | Norming | | |
| | | Performing | Problem Solving | Group Function & Maintenance |
| *End* | Decision Making | | Termination | Pretermination |
| | | | | Termination |

development has only three stages, whereas the model presented by Sarri and Galinsky (1974) has seven stages.

There have been attempts to integrate some of these conceptualizations of group development. For example, Whittaker (1976) selected the model of group development by Garland, Jones, and Kolodny (1976) shown in Table 3–1, as being the most complete. He then proceeded to fit several other models of group development to that model.

Although there have been attempts to integrate differing models of group development, there are very few empirical studies of particular models and little empirical evidence to support the notion that any one model accurately describes the stages through which all groups pass. Most of the empirical studies have relied on direct observation or tape recordings of a small number of groups or a series of similar groups led by the same leader. In many cases, the reliability and validity of the behaviors being recorded and analyzed have not been adequately established. The studies that have been conducted tend to suggest that groups move through stages but that the stages are not constant across different groups (Shaw, 1976; Smith, 1978). Stages of group development may be affected by the needs of group members, the type of group, the goals of the group, the setting in which the group meets, and the orientation of the leader (Shaw, 1976; Smith, 1978).

Despite the variable nature of the stages of group development described by different writers, it appears that many of the models contain similar

*Table 3–1 (cont'd.)*

| Klein (1972) | Tecker (1972) | Sarri & Galinsky (1974) | Garland, Jones, & Kolodny (1976) | Henry (1981) |
|---|---|---|---|---|
| Orientation | Beginning | Origin Phase | Preaffiliation | Initiating |
| Resistance | Emergence of Some Group Feeling | Formation Phase | Power & Control | Convening |
| | | | | Formation |
| Negotiation | Development of Bond, Purpose, & Cohesion | Intermediate Phase I | Intimacy | Conflict |
| Intimacy | Strong Group Feeling | Revision Phase | Differentiation | Maintenance |
| | Decline in Group Feeling | Intermediate Phase II | | |
| Termination | Ending | Termination | Separation | Termination |

stages. As can be seen in Table 3–1, we have divided the various stages of group development into three stages: beginning, middle, and end. Each of the models of group development is placed in relationship to these three broad stages.

Most writers suggest that the beginning stages of groups are concerned with planning, organizing, and convening a group. The beginnings of groups are characterized by an emergence of group feeling. Group feeling, however, often does not emerge without a struggle. For example, Klein (1972) emphasized the resistance of members to group pressure, and Garland, Jones, and Kolodny (1976) emphasized the desire of group members to become a part of the group while maintaining their autonomy. Thus, along with the tendency to approach one another, there is also a tendency for members to maintain their distance. This is what Garland, Jones, and Kolodny (1976) have identified as an approach-avoidance conflict. For a more detailed description of the approach-avoidance conflict that members often experience at the beginning of a group, see Chapter 6.

Middle stages are characterized by a continuation of conflict found in the beginning stages of group development. During middle stages, this conflict centers around testing and exploring the worker's role as the designated leader. At the same time, there is a deepening of interpersonal relationships and greater group cohesion. After this occurs, groups concern themselves with task performance. *Problem solving, performing, maintenance,* and *maturity* are the terms most frequently used to describe this process. Task accomplishment is preceded by a differentiation of roles and accompanied by the development of feedback and evaluation mechanisms.

The endings of groups are characterized by the completion and evaluation of a group's efforts. Bales' (1950) model of group development suggests that during this stage, task groups make decisions, finish their business, and produce the results of their efforts. Treatment groups, which have emphasized socioemotional functioning as well as task accomplishment, begin a process of separation, during which group feeling and cohesion decline. Often members mark termination by summarizing the accomplishments of the group and by celebrating together.

Models of group development serve a useful function by providing a framework to describe worker roles and appropriate interventions during each stage of the life of a group. They also serve a useful function in helping to organize and systematize strategies of intervention. For example, in the beginning stage a worker's interventions are directed at helping the group define its purpose and helping members to feel comfortable with one another. Models of group development can also serve a useful purpose in preparing the leader for what to expect from a group during a particular stage of development.

The usefulness of theories of group development for group work practices is limited by the uniqueness of each group experience. The developmental stages of groups vary significantly across the broad range of task and treatment groups that a worker may lead. It should not be assumed that all groups follow the same patterns of development or that an intervention which is effective during a particular stage of development of one group will automatically be effective in another group in the same developmental stage. Yet, because of similarities in worker practice across different groups in similar stages of development, this text is organized around the skills and techniques that workers use in the planning, beginning, middle, and ending phases of group work.

## SUMMARY

Groups are social systems made up of people in interaction. This chapter described some of the most important forces that result from the interaction of group members. In working with task and treatment groups, it is essential to understand group dynamics and to be able to use them to accomplish group goals. Without a thorough understanding of group dynamics, workers will not be able to help members satisfy their needs or help the group accomplish its tasks.

There are four types of group dynamics with which group workers should be familiar. These include (1) communication and interaction patterns, (2) the attraction of the group for its members, (3) social controls such as norms, roles, and status, and (4) the group's culture. Communication and interaction patterns are basic to the formation of all groups. Through communication and interaction, properties of the group as a whole develop and the work of the group is accomplished. This chapter presented a model of the communication process.

Groups are maintained because of the attraction they hold for their members. Members join groups for many reasons. The extent to which the group meets members' needs and expectations determines the attraction of the group for its members and this, in turn, determines the extent to which a group becomes a cohesive unit. As cohesion develops, group structures are elaborated and norms, roles, and status hierarchies form. Norms, roles, and status hierarchies are social controls. They take the form of shared expectations concerning appropriate behavior in the group. Conformity to expected behavior patterns results in rewards, and deviation results in sanctions. Social controls serve to maintain a group's equilibrium as it confronts internal and external pressure to change during its development but they can be harmful if they are too stringent.

As the group evolves, it develops a culture that is derived from the environment in which it functions as well as from the beliefs, customs, and values shared by its members. The culture of a group has a pervasive effect on its functioning. For example, a group's culture affects the objectives of the group, the task the group decides to work on, the way members interact, and the methods the group uses to conduct its business.

Although properties of groups are often discussed as if they were static, they are constantly changing throughout the life of a group. Many writers have attempted to describe typical stages through which all groups pass. Although no single model of group development is universally accepted, some of the major characteristics that distinguish group process during each stage of group development were discussed. These characteristics serve as a useful guide for group practitioners in the beginning, middle, and ending phases of work described in later portions of this text.

Overall, this chapter has pointed out the power of group dynamics in influencing group members and in contributing to or detracting from the success of a group. As workers become familiar with properties of groups as a whole, their appreciation of the effects that natural groups and formed groups have on the lives of their clients is enhanced. In addition, workers can utilize their understanding of group dynamics to enhance their ability to work effectively with both task and treatment groups.

# 4
# Leadership

Leadership, as a professional role is the process of guiding the development of the group and its members. A worker acts as leader in order to help the group as a whole and each of its members achieve goals that are consistent with the value base of social work practice. The purposes of this chapter are to help group workers understand the leadership role, and to help them work effectively with task and treatment groups.

Although the leadership role is most often associated with the designated leader, that is, the worker, it is important to distinguish between the worker's role as the designated leader and the indigenous leadership that emerges when members take on leadership roles as the group develops. Leadership is rarely exercised solely by the worker. The professional worker encourages members to exercise their own power, taking responsibility for themselves and for the development of the group as a whole. Thus, leadership can be exercised by the worker in guiding group processes, and it can also be exercised by members who are encouraged by the worker to take indigenous leadership roles. Workers share their leadership functions in order to divide labor, to encourage members to exercise their own power, and to help members to have some influence and control in the group situation. Workers should do as much as possible to stimulate, support, and encourage indigenous leadership among members so as to encourage their autonomous functioning and to ensure that their existing skills do not atrophy.

Some group work theoreticians eschew the power and influence of the worker in his or her role as leader, preferring to emphasize the leadership function that members take on as the group develops. (See, for example, Klein, 1970, 1972.) Others prefer to emphasize the worker's role as leader in structuring the group process and influencing group members. (See, for example, Rose, 1977.) We believe that both ways of viewing leadership are essential for effective group work practice. Throughout this chapter, we emphasize both the importance of the worker as the group's leader and the importance of members sharing in leadership functions as the group develops. In the next section, we examine the power bases that workers draw upon in their role as professional leaders. After this, we examine a number of theories of group leadership and develop a model of how leadership emerges in a group.

## THE PROFESSIONAL WORKER AS GROUP LEADER

### Leadership and Power

Workers use their influence as leaders within and outside of the group to facilitate group and individual efforts to achieve desired goals. Within the group, the worker intervenes to change the dynamics of the group as a whole or to help individual members to change. In exercising leadership outside the group, the worker intervenes to influence the environment in which the group and its members function. For example, the worker may attempt to change agency policies that influence the group or attempt to obtain additional resources so that a group can complete its work. In exerting leadership inside or outside the group, the worker is responsible for the group's processes, actions, and task accomplishments.

The worker is rewarded for taking on the responsibilities inherent in leading a group by having attributed to him or her the power to influence and the ability to lead. Power is attributed to the worker by group members, peers, superiors, the agency, and the larger social system. In considering a worker's power, the distinction between attributed power and actual power should be clear. *Attributed power* comes from the perception of group members, or others outside of the group, of the worker's ability to lead. *Actual power* refers to the worker's resources for changing conditions inside and outside the group. Workers should recognize that attributed leadership ability is as important as actual power in facilitating the development of the group and its members.

Workers can increase the power attributed to them by group members. Recent studies have shown that members' expectations about the group and its leader influence the group's performance (Bednar and Kaul, 1978; Lieberman, 1976; Garfield, 1978; Orlinsky and Howard, 1978). Preparing members with films, brochures, or personal interviews that include information about the group, its leader, and the success of previous groups has been shown to be effective in increasing the change-oriented expectations of members (Parloff, Waskow, and Wolfe, 1978; Fish, 1973; Frank, 1961) and in helping individuals and groups accomplish their goals (Frank, 1961). When formal preparation is impossible, informal preparation by word of mouth or reputation can be used.

When attempting to increase the power attributed to them, workers should keep in mind that they are doing this to increase their ability to help group members function independently and at an optimum level. As their attributed power increases, workers are more likely to be regarded with esteem by group members, to be looked to as models of effective coping skills whose behaviors are emulated and whose advice, suggestions, and guidance are given serious consideration. Workers should not attempt to gain power for its own sake. They should not attempt to control members' behavior or impose their own values, standards, and rules concerning conduct in or outside the group unilaterally.

The attributed power of the worker comes from a variety of sources. Among these are professional status, organizational position, experience, defined boundaries between worker and group members' roles, fees for service, access to resources, and the commonly held view that a group's success or failure is the result of its leadership. Gathering people together to work in a group can also contribute to the worker's power, because groups are more effective at completing certain tasks than individuals working alone. For example, it has been demonstrated that members are more motivated to carry out decisions made in groups than those made by individuals (Vroom, 1969), that groups can make more creative decisions than individuals (Collins and Guetzkow, 1964), and that certain kinds of groups are more effective than individuals for solving certain problems (Bunker and Dalton, 1972).

The actual power of the worker depends on the worker's power base. Seven power bases (French and Raven, 1959) that the worker may possess include:

1. Connection power—using the favor or disfavor of important people, resources, or situations to gain compliance.
2. Expert power—using knowledge or skill to facilitate the work of the group and to gain compliance.
3. Information power—using information that is valuable to and needed by others.
4. Legitimate power—using the position held and the rights that accrue to this position in the organization or larger social system to influence behavior.
5. Reference power—using personal traits such as being liked and admired and the desire of group members to be identified with the worker to gain the compliance of other members.
6. Reward power—using social or tangible rewards to influence the behavior of others.
7. Coercive power—using sanctions to induce compliance because failure to comply will lead to punishment.

Using power can have negative as well as positive consequences. For example, coercive power is sometimes used to compel clients to receive treatment. However, coercion can have negative effects such as hostility, anger, rebellion, and non-attendance at group meetings. Therefore, the worker should exercise his or her power judiciously, in a manner that is consistent with personal, professional, and societal values.

At the same time, the worker's power as leader can not, and should not, be denied. This is sometimes done by those who suggest that members should take total responsibility for leading the group. We believe that groups need leaders in order to avoid disorganization and chaos, and that leadership and power are inseparable (Etzioni, 1961). Anyone who has attended the first meeting of a new group recognizes the power that the worker has as the designated leader. This power can be illustrated most vividly by examining members' behaviors and feelings during the initial portion of the first group meeting. Members direct most of their communications to the worker or communicate through the worker to other group members. Members are often anxious and inquisitive, wondering what they can expect from the group and its leader. Members comply readily with requests made by the worker. Although members wonder about the worker's ability to help them and the group as a whole, they usually give the worker latitude in choosing methods and procedures to help the group achieve its objectives.

Beginning with the first group meeting, it is essential that workers move as rapidly as possible to share their power with members and the group as a whole. The worker can do this in a variety of ways such as (1) encouraging member-to-member rather than member-to-leader communications, (2) asking for members' input into the agenda for the meeting and the direction the group should take in future meetings, (3) supporting indigenous leadership when members make their first, tentative attempts at exerting their own influence on the group, and (4) encouraging attempts at mutual sharing and mutual aid among group members during the first meeting (Shulman, 1979).

## Theories of Group Leadership

Early theories about the best method to use in leading a group focused primarily on leadership style. Leadership was considered a trait rather than as a cluster of behaviors that could be learned (Halpin, 1961). Three positions on a continuum of leadership behavior, seen in Figure 4–1, laissez-faire, democratic, and autocratic, were the subject of early investigations (Lewin, Lippitt, and White, 1939; Lewin and Lippitt, 1938). Findings from these studies indicated that there was more aggression, hostility, and scapegoating in autocratic groups than in democratic groups. There were no differences in the tasks that the groups completed, although there was some indication that the products of democratic groups were qualitatively superior to those in groups that used autocratic or laissez-faire styles of leadership. Group members also preferred the democratic group's process, that is, they liked the leader better and were freer and more willing to make suggestions. These early findings seemed to suggest that allowing members to participate in the group's decision making process was the preferred leadership style. Recent findings have also suggested that a friendly, helpful, and rather permissive leadership style results in more effective and productive groups (Sherif and Sherif, 1969).

As findings began to accumulate, however, it became clear that situational factors influenced which leadership style was most effective. For example, Hare (1976) has cited a number of studies indicating that authoritarian leadership is better than democratic or laissez-faire leadership in some situations. Nixon (1979) has suggested that at least seven factors must be

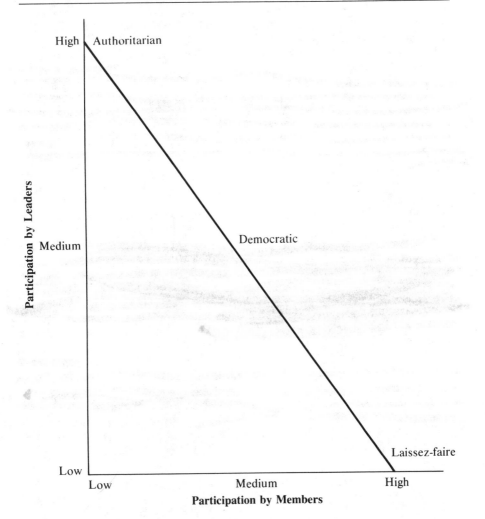

**Figure 4–1** Participation in Decision Making by Leaders and Members in Groups Using Three Leadership Styles

assessed in order to make predictions about what leadership styles or behaviors are most effective. These include:

1. The nature of leadership expectations held by groups members.
2. The way leadership has been attained.
3. Whether there is competition between formal and informal leaders.
4. The needs, tasks, and goals of the group as a whole.
5. The task and socioemotional skills of members.
6. The nature of authority in or outside the group.
7. The nature of environmental demands placed on the group and its leadership.

During this time, social workers were also developing models of leadership designed to help group work practitioners intervene effectively in a variety of practice situations. Papell and Rothman (1980a) outlined three major models of group work practice shown in Table 4–1. These three group work models are (1) the social goals model, (2) the remedial model, and (3) the reciprocal model. The social goals model is an early group work model. It was used, and continues to be used, in settlement houses and in group work with youth in organizations such as the Girl Scouts, YWCA, and Jewish community centers. The social goals model focuses on socializing members to democratic societal values, group interaction, and cultural diversity. It also has been used by community development agencies to change societal norms and structures and to improve the social welfare of all citizens. The worker is viewed as an enabler who uses program activities, such as camping, discussions, and instructions about democratic processes, to achieve the group's goals.

The remedial model focuses on restoring or rehabilitating individuals by helping them to change their behavior. The worker acts as a change agent and intervenes in the group to achieve certain specific purposes determined by group members, the group worker, and society. The remedial model uses a leader-centered approach to group work, with the worker actively intervening in the group's process. Recently, this model has been given a great deal of attention in the group work literature (see, for example, Vinter, 1967; Rose, 1977; Garvin, 1981).

In the third model presented by Papell and Rothman (1980a), the reciprocal model, group members form a mutual aid system for one another. The worker is a mediator and a resource person who attempts to facilitate the group's functioning in both task and socioemotional domains, that is, in achieving its goals and satisfying its members. Schwartz (1976) and Shulman (1979) are well known for this group-centered, process-oriented approach to group work practice.

## Factors Influencing Group Leadership

Any of the three models of group leadership may be appropriately used, depending on the situation facing the group, the capacity of its members, and the skill of its leader. The growing recognition that group leadership is situational and affected by a variety of interacting factors is based on recent empirical findings in social psychology, sociology, and business administration, as well as on data gathered in evaluating group work practice. (See, for example, Gibb, 1969; Fiedler, 1967; Vroom and Yetton, 1973; Nixon, 1979.)

Several investigators have found that in order to understand the dynamics of leadership in diverse treatment and task groups, a variety of factors in addition to the personality and leadership style of the worker must be considered. In their analysis of leadership in task groups, Hersey and Blanchard (1977) emphasize the importance of group participants. Others focus on the social environment, properties of the group as a whole, the type of problem the group is working on, and the purposes and functions of the group. (See, for example, Gibb, 1969; Nixon, 1979.) The relationship be-

## Table 4–1
### THREE MODELS OF SOCIAL GROUP WORK[1]

| Selected Characteristics | Social Goals Model | Remedial Model | Reciprocal Model |
|---|---|---|---|
| Purpose and goals | Social consciousness, social responsibility, informed citizenry, and informed political and social action | To restore and rehabilitate group members who are behaving dysfunctionally | To form a mutual aid system among group members to achieve optimum adaptation and socialization |
| Agency | Settlement houses and neighborhood center settings | Formal agency setting, either clinical outpatient or inpatient settings | Compatible with clinical inpatient and outpatient settings and neighborhood and community centers |
| Focus of work | Larger society, individuals within the context of the neighborhood and the social environment | Changing individual dysfunction | Creating a self-help, mutual aid system between all group members |
| Role of the group worker | Role model and enabler for responsible citizenship | Change agent who engages in study, diagnosis, and treatment to help group members attain individual treatment goals | Mediator between needs of members and between needs of the group and the larger society, enabler contributing data not available to the members |
| Type of group members | Citizens, neighborhood, and community residents | Clients who are not functioning adequately and need help in coping with life's tasks | Partners who work together sharing common concerns |
| Methods used in the group | Discussion, participation, consensus, developing and carrying out a group task, community organizing, and other program and action skills to help group members acquire instrumental skills about social action and communal living and change | Structured exercises, direct and indirect influence, in and outside of the group, to help members change behavior patterns | Shared authority where members discuss concerns, support one another, and form a cohesive social system to benefit one another |

[1]Adapted from Pappell and Rothman, 1980a.

tween a leader's power and members' performances has also been examined. These studies suggest that the type of power used when exercising leadership is affected by a variety of situational variables (Ivancevich and Donnelly, 1970; Bachman, Bowers, and Marcus, 1968; Jamieson and Thomas, 1974; Tannenbaum and Schmidt, 1972) arising from various sources including the leader, the group members, the group as a whole and the larger system the group is a part of (Tannenbaum and Schmidt, 1972).

Several social scientists have attempted to organize all situational factors affecting the group and construct a model of group leadership. For example, Fiedler (1967) and Gibb (1969) have both developed contingency models to explain leadership and decision making in groups. Fiedler considered three dimensions: (1) the degree of structure involved in the task, (2) the amount of power given to the leader because of the leader's position, and (3) the quality of interpersonal relationships between the leader and the members. Vroom and Yetton (1973) have developed a normative model of leadership that takes into consideration eight problem attributes that influence the type of leadership that emerges in a given situation. These include:

1. The importance of the quality of the decision.
2. The extent to which the leader possesses sufficient information and expertise to make a high quality decision by himself.
3. The extent to which group members have the necessary information to generate a high quality decision.
4. The extent to which the problem is structured.
5. The extent to which acceptance or commitment to the decision is critical to the effective implementation of the decision.
6. The probability, based on previous experiences, that an autocratic decision by the leader will be accepted by group members.
7. The extent to which group members are motivated to attain organizational goals as represented in the objectives of the task.
8. The extent to which group members are likely to disagree over preferred solutions.

Vroom and Yetton's (1973) normative model considers the interaction of all these factors when deciding what type of leadership will be most effective in solving a problem.

A number of group work practitioners have also suggested that leadership must be seen as a process that occurs within the context of the group and its environment. Tompkins and Gallo (1978) propose a model for goal formulation in social work groups that takes into account environmental forces. In his recent text, Garvin (1981) emphasizes the role of the agency in influencing the work of treatment groups. Vinter and Galinsky (1974) mention several methods workers can use to help members utilize relationships and the environment outside of the group to achieve their goals. These include interventions with significant others, social systems, and the social environment. For example, a worker might want to intervene with family members to change their attitudes and behaviors about a group member who was a former inpatient in a state psychiatric hospital. At the same time, the worker might want to suggest ways that the member could change his living arrangements so as to be able to cope more effectively with family members. Apart from the group, the worker may want to meet with other professionals in a task force convened to assess and plan for the aftercare needs of former psychiatric inpatients.

In examining group leadership, Heap (1979) suggests that the degree of activity of a worker is directly related to the social health of the group's members. Thus, a worker should be active in groups in which members are "out of touch with reality" or "withdrawn or very aggressive" (Heap, 1979, p. 50). In groups with interested, eager, and competent members, the worker should take on a less active enabler role.

The treatment and task group typologies given in Chapter 1 also suggest that leadership should vary depending on the purpose of the group and the group's membership. For example, a worker may need to be rather directive and structured in a remedial group for severely mentally impaired inpatients of a state hospital. The worker, as "expert," may work with each member for ten or fifteen minutes. Other members may be asked for their opinions or asked to provide feedback, but the primary focus is on an individual member who is helped to achieve particular treatment goals. Such an approach is similar to individual treatment in a group. This method of leadership is quite different from a group-centered method that may be more appropriate for educational or growth groups in which members are eager, competent, and nonimpaired. In using a group-centered method, the worker serves to facilitate communication, interaction, understanding, and mutual aid, and encourages members to help one another rather than to look to the worker as an expert who can solve their concerns or problems.

Over all, one conclusion that can be drawn from social science findings and from data accumulated from group work practice is that one method of leadership is not effective in all situations. Approaches that suggest one method of leadership for all circumstances are oversimplified. (See Hersey, Blanchard, and Natemeyer, 1979; Davis, Laughlin, and Komorita, 1976.) In her development of a broad-range model of group leadership, Lang (1972) underscores this point. She demonstrates how workers should vary their leadership depending on the characteristics of the group they are leading. The worker's leadership skills and intervention strategies should vary depending on the degree to which the group as a whole and its individual members can function autonomously. The less autonomous the group is, the more the worker must play a central role in leading the group. Conversely, the more autonomous the group is, the more the worker can act to facilitate the members' own self-direction and indigenous leadership abilities.

In addition to suggesting that leadership is situational, it is clear that the group has a significant impact on its own success. The worker must learn to recognize and use group forces that lead to effective outcomes. Lieberman (1975) points out five properties of groups that are particularly influential for the therapeutic experience of the participant. These properties are the capacity of the group (1) to develop cohesiveness and a sense of belonging for its members, (2) to control, reward, and punish behavior, (3) to define reality for the individual, (4) to induce and release powerful feelings in its members, and (5) to provide a contrast for social comparison and feedback. To these can be added the group's capacity (6) to universalize an experience (Yalom, 1975), (7) to provide behavior that can be modeled, and (8) to provide peers to participate in discussions and re-enactments of previous experiences as well as here-and-now encounters. Although these group properties were obtained from case studies and phenomenological analyses of treatment groups, it is not difficult to apply many of them to task groups as well. The effective worker helps members to facilitate the development of these properties in the group.

## Effectiveness of Leaders

Although most people assume that leaders exert considerable influence on the outcome of task and treatment groups, what is the empirical evidence to justify this faith in the group leader? As Lieberman (1975, p. 357) notes, "it is quite possible that the leader's behavior, personality, and skill level have taken on mythic proportions as basic causal forces explaining successful . . . change." Most theories of group work emphasize the role of the leader in helping the group achieve its objectives and helping group members to feel satisfied with the group's process. Many of these theories, however, have accumulated little or no evidence to substantiate these assertions.

Empirical evidence does not fully support the notion that group leadership is central in helping the group attain its objectives. Some evidence supports claims that leaders' behaviors are important for the success of the group (Feldman and Caplinger, 1977; Bendar and Kaul, 1978; Toseland, 1983), but other evidence suggests that this may not be so. Lieberman, Yalom, and Miles (1973), for example, found that tape-led (virtually leaderless) groups were more effective than three fourths of the leader-led groups they studied. McLaughlin, White, and Byfield (1974) found that a programmed tape format with the leader present as a member was a better method for achieving group objectives than five other leadership structures, including the traditional leader-led group format. Therefore, in considering leadership, workers should recognize that other factors in addition to their skills may affect group outcomes. Taken together, these factors may be just as important as a worker's skill in helping a group to achieve its objectives.

## LEADERSHIP AS AN EMERGING PHENOMENON

### An Interactional Model

Figure 4–2 represents our conception of factors that affect group leadership. We believe it presents an accurate picture of how systems interact to affect group leadership. The interactional model, presented in Figure 4–2, incorporates the empirical findings of others who have developed comprehensive models of group leadership (Tannenbaum and Schmidt, 1972; Likert, 1967; Vroom and Yetton, 1973.) Because the interactional model views leadership as being derived from the interactions of the group, its members, the

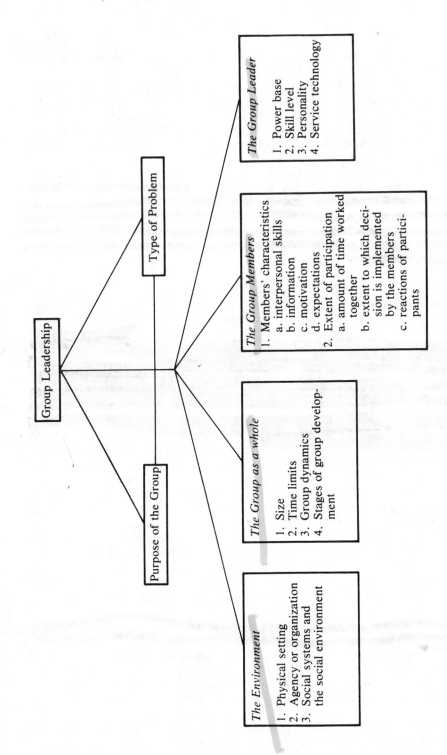

**Figure 4-2** An Interactional Model of Group Leadership

Group Leadership

Type of Problem

Purpose of the Group

*The Group Leader*
1. Power base
2. Skill level
3. Personality
4. Service technology

*The Group Members*
1. Members' characteristics
   a. interpersonal skills
   b. information
   c. motivation
   d. expectations
2. Extent of participation
   a. amount of time worked together
   b. extent to which decision is implemented by the members
   c. reactions of participants

*The Group as a whole*
1. Size
2. Time limits
3. Group dynamics
4. Stages of group development

*The Environment*
1. Physical setting
2. Agency or organization
3. Social systems and the social environment

leader, and the environment, the model is closely related to the ecological systems perspective of social casework proposed by Germain and Gitterman (1980) and by Siporin (1980a) as well as the interactional perspective presented by Maluccio (1979). The interactional model represents leadership as a shared function that is not solely lodged in the designated group leader. In addition to the worker's role as designated leader, the model shown in Figure 4–2 clearly shows that leadership emerges from a variety of interacting factors as the group develops.

As a heuristic device, the model can be useful in planning effective leadership methods for differing types of groups. The model shows six separate but interrelated factors that should be considered when leading a task or treatment group. These factors are (1) the purpose of the group, (2) the type of problem the group is working on, (3) the environment in which the group works, (4) the group as a whole, (5) the members of the group, and (6) the leader of the group.

*Purpose of the Group.*    When considering how leadership emerges in a group, it is essential to consider the purposes of the group. Purposes are the reasons for bringing group members together. They serve as a guide for the worker's interventions. According to Browning (1977), a group may be formed (1) to perform tasks that require more than one or two people to be completed, (2) to meet individual needs, (3) to bring people together who are involved in the same or similar problems, (4) to represent a larger collection of people, (5) to form the largest collection of people that can be managed together, (6) to help maintain an organization more economically than individuals, (7) to increase motivation, or (8) as a result of physical factors such as working together in the same office. To this list can be added the purpose of using the group to change conditions or situations outside of the group in an organization, a service delivery system, or an entire social system.

A group may have a single purpose or several purposes. The worker should consider how a group's purposes are perceived and interpreted by all systems that interact with that group. The worker should ensure that the purpose of the group and the type of problem to be worked on are consistent with one another. For example, if the purpose of a group as defined by the agency or the worker is to meet the needs of individual members, then the type of problems on which the group works should be related to the concerns of individual group members. The group should not be working on tasks developed by the agency or the worker that do not meet the needs of individual members.

The purpose of a group helps to determine the extent to which the worker uses power and influence to affect how work will be accomplished. In a group whose purpose is solely to complete a task or solve a problem, a worker may choose to encourage members to structure and focus the interactions more than in a group whose purpose is to have individual members share common concerns and ideas about a particular issue.

*Type of Problem.*    The type of problem or task a group works on has important implications. It has been found that groups do better than individuals on certain types of tasks, but individuals working alone do better on others (Bunker and Dalton, 1972). Generally, groups do better when the task is additive in nature, such as collecting information. Thus, it would be better to collect information about a client from all the professionals working with the client in a treatment conference group rather than individually from each professional. Groups also appear to improve on the decisions of individuals working alone in deciding between clearly delineated alternatives. For example, Toseland, Rivas, and Chapman (in press) found that groups improved the decision making ability of individuals working alone in deciding on funding priorities for medically underserved counties. Groups also do better on tasks requiring a wide range of responses (Thorndike, 1938). For example, it is preferable to have group members and the leader generate alternative solutions with a woman who is having trouble expressing her anger rather than to have the woman generate the alternatives with one worker. For these kinds of tasks, the worker should attempt to promote interaction, input, and feedback from all group members so that a wide range of responses are generated and evaluated.

Individuals working alone solve some problems or tasks faster and better than when these individuals work together in a group. Individuals working alone more readily solve complex problems requiring that many variables be synthesized to form a whole. In these cases, the group's product "frequently amounted to nothing but the best individual performance of a member of the group, turned in for the group" (Thorndike, 1938).

Workers can make effective use of the knowledge that individuals may solve some problems better by working alone than by working on them in a group. For example, in preparing a countywide plan for disseminating emergency energy allocation funds to low-income families, a worker decides to use a nominal group procedure (see Chapter 8) because this procedure encourages members to work alone before sharing their ideas with the entire group (Delbecq, Van de Ven, and Gustafson, 1975). The worker might also help members form small subgroups to work on specific ideas generated by the nominal group procedure before deliberating on them in the larger group.

Several other aspects of problems should be considered when leading a group. One of these is whether the problem is of concern to the group as a whole, some subgroup, or an individual. All members of the group may not be affected to the same extent by a particular problem or task being considered by a group. For example, when leading a group to teach parenting skills to foster parents, the worker should attempt to get all members involved in discussing parenting problems that are of interest to everyone in the group. When a member raises a problem unique to his or her particular situation, the worker should attempt to develop from this information generalized principles of child rearing of interest to all group members. This technique is often called *universalizing*.

Finally, in considering the type of problem confronting a group, workers should be aware of where their legitimate influence ends. It may not be appropriate for the worker to encourage discussion of certain topics. For example, it would not be appropriate for a worker leading a task group planning for an emergency housing shelter to encourage a group member to talk about his or her family life. In other situations, however, workers may want to encourage group members to discuss taboo areas. For example, when the type of problem being discussed is child abuse, it might be helpful for the worker to encourage all members to talk about how they were disciplined during their early childhood.

*The Environment.*   The environment in which the group conducts its work has a profound effect on how leadership emerges in the group. Environmental influences come primarily from three interrelated factors: (1) the immediate physical setting, (2) the agency or organization in which the group functions, and (3) other social systems and the social environment. Each helps create the group's culture, which in turn affects how the worker's interactions are perceived by the group.

THE SETTING.   The worker should ensure that the setting facilitates the group's work. The decor of the waiting room, the comfort of the meeting area, and the availability of equipment and supplies such as tables, blackboard, or newsprint needed by the group all influence the groups' leadership. It is important for the worker to match group members' needs and preferences to a setting that facilitates the group's work. Members of a gang, for example, may need to be met in their own environment before any suggestion can be made about doing an activity in a social agency or neighborhood community center. In contrast, a board member may be helped to better understand an issue in the setting of a conference room.

THE AGENCY CONTEXT.   In addition to the physical environment, the agency influences the group and its worker in a variety of ways. The worker, for example, must be aware of agency policies, rules, and regulations that govern the group's behavior, its process, and its product. The worker is given legitimate authority by the agency or organization to help the group perform its tasks. The agency's delegation of this authority to the worker is often somewhat contingent on the worker's using the method of service delivery currently existing in the agency. For example, two group workers attempting to help pregnant women stop drinking alcohol may use quite different means, depending on the type of program sponsored by each agency. One group leader may use a self-help group approach whereas the other may use a group format based on cognitive-behavioral self-control procedures.

Worker's positions within an agency or organization can also affect what role workers play in a group. For example, in a task group a worker may take four sub-roles: the meeting head, the administrator, the leader, and the spokesperson (Ttropman, 1980). As the meeting head, the worker facilitates group functioning. As administrator, the worker performs maintenance functions that are vital to the group's continuing effectiveness. As a leader, the worker sets the climate and direction for the meetings. As a spokesperson, the worker is called upon to publicize the official opinions, views, and statements of the group, relate to the administrative hierarchy of the agency, and represent the group at official functions. Workers should be aware of how their position in an agency influences their work in helping members of treatment groups achieve their goals. Some settings encourage the use of particular practice approaches or particular procedures whereas others do not.

OTHER SOCIAL SYSTEMS. The third way in which the environment influences group leadership is through large social systems such as the community environment in which the group operates. The worker's behavior is influenced by norms established by society. For example, in a group for abusive parents, the worker intervenes to help members comply with societal norms and values concerning appropriate parenting behaviors. Smaller social systems can also affect a group's work. For example, an agency committee might hesitate to become involved in a search for additional emergency housing if a delegate council formed by a community planning agency has already been set up to look at ways to develop additional emergency housing resources.

*The Group as a Whole.* Four properties of the group as a whole influence how leadership emerges in the group, including (1) the size of the group, (2) the time limit in which the group is expected to accomplish its goals, (3) group dynamics, and (4) the stage of a group's development. As the size of a group grows, the opportunity for participation among members decreases. Rules may increase as workers use them to maintain order and control in the group. Subgroups are more likely to form. Thus, increases in group size have important implications for how leadership skills should be used in the group. Techniques for leading large groups are discussed in Chapter 9.

Decreases in group size also affect leadership. For example, treatment groups in outpatient settings will often experience a drop in membership after a few sessions. Groups may have ten participants for the first session and six or seven members who continue with the group after the first three sessions. Reduction in membership provides a good opportunity to build group cohesion, because the potential for communication increases and those with little motivation or little interest drop out.

Time limits also influence how a group should be led. Time limits may be voluntary or mandatory. A treatment group, for example, may decide to use a time-limited method such as a behavioral group approach or a task-centered group approach. A task group such as a delegate council may feel responsible for making a speedy decision on an issue for an upcoming state-wide meeting. In either case, the time limits in both groups affect leadership behavior. Time limits generally lead to greater structuring of interactions and an increase in task-focused behavior so that the group can accomplish its goals within the given deadlines. The way that time limits are used depends on the purpose and function of the group, and the need of the group to make a rapid decision.

A third group as a whole property that can influence leadership is the dynamics that operate in a group. As discussed in Chapter 3, these include communication and interaction patterns, attraction, social control, and group culture. Workers should use their skills to foster the development of group dynamics that help the group accomplish its tasks and contribute to members' satisfaction. Interventions to change the dynamics of the group as a whole are discussed in Chapter 8.

The stage of a group's development is the fourth group as a whole factor
that has an impact on leadership behavior. If the group is to be successful in
its development, the worker must be aware of the developmental tasks that
face the group during each stage. A large portion of this text focuses on the
specific skills and methods that workers can use during each stage of a
group's development.

*Group Members.*    Group members influence how leadership emerges in the
group in three important ways: (1) through the unique characteristics and life
experiences they bring to the group, (2) by the extent to which they participate in the group, and (3) by the extent to which they share in leading the
group. Several characteristics of members affect their ability to have an
influence on the group. These characteristics include members' interpersonal skills, the amount of information they possess or have access to, their
perceived responsibility for the work of the group, their motivations, and
their expectations about the process and outcome of the group. The importance of these characteristics should not be overlooked when considering
how leadership develops in a group. It has been shown, for example, that
members' expectations influence outcomes in both treatment and task
groups (Bednar and Kaul, 1978; Gibb, 1969) and that interpersonal skills and
knowledge about a particular problem also help to determine how well a
group functions (Hersey, Blanchard and Natemeyer, 1979; Browning, 1977).

Members may share unequally in particular attributes. One member who
is knowledgeable about a particular topic may become the task leader in the
group while that topic is being discussed. Another member may serve as the
group's socioemotional leader by expressing feelings and responding to
other members' feelings. The worker's attempt to facilitate members' efforts
to take on leadership roles in the group should recognize members' leadership potential.

The extent of members' participation also influences how a worker leads
a group. Some members' lack of interpersonal skills or motivation may
prevent them from participating fully. In other cases, the worker may pur-
posefully prevent a group member from making verbal communications,
thereby limiting to nonverbal means a member's ability to influence the
group. For example, a worker leading a delegate council may decide to limit
discussion thereby effectively stopping some members from speaking out
about an issue.

The worker should anticipate members' reactions when they are encouraged or discouraged from active participation in a group. Generally,
discouraging or limiting a member's participation in a group leads to the
member's dissatisfaction with the group. In some situations, however,
members may be more interested in hearing what the worker or a guest
speaker has to say than in what other members have to say and may readily
accept limits on their participation. This is particularly true in educational
groups where members' participation may be limited to a discussion period
after a presentation by the worker. In task groups, members may not have an
interest in or a knowledge of certain issues, and the worker may therefore
want to encourage more knowledgeable or interested members to express

their views. In other cases, the worker may want to limit discussion among members in order to come to a speedy decision.

The extent of a member's participation in the group and the member's resulting willingness and opportunity to share leadership functions is affected in part by the amount of time the member has been a part of the group. A new group member will often have difficulty exerting leadership in a group in which the relationship among members has already been established. Similarly, a member of a street gang that has been together for several years has greater power to influence the gang than a worker who is just beginning to work with the gang.

The worker should also consider to what extent members will be required to carry out tasks or decisions made by the group. Members are more likely to carry out tasks and decisions that they have had a part in shaping, particularly if the members who have to carry out the task have agreed with the group's decision. For example, when it is suggested by the worker or other members that a member of a parent training group observe her child's behavior at home and report on it during the next meeting, the member should be encouraged to express her feelings about the task. The member should also be encouraged to become involved in determining the specifics of the task and in identifying any potential impediments to completing it. If the member does not agree that the task is feasible or if she feels that it will not be helpful in improving her parenting skills, she should not be encouraged to do it. Similarly, in task groups, it is particularly important to involve members in making decisions when their cooperation is needed for implementing a particular plan of action.

*The Group Leader.*     Although the purpose of the group, the type of problem being confronted, the environment, the group as a whole, and the group's members all influence how leadership emerges in the group, the worker, in the role of designated leader, also has influence over group processes and task accomplishments. As stated earlier, when group leadership was first examined closely in the early part of this century, most studies focused on the personal qualities of the leader and on styles of leadership, such as autocratic, democratic, or laissez-faire (Lewin, Lippitt, and White, 1939). Gradually, the studies broadened and attempted to show how leadership styles interact with the other components of the leadership model shown in Figure 4–2. Although our model of group leadership is based on findings that suggest leadership is an interactional process among each of these systems of influence, the model would not be complete without considering how qualities of the designated leader influence group leadership.

THE POWER BASE.     Probably the most important factor to consider about a worker is the basis of his or her power. Earlier, we indicated that seven types of power can be used to influence a group. These include coercive, connection, expert, information, legitimate, referent, and reward power bases. Most workers draw on a variety of power bases; it is important for workers to realize the power bases at their disposal when they are considering leading a group. With mandated clients, workers may want to use their influence to overcome members' resistance before beginning a group. For example, a worker planning to lead a group of alcoholics who have been referred because of a DWI (driving while intoxicated) offense may influence members by not certifying that they are fit to have their revoked licenses returned until they have successfully completed a group treatment program.

SKILL. The level of skill that workers possess also influences their ability to lead. Experience and training of workers have been correlated with effectiveness in working with individuals and groups (Parloff, Waskow, and Wolfe, 1978). Even when workers have a number of strong power bases that they can use to influence group members, unskillful application of their power will often result in members becoming angry and uncooperative or submissive and passive. Through the use of appropriate leadership skills, the worker can more readily achieve objectives and satisfy group members.

PERSONALITY. Workers' personalities also influence group leadership. A worker who is shy and sensitive about others' feelings is less likely to use confrontation as a technique when leading a group. Workers should be aware of how their personalities intervene in their attempts to objectively analyze what the group needs and in their attempts to intervene in the group's processes.

SERVICE TECHNOLOGY. The service technology that workers use also affects how they conduct their groups. *Service technology* refers to particular theories or methods of intervention used by a worker. Three leaders of groups for alcoholics, for example, will intervene in quite different ways, using transactional analysis, behavior therapy, or reality therapy. Workers' choice of service technologies may be influenced by their personal preferences, their training, or the ideology of the agency in which they work.

A worker's technological and ideological stance often serves as a useful way to organize interventions. Workers may wish to receive specialized instruction in a particular service technology, such as transactional analysis or behavior modification; however, it is essential that they become familiar with basic practice principles of leading groups before they receive specialized training.

## SKILLS OF GROUP LEADERSHIP

Group leadership skills are behaviors or activities that help the group to achieve its purpose and tasks and help members achieve their personal goals. Both workers and members use leadership skills, although the worker ordinarily uses them more than any other member of the group. Leadership skills are combined when conducting group meetings. For example, in utilizing a problem-solving method, a worker uses numerous leadership skills to help a committee arrive at a decision concerning personnel practices in a family service agency. In an aftercare treatment group for drug addicts, a worker uses many skills to help members remain drug free.

Although there has always been interest in the "skillful use of self" in social work (see Maloney, 1963), recently there has been a growing interest in training programs designed to teach practitioners and managers the skills necessary for practice with individuals and groups. (See for example Schinke, Blythe, Gilchrist, and Smith 1980; Toseland and Spielberg, 1982; Rivas and Toseland, 1981.) Most of the evidence for the effectiveness of specific skills has been gathered from evaluating work between two individuals rather than from work in task and treatment groups (Brammer, 1979; Orlinsky and Howard, 1978). Evidence about a worker's overall skill level, as measured by the training, experience, and performance of the worker, also suggests that skills can be learned and that they make a difference in performance (Meltzoff and Kornreich, 1970; Toseland and Spielberg, 1982). Evidence from these and other studies indicates that certain skills, such as listening and responding empathically and sharing personal thoughts and feelings, are directly connected to positive outcomes (Shulman, 1978). Results are tentative, however, because it is difficult to design studies that test for the independent effect of one particular skill on overall outcome.

Group leadership skills are somewhat different from skills used in working with an individual. Both members and the worker often have greater freedom about whether to participate in a group than they have when members are to meet with a worker individually. They have more choice in regard to how they will direct their participation. There is also a greater possibility for shared leadership and the delegation of various leadership responsibilities. There have been a few attempts to focus on the specific skills necessary to lead groups (see, for example, Bertcher, 1979; Egan, 1976; Shulman, 1979) and some recent programs designed to train group workers in specific skills (Oxley, Wilson, Anderson, and Wong, 1979; Rivas and Toseland, 1981). These studies suggest that training programs can be effective in increasing a worker's skill level.

Some of the basic skills necessary for group leadership are categorized in Table 4–2. Skills are listed in three categories: (1) facilitating group processes, (2) data gathering and assessment, and (3) action. These are three of the most common functions of a group worker. Skills are classified on the basis of their most likely functions in the group. However, skills listed under one category may, on occasion, be used in another category, particularly if they are combined with other skills. For example, responding is classified as a skill in facilitating group processes. Although responding to another group member's actions or words facilitates communication, responding may also lead to additional data gathering, assessment, or action. The functional classification scheme presented in Table 4–2 therefore is intended as a guide rather than a rigid method for using particular skills.

## SKILLS TO FACILITATE GROUP PROCESSES

As can be seen in Table 4–2, a number of different skills have been listed in the category of facilitating group processes. All these skills can be used by workers differentially, depending on their intentions when attempting to influence various group processes. For example, although some information suggests that a high degree of member-to-member communication leads to

*Table 4–2*

## A FUNCTIONAL CLASSIFICATION OF GROUP LEADERSHIP SKILLS

| Facilitating Group Processes | Data Gathering and Assessment | Action |
|---|---|---|
| 1. Attending to others | 1. Identifying and describing thoughts, feelings, and behaviors | 1. Directing |
| 2. Expressing self | | 2. Synthesizing thoughts, feelings, and action |
| 3. Responding to others | 2. Requesting information, questioning, and probing | 3. Supporting |
| 4. Focusing group communication | | 4. Reframing, redefining |
| 5. Guiding group interaction | 3. Summarizing and partializing information | 5. Resolving conflicts |
| 6. Involving group members in the communication pattern | 4. Analyzing information | 6. Giving advice, suggestions, or instructions |
| | | 7. Confronting |
| | | 8. Providing resources |
| | | 9. Modeling, role playing, rehearsing, and coaching |

better outcomes than minimal peer interaction (Coons, 1957), workers may not always want to increase communication. Instead, workers may want to focus group communication, clarify communication, or understand a communication. In general, skills in facilitating group processes contribute to positive group outcome when they improve understanding among group members, build open communication channels, and encourage the development of trust so that all members are willing to contribute as much as they can to the problem on which the group is working (Parloff, 1961; Cabral, Best, and Paton, 1975).

## Attending Skills

*Attending skills* refer to nonverbal behavior such as eye contact, body position, and verbal behavior that convey empathy, respect, warmth, trust, genuineness, and honesty. Attending skills are useful in establishing rapport as well as a climate of acceptance and cohesiveness among group members. Egan (1975) suggests, in addition to body position and eye contact, skills which indicate that a worker has heard and understood a member are part of effective attending. Such skills include repeating or paraphrasing what a member says and responding empathically and enthusiastically to the meaning behind members' communications. They also include what Middleman (1978) has referred to as "scanning" skills. In "scanning" the group, the worker makes eye contact with all group members, letting them know that the worker is concerned about them as individuals. Scanning also helps reduce the tendency of workers to focus on one or two group members.

## Expressive Skills

Expressive skills are also important for facilitating group processes. Workers should be able to help participants express thoughts and feelings about important problems, tasks, or issues facing the group as well as to reiterate and summarize them when necessary. Members should also be helped to express their thoughts and feelings as freely as possible in an appropriate and goal-oriented manner. Members of task and treatment groups can often benefit from an open discussion of formerly taboo areas that affect the group or its members. Self-disclosure is an expressive skill that can be used effectively for this purpose. Although self-disclosures should be made judiciously, according to their appropriateness for particular situations, they can often be useful in helping the worker promote open communication about difficult subjects.

## Responding Skills

Skillful responses facilitate a group's processes, helping the group as a whole and individual members to accomplish tasks. The worker may, for example, amplify or tone down what one member has said (Middleman, 1978). Workers should plan responses to elicit specific reactions that will affect future group processes. For example, if a worker's response supports a group member's efforts, the member is more likely to continue to work on a task or a concern. If the worker disagrees with a member's statement or action, the member is likely to react either by responding to the worker's statement or by remaining silent. The member is not likely to continue to pursue the original statement. Thus, by responding selectively to particular communications, the worker can exert influence over subsequent communication patterns.

## Focusing Skills

The worker can also facilitate group processes by focusing them in a particular direction. This can be done by clarifying, by repeating a particular communication or sequence of communications, or by limiting the range of discussion. Helping the group to maintain its focus can promote efficient work by reducing irrelevant communications and by encouraging a full exploration of issues and problems.

## Guiding Group Interactions

In addition to focusing the group's communication, the worker may want to guide the group's interaction in a particular direction. By limiting or blocking a group member's communications, by encouraging a particular member to speak, or by linking one group member's communication to those of other group members, the worker can guide the group's interaction patterns. Middleman (1978) refers to this as redirecting a message.

The skill of guiding group interactions can be useful to a worker for several reasons. For example, the worker may want to correct a dysfunctional aspect of the group's process, such as the development of a subgroup that disrupts other members. A worker who can skillfully guide group interaction patterns can limit the communication between subgroup members and increase their communication to other group members. The worker may also want to use skills in guiding group interaction to explore a particular problem or help members sustain their efforts in solving a problem or completing a task. At other times, the worker may want to encourage open communication. For example, by redirecting a communication, the worker can help members speak to one another. The worker might say "John, your message is really intended for Jill. Why don't you share your message directly with her rather than through me?"

## Involving Group Members

The last skill noted in Table 4–2 for facilitating group processes is that of involving group members. Ideally, all members should be involved and interested in the content of what is being discussed in the group. Yalom (1975) has called this universalizing a group member's experience. Involving members who have been silent helps to identify commonalities and differences in their life experiences. As members become involved they realize how particular problems affect them and how a solution to one member's problem can be directly or indirectly helpful to them. Involving others is also essential for building group cohesiveness, a sense of mutual aid, and shared decision making.

## DATA GATHERING AND ASSESSMENT SKILLS

Data gathering and assessment skills are useful in developing a plan for influencing communication patterns as well as in deciding on what action skills to use to accomplish the group's purposes. These skills provide a bridge between the process-oriented approach of facilitating group processes and the task-oriented approach of using action skills to achieve goals and to satisfy members' needs. Without effective data gathering and assessment skills, workers' interventions are not grounded in a complete understanding of the situation. This can cause workers to use premature, oversimplified, or previously attempted solutions that have not been carefully analyzed and weighed before implementation.

### Identifying and Describing Skills

Perhaps the most basic data gathering skill is helping members identify and describe a particular situation. This skill allows for the elaboration of pertinent factors that influence a problem or task facing the group. In using this skill, workers should attempt to elicit descriptions that specify the problem attributes as clearly and concretely as possible. In order to understand the problem, it is often useful for the worker to identify or describe historically as well as current aspects of the problem. It may also be helpful to share alternative ways of viewing the situation in order to obtain diverse frames of reference, interpretations, and potential solutions to a problem.

## Requesting Information, Questioning, and Probing

The skills of identifying and describing a situation are essential to workers' active attempts to gather data by requesting information, questioning, and probing. Using these skills, workers can clarify the problem or concern and broaden the scope of the group's work by obtaining additional information that may be useful to all members. The worker should be careful to ask questions that are clear and answerable. Double questions or value-laden questions may be met with resistance, passivity, anger, and misunderstanding. For some issues and for some group members, questioning or probing may be seen as a confrontation or as a challenge to what has already been stated. This is particularly true in areas where the group member is reluctant to give additional information because the information is perceived as emotionally charged or potentially damaging to the member's status in the group. The worker should be particularly sensitive to these concerns when seeking additional information from a member. Helping the member to explore fears or concerns about the potentially damaging effect of a disclosure is one intervention that can be helpful. Another is having a particular member ask for feedback from other members about the realistic basis of his or her fears.

## Summarizing and Partializing

When information has been discussed about the problems or concerns facing the group, a worker can use summarizing or partializing skills. Summarizing skills enable a worker to present the core of what has already been said in the group and provide members an opportunity for reflection about the problem. Summarizing skills give members and the worker an opportunity to consider the next steps to take in solving the problem and allow members to compare their perceptions about what has gone on in the group with the worker's summary. Partializing skills are useful for breaking down a complex problem or issue into manageable bits. Partializing is also helpful in determining group members' motivation to work on various aspects of the problem.

## Analyzing Skills

Once the data has been gathered and organized, the worker can use analyzing skills to synthesize data and make an assessment of how to proceed. Analyzing skills include pointing out patterns in the data, identifying gaps in the data and establishing mechanisms or plans for how to obtain data to complete an assessment. For example, in a treatment conference in a group home for adolescents, the worker can use analyzing skills to point out patterns used by staff members in previous work with a particular youngster. The group can then explore new methods and techniques that might be tried in future efforts to work with the youngster. In an educational treatment group for potentially abusive parents, the worker can use analyzing skills to link a parent's behavior patterns to the onset of physical abuse of the parent's child.

## ACTION SKILLS

### Directing

Action skills are most often used by the worker to help the group accomplish its tasks. Perhaps the most basic skill in this area is directing the action of the group. Whether the worker is clarifying the group's goal, helping members to participate in a particular program activity, leading a discussion, sharing some new information, or making an assessment of a particular problem, the worker is taking responsibility for directing the group's action. Directing skills are most effective when they are coupled with efforts to increase members' participation and input (Stogdill, 1974). The worker should not use directing skills without obtaining members' approval or without involving them in decisions about the direction the group should take to accomplish its goals. The worker should be aware of how each member reacts to being directed in a new component of the group's work. For example, in directing a role-play in a remedial group designed to help teenagers learn how to handle angry feelings more effectively, the worker should be aware of how the action will affect each member. Depending on the way they express their anger, some group members may benefit from playing certain roles more than other members. Others may benefit most from observing the action.

### Synthesizing

Another useful action skill for group leadership is synthesizing verbal and nonverbal communications. Skills such as making connections among the meanings behind a member's actions or words, expressing hidden agendas, making implicit feelings or thoughts explicit, and making connections between communications to point out themes and trends in members' actions or words are all examples of synthesizing skills.

Synthesizing skills can be useful in providing feedback to members about how they are perceived by others. Because these skills often involve a considerable amount of judgment and conjecture about the facts that are available to the worker, they should be used cautiously, and all members should have the opportunity for input into the synthesis. Ideally, when the worker synthesizes a number of interactions or points out similarities in group problem-solving or group communication patterns, all members should also be able to give feedback about their perceptions of the situation. For example, during a weekly staff meeting of an adolescent unit in a state mental hospital a worker mentions the pattern of interactions that have developed among team members. In describing these patterns, the worker asks members for feedback on how they perceived the group's interaction.

## Supporting Group Members

In both task and treatment groups, the ability to support members is a useful group leadership skill. The group's atmosphere should reflect a climate in which all members' experiences and opinions are valued. Members should be encouraged to be supportive of one another. The worker should support members by encouraging the expression of members' thoughts and feelings on topics relevant to the group, by soliciting their opinions, and by responding to their requests and comments. This may include encouraging the ventilation of feelings or thoughts by a member. In addition to encouraging members to share their concerns and support one another, the worker should point out members' strengths, demonstrate the effectiveness of the group in helping to resolve problems, and provide hope for continued progress or success.

Ventilation and support may be the primary goal of some groups. In a task group in a planning agency, for example, the worker calls a meeting to have members share their concerns and to support each other in the work they are doing on an arduous task. In a treatment group for recently widowed persons, ventilation of feelings about the loss of a loved one and support in the life transition that results from widowhood is therapeutic for those participating in the group.

## Reframing and Redefining

Beyond synthesizing and eliciting data, a worker may want to use skills in reframing and redefining an issue or concern facing the group. Often, one of the greatest obstacles to the work of a group or of an individual group member is failure to view a problem from different perspectives in order to find a creative solution. For example, in a group where one member is being used as a scapegoat, the worker might help members to redefine their relationship to that member. This can be done by having members talk about how they relate to the person who is being scapegoated and how they might improve their relationship with that person. In this case, reframing the problem from one that focuses on the scapegoated member as a problem to one that is a problem shared by all members is a useful way to change members' interactions with this particular member. As the problem is redefined and group members change their relationship with the member being scapegoated, the problem often diminishes or disappears. Redefining and reframing the problem can help members to examine the problem from a new perspective. Reframing is described in greater detail in Chapter 8.

## Resolving Conflicts

One of the most important action skills is helping to resolve conflicts among members and conflicts with forces outside the group. Group members may come into conflict with one another for a variety of reasons. For example, in a delegate council, members may represent quite different constituencies that have concerns, interests, and goals that conflict with one another. In a treatment team, group members' responsibilities for different work functions and different tasks may cause conflict or competition, particularly if resources for accomplishing a task are limited. Conflict may also occur between the group as a whole and some external entity, such as the agency sponsoring the group.

In helping to overcome conflict, workers can help the group develop and maintain rules for participation. These rules are frequently expressed in early contractual discussions with members. Sometimes these rules, which should be developed with participation from all group members, are stated in a written agreement that all members sign at the beginning of a new group. An example of such a written agreement is shown in Figure 3. We have found the process of helping members to identify and agree on rules for participation particularly helpful in children's groups. Children enjoy setting rules for their group and they appear more willing than many adults to help each other follow rules that they have been involved in making.

The worker may also use moderating, negotiating, mediating, or arbitrating skills to settle disputes. Moderating skills refer to keeping meetings within specified bounds so that conflict is avoided. Negotiating skills are used to help members come to an agreement or an understanding when initial opinions differ. Mediating skills are used when two or more members are in conflict and action is necessary to help them reach an agreement and resolve the dispute. Finally, arbitration skills are used in resolving conflicts by having an authorative third person meet with the group; the third person listens to the disputing persons and binds them to a settlement. Arbitration is sometimes used in task groups that have reached an impasse when working on a labor contract. Specific methods that workers can use to help resolve conflicts in groups are described more fully in Chapters 8 and 9 and by Bernstein (1976).

Members may also come into conflict with forces outside the group. For example, in attempting to be more assertive, members may receive hostile,

---

I the undersigned agree to:

1. Attend each group session or call one day prior to the group meeting to explain my absence.

2. Not talk about anything that occurs in the group to anyone outside the group, unless it applies only to myself and no other group member.

3. Carry out all assignments agreed to in the group between group sessions.

4. Speak in turn so that everyone gets a chance to talk.

5. Give the group two weeks' notice prior to deciding to terminate my participation.

|  |  |
|---|---|
| Mary Jones | Date |

**Figure 4–3** Rules for Group Participation

angry, or aggressive responses from family members or friends. When conflict develops outside the group, the worker can use his or her influence to reduce it by intervening directly in the situation or by helping members to develop the skills necessary to overcome the conflict by themselves. When the conflict is an inevitable by-product of a change the member wishes to make outside the group, the worker can help the member feel comfortable with the conflict until a new state of equilibrium is achieved.

Sometimes it is helpful for the worker to meet persons outside of the group in order to resolve a member's conflict. For example, a worker meets with the parents of an adolescent group member to discuss the ways in which the parents set limits and rules for their child. In other cases, workers can prepare members for the reactions they may encounter outside the group. For example, a worker can help members learn how to respond to the rejection or hostility they may receive when they are more assertive than they have been in past encounters with a particular person. Preparing members for what to expect in a wide range of situations and settings also helps to ensure their success when they are using newly learned behaviors in unfamiliar settings or situations.

## Advice, Suggestions, Instructions

Another cluster of action skills that both workers and members can use include giving advice, suggestions, or instructions. Workers use these skills to help group members acquire new behaviors, understand problems, or change problematic situations. The giving of advice, suggestions, or instructions are infrequently used skills in practice, estimated to be between 1 and 5 per cent of all communications made by practitioners (Boatman, 1975; Mullen, 1969; Pinkus, 1968). Despite this, advice is expected and wanted by many clients, especially those of lower socioeconomic status (Aronson and Overall, 1966; Davis, 1975; Mayer and Timms, 1970). Further, these skills appear to have some beneficial effects in helping clients formulate new ideas and approaches to resolving problems. (See Reid and Shapiro, 1969; Davis, 1975, Ewalt and Kutz, 1976; and Fortune, 1979.)

Advice, suggestions, or instructions should be timed appropriately so that group members are ready to accept them. They must be clear and geared to the comprehension level of the members for whom they are intended. For example, in an educational group for training Department of Social Service workers to lead parenting groups, the group worker should be sure that the material being presented is at a level that will be readily understood by workers' clients. Similarly, a group of teenage parents who have not completed high school requires a presentation of ideas, advice, suggestions, and instructions quite different from that to a group of highly educated women who have delayed child rearing until their early thirties. Advice or instructions given to children in a group should be more simplified than those given to adults. Workers should also be sensitive to the language and culture of the members of their groups. Certain words in our language may not translate appropriately or with the same meaning in another language. Further, the cultural heritage of a population may influence how such individuals receive and decode messages sent from the worker.

The worker should not act alone in giving advice, suggestions, and instructions. This sets the worker off as an expert who may be seen as too directive. The worker should encourage members to share information, advice, and instructions with each other. Middleman (1978) and Shulman (1979) refer to this as the worker reaching for feelings and information that members may be hesitant to disclose.

To encourage members to share information and advice with each other, the worker should facilitate the development of helping networks in which members share their life experiences, information, and resources, as well as their opinions and views. One of the distinct advantages of group work as compared to individual work is the ability of group members to rely on one another for help in solving problems and accomplishing goals. Our experience suggests that well-established helping networks often continue outside the group long after the group experience has ended. For example a group of single parents formed a child-care cooperative that continued after the twelve-week parenting skills group ended. Similarly, members of another group formed a local chapter of a welfare rights organization that continued after the group experience ended.

## Confrontation Skills

Confrontation is a useful action skill in attempting to overcome resistance and to motivate members. Confrontation is the ability to clarify, examine, and challenge behaviors so as to help members overcome distortions and discrepancies between behaviors, thoughts, and feelings (Egan, 1975; Toseland and Spielberg, 1982). Confrontation skills should be used only when the worker has carefully assessed the situation and decided that the confrontation will not be rejected by a member. If a member is not ready to examine thoughts, behaviors, or feelings, the member may react negatively to a confrontation by becoming passive, angry, or hostile.

Because confrontations are potent and emotionally charged, workers should be prepared for reactions when using them. In certain circumstances, workers may want to make gentle or tentative confrontations to explore a member's reactions before a direct, full-scale confrontation. Although confrontations are often associated with pointing out a member's flaws or weaknesses, they can be used to help members recognize strengths and assets. For example, in a remedial group for psychiatric inpatients, a depressed group member who is self-deprecating is confronted with this and challenged to begin to recognize her strengths and assets. Similarly, a member of a growth group may be confronted by pointing out how the member's verbal assertions differ from her actual behavior.

## Providing Resources

The agency has access to a wide variety of resources that the worker can make available to members, such as medical treatment, home health care, financial assistance, job and rehabilitation counseling, family planning, and financial management consultation. Making skillful use of these resources by accurate assessment and referral can be helpful to group members. The worker can also help members to explore resources used by other members of the group. In this way, the cumulative knowledge of all group members can be used to help connect a member to needed resources and to help the member gain some insight about what might be expected when attempting to utilize a particular resource.

In task groups, workers can also provide a variety of resources for members. Workers can influence the environment in which a group works, either directly or indirectly, to make it easier for the group to accomplish its tasks. Workers may have access to important people or action groups, where the group's work can be given proper consideration. Since task groups are often composed so that they contain members with a variety of different skills and resources, members of task groups can also help one another achieve the group's goals.

## Modeling, Role Playing, Rehearsing, and Coaching

The action skills of modeling, role playing, and rehearsing situations in the group can be helpful in both task and treatment groups. *Modeling* refers to the worker or a member demonstrating behaviors in a particular situation so that others in the group can observe what to do and how to do it. For example, the worker in an assertion training group demonstrates how to respond to a spouse who has become quite angry. In another group, the worker models caring and concern by going over to a group member who has begun to cry and placing her arm around the member's shoulder.

*Role playing* refers to having the group members act out a situation with the help of each other. The two primary purposes of role playing are to assess a member's skill when responding to an interpersonal situation and to help the member improve particular responses. Responses can be improved by receiving feedback, by rehearsing a new response, and by receiving coaching from the worker or other group members during rehearsals (Etcheverry, Siporin and Toseland, 1984).

Although role plays are commonly used so that members gain experience in the protected environment of the group before attempting a new response outside the group, role playing can also be used to improve responses that have already been made to prepare members for future situations in which similar responses will be required. For example, in a group for couples trying to improve their relationships, the worker asked each member to role play an argument they had with their spouse during the past week. During the role play, the worker asked the members of each couple to switch roles so that each partner experiences how the other felt, thought, and acted in the situation. The role play helped each couple to understand their partner's behavior and how their own behavior influenced their partner. The couples were given enough support in the group to use the feedback they received about their behavior to experiment with new and better ways to communicate during an argument. In this way, the couples learned new communication skills and began to use new, improved ways of responding to each other during disagreements.

*Rehearsing* refers to practicing a new behavior or response based on the feedback received after doing a role play. Because it is difficult to learn new behaviors, or to diminish less adaptive but habituated behavior patterns, a member may have to practice a new response several times. Coaching is the use of verbal and physical instructions to help members who are having difficulty reproducing a particular response. For example, members of a group for the mentally retarded practice skills in expressing their feelings during interpersonal interactions. As members practice, the worker coaches them by giving instructions and by demonstrating how to improve their responses. Additional information about different types of role playing techniques that can be used by group workers is given in Chapter 8.

## LEARNING GROUP LEADERSHIP SKILLS

Those who are training to become group workers should become familiar with knowledge about groups as a whole, understand the way individuals function in groups, and become involved in a variety of groups, both as members and as leaders, to integrate theoretical knowledge learned about group dynamics with practical experiences. Ways to learn about leading groups include (1) gaining knowledge about group leadership, (2) practicing this knowledge through exercises and role plays, (3) becoming a member of a group, and (4) leading a group.

In the classroom, trainees can learn to lead groups under a variety of conditions and circumstances by combining didactic and experiential methods of learning. Didactic material should expose trainees to the array of groups that they may be called upon to lead. Therefore, lectures, discussions, and examples should include groups in a number of different settings with divergent purposes and differing clientele. Lecture material can be supplemented with video tapes of different kinds of groups in action.[1]

Cognitive knowledge is, by itself, insufficient to train effective workers. Exercises and role plays should be used to illustrate and to demonstrate the material presented during lectures. Often one or more lab groups can be formed to help trainees practice the material that has been presented. Lab groups give trainees a sense of what it is like to be a member of a group. It is also possible to rotate leadership in a lab group so that all members are responsible for leading a group at least once.

Laboratory group experiences can be enhanced by the use of video and audio equipment. These devices give trainees feedback about their verbal and nonverbal behavior as they participate in or lead a meeting. Tapes made during labs can be reviewed by trainees and the lab's leader during supervisory sessions to help members develop their group leadership skills.

Learning about how to lead a group can also occur by becoming a member of an existing group in the community. Participation as a member of

---

[1]Sheldon Rose at the University of Wisconsin, Madison, Lawrence Shulman at the University of British Columbia, and Ronald Toseland at the State University of New York at Albany, have video tapes available for distribution.

a group encourages vicarious learning as the trainee observes a leader's behavior. The leader acts as a model of leadership skills for the member.

Learning also occurs by critiquing the group's process. Critiquing the group helps to ensure that members do not accept all the activities of the group's leader without question. It gives the member an opportunity to examine the development of a group over time and an opportunity to observe the effects of leadership skills in action. It is relatively easy to structure lab groups so that part of the group's time is spent analyzing the group process, but trainees may not have this opportunity in community groups. Therefore, in order to achieve maximum benefit from participation in a community group, trainees should have an opportunity to discuss their experiences as members of the group in supervisory sessions.

When trainees become familiar with basic skills in leading a group through these experiences, they are ready for a field practicum. The field practicum may include leading several sessions of a group, co-leading a group, or leading an entire group while receiving supervision. For purposes of learning about group leadership skills, group supervision is preferable to individual supervision because the supervisor models group leadership skills while reviewing a trainee's work with a group. Rivas and Toseland (1981) have found that a training group is an effective way to provide supervision. Methods for conducting group supervision are discussed by Rose (1977). If enough practicum sites are not readily available, students can be encouraged to form their own task or treatment groups by providing group services for students or community residents (see, for example, Rivas and Toseland, 1981).

## CO-LEADERSHIP

Co-leadership presents a dilemma for the practicing group worker (Kolodny, 1980). Do the benefits of co-leadership exceed its potential disadvantages? An entire issue of the journal *Social Work With Groups* has been devoted to this topic.[2] Although there is little empirical evidence to suggest that two leaders are better than one (Yalom, 1975), there are many clinical reports of the benefits of having two leaders. (See, for example, Levine, 1980; Starak, 1981; MacLennon, 1965; McGee and Schuman, 1970; Davis and Lohr, 1971; Schlenoff and Busa, 1981; Cooper, 1976.)

Among the most frequently cited benefits of co-leadership are that it:

1. Provides a leader with a source of support.
2. Provides a leader with a source of feedback, and an opportunity for professional development.
3. Increases a leader's objectivity by providing alternative frames of references.
4. Is an excellent way of training an inexperienced leader.

---

[2]*Social Work With Groups*, Vol. 3, No. 4 is devoted to the topic of co-leadership.

5. Provides group members with models for appropriate communication, interaction, and resolution of disputes.
6. Provides a leader with assistance during therapeutic interventions, particularly during role plays, simulations, and program activities.
7. Aids in setting limits and in structuring the group experience.

The above list suggests several ways in which co-leadership can be helpful. For the novice worker, probably the greatest benefit of co-leadership is having a supportive partner who understands how difficult it is to be an effective leader. As Galinsky and Schopler (1980, p. 54) point out, "the support of a compatible co-leader lessens the strains of dealing with difficult and often complicated group interactions." During group meetings, co-leaders help each other facilitate the work of the group. In between group meetings, co-leaders share their feelings about the group and their roles in it. In addition to supporting each other's efforts at group leadership, co-leaders can share feedback with each other about their mutual strengths and weaknesses, thereby fostering each others' professional growth and development.

Co-leadership can also be helpful because it allows workers to share alternative frames of reference regarding the interaction that has taken place in the group. These help to fill in gaps in each worker's memory of events and helps each view the interaction from a different perspective. This may lead to a more complete and accurate assessment as well as to more adequate planning when preparing for future group meetings.

Another area in which co-leadership has potential benefits is in intervening in a group. Co-leadership provides a group with the benefit of having two experts who can help in problem solving. It provides two models of behavior for members to identify with, and helps in role plays, stimulation, and program activities engaged in by the group. Co-leadership can increase workers' abilities to establish and enforce limits as long as they share common goals (Davis and Lohr, 1971). Co-leaders also have the opportunity to structure their roles to meet the needs of members. For example, one worker can focus on members' socioemotional needs while the other worker can focus on members' task needs.

Despite these benefits, co-leadership has some potential disadvantages. Because it requires the time of two leaders, co-leadership is expensive. Leaders must coordinate their actions in planning for the group. Between group sessions, communication can be a problem if workers do not make a concerted effort to find the time needed to discuss their work together (Herzog, 1980). If leaders do not function well together, they may not serve as therapeutic role models for members (Davis and Lohr, 1971). Yalom (1975) recommends that co-leaders have equal status and experience. He suggests that the apprenticeship format, that is, training new group leaders by placing them in groups with experienced leaders, may create conflict and tension.

Although we have not found conflict to be a problem in the groups we have led with students and other less experienced co-leaders, conflict between leaders can have detrimental effects on the outcome of a group (Cooper, 1976; Yalom, 1975). Members may be able to play one leader against the other, or avoid working on difficult issues. When co-leaders experience conflict with one another, we have found that it can be helpful to resolve the conflict in the group. Resolving the conflict in the group lets members know that the leaders are aware of the conflict and are able to work together to resolve it. Workers also act as models, demonstrating appropriate conflict resolution strategies.

Galinsky and Schopler (1980) caution that, in some situations, it may not be helpful to resolve a conflict between co-leaders in the group. Certainly, members should not be drawn into a conflict. It is not a good idea to express conflict in early group meetings because this may add to the tensions that members are experiencing (Yalom, 1975). The decision about whether to resolve a conflict in a group should depend on its potential impact on members. Since members are usually aware of a conflict, it may be preferable to resolve it within the group, especially if it is not too distressing. When conflict is resolved outside of the group, some members may not be aware that this has occurred.

Because of the lack of empirical evidence about its effectiveness, the benefits and drawbacks of co-leadership should be carefully considered before two leaders are used in a group. In situations where it is especially important to have models who represent different points of view it may be important to have co-leaders. For example, in a couple's group it may be useful to have male and female co-leaders. In other situations, however, the expense of co-leadership, or the incompatibility of potential co-leaders, may negate any potential benefits.

When the decision is reached to co-lead a group, it is essential that co-leaders meet together on a regular basis both to plan for the group and to discuss group process issues that arise as the group develops (Davis and Lohr, 1971). To avoid co-leaders becoming too busy to meet together, it is helpful if they schedule a specific time to meet after each group meeting. During these meetings, co-leaders should review what they did well in working together, what difficulties they experienced, how they plan to work together during the next meeting, and how members and the group as a whole are progressing. Co-leaders should be particularly aware of any attempts to divide their effort so that they are working toward different purposes, or on behalf of two different group factions. We recommend that co-leaders schedule their review meeting soon after a meeting because they are more likely to remember what has occurred, and they have more time to prepare for the next meeting.

To avoid the difficulties that may be associated with co-leadership, it is recommended that co-leaders should feel at ease with one another's leadership style (Yalom, 1975). According to Davis and Lohr, (1971), co-leaders should be selected for their complementarity rather than their similarity. This helps to broaden the perspective used to assess the group and its members. It also provides an additional model of ways to handle problematic behaviors and widens the scope of intervention strategies that may be used in the group.

In our experience in leading groups and supervising students who have led groups, we have found that it is worse to have a co-leader with whom you do not agree than to lead a group by yourself. Therefore, group workers should be cautious in choosing a co-leader. Difficulties may arise when workers agree to co-lead a group without carefully considering whether they can work together effectively. Potential co-leaders may want to examine each other's styles while leading a group or during team meetings, before agreeing to co-lead a group.

## SUMMARY

This chapter focused on leading task and treatment groups effectively. Although leadership is sometimes viewed as a function exclusively executed by the worker, leadership functions should be shared with group members. In this regard, we distinguish between the worker's role as the designated leader of the group and the leadership roles of group members that emerge as the group develops.

Leadership has been defined as the process of guiding the development of the group and its members in order to achieve goals that are consistent with the value base of social work practice. Workers' ability to guide group members depends on the power attributed to them by group members as well as by the agency or organization and the larger society that sanctions the work of the group. The power bases that can be used to guide the development of the group and its members include (1) connection power, (2) expert power, (3) information power, (4) legitimate power, (5) referent power, (6) reward power, and (7) coercive power. Leaders vary in the degree to which they have access to each of these power bases and the extent to which they use each power base to guide the group.

Leadership is affected by a variety of situational factors that act in combination. Thus, there is no one correct way to lead all groups. Rather, leadership methods should vary depending on the particular group a worker is leading. This chapter reviewed the remedial, social goals, and reciprocal models of group leadership and examined a number of variables that affect group leadership.

To help workers examine situational variables, an interactional model of group leadership was developed. This model includes (1) the purpose of the group, (2) the type of problem the group is working on, (3) the environment in which the group is working, (4) the group as a whole, (5) the members of the group, and (6) the leader of the group. In utilizing this model, three areas of worker skills are essential for effective group leadership. These include skills in (1) facilitating group processes, (2) data gathering and assessment, and (3) action. Together, they form the core skills needed for the effective leadership of task and treatment groups. The chapter ended with a discussion of methods for training group workers and an examination of the benefits and the drawbacks of co-leadership.

PART **II**

# The Planning
# Phase

# 5

# The Planning Process

The planning phase of group work marks the beginning of the worker's involvement in the group endeavor. Planning precedes those important first encounters that take place when the worker and group members meet together for the first time as a group. This chapter deals with what is referred to in the literature as pre-group planning. Specifically, it considers all the worker's actions directed toward forming the group.

In practice there are two distinct aspects of the planning process. The first is pre-group planning directed at forming the group. This chapter is primarily concerned with this aspect of the planning process. The second aspect is planning that takes place during the beginning, middle, and ending phases.

In planning directed at forming the group, the worker focuses on the individual member, the group as a whole, and the environment. In focusing on individual members, the worker considers their motivations, expectations, and goals for entering the group. The worker focuses on the group as a whole by considering the purpose for the group and how the group may develop as a result of the members' interaction. The worker also focuses on the environment in which the group will function by examining how the sponsoring agency and the larger community affect the group.

The second aspect of planning is carried on throughout the life of the group. During the beginning phase, the worker and the members plan in more detail how to accomplish the overall group purpose. During the beginning phase, the worker carries out detailed assessments of individual members of the group. These assessments lead to additional planning activities throughout the middle and ending phases of the group. For example, in treatment groups, the worker uses assessments to refine and reformulate individual goal planning and to contract with individual members for further work. In task groups, the worker uses data collected during assessments to formulate procedures for accomplishing the group's work, such as developing session agendas, dividing labor and responsibility, and determining methods to be used in making decisions and solving problems. Information about this progressive aspect of the planning process is included in Part III of this text.

Although this chapter emphasizes the need for pre-group planning, there are instances in which the worker has little control over the way a group is planned. For example, it is not uncommon for a worker to inherit leadership of an existing group. In some agencies, group membership is mandated, and the worker must accept all members who are referred to the group. Other groups such as delegate councils, treatment conferences, or administrative staff groups are composed through a mandated plan or formula. For example, bylaws may specify that members of a delegate council are chosen by an election. In these examples, the worker does not plan the group's membership.

Although not all types of groups can be planned by the worker, whenever possible, the worker should attempt to plan by following an orderly set of procedures that will contribute to a rational and purposeful experience for members. In planning, the worker can ensure successful individual and group outcomes by dealing with obstacles that are present in the agency environment. The worker can use his or her expertise to overcome these obstacles and to apply the planning process differentially, according to the needs of the members and the needs of the group.

## Elements of Treatment Group Planning

A number of models of planning for treatment groups have been conceptualized. (See Hartford, 1971, Sarri and Galinski, 1974, Vinter, 1974a, Garvin, 1981, Schwartz, 1976, Tropp, 1976, Bertcher and Maple, 1977, Kurland, 1978, 1982.) As illustrated in Table 5–1, several elements of these models are similar. One of the most important is establishing a group's purpose. Many writers stress the importance of group purpose, but there appears to be little conceptual agreement about the purposes of treatment groups (see Chapter 1, "Typology for Treatment Groups"). Most writers also mention the importance of a group's sponsoring agency and environment, stressing the necessary worker actions needed for a good fit between the group and the agency. All writers mention assessing member characteristics so as to compose the group in a planned way. Differences exist among writers about how much emphasis to place on systematic member selection, and some writers emphasize such issues as group procedures, group size, and the number and frequency of meetings, whereas others devote relatively little attention to these elements of planning.

## Elements of Task Group Planning

Table 5–2 compares selected planning elements for some of the types of task groups discussed in Chapter 1. One common element is the need for planning

## Table 5-1
## MODELS FOR PLANNING TREATMENT GROUPS

| Author | Planning Process | Selected Planning Concerns |
|---|---|---|
| Hartford (1971) | Private pre-group phase<br>Public pre-group phase<br>Convening phase | Clarify group's role with sponsoring body, spell out service objectives, justify group work as method of choice, determine composition, assess duration, frequency, and number of meetings, set feasible time limitation, consider location, determine open or closed nature of membership, examine worker's work response in relation to all of these aspects. |
| Sarri & Galinsky (1974) | Origin phase | Size of the group, members' characteristics and initial orientations, environmental location of the group. |
| Vinter (1974a) | Treatment sequence | Intake, diagnosis, and treatment planning, group composition considerations, preparing for group meetings. |
| Garvin (1981) | Pre-group phase | Establishing group purposes, group composition considerations, preparing for group meetings. |
| Schwartz (1976) | Tuning in | Preliminary empathy, anticipating possibilities and rehearsing expectations, generalizing and partializing data, preliminary contracting. |
| Tropp (1976) | Group formation | Organizational auspice, identification of population, type of group and nature of the participants, form of the group, i.e., size of group, number, length, and frequency of sessions, time and place. |
| Bertcher & Maple (1977) | Group creation and modification | Identify and define common client problems, specify preliminary group objectives, determine critical attributes of potential members, determine given group attributes, obtain information on critical attributes for each potential member, interview client, select tentative group members, obtain members' commitment to group objectives. |
| Kurland (1978; 1982) | Group formation | Need, purpose, composition, structure, content, pre-group contact, agency context. |

## Table 5–2
## MODELS FOR PLANNING TASK GROUPS

| Author | Planning Process | Selected Planning Concerns |
|---|---|---|
| Brilhart (1974) | Preparation (discussion groups) | Planning an agenda, notify discussants, planning the pattern for guiding the discussion of each problem, making resource materials available, making clear what is expected of each participant, physical arrangements. |
| Brown (1952) | Goal setting and planning (committees) | Selection of group goals, discovering resources, selecting activities, building a general plan. |
| Tropman (1977) | Elements of planning (committees) | Goal determination, program development, program implementation, program planning. |
| League of Women Voters Education Fund (1977) | Establishing planning committees (conferences, delegate councils) | Arrangements, program content, recruitment, finance, secretary, kits, printing, publicity, follow-up. |
| Pincus and Minahan (1973) | Forming action systems (action systems, teams) | Determining ideal size of action system, composition, operating procedures. |
| Tecker (1980) | Planning principles (administrative groups) | Composition and member background, defining and understanding group purpose; achieving group interdependence, balance, organization; planning meetings, evaluation. |

group goals. Almost all writers identify this element of planning as important. The emphasis on goals in task groups corresponds to the importance of determining group purposes in planning for treatment groups. A second common element often mentioned by task group writers is planning for task group membership so as to build into the group the necessary resources and levels of expertise. A third frequently mentioned aspect of task group planning is preparing for meetings. Most writers suggest extensive use of program materials, specific meeting activities and procedures, and the use of a meeting agenda. Such pre-meeting planning activities are not as highly emphasized in most models of planning for treatment groups.

## Planning Model for Group Work

The remaining portion of this chapter is devoted to explicating a model of planning for group work that can be used for either treatment or task groups. This model includes:

1. Establishing the group's purpose.
2. Assessing the potential sponsorship and membership of the group.
3. Recruiting members.
4. Composing the group.
5. Orienting members to the group.
6. Contracting.
7. Preparing the group's environment.

This planning model represents a logical set of procedures. In some situations certain of these steps cannot be utilized, such as when a worker enters an already existing group or if the realities of the practice situation make it impractical or impossible to control composition, recruitment, or orientation. In most situations, however, utilizing a planning model can help to avoid unanticipated difficulties in the group and can help to achieve positive group and member outcomes.

The steps suggested in the planning model are not necessarily sequential. In practice, the worker may become involved in several procedures at the same time. For example, recruiting, contracting, and preparing the environment can occur at the same time. Similarly, determining purpose and assessing potential membership can sometimes be done simultaneously. Carrying out one step may influence how another step is handled. For example, in assessing the potential membership of a committee, the worker may realize that a budget item for travel is required for certain members of the group. Thus, the information gained in carrying out one procedure (assessing membership) influences action taken in another (preparing the group's environment and financial arrangements). Although the procedures contained in this chapter appear in a sequential order, this is to organize the material to be presented. In practice, few workers have the luxury of planning a group in a step-by-step fashion.

## ESTABLISHING THE GROUP'S PURPOSE

The first and most important question that can be asked about a proposed group is, "What is the group's purpose?" A statement of the group's purpose should be broad enough to encompass different individual goals, yet specific enough to define the common nature of the group's enterprise. The worker should provide a clear statement of group purpose. According to Shulman (1979) and Klein (1972), a clear statement of purpose assists members in answering the question, "What are we doing here together?" It can help to prevent a lack of direction that can be frustrating to the group.

A brief statement of the group's purpose generally includes information on why the group is meeting, how the group might conduct its work, and what the range of individual goals or tasks might be in the group. Some examples of statements of purpose follow.

1. The group will provide a forum for discussing parenting skills, where each member can bring up specific issues about being a parent and can receive feedback from other group members.
2. The group will study the problem of domestic violence in our community, and each member will contribute to a final task force report.
3. The group will review and assess all proposals and decide what projects should receive funding.

Such statements are broad in nature, but they provide information to members that will assist them in identifying with and committing themselves to the group. As will be seen in Chapter 6, the members of the group will usually discuss and clarify the group's purpose in the early group sessions, producing more specific aims of the group through interaction with each other and with the worker. It is, nonetheless, helpful for the worker to prepare for these early discussions by anticipating questions that members might raise, identifying potential obstacles to effective group functioning, identifying potential agenda items, and clarifying the role that the worker will play in the group.

The purpose of a group can frequently be determined by considering how the idea for establishing the group was generated. The idea of establishing a group can be generated from a number of sources, such as the group worker, agency staff members, or potential clients. Frequently, a worker will detect an unmet need for service or a population that might be underserved in an agency. In other cases, the worker collects data to verify a need for service or to identify a particular problem to be solved, and uses this information as a basis for defining the purpose of a group. Staff members can also begin the process of planning for a group by suggesting that certain clients or certain tasks of the agency might best be served in a group. Finally, potential group members can suggest that their personal needs or their need to accomplish certain tasks might best be handled in a group. The following examples illustrate how ideas for groups are generated.

*Group-Worker Generated*
1. The worker proposes an educational group for children, based on the worker's perception of the need for adolescent sex education.

2. The worker proposes an advising delegate council in a hospital, based on a survey of workers' job satisfaction, which indicates the need for better communication among professional departments.

*Agency Staff-Generated*
1. A number of agency caseworkers, concerned with statistics showing rising family violence, suggest that clients from their caseload participate in a remedial group for child abusers.
2. The chairperson of the agency board of directors requests that a committee be established to study and suggest alternative sources of funding for the agency.

*Member-Generated*
1. The parents of children in a day-care center request a series of educational group meetings to discuss concerns about their children's behavior at home.
2. A number of clients receiving public welfare assistance suggest to the director of the agency that a social action group be formed to combat poor housing conditions in a neighborhood.

## ASSESSING POTENTIAL SPONSORSHIP AND MEMBERSHIP

Although assessment of potential sponsorship and membership for the group might be seen as separate, in reality, the agency and its clients are intrinsically linked. The worker must assess both the sponsoring agency and potential membership base in order to plan for the group. Agency sponsorship determines the level of support and resources available to the group. The assessment of potential membership assists the worker in making an early estimate of the group's potential viability.

### Assessing Potential Sponsorship

In Chapter 1, it was noted that group work was carried out in conjunction with a system of service delivery, such as a social service agency. The nature of the sponsoring agency, its mission, objectives, resources, and clientele have a significant impact on the formation of the group. Hartford (1971) suggests that the purpose, focus, goals, and sanctions of the group service are conditioned by the setting and the clientele. Wilson and Ryland (1980, p. 172) also emphasize the impact of the sponsoring agency, particularly on its task groups, noting that, "whatever is defined as the purpose of the agency has a direct bearing on the decision-making process within the agency's constituent groups." Most group work writers mention the importance of the agency, but few discuss this in as great detail as Garvin (1981), who points out how agency conditions affect the group and how agency purposes suggest a typology of groups that can be used for meeting human needs. Treatment groups rely on agency administrators and staff for sanctions, financial support, member referrals, and physical facilities for the group. Similarly, task groups are intrinsically linked to the functioning of their sponsoring agencies and must continually refer back to the agency's policies for clarification of their task, charge, and mandate.

In assessing the agency as sponsor for the group, the worker studies the fit between agency policies and goals and the purpose of the proposed group. The proposed group should fit within the overall operating goals of the agency. If the group represents a new form of service or suggests a problem area or a population not addressed by agency policy, the worker will have to take special measures to ensure the support of the agency and its staff. Interviews with agency administrator or staff can help to introduce the idea for group service and can assist in gaining suggestions about how to proceed. The worker may also wish to carry out a needs assessment or to present research findings to document unmet needs. An agency's administrator and board of directors may be particularly interested in the cost versus the benefits of the proposed group service. A brief review of the efforts of others who have led similar groups can help to clarify the possible costs or benefits associated with proposing a group endeavor. In other cases, an agency may decide to offer the group service on a trial basis while conducting a cost analysis, such as that described in Chapter 8.

The worker's assessment of the agency is carried out to determine the overall level of support for the group. In some instances, the worker and the agency may decide that the proposed group does not fit within the policies or operating goals of the agency and that the proposed group is not appropriate. In a county-funded rape crisis center, for example, groups may be proposed for battered women who have been victims of family violence but who have not been raped. Such an expansion of services, although appropriate and related to the agency's purpose, may be viewed as beyond the scope of the agency's mission, beyond staff resources, or in violation of regulations of the agency's funding sources. When the worker encounters a lack of support or resistance to a proposed group service, a great deal of research, public relations, or social action efforts may be required both in the agency and the community to increase receptiveness.

## Assessing Potential Membership

Along with assessing the extent of agency sponsorship, the worker should begin to assess the potential membership of the group. Such a beginning assessment does not involve extensive procedures such as arriving at goals for members or agreeing on individual contracts. Rather, this early assessment assists the worker in thinking about the purpose of the group and the possible membership that might be recruited.

In planning for a treatment group, the worker begins by considering the idea for the group. The worker can then collect data about clients by observing and interviewing them, and by asking collaterals such as family members, or other staff who are familiar with members outside of the group. As potential members are identified, the worker begins to gather specific information about their problems, needs, and concerns. The worker relates this information to the proposed group's purpose. For task groups, the worker considers potential members according to their interest in the task and the expertise they possess that might assist the group in accomplishing its task. Members might also be sought on the basis of their importance to the sponsoring agency, their status in the community, and their identification with the purposes and tasks of the group.

An important aspect of assessing potential membership is determining whether or not potential members share the worker's perception of the tasks facing the group. Shared perceptions lead to group cohesion and increase members' satisfaction with group functioning. In addition, the worker spends less time in overcoming obstacles and resistance to accomplishing the group's goals when members share similar perceptions of the concerns facing their group.

Information should be gathered about the extent to which potential members recognize the need for the group, its purpose, tasks, and goals so as to anticipate some of the issues that might arise during group meetings. There are some practice situations that require the worker to lead groups of people who are resistant because they are not participants in the group by their own choice. In some agencies, such as probation departments, mental health institutions, or correctional facilities, membership in a treatment group may be mandatory. Certain types of task group participation such as in teams, administrative staff groups, and committees may also be mandatory.

If the assessment of potential members indicates that some are mandated to participate, the worker should anticipate possible resistance and plan interventions that will help to overcome it. For example, members of a group in a correctional facility might use nonverbal exercises to overcome initial difficulty in establishing trust. Discussions that center on the reasons for the mandatory nature of the group are also sometimes helpful in overcoming resistance. The worker can ask members to discuss their perceptions of why they are required to attend, their feelings about mandated participation, and how they might best use the group experience that they are required to attend.

To prepare for recruiting and orienting members in both voluntary and mandatory groups, the worker should list the benefits of participating. In treatment groups, benefits include meeting personal needs, accomplishing personal goals, and resolving concerns and problems. In task groups, members benefit by engaging in a satisfying group experience, working closely with others, and achieving feelings of personal competency by accomplishing tasks. There may also be indirect benefits of participation that can neither be planned for nor predicted prior to the beginning of the group. For example, the results of an ad-hoc committee to review program offerings resulted in policy changes and the implementation of a new program that benefited group members as well as the clients of the agency.

## RECRUITING MEMBERS

Recruitment procedures should ensure an adequate number of potential members for the group. In recruiting members, the worker considers sources from which potential members can be identified and referred to the group. Members can be recruited within the worker's agency or outside of the agency in other organizations or the community.

For treatment groups within the worker's agency, potential members can be identified from the caseloads of colleagues, from agency records, or from agency mailing lists. In some groups, current members may be able to assist in identifying potential members. Potential members might also introduce themselves to the worker, individually or in a group, in order to suggest that the agency initiate a particular group service. Finally, the worker might consider reviewing the agency's waiting list to determine if any of those waiting for service would benefit from group treatment.

For certain treatment groups, the worker's own agency may not have a large enough potential membership base. In planning for these groups, the worker can contact other social service agencies to obtain referrals. This is particularly true for specialized groups composed of members with particular demographic characteristics, for groups composed around a highly specialized problem area, or working on a problem or task that affects a broad segment of the community. In contacting other social service agencies for referrals, the worker should communicate with the administrators of those agencies and inform them of the purpose of the proposed group to elicit their support and, if necessary, gain access to line workers who can identify potential group members.

The community can also be a source of group members. The worker should assess the community to locate concentrations of potential members. Census tract data can be helpful in locating people with certain demographic characteristics (Toseland, 1981a). The worker might also get information about the community from talking to community leaders, politicians, police, school teachers, or clergy.

For task groups, the type of group and its purpose often suggest excellent sources for member recruitment. For example, members of a committee to study an agency's employee benefit package can be recruited from employees of the agency and from the agency's board of directors. A task force to study the problem of refugee resettlement can recruit members from all agencies serving that population in the community. For certain types of task groups, membership recruitment is automatically determined by the nature of the group. Administrative staff groups, for instance, recruit members from within the agency. Boards of directors usually recruit members from the community because the board "stands in" for the community and is accountable to the community for the services the agency provides.

## Methods of Recruiting Members

When the worker has identified sources for member recruitment, decisions must be made about how to reach these sources. A variety of recruitment techniques will help potential members understand the purpose of the group and assist members in deciding whether or not to join. They are (1) contacting potential members directly, (2) posting announcements, (3) preparing television and radio announcements, and (4) issuing press releases and making appointments with feature writers of local newspapers.

Some evidence suggests that direct contact with potential clients is the most effective recruitment method (see, for example, Toseland, 1981a). When potential group members can be identified from agency records or from caseloads of colleagues, the worker may wish to set up an initial appointment by letter or telephone contact. The interview should be followed up by another contact to ensure maximum effectiveness of the recruitment effort. Person-to-person contact can be quite expensive in terms of the worker's time and therefore may not be feasible. Less expensive methods of direct contact include telephoning potential members, or speaking at church or community meetings and social events.

Posting announcements can also be effective for recruiting group members. Appendix B contains two examples of announcements for groups. An announcement should include a clear statement of a group's purpose. The proposed meeting place, dates, times, length and frequency of meetings, and any service fees should also be clearly specified. To provide basic information about a group's sponsoring agency and a group's leader, appropriate agency and worker names should be listed along with telephone numbers for members to obtain further information. It is sometimes helpful to list any special arrangements that are planned for members such as child care services, transportation, or refreshments.

If the worker has a list of potential members, announcements can be mailed. The worker may mail announcements to other social service agencies and they can also be posted on community bulletin boards, in housing projects, public gathering places, or in local businesses. In rural locations, announcements can be posted at volunteer firehouses, church halls, schools, general stores, or post offices. Such locations are frequently the best places to post announcements because people gather there to discuss information about their community. The worker also can ask that announcements be made at meetings of community service groups, church groups, business associations, and fraternal organizations.

The worker might also want to make information about the group available through local television or radio stations. All television and radio stations broadcast public service announcements that are deemed to be in the public interest, and the proposed group might be eligible for inclusion in such broadcasts. Television and radio stations frequently produce their own local public interest programs, such as talk shows, public discussions, special news reports, and community news announcements. Such forums can be used by the worker to discuss a group service and invite members to join.

The worker can also use press releases and newsletter articles to recruit members. Most newspapers include a calendar of events for a specified week or month in which brief announcements can be placed. An excellent source of reaching potential members is the feature newspaper article. Newspapers frequently feature news articles about new forms of group services or about particular social problems. The worker should consider whether or not the group qualifies as a newsworthy item and, if so, the worker should contact a local editor and arrange for an interview with a reporter.

## COMPOSING THE GROUP

After recruiting the potential membership of a group, the worker should compose the group. In carrying out this process, the worker chooses members according to their needs and according to the requirements of the group as a whole. Group composition is also carried out according to a set of established principles that the worker decides upon prior to actual composition. Several important principles of composition are that there should be:

1. A homogeneity of member purposes and certain personal characteristics.
2. A heterogeneity of member coping skills, life experiences, and expertise.
3. An overall structure that includes a range of member qualities, skills, and expertise.

In addition to these principles, the worker considers the issues of group size, open or closed membership, and the demographic characteristics of members when composing a group.

### Homogeneity

The principle of homogeneity suggests that members should have a similar purpose for being in the group and that members should have some personal characteristics in common. Common purpose and common characteristics among members help to facilitate communication and help members to identify with each other's concerns, problems, and tasks. Additionally, commonalities among members assist them in building relationships with each other.

It is important for members to accept and to identify with the major purpose for the group so that they can utilize the group meetings to their full advantage. The worker should assess the extent to which members' purposes coincide with one another and the group as a whole. Without some common purposes for being in the group, members will have little basis for interacting with each other.

It is also important that members share some similar personal characteristics such as age, level of education, cultural background, degree of expertise relative to the group task, communication ability, or type of problem in common. The worker should determine that all members have enough characteristics in common to facilitate the work of the group. The extent to which members should possess common characteristics varies with the type of group. In an educational group for new parents, it might be important that all members be able to read English at a sixth-grade level in order to understand program materials recommended for reading at home. In an educational group about the principles of transactional analysis, it might be necessary for all members to read at high school level to understand the material they will be asked to read. In a program-oriented group for youngsters residing in a treatment center, the most important common characteristic for members may be their common living situation. Groups of alcoholics, drug abusers, and delinquents all have a problem in common.

## Heterogeneity

For most groups there should be some diversity of member coping skills, life experience, and levels of expertise. It has been noted that differences in members coping patterns "opens the eyes of members to options, choices, and alternatives, and makes it possible for them to learn from one another" (Klein, 1972, p. 6). In treatment groups, it is important for members to be able to hear how others have coped with their problems. Members may also learn by observing different problem-solving approaches carried out by other members.

In some groups, the worker chooses members with differing life experiences or diverse characteristics to foster learning among members. A growth group, for example, might be composed of members from different cultures, social classes, occupations, or geographic areas to expose members to the benefits of differing viewpoints, differing life-styles, and differing styles of communication. The differences among members can provide multiple opportunities for support, mutual aid, and learning.

Heterogeneity is also frequently built into the membership of task groups. This practice ensures an adequate range of resources and provides for an efficient division of labor when dealing with complex tasks. For example, agency boards of directors are usually composed of members who represent a variety of professions, agencies, and occupations. They bring different kinds of expertise to the board. Some other task groups such as delegate councils and task forces are also composed of members who represent differing constituencies with diverse interests and needs. For example, a task force to study the problem of youth is composed by choosing members from diverse parts of a city; i.e., members from the business district, the inner city and residential neighborhoods. Such heterogeneity is an important asset to the group in accomplishing its tasks.

## Group Structure

The worker structures group composition so that members will be able to meet their needs and so that the group will be able to accomplish its purposes. Bertcher and Maple (1977) and Pincus and Minahan (1973), for example, advocate a systematic composition procedure aimed at finding an optimal mix of descriptive and behavioral characteristics of members. Although a highly structured procedure for composing a group is not always appropriate, there are some general qualities the worker should seek in members to aid interaction and build group cohesion.

Members of treatment groups should have the ability and the desire to communicate with others in the group (Klein, 1972, p. 63). Mahler (1969, pp. 18–20) suggests that a member who is grossly ineffective in communicating with peers could engender more antagonism than support from fellow members and is best excluded from group treatment. The worker should seek members who can accept each other's behavior. Members should be able to get along with each other despite differences of opinions, viewpoints, or positions. Members should also have some capacity to understand their own behavior. Persons who cannot accept feedback or utilize it are poor candidates for treatment groups.

It is also helpful for the worker to consider the level and the source of member motivation when composing a treatment group. Members of treatment groups should be motivated to work on their problems or concerns. Motivation can originate from internal or external sources. Internal motivation is based on personal desire to change, grow, or deal with one's problems. External motivation stems from a member's compliance with an external influence such as from a spouse, from an employer, or from the court system.

In composing task groups, other qualities should also be sought in members. Likert (1961) suggests that task groups be composed by seeking members who are (1) skilled in various roles of membership and leadership, (2) attracted to the group, (3) highly motivated to abide by the group's values and to achieve group goals, and (4) strongly motivated to communicate fully and frankly all information that is relevant to the group's activity. Scheidel and Crowell (1979, p. 122) suggest that members of a task group should "together possess all the information necessary to the performance of their task plus the ability to interpret and use it."

The worker should choose members who will be able to put the needs of the group or the requirements of the task before their own personal needs. Klein (1972, p. 335) notes, for instance, that "committee productivity is curtailed when members use the committee for the meeting of personal needs rather than the fulfillment of group goals."

In addition to these qualities, the worker should seek members who demonstrate ability to cooperate with one another. Although a task group can be composed of members with motivation and expertise, it can be hampered by a lack of cooperative effort. It is not always possible to predict how people will work together, but it is necessary to give this some consideration when composing a group.

### Size

There is no optimal size for treatment or task groups. The worker determines the size of the group according to a number of criteria. Bertcher and Maple (1974, p. 196) suggest that size "should depend on the objectives of the group and the attributes of the members." The group should be small enough to allow it to accomplish its purpose, yet large enough to permit members to have a satisfying experience.

Studies of committees have shown that the most common sizes are five, seven, and nine members (Brilhart, 1974). Bales (1954) suggests that five is the optimum number of members for task groups. For decision-making groups, it has been suggested that seven members are desirable (Scheidel and Crowell, 1979). With the exception of larger task groups, such as delegate councils, the optimum range for task groups appears to be between five and seven members.

Similar suggestions appear in the literature for the size of treatment groups. Bertcher and Maple (1974) suggest a range of more than three but less than fifteen members. Klein (1972, p. 65) notes, "five to seven is often given as ideal . . . developmental groups of fifteen are viable." In general, the literature indicates that a group size of seven members is ideal (Garvin,

1981; Yalom, 1975). Despite suggestions about the ideal size for a treatment group little empirical research has been conducted to determine the relationship between group size and group effectiveness (Yalom, 1975).

In determining the size of treatment groups, the worker should consider how the members will be affected. For example, will members feel satisfied with the attention given to their concerns or problems? The amount of attention given to members' concerns is an issue for the worker, because "as group size increases, the complexity increases rapidly: the number of interpersonal relationships increases geometrically as the number of members increases arithmetically" (Brilhart, 1974, p. 30).

In determining the size of task groups, the worker must consider how many members are needed to accomplish tasks in an efficient and effective manner. Although smaller groups are not always best for accomplishing complex tasks, Thelen (1954, p. 187) suggests that the worker compose the smallest group "in which it is possible to have represented at a functional level all the social and achievement skills required for the particular activity."

The worker should consider the advantages and disadvantages inherent in different group sizes. Larger groups offer a greater number of ideas, skills, and resources to members than smaller groups (Douglas, 1979). In general, larger groups can handle more complex tasks (Bertcher and Maple, 1974). Members have greater potential for learning because of the presence of additional role models. Members have more opportunity for support, feedback, and friendship. There is less pressure on members to speak or to perform. They can engage in what Shulman (1979) refers to as "occasional withdrawal," which is needed by all members to reflect on their participation. In larger groups, fewer difficulties arise when one or more members are absent. There is less danger that the group will fall below the size needed for meaningful interaction (Yalom, 1975).

Despite the advantages, larger groups have certain disadvantages. The larger the group, the less individualized attention each member can receive. Larger groups make it more difficult to achieve close, face-to-face interaction. There is more danger of harmful subgroups forming. Large groups encourage withdrawal and anonymity by silent members. They create less pressure to attend because members' absence will be less conspicuous than in smaller groups.

Larger groups are also more difficult for the worker to manage. They frequently require more formalized procedures to accomplish their meeting agendas. Brilhart (1974) notes that in tasks requiring discussion, larger groups have more difficulty in achieving cohesiveness, and Scheidel and Crowell (1979) suggest that large groups have greater difficulty reaching consensus.

Deciding on the optimum number of members for a treatment or task group is difficult. At best, the worker can consider the purpose of the group, the needs of the members, and the particular requirements needed to accomplish tasks. Beyond this, the worker can consider the advantages and disadvantages of large and small groups. If a group's purpose is narrow or if the common problem area among members is highly specialized (for example, parents of children with Down's Syndrome), the group will necessarily be small. In other instances, the worker might have the luxury of choosing members from a large potential membership base.

## Open or Closed Membership

The worker should also determine if the group will be open or closed to new members. Open groups maintain a constant size by replacing members as they leave (Yalom, 1975). Members enter and terminate throughout the life of the group, ensuring the group's continuance as members drop out. Closed groups ideally begin and end with the same membership. The closed group "accepts no new members and usually meets for a predetermined number of sessions" (Yalom, 1975, p. 277).

Often the choice between open or closed membership depends on the purpose of the group and the environment in which the group will function. A cottage-based treatment group in a residential treatment facility has members added automatically as space in the cottage is available. A committee formed to study deinstitutionalization of psychiatric patients discovers that it is necessary to add representatives from local halfway houses in order to make more comprehensive recommendations.

In other situations, closed groups may be preferable to open groups. An educational group for those who wish to learn to be more assertive might find it helpful to begin and end with the same membership so that new members will not impede the progress of the original members. A closed group might also be necessary for teenage mothers learning parenting skills so as to follow a prescribed curriculum that covers the content in a competency-based, step-by-step manner.

Workers should be guided in opting for an open or closed group by reviewing some of the following advantages and disadvantages of each membership option. Open membership allows new ideas and new resources to be brought to the group through new members. Hartford (1971, p. 135) notes that the "influx of new ideas, beliefs and values" can make open groups more creative than closed groups. The worker can change the entire character of the group by adding new members. The difficulties involved in adding new members to an already functioning group are not insurmountable. Klein (1972) and Yalom (1975) note the ease in which members can be assisted in entering the group, learning group norms, and participating in a meaningful way without requiring the group to regress to earlier stages of its development.

There are some potential disadvantages to open group membership. Hartford (1971, p. 135) suggested that "instability is the basic shortcoming of the open group, resulting from loss of leadership, turnover in personnel, exodus of members, loss of group identity." Adding new members may disrupt work on members' problems or on group tasks.

Members of closed groups may form a greater sense of cohesion because they have all attended the group since its beginning. There is often a greater stability of roles and norms in closed groups. The benefits associated with a stable membership include higher group morale, more predictability of role behaviors, and an increased sense of cooperation among members. Planning for group sessions can also be easier because of the stability of membership.

One disadvantage of a closed group is that when members drop out or are absent the number of members in the group may fall below that required for meaningful group interaction. Without the benefit of new ideas, viewpoints, and skills from new members, a closed group can run the risk of engaging in what Janis (1972) refers to as "group think," or "the avoidance of minority or outside opinions" (Kiesler, 1978, p. 322). Such avoidance of new ideas can create an extreme form of conformity within the group that can reduce its effectiveness (Janis and Mann, 1977).

### Demographic Characteristics

Although demographic characteristics alone are not predictive of successful group outcomes (Yalom, 1975), they are important to consider when composing a group. In selecting members, the worker usually considers three major characteristics: (1) age, (2) sexual makeup of the group, and (3) sociocultural factors.

It is not sufficient to consider only age when composing a group. The worker should seek members who are similar to each other in terms of their stage of development and their life tasks. The worker should consider that the level of member maturity, self-insight, and social skills can vary considerably within age groups. Neither children nor adults acquire maturity, insight, and skills on the basis of age alone, but rather through multiple experiences with their environment, family, peer group, and culture. For example, in composing a children's groups, it is helpful to consider the level of member development rather than to rely on age alone. Care should be taken to assess each potential member to determine that all have a common basis for interaction and communication.

Research suggests that the behavior of members will vary with the sexual composition of the group (Carlock and Martin, 1977). The worker should consider the purpose of the group as well as other factors such as age range and level of maturity to determine the most appropriate sexual makeup of the group. In a men's or women's support group, for instance, an atmosphere of support and openness can often be created through homogeneity of composition. In a remedial group for children, a co-ed group might add to the difficulties of members and interfere with interaction because of the tendency of children at certain ages to either impress or ignore members of the opposite sex.

In other situations, co-ed groups are more effective. For example, in a task group such as a teen club planning meeting, a mixed group is most appropriate to help members of the opposite sex learn to relate to one another. Similarly, an assertiveness group might include both men and women to be able to realistically role play assertiveness training exercises.

Another demographic characteristic that should be considered is the sociocultural background of potential members. The worker should be sensitive to the needs of each member as well as to the overall needs of the group.

In general, there should not be wide sociocultural differences among members that would severely interfere with interaction and communication (Klein, 1972). One finds a great deal of support and high levels of interaction and communication among members who have a common sociocultural background. For example, support groups for foreign-born students in U.S. colleges are frequently composed on the basis of the similarity of cultural backgrounds of the members.

In other instances, the worker may deliberately plan a group composed of members with diverse sociocultural backgrounds. Diversity can foster mutual understanding and learning among members. For example socialization groups in neighborhood centers and youth organizations might be composed by the worker so that they encourage members from different ethnic, cultural, and racial groups to interact.

## ORIENTING MEMBERS

After potential members have been recruited and selected, the worker should orient them to the group. The way members are oriented is important because this process begins the relationship between the worker and the members. Orientation can also motivate members and clarify their expectations.

The primary method for orienting members is the intake interview (Klein, 1972), which can be carried out with each member or with a small group of potential members. Interviews usually explore how members view their problems or the group's task, how and why members were selected for the group, and what benefits the members expect to gain from participating in the group. Other methods for orienting members include discussions, role plays, observing actual groups or tapes of groups, as well as didactic instruction in group dynamics.

Some workers use rehearsal procedures with individual members or with small groups of members to teach communication skills that can be useful to members in group participation. Other workers use group interviews to model behaviors for members. In some communities, agencies offer training programs for new members of community boards and other task groups. Orientation methods are designed to (1) explain the purpose of the group, (2) familiarize members with group procedures, and (3) screen members for appropriateness.

### Explaining the Purpose of the Group

The worker should begin orienting members by stating the group's purpose. The worker's statement should be specific enough to allow members to ask questions about the group and to clarify what will be expected of them. At the same time, it should be broad enough, and tentative enough, to encourage input and feedback. Orienting members in this way helps to prepare them for a more extensive discussion of the group's purpose during the first group meeting.

## Familiarizing Members with Group Procedures

Group members frequently have questions about how the group will work. Through these questions, members try to understand some of the general rules of group functioning. It is helpful for the worker to explain procedures for member participation and for how the group will conduct its business. Shulman (1979) suggests that members be given a job description of the leader, including a statement that the leader will make sure that everyone who wants to talk has a chance to contribute ideas to the group.

Leaders of both treatment and task groups often establish routine procedures for meetings, either during the planning stage or the beginning stage of the group. Some treatment group meetings, for example, use a short review period for the first few minutes to discuss the major points of the last session. Time is then allotted for identifying particular member concerns to be discussed during the session. Some groups use the final few minutes to summarize, to discuss between-meeting assignments, or to talk about the group's progress. Task groups also frequently follow routine procedures, such as reading the minutes of the previous meeting, discussing old business, and bringing up new business. Many of these procedures are decided upon by the group in its early meetings, but discussion of group procedures during the planning phase helps members see how they can participate in or contribute to the group.

## Screening Members for Appropriateness

During the orientation, the worker screens members to ensure that their needs are matched with the purposes of the group. The worker has the opportunity to observe members and collect impressions and information about them. During this time, members are also screened by using any criteria for inclusion or exclusion that the worker may have developed. The orientation interview allows the worker to assess if membership in the group is really appropriate. Members will often display impaired functioning during the orientation interview.

Some factors that may render persons inappropriate for group membership include (1) problems with scheduling transportation or other practical considerations, (2) personal qualities, such as level of social skills, that are extremely dissimilar to those of other group members, and (3) needs, expectations, or goals that are not congruent with those of the other group members. Such factors as these have been linked to members dropping out of treatment prematurely (Yalom, 1975). In considering members' appropriateness for a group, Klein (1972, p. 60) takes a pragmatic view, suggesting that members should have "the ability to communicate with each other, motivation to work on their problems, no behavior so bizarre as to frighten the others, and no wide differences that are personally or culturally beyond acceptance." Such a view is helpful, because it focuses on behavior that is observed during the orientation process rather than on labels or classifications of disorders that are difficult to observe.

## CONTRACTING

During the planning phase, the worker begins the contracting process. Contracts usually result from the dynamic interaction of the worker and the members during the beginning stage of the group, but certain contracting procedures are initiated prior to the actual beginning of the group.

Two forms of contracting take place during the planning phase of group work: contracting for group procedures and contracting for individual member goals. The worker should make some preliminary decisions about group procedures before beginning. These decisions include the duration and frequency of group meetings, attendance requirements, procedures to ensure confidentiality, and other considerations such as time, place, and fees for meetings. The worker should also begin the process of contracting for individual member goals, although this type of contracting takes place primarily during the beginning phase of group work.

A contract is a verbal or written agreement between two or more members of a group. In a legal contract, each party agrees to provide something, although what is provided by each does not have to be equal, and penalties are specified if either party does not fulfill the contract. Recently, there has been an increase in interest in the use of contracts in group work practice (Rose, 1977; Croxton, 1974).

In most task and treatment groups, contracts are verbal agreements. For example, the leader of an educational treatment group for foster parents agrees to meet with the group for five two-hour sessions to explain the purposes of the agency. The worker also agrees to explain the help that the agency can offer as well as how the legal rights of foster children can be safeguarded. Members agree to attend each session and to use the information that is provided to become better foster parents. Similarly, the leader of a treatment conference verbally agrees with group members about the procedures for reviewing cases, the responsibility of each staff member in the review process, and the ways in which the information presented during the meeting will be used in case planning.

As shown in Figure 5–1, a written contract may be used at times for a group. A written contract helps to clarify a group's purpose. It also helps members clarify expectations about the worker and the agency, and it allows the worker to specify what is expected of group members. A written contract can be referred to in group meetings if either the members or the worker need to be reminded of the purpose, expectations, or obligations to which they agreed. Generally, written contracts specify basic ground rules for participation that do not change during the life of the group. However, it is possible to renegotiate a contract by mutual agreement at any time during the group's life.

Written contracts are rarely used in task groups. The meeting agenda and the by-laws or other governance structure under which the task group operates are usually the only written agreements binding group members together. Ordinarily, task groups rely on verbal contracts about the tasks to be accomplished, the roles of group members, and the division of labor in the group.

## Contracting for Group Procedures

The worker begins to determine group procedures by deciding on the duration and frequency of meetings. The length and frequency of meetings is closely related to the group's purpose and the needs of its members. In treatment groups, the optimal length of time for each meeting varies, with some groups needing one and one-half hours, and others needing as much as three hours. Some groups, such as encounter or sensitivity training groups, use frequent meetings within a short space of time so as to achieve high communication levels and to reduce member defenses. Others such as marathon groups meet for long periods of time—for a whole day or for one or more consecutive days.

---

As a group member I agree to:

1. Attend all group sessions.

2. Arrive on time for each group session.

3. Refrain from repeating antying that is said during group sessions to anyone outside of the group meeting.

4. Complete any readings, exercises, treatment plans, or other obligations that I agree to in the group prior to the next group session.

5. Participate in exercises, role plays, demonstrations, and other simulations conducted during group meetings.

As the group leader I agree to:

1. Be prepared for each group session.

2. Begin and end all group sessions on time.

3. Provide refreshments and program material needed for each session.

4. Discuss the group only with my colleagues at work and not outside of the work context.

5. Evaluate each group session to ensure that the group is helping all members to resolve their problems and is personally satisfying to all group members.

6. Provide members with agency and community resources, where appropriate to help them resolve their problems.

| | |
|---|---|
| *Group member* | *Date* |
| *Group leader* | *Date* |

---

**Figure 5–1** An Example of a Treatment Group Contract

There is no standard length of time recommended for either treatment or task group meetings. Meeting length should vary according to the needs of members. For example, a worker limits the duration of meetings of a cancer patients' group because of members' physical limitations and discomfort. Similarly, members of an administrative staff group limit their meetings to forty-five minutes because of their busy schedules.

The frequency of group meetings should also be considered when contracting for group procedures. In general, weekly sessions are recommended for treatment groups, although this does not preclude meeting more frequently when needed. The frequency of task group meetings depends on the requirements of the task and any time limits or deadlines that need to be considered. The worker must also consider how much time each member is able to devote to the group.

Numerous other group procedures should be considered. The worker can specify attendance requirements, confidentiality of discussions, or other rules governing behavior in the group, such as how discussions will take place and how decisions will be made. Additional details appropriate for inclusion are the time and place for meetings, the fee involved, and the monitoring and evaluation procedures to be used by the worker.

### Contracting for Member Goals

During the planning stage, workers also begin contractual arrangements with individual members. When contracting for goals with members, it is advantageous to be as specific as possible so that they will know what is expected of them. Bertcher and Maple (1977, p. 51–52) refer to this process as writing behaviorally specific objectives for group members. They outline the following basic steps: (1) determining the condition under which the desired behavior will occur, (2) stating the desired behavior in terms of what a person will be able to do, and (3) determining the standards by which results are to be measured. This method can be used when contracting with members of both treatment and task groups and is explained in more detail in Chapter 6.

## PREPARING THE ENVIRONMENT

Three factors should be considered when preparing a group's environment: (1) preparing the physical setting, (2) securing financial support, and (3) securing special arrangements. The extent to which the worker can control these factors of the environment is sometimes limited. However, attempts to consider these factors and incorporate them into the planning process will enhance chances for successful group development.

### Preparing the Physical Setting

The physical setting in which the group meets can have a profound effect on the behavior of group members and the conduct of group meetings. Room size, space, seating arrangements, furnishings, and atmosphere should all be considered when preparing a place for the group to meet. Difficulties encountered in early meetings, inappropriate behavior by members, and unanticipated problems in the development of the group can sometimes result from inadequate attention to these aspects of a group's physical environment.

Room size can influence how active or involved members become with the business of the group. Generally, a small room engenders positive feelings of closeness among members and helps to limit potential distractions. A large room can allow for too much distance among members, encouraging some members to "tune out." A small group of people meeting in a large room may have difficulty in concentrating on processes occurring in the group because of the open space around them.

Choosing an appropriate room frequently depends on the worker's judgment about how physical space will affect members. For example, a small room may not allow enough space among members. This may lead to discomfort, irritability, anxiety, or acting out. Certain populations are particularly reactive to the size of the meeting room. Young children, for example, often benefit from a large, open area in which to engage in activities.

Comfortable seating should be available for the group. Sometimes group members prefer to sit on the floor to create an informal atmosphere. Carpets, lamps, worktables, and wall pictures should also help to create a comfortable atmosphere. The physical environment conveys a message to group members about the agency's regard for them as clients.

Overall, the worker should consider the total impact of the physical setting on a group's ability to accomplish its tasks. If a group is to engage in informal discussion, the worker can help to create an informal atmosphere with comfortable couches or pillows for sitting on the floor. If a group is to work on formal tasks, such as completing a research project or a report, the worker should create a more formal atmosphere. For example, a room in which the group can sit around a well-lighted table may be most appropriate.

## Securing Financial Support

The worker should be concerned about how the expenses associated with the group will be financed. For this reason, the worker should explore the financing arrangements with the group's sponsoring agency, beginning with an assessment of the agency's total financial statement. The costs associated with treatment and task groups vary, but major items include the salary of the worker, the use of the meeting room, and the expense of supervision for the worker. Other expenses may include duplicating, telephone, mailing, refreshments, and transportation.

Expenses such as the worker's salary and the meeting room are often paid for by the agency in a routine manner. For expenses necessitating an outlay of cash, the worker should submit a budget request to the sponsoring agency. A petty cash fund can provide a flexible means to cover expenses incurred by the group.

For some treatment groups, income may be generated by fees collected from members, or income may be produced from outside sources, such as from grants or contracts. Although most task groups do not usually generate income, some are formed to generate funds for new programs or to do agency fund-raising. Others generate financial savings to an agency through creative problem solving or decision making. Utilizing information about costs and income, the worker can determine what financial support must be obtained for the proposed group.

## Securing Special Arrangements

The worker should be particularly sensitive to any special arrangements that may have to be made to accommodate group members. The worker should be sure that barriers will not prevent particular members from being able to attend meetings. For a group of senior citizens, for example, the worker should consider transportation needs, the safety of the meeting place, the comfort of chairs, and access to the agency and the meeting room (see, for example, Toseland and Coppola, 1984). In working with the physically handicapped, the worker should plan a barrier-free location for meetings. If a group for parents is planned, the worker should consider child care arrangements. The worker should discuss transportation arrangements and obtain parental consent for children's involvement in a group. In working with a population for whom English is a second language, the worker may need to arrange for the services of an interpreter during meetings.

## WRITING A GROUP PROPOSAL

In planning for a group, the worker might find it useful to prepare a written proposal. Such a proposal is sometimes required for obtaining agency sponsorship for the group or in obtaining funding from various sources. A written proposal can also inform potential members about the group. Spending time to organize and write a group proposal can also aid the worker in preparing for meetings.

Sources that explain proposal writing (Lauffer, 1977) can be utilized when proposing a treatment or task group. Although these sources suggest rather detailed outlines, for most groups, we recommend a brief summary (one to two pages) based on the outline in Appendix C. Two sample proposals, one for a treatment group and one for a task group, are presented in Appendixes D and E.

## SUMMARY

This chapter stresses the need for planning in group work. When planning for a group, workers consider many variables and exercise control over as many of them as possible. The planning process should be guided by the purposes of the group, the needs of the members, and the requirements of the task.

This chapter presented a model for planning treatment and task groups. Steps in the planning model include (1) establishing the group's purpose, (2) assessing the potential sponsorship and membership, (3) recruiting members, (4) composing the group, (5) orienting members, (6) contracting, and (7) preparing the group's environment. This model, useful in planning for the many different types of groups a worker may lead, points out the similarities in planning for a variety of groups. Although all planning models represent an idealized, step-by-step set of procedures that may vary, depending upon the realities of agency practice, following a logical model of planning can assist workers in helping groups to meet members' needs and to accomplish established goals.

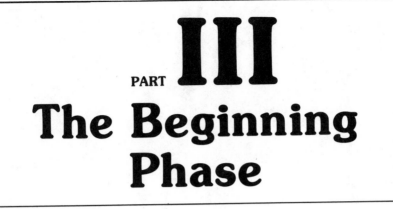

PART **III**
# The Beginning Phase

# 6

# The Group Begins

## The First Meeting

The first meeting of a group is often a stimulating experience. Before beginning, the members have certain expectations about the group. These are based on their previous experiences with other groups, their previous relationships, and the role expectations and characteristic ways of interacting that they bring to the group (Berne, 1963). Usually, the participants realize that there is an important purpose for their face-to-face contact in the group. They may have met with the worker before the first group meeting or received information on the purpose of the group through other agency workers, from other group members, or from previous group members. Despite this, at the beginning of any group, members are not fully certain about the purposes of the group. They wonder how the group will accomplish its tasks, what demands will be placed on them, and how the worker will interact with them.

The beginning of a group is characterized by caution and tentativeness. As Shulman (1979, p. 138) points out, each member asks, "what are we doing here together?", "What kind of person will the worker be?", "what kind of people will these other group members be?" and "what is expected of me?" From the very first contact, participants make assessments of one another. These assessments are based largely on non-verbal cues such as dress and personal appearance. The first interchanges are often stereotyped conversations in which participants attempt to become familiar with one another through mutual interests in places, people, events, and common experiences (Hartford, 1971).

As the group meeting progresses, an approach-avoidance conflict becomes more evident (Garland, Jones and Kolodny, 1976). Members approach each other in their striving to connect with one another, but they avoid getting too close to one another because they fear the vulnerability that such intimacy implies. Discussion of emotionally charged issues can be detrimental in the beginning of a group. When a member self-discloses emotionally charged issues very early in the group's development, other members sometimes become threatened and disclose little personal information for a time. This occurs because few norms have developed about how to behave in the first few meetings and members are unsure about how to respond. Members may feel threatened if they believe they will be asked to self-disclose at similar levels. Members may not be ready to do so, or they may believe that others will not be receptive or supportive if they disclose personal details that they consider to reflect poorly on themselves. Members are concerned about the way they present themselves early in a group and often prefer to proceed with caution.

Through their initial interactions, members attempt to find their place within the group. As the group develops norms, members begin to find out what is acceptable and unacceptable behavior in the group. The tentative interactions found in the beginning of most groups are a testing ground for developing relationships. Group members attempt to reach out to find who in the group they can trust with their thoughts and feelings and who they can seek out to form a continuing relationship.

At the beginning of the group, members are cautious about how they expose themselves. Concerns about their own adequacy are heightened because all interactions occur within the public view of the worker and a number of other group members. All members have had a variety of experiences in other groups and these past experiences affect members' reactions to a new group. Members recall how they were received in other groups. They use those experiences as a basis for their behavior in the current group. A useful exercise that can be done early in the group's life is to have each member describe an experience they had in a previous group, emphasizing how that group experience affected their participation in the current group.

Members react in a variety of different ways to the group situation. Some will remain silent, taking a wait-and-see stance toward the other group members. Others will try to reduce their anxiety by engaging in conversation or by asking questions to help them clarify their position in the group. Gradually, a pattern of relating develops within the group. As Hartford (1971) points out, this pattern of relating includes affectional acceptances or rejections, alliances and subgroups, status ratings, leader and follower patterns, and characteristic communication patterns. These patterns crystalize as the group develops. It is important for the worker to be aware of patterns of relating as they develop. The worker can point these out to group members and encourage the development of those that will help the group and its members accomplish their purpose. For example, open patterns of interaction that allow all members to participate lead to member satisfaction and successful task accomplishment. These should be encouraged by the worker.

## OBJECTIVES IN THE BEGINNING STAGE

The beginning stage is often considered by novice and experienced workers alike as the most difficult stage of group work because members are seeking direction, yet are suspicious of workers' attempts to impose goals on them. In the beginning stage, members develop their impressions and assessments of the skills of the worker. Because members' commitments to become participants in a group are often more tentative in earlier than in later stages, workers who lack skills in the initial phase of a group's development are likely to find that members will not continue with the group.

All group workers should focus on certain objectives as they begin a group. These include:

1. Introducing members of the group so they feel comfortable with one another.
2. Stating the purpose and function of the group as it is perceived by the worker and the agency.
3. Balancing task and socioemotional aspects of the group process.
4. Providing the opportunity and the climate for members to give feedback about the fit between their needs, the worker's view of their needs, and the services provided by the agency.
5. Setting goals.
6. Contracting.
7. Facilitating member motivation and ability to work in the group.

In the following pages, these objectives and the skills necessary to carry them out are presented sequentially. Despite their sequential presentation, in actual practice, the group worker should be concerned about these objectives simultaneously.

### Introduction

When the participants have arrived and the group is ready to begin, the first task of the worker is to introduce members to one another. Introductions help members to share their mutual concerns and interests. They also help to develop trust among members. The worker should decide what information would be important for members to share with the group. Beyond each member's name, the information revealed by each member should depend on the purpose of the group. For example, if the group is an interagency task force to study the problem of battered women, members might be expected to share their position in their agency, their experiences with services to battered women, and their reasons and purposes for becoming involved in the task force. If the group is for parents with children who have behavior problems, in addition to information about themselves, parents might briefly describe their children and the behavior problems they are experiencing.

In addition to acquainting members with one another, introductions should give members a starting point for interaction. Therefore, the information that is shared should attempt to bring out commonalities. The worker can facilitate this process by noting commonalities among the characteristics and the concerns disclosed by different members. Rather than proceeding through the introduction in a mechanical fashion, the worker should encourage members to discuss these commonalities. This helps members to feel at ease with one another. It also helps in developing group cohesion and demonstrating to members that they are not alone with their problems and concerns.

The fact that members can share common concerns and issues with one another is one of the unique aspects of the group as a practice method. Yalom has called this phenomenon "universality" (Yalom, 1975, pp. 7–9). People who come to treatment groups often believe that they are alone with their problems, that they are unique, and that no one else faces the same troubles. In reality, although they have been experiencing problems by themselves, other people experience similar concerns. As individuals, they are isolated and alone. In a group, they begin to see that their problems are experienced by many others.

In treatment groups, the first group meetings provide members with feelings of support and comfort as they realize they are not alone. A similar process occurs in task groups. For example, workers from different community agencies often experience similar frustrations and similar problems in serving clients with particular social service needs. Alone, workers feel they can do little to change the system to make it more responsive to clients. Together, in a task force, a treatment conference, or in the variety of other task groups described previously, workers can begin to share their concerns, coordinate their efforts, and work to change problematic situations.

The most common method of introducing members to one another is to have them introduce themselves one after another in "round robin" fashion. If this method of introduction is used, it is helpful for workers to introduce themselves first. In the early stages of the group, members take many of their cues from the worker. Workers serve as models by disclosing characteristics about themselves. Once members have the opportunity to hear how the worker introduces himself or herself, members are likely to focus on these disclosures as they introduce themselves. Sometimes, the worker may want members to disclose information about areas of concern that the worker does not share. For example, in a group of parents, the worker may not have children. Workers should note the absence of this characteristic in their own lives, state how it might affect their work in the group, and ask members to mention it in their introductions.

When they introduce themselves, it is rare for members to disclose more than the worker discloses. Members initially tend to disclose themselves to a lesser extent than the worker. Therefore, if workers expect a certain level of self-disclosure or want to foster disclosures in a certain area, their introductions should serve as models of what is expected of each group member. This is not to suggest that the introduction should call on members to reveal in-depth, personal life experiences. In the early stage of the group, members are often reluctant to reveal themselves and asking for in-depth, personal self-disclosures during the beginning of a group may increase rather than decrease barriers to open communication.

Group workers may find several variations on the "round robin" useful in opening different types of groups. In order to increase member interaction, the group can be asked to divide into pairs. One member of each pair interviews a partner for five minutes, asking about details specified by the worker. After five minutes, members of the pair reverse roles and continue getting to know one another for another five minutes. When the group reconvenes, the partner of the member who was first interviewed introduces that member to the group by recalling the facts learned during their conversation. The process is repeated with each member introducing the partners whom they interviewed. In addition to helping members develop a relationship with a partner, group workers will find that this method of introduction sometimes leads to a greater depth of self-disclosure than the "round robin" because new group members are likely to reveal more about themselves on a one-to-one basis than when asked to introduce themselves to the group.

A variation on this opening is what Shulman (1979, p. 143) has called "problem swapping." In this opening, pairs volunteer to discuss their problems or concerns openly before the group. This opening is useful because common problems often emerge from this discussion and they can form the basis for the group's work.

An opening that is useful in growth-oriented groups is known as "top secret." In this opening, members are asked to write down one thing about themselves that they have not or would not ordinarily reveal to new acquaintances. The leader collects these "top secrets" and reads them to the group. Members attempt to identify the person who made each revelation, giving a reason for their choice. This exercise can be repeated in a later group session. It illustrates the extent to which trust and cohesion have increased in the group because members will often reveal more intimate or personal "top secrets" after they come to know and feel comfortable with the members of their group.

Other openings such as "treasure hunt" can be useful in beginning a children's group. Members are asked to find out two or three facts about each of the other group members. In doing so, there is a great deal of structured, but informal, group interaction that helps members overcome initial anxieties. The facts obtained are shared when the group reconvenes. Another opening is to have members state their name and what they like and dislike about it. This opening often leads to self-disclosures focused on members' feelings about themselves and about their family heritage.

Program activities can also be used in opening a group. For example, in children's groups, members may be asked to pick an animal that represents them. When introducing themselves, members can name the animal they have selected and state what characteristics of the animal they identify with. Another program activity for children or adolescent groups is to have members stand in a circle and hold hands with two members who are not next to them. Members are then asked to untangle themselves and form a circle without letting go of each other's hands. For additional program activities that can be used to open a group, see Pfeiffer and Jones (1962–1982) or Middleman (1968).

*Variations in Group Beginnings.*   A number of factors can change the way a worker begins a group. Sometimes, for example, workers become involved with groups of people who have known each other before the group was formed. This can occur when the members are clients of a neighborhood center, a residential treatment facility, or are friends in the community. Similarly, in task groups, members may be familiar with one another as co-workers in the same agency or as co-workers in a network of agencies working with similar clients or a similar social problem. When members know one another, the challenges for the worker are different from those that occur in a group of strangers.

Members who have had previous contact with one another are more likely to relate in ways that are characteristic of their previously established patterns. Roles and relationships established earlier may be carried into the new group, regardless of their functional or dysfunctional nature in the current group situation. In groups where only a few members know one another or where previous relationships between members vary from friendly to neutral or unfriendly, there is a greater likelihood for subgroups to develop than in groups whose members have had no previous contact. There is also a natural tendency for members who know one another to interact with one another and to exclude strangers.

When it is possible to obtain information about potential group members, it is often helpful if the worker can find out about any relationships that may exist among them. This will give the worker some indication of what form members' relationships are likely to take as they begin the group. It also gives the worker an opportunity to plan strategies to intervene in dysfunctional relationship patterns. The worker may wish to use information about members' previous relationships to reconsider the composition of the group or discuss members' interactions as the group begins. For example, a worker in a group home uses knowledge about the relationships that have developed among residents when deciding on how best to intervene to change communication patterns in a governance group that has just been established within the facility.

Another common variation in beginning a group occurs when the worker becomes involved in a previously formed group. This can include a worker who reaches out and works with a gang of adolescents, a worker who serves as a consultant to a self-help group, a worker who is asked to staff a previously formed committee, or a worker who is asked to replace the leader of an intact treatment group. Here the worker faces a different situation from one in which all of the members are new to the group (Northen, 1969). Instead of members looking to the leader for direction, as in a new group, the worker in previously formed groups is the newcomer in a group with established patterns of relating. Members of previously formed groups are concerned with how the worker will affect the group, what they will have to do to accommodate the worker, and what the worker will expect of them. Members may also act on feelings resulting from termination with a previous worker.

In working with previously formed groups, the worker should attempt to become familiar with the group's structure and its current functions and processes. It is especially important that the worker become familiar with the formal and informal leadership of the group, members' relationships with one another, and with the tasks that face the group. Information obtained from a previous leader or from agency records may be helpful in giving the worker some indication of how to approach the group. In working with gangs or other community groups where little information is available, the worker may find it helpful to spend some time gathering information about the group. Any information obtained before contact with the group should be considered tentatively, however, because it is difficult to predict how an ongoing group is likely to react to a new worker. The worker may also want to observe the group before attempting to intervene.

Whether or not the worker is able to obtain information about the group's functioning, the worker's presence will cause adjustments in it. A process of accommodation to the new worker and assimilation of the worker into the culture of the group will occur. In general, cohesive and autonomous groups that have functioned together for some time will find it difficult to accommodate to a worker and will expect the worker to become assimilated into the ongoing process of the group. Groups that are less cohesive, less autonomous, and have been meeting for a relatively short duration will find it easier to adjust to the worker's influence. A worker from a neighborhood center who is interested in working with a closely knit gang of adolescents who grew up together, for example, has to spend a considerable amount of time developing trust and rapport with the group, before members would consider participating in a recreational activity at the neighborhood center.

## Defining the Purpose of the Group

After the introduction, the worker should make a short statement about the group's purpose and the worker's function in the group. When members are not clear about the purpose of the group or the motives of the worker, their anxiety is heightened and they are less likely to become involved in working on their concerns and problems. Garvin, Reid, and Epstein (1976), for example, found that when objectives are clearly specified, the group is more likely to be successful in achieving its goals. Evidence suggests that workers often fail to define the purposes of the group they are leading (Hartford, 1962b). Even when the purpose has been explained to members during a pre-group intake interview, the worker should restate the purpose during the first meeting.

The group's purpose should be presented in as positive a way as possible. Jerome Frank and other cognitive psychologists have pointed out that importance of persuasion, expectancy, and placebo effects in psychotherapy (Frank, 1961). These factors are also present in group work practice. Presenting a positive, hopeful image of what can be accomplished in the group makes use of the beneficial effects of these cognitive expectancies. Rather than focusing on members' problems or concerns, the worker can express the group's purpose in terms of the goals to be accomplished. Thus, statements that focus on positive objectives and goals such as "through this group experience you can learn to . . . ," "you can stop . . . " or "through all of our efforts in this task force we can . . ." are preferable to those that focus on the negative aspects of problems or concerns.

If the worker has had a successful experience in leading a previous group that focused on similar concerns, the worker can mention this success. In treatment groups, this offers members the hope that the group will be useful in helping them to resolve their own concerns. In task groups, members are more likely to be motivated and to persist in goal achievement. In open-ended treatment groups where new members replace old ones, it is often helpful to have members who have been in the group for some time state how the group has been helpful to them. Professional group workers can learn from the way that self-help groups such as Alcoholics Anonymous and Recovery Incorporated rely on the testimony of "cured" members as a major component of their group program. In task groups, members who have had some experience in the group can be used to orient new members.

The opening statement about the group's purpose should include a brief description of the functions of the agency sponsoring the group. In treatment groups, it should define the limits of service so that members will have a clear notion of what services they can expect and what services are beyond the scope of the agency. There is nothing more frustrating for members and workers alike than having members' implicit or explicit expectations go unfulfilled. The opening statement should include a brief statement about how the worker intends to function in the group, the role that the worker has in helping members obtain agency services, and any brokerage or advocacy services the worker will provide if resources or services are unavailable within the agency.

In task groups, relating the agency's function and mission to the group's purpose helps members to understand why they were called together to participate in the group. The opening statement allows members to see how the agency's functions are related to the group's task. It is not uncommon, for example, for members of task groups to ask about how and to whom the results of their work will be reported. Task group members may also be interested in the extent of power that their group has to make permanent changes in policies, procedure, and practices through its findings and recommendations.

In all treatment groups, and in task groups where data on clients may be discussed, the worker should spend a few minutes discussing issues of confidentiality. In treatment groups, members are often concerned about how information they share with the group will be used outside the group meeting by the worker and other group members. Members can not be expected to disclose intimate concerns or develop a sense of trust unless they can be assured that discussions within the group will not be shared outside. In some cases, the worker may have an obligation to share information discussed in the group with other staff members in treatment conferences or with law enforcement officials. In these cases, the worker should be clear about the limits of confidentiality, with whom and under what circumstances data may be shared.

Confidentiality is also an important issue in many task groups. Members are often unsure about what issues, proposals, and facts can be shared with their colleagues. For example, a state-level task force designed to study ways to improve services to older persons who are attempting to maintain themselves in the community deliberates for several months on a variety of proposals before issuing press releases and meeting with the governor's staff and members of the legislature in a coordinated effort to have its proposals implemented. Premature and partial releases of information do a disservice to the work of the task force. The worker should make the issue of confidentiality clear from the beginning so as to avoid releases.

## Task and Socioemotional Focus

Another objection facing the worker in the beginning phase of both task and treatment groups is balancing the task and socioemotional aspects of group process. Through systematic observation of group process in leadership training groups, committees, juries, classes, therapy groups, and labor relations teams, Bales (1950) established a set of twelve categories to describe group interactions. Half of the categories are in problem-solving or task-focused areas, and the other half pertain to socioemotional areas. Bales' scheme (1950) for observing a group is instructive because it points out that in all groups the worker must be conscious of both task and socioemotional aspects of group process. In task groups, it has been found that about two thirds of the group interactions are focused on task accomplishment and one third on socioemotional aspects such as giving support and releasing tension (Bales, 1955). Evidence concerning treatment groups suggests that they may spend a considerably greater amount of time on socioemotional rather than task-focused areas (Munzer and Greenwald, 1957).

The evidence presented by Bales (1950; 1955) also suggests that in both task and treatment groups, neither the task nor the socioemotional aspects of group process can be neglected. An exclusive focus on tasks in any group may lead to members' dissatisfaction with their social and emotional interactions in the group. Focusing exclusively on tasks can lead to conflict among members and may result in a less effective group. An exclusive focus on the social and emotional aspects will lead to a group whose members will be satisfied with their relationships with one another but will be dissatisfied about what has been accomplished. Thus, a balance between the task and the socioemotional aspects of group process is essential.

No magic formula exists for achieving the appropriate balance between task and socioemotional aspects of the group. Writers such as Coyle (1930), Schwartz (1971), Klein (1970), Tropp (1968), and Shulman (1979) tend to focus on the socioemotional side of group interaction. Vinter (1967), Sarri (1974), Rose (1977), and Feldman and Wodarski (1975) are more concerned with group and individual tasks. Through a careful assessment of the group needs and the members' needs, the worker can decide on an appropriate balance and help the group to achieve it.

## Member Feedback and Group Structure

One of the major tasks of the worker in the beginning of the group is to provide members the opportunity to discuss the purposes of their meeting together. Open communication, particularly when it may conflict with the purposes or the goals articulated by the worker, is often difficult to achieve. In the beginning stage, members are reluctant to risk their own tentative position within the group or to express opinions that may differ from those expressed by the worker or other members. Therefore, in addition to providing members with an opportunity to express their opinions and concerns regarding the group's purpose and goals, the worker should reach out for members' input.

The worker should state the group's purposes and goals with sufficient breadth to allow members to formulate their own purposes and their own goals (Northen, 1969). This does not mean that the worker's opening statement should be so broad that almost any purpose or goal can be contained within it. Statements about improving members' social functioning or coping ability are too abstract and will not clarify the group's purpose. At the same time, if the worker states the purpose and goals without encouraging members' feedback, the group may not serve the needs of its members or may miss one or more important aspect of members' concerns.

Workers can reach out for members' input and feedback in a variety of ways. First, the worker should state clearly that the group is meant to serve the needs of its members who ultimately determine the group's purpose and goals. Members are asked in turn to state their own purposes and goals, as well as to comment on the broad purposes and goals articulated by the worker. Workers can encourage members' feedback by taking all feedback seriously and by praising members for sharing their feelings and thoughts.

Members can sense if the worker's call for feedback is genuine or perfunctory. If the worker makes a continuous effort to solicit feedback by encouraging all members to express their thoughts and feelings, members are more likely to feel that their input is welcome. Members can be asked to make a statement about how the group's purposes and goals meet their needs and to suggest how the group could be improved.

Some writers indicate that the worker should provide little or no direction at the beginning of a group, allowing the group to struggle with its purposes and goals until it develops them by itself (Klein, 1970). An unstructured beginning can be a useful way to enable members to examine their own interpersonal styles. This approach is often used in t-groups where one of the group's purposes is to explore its own process of development. It may serve a useful function for members who are particularly interested in examining interpersonal interactions and group dynamics, but it has some drawbacks. The process of struggling to develop purposes and goals is time consuming. Without clear purposes and goals, task groups would be severely delayed and hampered in their efficient functioning. In treatment groups, little or no direction at the beginning of the group increases anxiety and uncertainty about each member's role. In groups whose members have moderate to severe psychological, social, environmental, or physical disabilities, the worker should take some responsibility for providing direction and structure to reduce members' initial anxiety and uncertainty.

To a certain extent, the degree of structure imposed on the group and the degree to which feedback and input about the group's method of functioning is encouraged depend on the group's purposes and goals. In groups that are clearly advertised and set up for a specific and relatively narrow purpose, such as assertiveness training or weight loss, members may only need an opportunity to discuss the means to be used to reach the group's goals. Members of time-limited groups that have a narrow focus expect workers to provide direction and leadership. They are interested in combining a mutual sharing of their concerns with specific methods and directions that will help them cope with and alleviate specific problems. Rose (1977), for example, proposes that workers come to groups with relatively set agendas for work, concentrating their efforts on time-limited groups focused on specific problem areas rather than on long-term, less structured groups that do not limit the scope of problems dealt with by the group.

An example of a session agenda for a time-limited, structured parenting group is presented in Figure 6–1. As can be seen, the agenda provides the organizing framework for the first group meeting. It indicates the goals for the session, the material to be covered during the group meeting, as well as the reading assignments and tasks required of each parent during the following week. Similar session agendas are prepared by the worker for each of the ten sessions in the time-limited parenting group.

In structured, time-limited groups it is quite common for the agenda to be developed before the group session. As compared to less structured, process-centered approaches, structured group approaches give the worker greater responsibility for group goals and the way the group conducts its work (Papell and Rothman, 1980b). Process-centered approaches encourage members to take informal leadership roles and develop their own goals, agendas, and contracts. In structured groups, members' input is generally limited to modifying goals, agendas, and contracts developed by the worker. Workers often make less active attempts to encourage informal leadership.

Drum and Knott (1977), Rose (1977), and others describe a variety of time-limited, structured groups for acquiring skills, managing anxiety, coping with life transitions, and learning parenting skills. These groups last for at least six and usually not more than fourteen meetings. Meetings usually contain a mixture of (1) educational material, (2) exercises, role play, and simulations to help members practice the material, (3) discussion of the material and the problems members are experiencing outside of the group, (4) a brief period to go over weekly assignments for members to do outside the group, and (5) an evaluation of the meeting.

Many structured, time-limited groups are educational, treatment groups. These are becoming increasingly popular and important sources of help for many clients (Papell and Rothman, 1980b). Perhaps the greatest asset of these groups is that they provide a carefully planned framework that can be replicated intact, or modified and adapted by workers to fit different types of client groups in a particular setting. For example, a worker who decides there is a need for a social skills training group in a particular setting can use

---

**AGENDA**

**Session 1**                                        Date _____

*Goals*
By the end of this session each parent will be able to

    1. Describe the purpose of the group program.
    2. State how behavior is learned.
    3. Describe specifically one behavior of his/her child.
    4. State the behavior he/she will monitor during the next week.
    5. Describe how each behavior will be monitored.

*Agenda*

    1. Introduction
      A. Leaders introduce self to group.
      B. Each member introduces self to group (name, number of children, present problems you would like to work on).

    2. Orientation to the group program
      A. Purpose of the group session
        1. Goals.
        2. Why should parents be trained in parenting skills?
        3. Who is responsible for what?
      B. Group Contracts
        1. Read over, modify, sign.

    3. Introduction to behavior modification—lecture
      A. Behavior is learned
        1. Reinforcement.
        2. Extinction.
        3. Punishment.
      B. Role-play demonstration

*Break*

    4. Assessment
      A. Discussion of behavior checklist.
      B. Describe one behavior of your child.
      C. Develop monitoring plan: what, who, how, when.

    5. Buddy system
      A. Description.
      B. Choose buddy, exchange numbers, arrange calling time.

    6. Assignment
      A. Monitor chosen behavior and begin to chart it.
      B. Call buddy.
      C. Read units 1 and 2 (exercises at the end of each chapter are optional).
    7. Evaluation

---

**Figure 6–1** Example of a Session Agenda for a Time-limited, Structured Parenting Group

the framework presented in Rose (1980) to lead this type of time-limited, structured group. Some other agendas for structured, time-limited groups appear in Drum and Knott (1977).

In other groups, however, members' concerns and needs are not appropriately served by a time-limited, structured group approach. Workers who impose purposes, goals, and a specific agenda on members without first consulting with them may find that they have failed to meet the members' needs. In a series of studies on the efficacy of group work, Toseland and others have found that in groups with specific purposes and homogeneous concerns, previously developed agendas providing a structured group meeting are more effective than less structured groups (Toseland, 1977; Toseland and Rose, 1978; Toseland, Kabat and Kemp, 1983). In these groups, the leader provides specific information and exercises to help members with their concerns.

In groups that are focused on mutual support and aid, promoting an open, flexible structure by encouraging member input appears to be more effective in meeting members' needs than less flexible agendas (Toseland, Sherman, and Bliven, 1981; Toseland, Decker and Bleisner, 1979; Toseland and Hacker, 1982). In these groups, members are encouraged to reach out to one another as much as possible. Goals and specific agendas for each meeting are determined on the basis of feedback and mutual agreement among all members during meetings.

*Structure and Feedback in Task Groups.*   In task groups, members' feedback is encouraged in several ways. Members are encouraged to submit formal agenda items prior to the next group meeting. These items are then placed on the agenda and the member has an opportunity to have the group address the agenda item he or she has submitted. During meetings, members' feedback is usually limited to a discussion of the specific task or agenda item currently being discussed by the group. Members have a chance to add new agenda items to the group's order of business during a meeting but only if the group's predetermined order of business can be concluded in time to discuss new business.

Agendas are frequently used in task groups to keep groups focused on the work that is to be accomplished. Figure 6–2 is an example of an agenda for a meeting of a delegate council. It is standard procedure to (1) approve the minutes of the previous meeting, (2) receive reports from standing committees and administrative officers, (3) work on current business, and then (4) to discuss any new business that might be introduced. As shown in Figure 6–2, agenda items are divided into three categories; those for information, those for discussion, and those requiring action. Often, agendas are accompanied by attachments (for example, attachment A and B are listed in Figure 6–2) to explain the agenda items. Agendas with their attachments are usually given to all group members several days before the meeting so they can become familiar with the business that will be discussed during the meeting.

## Goal Setting in Group Work

In the first few meetings, groups often spend a considerable amount of time discussing goals. When the worker discusses the group's purposes, the pro-

Meeting Date _____

**CYPRUS HILLS DELEGATE COUNCIL**

| Order of Business | Information | Discussion | Action |
|---|---|---|---|
| 1. Call to order | | | X |
| 2. Approval of the minutes for the previous meeting | | | X |
| 3. Treasurer's report | X | | |
| 4. Program committee's report | X | | |
| 5. Director's report | X | | |
| 6. Emergency housing proposal | | X | |
| 7. Proposed changes in by-laws (see attachment A) | | | X |
| 8. Election of members of the women's issues task force (see attachment B for slate of candidates) | | | X |
| 9. Proposal to develop an ad hoc committee on community health care | | X | |
| 10. New business | | X | |

**Figure 6–2** An Example of an Agenda for a Delegate Council, Task Group

cess of goal formulation begins. Goals continue to be defined and modified as the functioning of the group and its members are assessed.

Group workers differ in their opinions about who should take responsibility for formulating goals. Klein (1970) and Tropp (1968), for example, believe that goals emerge from the group and that the worker's role is to facilitate the development of these goals. Northen (1969), Vinter (1974a), Rose (1977), and Konopka (1963) believe that through diagnosis and assessment the worker formulates goals for the group. Phillips (1951), Trecker (1972), and Schwartz (1971) emphasize that the worker helps to formulate goals by finding a common purpose between the individual members' goals and the agency's function and purpose. It is our position that goals in group work practice emerge from the interaction of individual members, the worker, and the system in which the group functions.

Both workers and members formulate goals for the group. As professionals, workers' goals are influenced by the values and aims of the social work profession. As members of social service agencies, workers are aware of the aims and the limitations of agencies, services, and their functions in communities. Workers' formulation of goals reflect what they believe can be accomplished, given the support, resources, and limitations within which the group operates.

Workers' goals are affected by what they know about the group's members. In treatment groups, workers often have an opportunity to meet each member during the planning phase. Potential members are selected, in part, because of their compatibility with the purposes and goals developed for the group. Workers make preliminary assessments of members' needs and capacities as well as the tasks that face each group member. Goals are formulated on the basis of this assessment process.

In task groups, a similar process occurs. Goals are formulated by the worker in relation to the capacities of members. For example, a worker who is chairing a committee to examine problems of inter-departmental coordination would be reluctant to set a goal of changing agency procedures if none of the committee members are in policy-making positions in their respective departments. However, given the status and role of the members, the worker might help the group to formulate a goal that includes making recommendations to respective department heads about steps that could be taken to improve coordination between departments. In this way, goal formulation is affected by the characteristics of the members who compose the group.

Goals are also formulated by individual group members who have their own perspective on the particular concerns, problems, and issues that affect them and their fellow group members. In previously formed or natural groups, members have the advantage of knowing more about the concerns of the other group members than the worker. In formed groups where members do not know each other prior to the first group meeting, members' goals are based on (1) their assessment of their own needs, (2) their previous experiences in trying to accomplish these goals, (3) the environmental, social, and familial demands placed upon them, (4) their assessment of their own capacities and capabilities, and (5) their impressions or experiences of what the social service agency sponsoring the group has to offer.

Goals for the group are formulated through a process of exploration and negotiation in which the worker and the group members share their perspectives about the goals they wish to attain (Schopler and Galinski, 1974). In this process, it is important for members and the worker to communicate openly about the goals they have formulated individually. There is some evidence to suggest that members should share the variables that they believe are important in arriving at a decision, and engage in a mutual process of examining and agreeing upon a common set of criteria before arriving at a decision (Toseland, 1983; Toseland, Rivas and Chapman, in press). Such a process helps to avoid disagreements concerning preferred solutions, to increase group cohesion, and to increase members' willingness to implement decisions.

The extent to which common goals can be developed for all group members varies from group to group. In some groups, members have one overriding concern in common. For example, a group of cigarette smokers who suffer from chronic lung diseases may be able to move quickly to a discussion of a specific contract to reduce cigarette smoking. In groups that are more diverse, such as outpatients in a mental health setting, it is more difficult to develop common goals. In these groups, common goals are often formulated on a general level, for example, to improve the interpersonal social skills of members. Goals for individuals in the group are formulated at a more specific level, for example, to improve the skills of John Jones when confronting others about behaviors he finds unacceptable.

The process of goal setting, therefore, is one in which the goals of the worker and the members are explored and clarified. Three types of goals emerge from this process: (1) group-centered goals that focus on the proper functioning and maintenance of the group, (2) common group goals that focus on the problems, concerns, and tasks faced by all group members, and (3) individual goals that focus on the specific concerns of a group member or the worker. For example, in an educational treatment group for parents of young children, a group-centered goal is to increase the group's attraction for its members. A common group goal is for the parents to learn about the normal growth and development patterns of young children. An individual goal is for Mr. and Mrs. Samuel to reduce their son's temper tantrums.

In task groups, three levels of goals can also be identified. For example, in a committee mandated to review intake procedures in a family service agency, a group-centered goal is to establish open, member-centered interaction patterns. A common group goal is to make a number of recommendations to the program director to improve admission procedures. An individual goal for a committee member is to conduct interviews with workers in two other agencies to find out about different approaches to intake procedures that can be shared with the committee at the next meeting.

It is important for the worker to help members develop clear, specific goals. Early in the process, members formulate general goals they would like to achieve. Statements such as "I would like to be less depressed," or "the group should try to reduce the paper work involved in serving our Medicaid clients" are common. After members have had an opportunity to state their goals for the group, workers should help specify and clarify them. This can be done by helping members identify objective and subjective referents of their goals and the criteria that will be used to evaluate goal achievement. For the goal statement "I would like to be less depressed," a member might define the referents of depression as sleeplessness, lack of appetite, and so on, and suggest criteria for improvement, such as sleeping seven hours each night and eating three meals a day.

Defining goals in clear terms helps workers and members alike to focus on what they are attempting to achieve in the group. Developing clear goals is a prerequisite for entering the middle phase of group work. Before goals can be prioritized and a contract between worker and clients can be developed, goals should be stated as clearly as possible. All members of the group should have input into the development of these goals giving them an opportunity to influence the direction the group will take to accomplish its tasks.

In previously formed groups, the worker has a different role in goal formulation than in newly formed groups. Groups that have existed before the worker's involvement have pre-existing goals. In some of these groups, goals have not been clearly defined and the worker's task is to help members clarify their goals. This is often so when working with groups of teenagers and children who have not carefully considered their goals. In other previously formed groups, clear goals may exist. The worker's task is to become familiar with these goals and to help the group develop methods to achieve those that are beneficial to themselves and society and to change or modify those that are not beneficial.

Sometimes a worker is asked to consult with a group when the group is blocked in its attempt to achieve its goals. The worker should help the group reassess its goals to ensure that they are clear and mutually agreed upon by members, that they do not conflict with one another, and that they are achievable. Achieving consensus about purposes and goals can be a particularly difficult process to accomplish with involuntary members who are often pressured into participating in a group. Still, there is usually some common ground in which mutually agreed upon goals can be developed. For example, youthful offenders are sometimes given the choice of participating in group treatment or being sentenced through the usual juvenile court system. The worker can begin by stating the conditions and standards for continued participation and then encourage members to develop their own goals within these minimally acceptable conditions and standards. Trust takes longer to develop in such groups, but if the worker consistently shows interest in the members' goals, concerns, and aspirations, the group can serve as a useful treatment modality.

## Contracting

In the group work context, contracts are mutual agreements that specify expectations, obligations, and duties. Most commonly, a contract is developed between group members and the worker who acts as the representative of the agency. However, as Garvin (1981) indicates, contracts can be developed between (1) the group as a whole and the agency, (2) the group and the worker, (3) a group member and the worker, (4) two or more group members, and (5) the member and the group. Generally, contracts involving the group as a whole are developed around group procedures (see Chapter 5). Individual member contracts with the agency, the worker, or with other members are usually developed around individual treatment goals or individual task assignments.

The most common form of individual member contract is one made between a member and the worker. For example, a member may contract with the worker to stop smoking, to become more assertive, or to make more friends.

Contracts can also be developed between two or more group members. They help one member to assist another in achieving a particular goal. For example, a member decides to practice being assertive in two situations during the group meeting and in one situation during the week. The member may ask another member to praise her if she is assertive in the group and to telephone her during the week to see if she has been assertive in a situation outside the group. In return, the member agrees to help the other member to achieve a particular goal.

A third form of individual contracting occurs between the member and the group. The member, for example, can agree to obtain information about a resource for the group or can promise to report back to the group about the results of a particular meeting. In an attractive, cohesive group, member to group contracts can be quite effective because the member does not want to let other members down by failing to follow through on the contract.

When contracting with individual members for goals or tasks it is important to be as specific as possible in stating what is to be accomplished, who will be involved in the effort, and how success or failure will be determined. Bertcher and Maple (1977) refer to this process as formulating behaviorally specific outcome goals. Goals specified in a written or verbal contract should state briefly who will do what, under what circumstances, and how it will be measured. The following examples contain outcome goals for a treatment group and a task group:

*Treatment Group* (To help members stop smoking)

| Who: | Mary Jones |
|---|---|
| Will do what: | will refuse the offer of a cigarette |
| Under what circumstances: | when it is offered at a social gathering |
| How will it be measured: | and will report this offer to the group |

| Who: | John Franks |
|---|---|
| Will do what: | will smoke less than three cigarettes |
| Under what circumstances: | at home, during each day of next week |
| How will it be measured: | as reported by spouse |

*Task Group* (Committee to study juvenile crime)

| Who: | Bill Evans |
|---|---|
| Will do what: | will interview the local family court judge |
| Under what circumstances: | prior to the next meeting |
| How will it be measured: | and prepare a written report for the committee |

| Who: | Ann Murphy |
|---|---|
| Will do what: | will read five articles on juvenile crime |
| Under what circumstances: | within the next two weeks |
| How will it be measured: | and report significant findings to the committee |

## Motivation, Expectations, and the Demand for Work

After an initial clarification of the broad purpose and goals of the group, the worker's task is to help members increase their motivation to begin accomplishing mutually agreed upon purposes and goals. The key to the successful achievement of the group's goals and members' own personal goals is motivation. To a large extent, motivation to work toward accomplishing a goal is determined by members' expectations about the worker's role in the group, expectations about the processes that will occur in the group, and expectations about what can be accomplished through the work of the group. Members bring a set of expectations to any group experience and they have a powerful influence on the way members behave in the group. For example, if a member expects the worker to tell him or her how to proceed, it is unlikely that the member will take much initiative in the group. If the member has been involved in a previous group experience where little was accomplished, the member's expectations and motivations to work hard to achieve individual and group goals is likely to be diminished.

As the worker and the members begin to explore how they can work together, members should be helped to identify their expectations and motivations. The worker can do this by asking members direct questions about what they feel they can accomplish in the group and how they expect the group to function. It is surprising how often a worker who asks these questions will be able to uncover ambivalence about giving up old ways of doing things and fear about what new and unknown changes will bring. Ambivalence frequently accompanies members' plans to attain desired goals.

Sometimes, members will respond evasively to direct questions about their motivations and expectations. This is particularly true when the worker has made an early and clear "demand for work" before assessing members' expectations and motivations (Schwartz, 1971, p. 11). In the face of a clear demand for work, the worker may find members reluctant to state ambivalent feelings about their ability to accomplish the goals for which they have contracted, fearing that the worker will disapprove of their ambivalence. Before the worker states his or her expectations about what members need to do to accomplish their goals, the worker should be careful to tune-in to the overt and covert messages members give about accomplishing the group's work. If the worker picks up an overt or a covert message indicating a lack of members' motivation to accomplish goals, the worker should check his or her perception of the meaning of the message with the group members.

Ambivalent feelings about change are common and should not be viewed as an obstacle to accomplishing the group's work. It is rare for changes to be proposed and worked on without some ambivalent feelings. It is often a difficult and painful task to change problematic areas of one's life. At the very least, it requires giving up the security of old ways of doing things.

A realistic appraisal of the chances for success is much preferred to covering up barriers to task achievement. Acknowledging members' ambivalence about changing their own behavior or about working on the group's task is a helpful way to get members to recognize their reactions to change. A frank discussion of a member's ambivalence about changing and about their perceived ability to achieve a goal will help all members see that this is a common reaction to planned change.

One exercise that is useful in uncovering motivations and expectations is to have each member focus on a goal and list the psychological, social, and environmental factors that mitigate against and promote its achievement. A variation on this exercise done with individual clients has been called "force field analysis" (Egan, 1975). In task groups, all members focus on one group goal. In treatment groups, it is more common for members to focus on one member's goal, but occasionally it is possible to select a common group goal upon which to focus. The exercise can be done by all group members, in pairs, or at home between sessions.

If the group decides to focus on the concerns and the goal of one group member or a goal that several members have in common, the worker can list the positives and negatives for attaining the goal on newsprint or a blackboard and display the results before all group members. This facilitates an organized discussion of factors that help to achieve goals and those that prevent goal achievement. Such a visual display will often result in members' surprise as they realize that despite their verbal assertions about achieving a goal, there are factors that detract from their motivation. An example of a list of positive and negative factors that influence a group member's decision about whether or not to separate from her husband is shown in Figure 6-3. The list was made after a lengthy discussion of the member's situation. An examination of a list of factors can help group mem-

---

**Problem: Whether or not to separate from my husband.**

**Factors Increasing Motivation**

1. Tom drinks too much.
2. Tom has become physically abusive twice in the last year.
3. There is almost daily verbal conflict between Tom and myself.
4. Staying in the relationship causes me to feel angry and depressed.
5. My relationship is interfering with the quality of my work at my job.
6. Tom and I have infrequent sexual relations.
7. The kids are being affected by our constant fighting.

**Factors Decreasing Motivation**

1. Concern about what breaking up will do to the kids.
2. Worried about whether I can live on only my salary.
3. Wonder if I can care for three kids and keep working forty hours a week.
4. Feeling like I would be breaking my commitment to Tom.
5. I'll have to explain the separation to my parents, friends, etc.

---

**Figure 6–3** Analysis of Factors which Increase and Decrease the Motivation of a member of a Treatment Group

bers decide whether there are sufficient positive motivations for achieving a particular goal as against the number of factors that suggest change is not desirable.

If a decision is reached to pursue a goal despite numerous factors that reduce motivation, the task of the worker and the members is to suggest ways to decrease those factors and increase others that contribute to a member's motivation. For example, in the situation outlined in Figure 6–3, the member decides to separate from her husband. To help the member attain that goal and change some of the factors that reduce her motivation, the group helps the member to (1) overcome her ambivalence about the effects of the separation on her children by suggesting that the children may be harmed more by seeing mom and dad constantly fighting then by experiencing their parents' separation, (2) examine her finances, her plans for child care, and other practical needs that she may have as she considers living independently, and (3) build her self-confidence and self-esteem by providing support and positive feedback during the separation process. Through this process, the member is helped to become motivated to achieve her goal with as little ambivalence, fear, and anguish as possible.

## SUMMARY

Although all aspects of group work are important for the successful functioning of a group, work with the group in its initial stage sets the tone for its future development and is therefore quite important. In the beginning stage, the worker's central task is to ensure that a group develops patterns of relating and patterns of task accomplishment that facilitate functioning as the group moves toward its middle stage of development.

To accomplish this task, workers should focus on achieving certain objectives in the beginning stage of task and treatment groups. These include (1) introducing members to one another, (2) stating the group's purpose and function, (3) balancing task and socioemotional aspects of group process, (4) obtaining group members' feedback about their own needs and the stated purpose and functions of the group, (5) setting goals, (6) developing contracts, and (7) helping members to develop motivation to work in the group. Each of these objectives is central to the success of a group during its initial stage of development.

Workers who are able to help their groups achieve these objectives in the initial stage of the group will find themselves in a good position to help the group function effectively as it moves from the beginning to the middle stage of its development. To the extent that these objectives are not achieved early in the group's development, they will have to be reconsidered later as the group encounters difficulties in its functioning during the middle stage.

# 7

# Assessment

Because of the complexity of human behavior as well as the complexity of group dynamics, assessment is one of the most challenging aspects of group work practice. The worker makes assessments to understand particular practice situations and to plan effective interventions. For a complete and thorough assessment, the group worker assesses (1) individual group members, (2) the group as a whole, and (3) the group's environment. Workers begin to make their assessments during the planning stage and continue to assess and reassess until the group ends.

Although assessments are made in all stages of a group's life, the process dominates a worker's time in the beginning phase of group work after the tasks discussed in the previous chapter concerning beginning a group are completed. It is at this time that the worker is most actively engaged in understanding the functioning of the group and its members.

## Assessment Defined

As Siporin (1975, p. 219) notes, "assessment is both a process and a product upon which the helping process is based." As a process, assessment involves gathering, organizing, and making judgments about information. As a product, assessment is a verbal or written statement of the functioning of the group and its members, which is useful in the development of intervention plans.

There is little agreement in the group work literature about the process of assessment. There are differences in assessment terminology (for example, assessment, diagnosis, ego assessment), differences in assessment focus (individual member versus group as a whole), and differences of opinion about the usefulness of the assessment process. Some writers use the term *diag-*

*nosis* to describe the process of identifying and analyzing problems faced by individual group members (see, for example, Sundel, Radin, and Churchill, 1974; Sarri and others, 1967). The term *diagnosis* has also been used to describe the process of analyzing problems in group functioning, (Klein, 1970; Bradford, Stock, and Horwitz, 1953). Other writers use the term *assessment* to refer to planning interventions with individual group members (Rose, 1977; Levine, 1979) and some prefer not to use either term because both are problem-focused (Schwartz, 1976; Shulman, 1979; Tropp, 1976).

Differing conceptions of assessment are the result of the broad scope of group work practice. As with other aspects of group work practice, assessment varies according to the type of group being conducted. In treatment groups, for example, workers frequently focus their assessments on the problems experienced by individual members, whereas in task groups workers' assessments are often focused on the group's productivity.

Despite differences in emphasis, there are many commonalities in the assessments made by workers leading different types of groups. For example, in leading both task and treatment groups, most workers make assessments of the strengths and weaknesses of the group as a whole, its members, and the external environment in which the group and its members function. There are also some commonalities in the assessment of different groups that are at the same stage of development. For example, in planning for any group, a worker assesses the compatibility of prospective members with the purposes of the proposed group. In the beginning stage, workers make a systematic assessment of the functioning of their group and its members. During the middle stage, workers test the validity of their initial assessments and modify their intervention plans on the basis of the success of early interventions. In the ending stage of the group, the worker makes an assessment of group and member functioning to highlight the accomplishments made by the group and its members and to focus attention on areas where work remains to be done.

## THE ASSESSMENT PROCESS

Fisher (1978) has aptly described assessment as a funneling process. In the early stages of assessment, the worker is confronted with amorphous and sketchy data about the group and its members. Initially, the worker fills in gaps in information by collecting missing data. As information is collected, the worker begins to sort through it, organizing it in a systematic fashion. As much as possible, the worker involves the group and its members in judgments about the data in order to select goals and decide on targets for intervention.

Gradually, the assessment process is narrowed as data are collected and organized and judgments are made about how to intervene, cope with, or alleviate a problem. For example, early in the assessment process, a worker asks members of a group for separating and divorcing persons to describe their feelings about their spouses. Information gathered from this preliminary assessment leads the worker to a further assessment of members' feelings of loss and feelings of anger toward their spouses. The worker facilitates members' discussion of these feelings and helps them to make judgments about what interventions would be most helpful. Results of the assessment process are used to develop an intervention plan, which includes helping members to express their feelings, to share effective coping skills, and to practice using coping skills to help them work through their feelings during and between group meetings.

Several issues arise when workers make assessments of the functioning of the group and its members. One of the most basic of these is how much information to collect. Although it is often recommended that workers collect as much information as possible (psychosocial histories for members of treatment groups or extensive information gathering efforts in task groups), increasing information beyond a certain point may not lead to better interventions (see Miller and Tripodi, 1967; Tripodi and Miller, 1966). For example, Wolins (1959) found that beyond a certain point more information reduced rather than increased the reliability of clinical judgments, and Brieland (1959) found that workers tended to formulate judgments before accumulating all available information.

When making an assessment, the worker should balance the need for detailed information with the need for action to relieve a problematic situation. When workers are not faced with urgent situations that require immediate intervention, they should take the opportunity to examine all the available data about a situation. Whether workers collect a great deal of information or are more circumspect in their data collection efforts, they should suspend their judgments concerning what to do about a problematic situation until they have reflected on all the data they have time to collect. In our experience in practice and in supervising students, we have noticed that a widespread and potentially damaging mistake of novice workers occurs when they make judgments and offer suggestions concerning intervention strategies before they fully understand a problematic situation and have checked to find out what members have already done to alleviate or cope with the situation. When making premature suggestions, the novice is often confronted by a group member who says, "I tried that and it didn't work." The result is that the worker is at a loss as to how to proceed and the member's faith in the worker's ability to help is shaken.

Workers are sometimes confronted with urgent situations that preclude extensive data collection. When considering what data to collect, the worker should be guided by goals formulated during the planning and the beginning phases of group work. The worker should be as clear as possible about the relevance of the information being collected. Extensive data collection that has little relation to the group's goals is an invasion of members' right to privacy and of dubious value for accomplishing group and individual member goals.

Pincus and Minahan (1973) have suggested some other principles to guide workers in their data collection efforts. These include (1) using more than one mode of data collection whenever possible, (2) distinguishing between the problem, concern, or task about which information is being collected and the source from which the information is collected, (3) obtaining relevant samples of data from several sources, (4) structuring data collection so that relevant information can be obtained quickly and efficiently, (5) developing an information collection system that will not place overwhelming demands on those who are collecting information or on those who are asked for information, and (6) avoiding biasing data despite the selectivity and subjectivity that is an inherent part of any data collection and assessment effort. In regard to the last point, involving all group members in the assessment process provides other points of view that can help to overcome limitations of the worker's subjective point of view. It can also be helpful to discuss assessment data with a co-leader or a supervisor between group meetings.

Another issue that often arises when making assessments of the members of treatment groups concerns the use of diagnostic classification systems and labels. Classification systems, such as the DSM III, are used in many mental health settings for assessment and for reimbursement purposes. The social stigma attached to diagnostic labels may be harmful to clients by tending to create a self-fulfilling prophecy in which clients behave in ways that are consistent with the labels ascribed to them (Fisher and Gochros, 1975; Hersen and Bellack, 1976; Cone and Hawkins, 1977). Previous versions of *Diagnostic Statistical Manual (DSM-I, DSM-II)* have been criticized for unreliability and for irrelevance in relation to the selection of intervention procedures (see, for example, Hersen and Bellack, 1976). However, the specificity of the new version, *DSM-III*, appears to overcome many of the problems noted in earlier versions. Although group worker practitioners should be wary of the indiscriminate use of diagnostic labels in mental health settings because of the social stigma attached to them, an understanding of DMS-III can be helpful in making differential assessments and arriving at subsequent treatment plans for group members.

While an in-depth examination of the applications of the DMS-III to group treatment is beyond the scope of this text, one example may help to illustrate its usefulness. If not diagnosed properly, a confused person, age 71, could quite conceivably be diagnosed as having organic brain syndrome and be recommended for treatment in reality orientation and program activity groups in order to prevent further deterioration. Using the criteria stated in the DSM-III, however, the person's confusion may be diagnosed properly as a major depressive episode compounded by isolation and malnutrition. Given this proper diagnosis, a quite different form of group treatment would be recommended after the person's malnutrition had been remedied. For example, the person might be encouraged to attend a remedial group for those suffering from problems of depression and to expand his or her friendship network by becoming involved in an activity group at a senior center or a social group at a church or synagogue.

A third issue that often arises when making an assessment concerns data collection. Fisher (1978), for example, suggests that assessment should be focused on the present. Others suggest it is important to obtain a developmental perspective that includes historical data (see, for example, Siporin, 1972). Each of the many different models of social work practice suggests slightly different foci. For example, Germain and Gitterman's life model focuses on (1) life transitions involving developmental changes, status role changes, crisis events; (2) the unresponsiveness of social and physical environments; and (3) communication and relationship difficulties (Germain and Gitterman, 1980). Similarly, Reid proposes a problem typology upon which assessments and interventions are focused (Reid, 1978).

Recommendations about how to focus assessments are useful in helping workers to become aware of the many approaches available to them when working with different types of groups. Workers should not, however, become locked into one consistent assessment focus. Premature allegiance to a particular view of a situation results in workers ignoring important data or attempting to fit all data into a particular conceptualization of the situation (Bieri, Bieri and others, 1966; 1962). Workers should be guided in focusing their assessments by the unique needs and particular circumstances of specific groups. In one case, for example, it may be important to focus on members' family situations while in another case it may be more beneficial to assess members' problem-solving skills. In this way, the focus of assessment should change with the changing needs of the group and its members.

Despite the need for the assessment process to be responsive to each unique situation as it arises, several practice principles can help a worker make an accurate assessment of the group and its members. One practice principle is that workers should strive to obtain objective facts. One way for a worker to help ensure that objective facts are being used in an assessment is to separate subjective impressions from observed events. Inferences about observed events should be based on logic and evidence. Another way for the worker to strive for objectivity is to share observations and inferences with group members. They can provide confirmation that observations and inferences are valid and they can give the worker an alternative perspective. Workers can also check the validity of subjective inferences by reviewing the data on which these are based with a supervisor or consultant. Obtaining alternative perspectives in this manner can be helpful to the worker in making assessments and formulating intervention plans.

Another practice principle for assessment is that in leading any group the worker should examine the functioning of individual group members, the group as a whole, and the group's environment. In this way, the worker makes a thorough assessment that is invaluable for treatment planning and intervention throughout the entire group experience. In the following sections of this chapter, we will examine these three areas of assessment.

## ASSESSING THE FUNCTIONING OF GROUP MEMBERS

Workers assess the functioning of group members in order to identify: (1) what they can contribute to the group, (2) what needs they bring to the group, and (3) what intervention plans help them to cope with or alleviate their problems and concerns. As a context for assessment, the group provides a natural laboratory where the worker can observe the functioning of each member as he or she interacts with other group members.

Despite the extensive coverage given to the assessment of individual clients in the literature, it may be helpful to review some of this material as a framework for selecting among the interventions discussed in the following two chapters.

When making an assessment of the functioning of members, workers should examine three broad areas including the (1) intrapersonal life of the member, (2) interpersonal interactions of the member, and (3) environmental context in which the member functions. In the assessment process, the worker should consider the current functioning of the member, and whenever possible, also examine members' functioning from a developmental perspective. Acquiring a developmental perspective can help the worker assess whether a member's current functioning manifests itself in a transitory, acute pattern of behavior or a long-term, chronic pattern.

In examining the intrapersonal lives of members, workers focus on emotional states, cognitions, beliefs, motivations, expectations, and sensations. When examining the interpersonal interactions of group members, workers should help them become aware of the level of their social skills and the extent and quality of their social networks. The worker should pay particular attention to members' interpersonal interactions with family and close personal friends because these relationships often have a significant impact on the member.

Workers should also examine the environmental context in which members function. Questions such as, "Is the environment supportive or does it hinder members' ability to work on group and individual goals?" and "What resources can members draw on from their environment to help them achieve their goals?" are often pertinent when making an environmental assessment. In addition to examining the environmental context in which a member functions, it can also be helpful for workers to assess how specific environmental contingencies affect members' behavior. In task groups, the worker may want to assess what factors influenced members to join a group and what consequences will occur as a result of members' participation in a group. For example, will a committee's report influence how a member's colleagues treat him or her in day-to-day interactions? Will the rules and regulations proposed by an administrative group have positive or negative consequences on the personnel whom group members supervise?

In treatment groups, an assessment of specific environmental contingencies that precede and follow members' problems and concerns can be useful in determining how particular problematic behaviors are maintained. For example, the antecedents of a member's anxiety, such as the self-statements he makes to himself about his lack of anything interesting to say, help to maintain his anxiety in social situations. To gain a greater understanding of the meaning of symptoms, as well as to find out about their intensity, duration and scope, it is useful to investigate the history of members' presenting problems in relation to their psychosocial development. Assessments are more likely to be accurate and complete if they consider the developmental context in which members' problems have developed.

## Methods For Assessing the Functioning of Group Members

A variety of different methods exist to help workers assess the functioning of group members. Although some of these methods can be adapted to assess the functioning of members in task groups, they have been developed for making assessments in treatment groups. Among the most commonly used methods for assessing members' functioning are (1) members' self-observations, (2) workers' observations, (3) reports by others who have seen the member function outside of the group, and (4) standardized assessment instruments.

## Members' Self-Observation

Self-observation refers to members' examining and recording their own behavior. Usually, members examine their own behavior outside of the group and the data obtained is reported during the following group meeting. This process is referred to as *self-monitoring*. Some evidence indicates that self-observation can be reactive, that is, the act of self-monitoring may, by itself, increase desired behaviors and decrease undesired behaviors (Thoresen and Mahoney, 1974; Stuart, 1977). Self-observation can also have therapeutic benefits by heightening members' awareness of their current behavior patterns. Awareness of behavior patterns is a prerequisite for initiating interventions.

Workers should first help members decide exactly what it is they are going to monitor. It is often helpful to have members monitor behaviors they would like to increase as well as those they would like to decrease so that they learn to replace problematic behaviors with those that are adaptive. In deciding what to monitor, workers should help members determine what is feasible and realistic, given their life circumstances. We have found, for example, that members often indicate their willingness to monitor several different problematic behaviors at the same time. Our experience has shown, however, that members are rarely capable of following through on such ambitious plans. Therefore, initially, it is important to encourage members to develop realistic plans for monitoring behavior that they can readily accomplish. Later, they may wish to develop more ambitious monitoring plans.

In deciding on a realistic plan, it should be clear where, when, and under what conditions a particular behavior will be monitored. For example, it is unrealistic for a single parent with four children to expect to monitor the behavior of one of her children just prior to dinner time when she is preparing dinner and taking care of the needs of all her children. However, there may be a particular time during the afternoon or evening when the parent may have the time to observe her child's behavior for a short period of time without being interrupted by household chores or the needs of her other children.

In most groups, members make a mental note of what they have observed by self-monitoring between meetings and share their observations with other members during the next group meeting. Because it is sometimes difficult for members to accurately recall the data they have monitored, methods for recording self-monitored data have been developed. These include charts, logs, diaries, problem cards, and self-anchored rating scales.

*Charting.* Some members find it useful to record monitored data on a chart. This helps members by providing an organized, visual display of the data which has been collected. It allows them to see trends in the data, that is, whether a behavior is increasing or decreasing. It also may serve as a reminder for members to perform tasks that they agreed to complete between meetings.

Workers should help members be creative in designing charts. For example, in helping a parent develop a monitoring chart that will be shared with a young child, smiling faces, signifying that a behavior was performed correctly, can take the place of checkmarks or tallies.

The format of a chart depends on the method used to collect self-monitoring data. The simplest format uses a tally to count the frequency of a behavior. More complicated formats are sometimes used to get an accurate assessment of the frequency of a behavior without having to count each occurrence. A chart divided into a number of time intervals can be used to count behavior. For example, a member can count behaviors that occur in a five-minute interval at the beginning of each hour between 6 P.M. and 10 P.M. every evening. Charts can also be made that allow a member to record whether or not a behavior occurred at particular intervals during a designated time period, for example, at the beginning of every 30-minute time interval. For further discussion of methods to chart self-monitored data, see Thoresen and Mahoney (1974) or Bloom and Fisher (1982).

Members sometimes fail to follow through on charting self-monitored behaviors. For some, charting may require too much organization. Others find it inconvenient to monitor and record their behavior immediately after it occurs. When members look for alternative methods for collecting data about their own behavior, we have found that they sometimes prefer to use one of the methods described in the following section.

*Logs, Diaries, and Problem Cards.* Another way to record self-observed data is by using a log or a diary. Logs and diaries are often less accurate than monitoring charts because members rely on their memory of events to record behaviors at some convenient time after they occur rather than as they occur. However, because of their convenience, members sometimes prefer keeping a log or diary to keeping a chart. Logs and diaries require members to record events in a descriptive fashion. To avoid logs and diaries becoming too idiosyncratic, the worker should give members a clear indication of what data they are to record. For example, a worker may ask members to record problematic situations and their immediate cognitive, affective, and behavioral responses to them. For some examples of logs and diaries and more information about how to use them, see Bloom and Fisher, 1982; Gottman and Leiblum, 1974; and Rose, 1981.

A variation of diaries and logs is the problem card (Goodman, 1969;

Flowers, 1979; Rose, 1981). Group members are asked to fill in one or more problem cards between group sessions. On each card, the member is asked to briefly describe a problem he or she has experienced between sessions that is relevant to the group's theme. The member is also asked to name a judge or rater who is willing to assess the member's progress in ameliorating the problem. At intervals throughout the group's life, these judges are asked to rate group members' progress in ameliorating problematic behavior. Because of the evaluation component, the problem card procedure can be used for either assessments or for evaluations.

*Self-anchored Rating Scales.* Members can also record their observations by using self-anchored rating scales. A self-anchored rating scale is a measurement device made by the worker and a group member specifically for the purpose of recording data about a problematic behavior that has been identified as the target of an intervention. To develop a self-anchored rating scale, the worker helps a group member to identify behaviors, feelings, and thoughts that are associated with various levels of the problematic behavior. For example, in developing a self-anchored rating scale to measure depression, a member suggests that severe depression occurs when he has suicidal thoughts and does not eat or sleep. Moderate depression occurs when the member has thoughts that he is not a good father or husband, when he has little appetite and eats only one meal a day, and when he falls asleep after lying awake for a long period of time. The member suggests that he is not depressed when he has a good appetite, can sleep well, and has thoughts that he is a good father and husband. An example of a self-anchored scale to rate depression is shown in Figure 7–1. For further information about developing self-anchored rating scales, see Bloom and Fisher, 1982.

## Worker Observations

Another method that workers can use to assess the functioning of group members is their own observation of members' behavior during group meetings. A worker can rely on naturalistic observations of a group at work or can design specific activities to assess members' functioning in a particular area. Such activities include simulation tests and program activities.

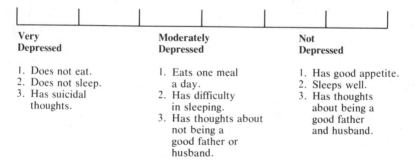

| Very<br>Depressed | Moderately<br>Depressed | Not<br>Depressed |
|---|---|---|
| 1. Does not eat.<br>2. Does not sleep.<br>3. Has suicidal<br>   thoughts. | 1. Eats one meal<br>   a day.<br>2. Has difficulty<br>   in sleeping.<br>3. Has thoughts about<br>   not being a<br>   good father or<br>   husband. | 1. Has good appetite.<br>2. Sleeps well.<br>3. Has thoughts<br>   about being a<br>   good father<br>   and husband. |

**Figure 7–1** Example of a Self-anchored Rating Scale

*Simulation Tests.*   Simulation tests assess members' functioning in specific role-played situations. Members are asked to act in roles that simulate real life situations, and the member whose behavior is being assessed is asked to respond to these members' real life roles. For example, in an assertion training group, two or three members are asked to role play, standing in a line at a grocery store. The unassertive member whose behavior is being assessed stands at the end of the line. Another group member who is not in line is asked to try and get ahead of the member at the end of the line. The worker and the other group members observe how the unassertive member handles the situation. Similarly, in a parenting group, a simulation test involves having two members play the roles of siblings in an argument about who is to play with a toy truck. The parent whose behavior is being assessed is asked to act as she would if such a situation occurred in her own home.

Assessments of a member's behavior in a simulation test are made by all group members. Scales to rate a member's response are designed specifically for the objectives and goals of a particular group. For example, in the assertiveness training group in which all group members were trying to reduce their anxiety and improve their responses, ratings focused on (1) the anxiety level that a member demonstrates while making a response, and (2) the effectiveness of the response in asserting the member's rights in the situation.

Simulation tests have been developed for measuring the skills of a number of different populations, including psychiatric inpatients (Goldsmith and McFall, 1975; Clark, 1971) and outpatients (Schinke and Rose, 1976), women (Delange, 1977), the aged (Toseland and Rose, 1978; Berger, 1976), social workers (Rose, Cayner, and Edleson, 1977), adolescents (Freedman, 1974; Rosenthal, 1978), the mentally retarded (Bates, 1978), and parents (Rose and Hanusa, 1980). These simulation tests were developed using the model described by Goldfried and D'Zurrilla (1969), which includes (1) analyzing a problematic situation and developing several realistic situations that members are likely to confront in their daily lives, (2) enumerating possible responses to these situations, (3) evaluating the responses in terms of their efficacy in handling the problematic situation, (4) developing a measurement format, and (5) evaluating the measure's reliability and validity. Workers can use this model to develop simulation tests for populations and problems for which simulation tests have not yet been developed.

Role play simulation tests have the inherent limitation that group members know they are "acting" rather than actually performing in real life situations. In most cases, however, members appear to forget that they are "acting" and perform as they would in real life situations. Other simulation tests have been invented to avoid the limitation of role play tests. These simulation tests, which have primarily been used in research projects, involve setting up a situation within or outside the group that assesses a member's skill in a social situation without his or her knowledge. Rose (1977), for example, reports on the use of a Simulated Dating Interaction Test (SDIT), in which a female confederate is asked to interact with a male group member in a waiting room. The interaction is tape recorded and the group member's appropriateness, anxiety, assertiveness, and overall pleasantness are rated. Because of the deception involved in such "real life" simulations, the difficulty in designing and setting up "real life" simulations, and their specificity, that is, assessing behavior in only one particular situation, they have been used infrequently in clinical settings.

*Program Activities.*    Many different types of program activities can be used for assessing the functioning of group members. The selection of appropriate program activities for assessment purposes depends on the type of group the worker is leading. In children's groups, the worker can have members participate in play activities and games. For example, the game charades can be used to assess how members act out particular situations. Games requiring cooperation can be used to assess the extent to which members are able to negotiate differences.

In adolescent groups, having a party, a meal, or a sports activity can often help the worker make an assessment of members' social skills and their level of social development. In adult groups containing moderately or severely impaired members, making a meal together or going on an outing together can help the worker assess members' daily living skills. Program activities should be carefully selected so they are age appropriate. They should also give members the opportunity to demonstrate behaviors that they would like to improve through their participation in a group. For more information about using program materials in groups, see Middleman (1968), and the section on program activities in Chapter 8.

## Reports by Others

In addition to members' self-observations and workers' observations of members, workers often rely on the reports of those who are familiar with members' behavior outside the group when making assessments. When considering data reported by others, the worker should assess its reliability and validity. This may include assessing the relationship of the person reporting the data to the group member about whom data has been collected. The reliability and validity of data reported to the worker by others can vary considerably from person to person and from one report to another. For example, some data may be based on rumors, assumptions, or the statements of unidentified third parties, whereas other data may come from direct observations. Obviously, the worker should place less confidence in the reliability and validity of rumors than in the reliability and validity of observations. The clarity of a person's report and the extent to which the data reported are based on objective facts and observations rather than subjective judgments can also help the worker make a determination about the reliability and validity of the reports received.

In assessing data collected from others, the worker should also consider the relationship of the person reporting data to the group member about whom data has been collected. Is the person reporting data interested in the well-being of the group member or is he or she motivated by ill-feeling, personal gain, or rivalry? By examining a person's motivation for reporting data about a group member, the worker can assess possible sources of bias in the data.

When a worker has an ongoing relationship with someone who regularly reports data about group members' behavior, such as mental health therapy aides, child care workers, or teachers who have extensive daily contact with group members, the worker should assist these persons in using reliable and valid data collection systems. For example, the worker can help a mental health therapy aide to develop a chart to monitor data within the therapeutic environment of an inpatient setting, or help an elementary school teacher to use the Walker (1970) or the Devereaux (Spivack and Spotts, 1966) checklists, which are standardized instruments to measure children's social behavior. In this way, the worker can build a relationship with those who have daily contact with group members and, at the same time, can ensure that accurate data are reported about members' behaviors outside the group.

## Standardized Instruments

A fourth way that workers can assess the functioning of group members is by using standardized assessment instruments. Because most brief assessment instruments are focused on particular problem areas, the type of assessment instrument selected depends on the group's focus. Levitt and Reid (1981) describe a number of "rapid assessment instruments" for measuring anxiety, depression, assertiveness, social interaction, and marital problems. In his recently developed Clinical Measurement Package, Hudson (1982) describes nine scales that can be used to assess (1) depression, (2) self-esteem, (3) marital discord, (4) sexual discord, (5) parent-child relationships, (6) child's relationship with mother, (7) child's relationship with father, (8) intrafamilial stress, and (9) peer relationships. Walls, Werner, Bacon, and Zane (1977) briefly describe more than 200 behavior checklists that can also be useful in assessing the problematic behaviors of children and adults. For additional information about the wide range of standardized assessment instruments that are available to assess group members' behavior, see Cone and Hawkins, 1977; Hersen and Bellack, 1976; Buros, 1966; and Robinson and Shaver, 1973.

## ASSESSING THE FUNCTIONING
## OF THE GROUP AS A WHOLE

Methods for assessing the group as a whole have been given less attention in the group work literature than methods for assessing individual members' problems and concerns. Klein (1970) and Bradford, Stock, and Horwitz (1953) proposed schema for diagnosing and correcting group problems. The many different conceptualizations of group development mentioned in Chapter 3 are also attempts at assessing "normal" group functioning. In recent years, however, the group work literature has tended to emphasize assessing and treating the problems of individual group members within the group context and has deemphasized the functioning of the group as a whole. In assessing the group as a whole, the worker should be guided by the four major areas of group dynamics that are mentioned in Chapter 3. These include the group's (1) communication and interaction patterns, (2) attraction, (3) social controls, and (4) culture.

Communication and interaction patterns are established early in the beginning stage of a group. Therefore, the worker should be especially concerned about these patterns as they develop during the beginning of a group. A careful assessment of communication patterns can alert the worker to potential problems and prevent them from becoming established as a routine part of group functioning. It can also help to facilitate intermember communication and disclosure of important information that may be helpful in attaining group or individual member goals.

A pattern that is often of concern to workers in the beginning of the group is too many member-leader interactions and too few member-member interactions (Toseland, Krebs, and Vahsen, 1978). There is a natural tendency in newly formed groups for members to look to the worker for direction. The worker may feel gratified by this and encourage members' communications. Unfortunately, this pattern of communication may serve to undermine the mutual aid and group problem solving that occurs when members direct their communication to everyone in the group rather than exclusively to the worker.

Other communication patterns can develop in a group that may also alert the worker to potential problems. For example, one member may attempt to dominate group discussion, preventing other members from interacting. Another potential problem is a lack of communication by a particular member. Although it is not unusual for some members to communicate less frequently than others, the worker should be aware of the potential for isolation when a particular member says little or nothing during the beginning phase of the group.

The initial attraction of a group for its members may come from a variety of sources. In treatment groups, for example, it may come from members' hope that the group will help them solve their problems, reduce their emotional distress, or educate them to perform new or more effective roles in their everyday lives. In task groups, it may come from the status or prestige associated with membership, the importance of the task on which the group is working, or a rare chance to share ideas with colleagues.

It is important for a worker to understand what attracts members to the group. The worker assesses the group's attraction for its members in order to maintain and increase these forces and help the group become a cohesive unit in working toward group and individual goals.

When workers assess group attraction, they sometimes find that its development has not progressed satisfactorily. There are many indications that the group is not attractive to one or more of its members. These indicators can include apathy or hostility toward group goals, the failure of members to listen to one another, and the growth of allegiances to other reference groups. By observing these indicators, the worker can gain much information about the attraction of the group for its members. Group attraction can also be measured by using a sociometric scale, the semantic differential, or the SYMLOG method, described later in this chapter. Once a worker determines that changes are needed in the group's attraction for its members, one of the methods described later can be used to prevent the group from decomposing.

Workers should also assess the social controls, that is, norms, roles, and status hierarchies, that develop in newly formed groups. The norms that develop in a group are extremely important because they define acceptable and nonacceptable behavior in a group. Schopler and Galinsky (1981) found that the norms have an important influence on members' satisfaction with their group experiences. Both members and observers indicated that inappropriate norms were more important than cohesion, roles, goals, leadership, composition, or extra-group relations in negative group experiences. The worker should be aware of the norms that develop in the groups with which they are working. They should help members to modify norms that detract from individual and group goals, and promote and protect those that are beneficial for goal achievement.

Roles for members also begin to develop early in the group. According to Levine (1979), initial role taking in a group is a tentative process and may not reflect the roles members will occupy later in the group. Members try out roles and often vacillate between one or another role, such as the socio-emotional leader, task leader, dominator, and so on. During this stage of the group, the worker can point out the functional and dysfunctional characteristics of these roles to members and help them develop role behaviors that will facilitate the group's functioning and their own functioning in the group.

Several typologies of role behavior have been developed to help workers assess members' roles. Benne and Sheats (1948), for example, have classified members' roles into three broad categories: (1) group task roles that are related to helping the group decide on, select, or carry out particular tasks; (2) group building and maintenance roles that help the group function in a harmonious manner, and (3) individual roles that are related to individual members' goals. Group task roles include the instructor, opinion seeker, information giver, elaborator, energizer, evaluator, procedural technician, and the recorder. Group building and maintenance roles include the encourager, harmonizer, compromiser, gatekeeper, expediter, standard setter, group observer, and the follower. Individual roles include the aggressor, blocker, recognition-seeker, confessor, dominator, and the help seeker.

Focusing on problematic role functioning, Shulman (1979) has identified the scapegoat, deviant member, gatekeeper, internal leader, defensive member, and the quiet member as common dysfunctional roles. Most of these roles are not difficult for the worker to identify. The scapegoat, for example, receives much negative attention and criticism from the group as he or she is blamed for a host of defects and problems. According to Shulman (1979), members attack the portion of a scapegoat's behavior that they least like about themselves. Although Shulman and others (see, for example, Garland and Kolodny, 1967) mention that scapegoating is a common role, we have found it to be relatively rare in the treatment groups we have conducted.

When one or more members of a group assume dysfunctional roles, it is a signal that the group as a whole is not functioning at an optimal level. For example, when an assessment reveals that a member functions as a "gatekeeper," that is, a member who does not allow the group to discuss sensitive issues, the worker should help the group as a whole examine how to change its overall functioning rather than focusing only on the member who has assumed the dysfunctional role. The gatekeeper function is to protect the group as a whole from discussing difficult issues. A quiet member may signal difficulties in the communication and interaction patterns established in the group as a whole. It is rare that a problematic group role is an expression of only individual rather than group dysfunction.

The status of individual group members and the power that the leader and other group members have at their disposal also affect the development of social controls within the group. For example, although high-status members are likely to adhere to group norms and procedures, they are also much more likely to influence the development of a group than are low-status members. Members in the middle of the status hierarchy are likely to strive for greater status within the group by adhering to group norms and upholding the status quo (Nixon, 1979). Low-status members are less likely to conform to group norms than either high- or middle-status members (Nixon, 1979). An accurate assessment of the status hierarchy in the group can help workers to understand and anticipate the actions and reactions of members when the worker intervenes in the group.

An accurate assessment of the power bases that the worker and the members have at their disposal can also be important in the beginning phases of group work. Workers who understand the limits of their influence over group members are able to use it effectively and avoid using it when it will be ineffective. An accurate assessment of the sources of members' power can also be useful to the worker in planning strategies for intervening in the group as a whole and for helping members to form a mutual aid network of shared resources within the group.

A fourth area that workers should assess when examining the functioning of the group as a whole is the group's culture. Ideas, beliefs, values, and feelings held in common by group members have a profound impact on the therapeutic benefits that can be achieved in the group. Just as some societal cultures promote the public expression of emotion and others do not, groups develop cultures that value certain ways of behaving.

In the beginning phase of group work, the worker should examine the culture that is developing in a group. Does the culture help the group and its members achieve their goals? Because group culture develops more slowly than the other group dynamics discussed previously, the worker's initial assessment of a group's culture should be viewed as a tentative indication about how it might develop as the group progresses. It is difficult to change a group's culture after it is well established, so the worker may wish to share his or her initial impressions with members before it has become fully established. For example, the worker may wish to point out in the first or second meeting that most members' communications are problem-oriented rather than growth-oriented, or that few supportive comments are made within the group. Methods to modify or change a group's culture are described in Chapter 8.

## METHODS FOR ASSESSING
## THE GROUP AS A WHOLE

In most practice situations, workers reflect on group functioning in between meetings and rely on their own subjective observations to assess the functioning of the group as a whole. Observation and reflection are the primary methods workers use for such assessments, but it can be beneficial to involve the group as a whole in a more structured assessment. In addition to helping members become aware of and involved in improving the group's functioning, using one or more of the following structured assessment methods can help to confirm or disprove workers' subjective impressions of group functioning.

### Measuring Communication and Interaction

There are many ways to measure the meanings that underline communications in the group. One measure that has been widely used is the semantic differential. Using this method, members are asked to rate the meaning of any object or person on a series of seven-point bipolar attitude scales, such as good/bad, valuable/worthless, and so on. Three dimensions of attitudes that can be assessed by the semantic differential include individual group members' (1) evaluation, (2) perceptions of potency, and (3) perceptions of the activity of objects, concepts, or persons being rated (Osgood, Suci, and Tannenbaum, 1957). An example of a semantic differential scale is shown in Figure 7–2.

By having members use the semantic differential to rate their fellow group members, the worker can begin to understand how members perceive one another. For example, using the activity scale, group members may rate a member as being particularly active and another member as being particularly inactive. Similarly, the scales can be used to obtain members' attitudes about specific concepts that may be relevant to group functioning, such as self-disclosure, communication, or leadership. The method can also be used to assess members' attitudes and perceptions regarding their presenting problems or the group's task.

Sometimes the worker may be less interested in the meaning of members' communications than in the distribution of communication within the group. Rose (1977) suggests that an observer can use a chart such as the one shown in Figure 7–3 to record interactions. A similar procedure has been used by Toseland, Krebs, and Vahsen (1978) to record member-member and member-leader interactions.

To avoid observer fatigue, a sampling procedure may be used instead of

**INSTRUCTIONS:** On each of the scales below please place a check mark in the space that best describes how you feel about _____.

|  | 7 Extremely | 6 Quite | 5 Slightly | 4 Neither or in Between | 3 Slightly | 2 Quite | 1 Extremely |  |  |
|---|---|---|---|---|---|---|---|---|---|
| 1. Large | — | — | — | — | — | — | — | Small | (Potent) |
| 2. Worthless | — | — | — | — | — | — | — | Valuable | (Evaluative) |
| 3. Fast | — | — | — | — | — | — | — | Slow | (Active) |
| 4. Cold | — | — | — | — | — | — | — | Hot | (Act) |
| 5. Happy | — | — | — | — | — | — | — | Sad | (Evaluative) |
| 6. Weak | — | — | — | — | — | — | — | Strong | (Potent) |
| 7. Good | — | — | — | — | — | — | — | Bad | (Evaluative) |
| 8. Tense | — | — | — | — | — | — | — | Relaxed | (Active) |
| 9. Tough | — | — | — | — | — | — | — | Soft | (Potent) |
| 10. Active | — | — | — | — | — | — | — | Passive | (Active) |
| 11. Heavy | — | — | — | — | — | — | — | Light | (Potent) |
| 12. Fair | — | — | — | — | — | — | — | Unfair | (Evaluative) |

$$A = \frac{}{3} + \frac{}{4} + \frac{}{8} + \frac{}{10} =$$

$$P = \frac{}{1} + \frac{}{6} + \frac{}{9} + \frac{}{11} =$$

$$E = \frac{}{2} + \frac{}{5} + \frac{}{7} + \frac{}{12} =$$

**Figure 7–2** Example of a Semantic Differential Scale

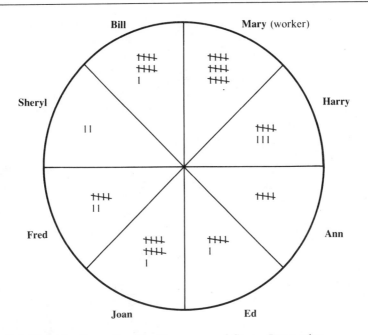

**Figure 7–3** Chart for Recording the Frequency of Group Interaction

continuous recording. Types of sampling procedures include (1) frequency recording where every time a behavior occurs it is recorded, for example, every communication in the group is recorded; (2) interval recording where behavior is recorded for a specified interval of time, for example, the first two minutes of every five minute time interval; and (3) time sample recording where behavior is recorded at a particular time, such as every five seconds.

## Measuring Attraction

Sociometry is a widely used method to measure interpersonal attraction. Originally developed by Moreno in the 1930s (see, for example, Moreno, 1934), sociometry refers to the measurement of social preferences, that is, the strengths of members' preference or rejection of each other. Sociometric measures are obtained by asking about each member's preference for interacting with other members in relation to a particular activity (Crano and Brewer, 1973; Selltiz, Wrightsman, and Cook, 1976). They can also be obtained by having observers rate members' preferences for one another. Patterns of choices can differ significantly, depending on the particular activity on which members' preferences are being evaluated (Jennings, 1950). For example, in relation to the activity "playing together" a member of a children's group expressed great willingness to play with a particular member, whereas in relation to the activity "working on a project together" the member expresses less willingness to interact with the same member.

Sociometric ratings can be made concerning any activity of interest to a worker. For example, a worker may want to assess members' preferences for other members in relation to the activity of socializing between group meetings or in relation to the activity of choosing a partner to complete a task. To obtain sociometric ratings, members are usually asked to write the names of the other members on one side of a sheet of paper next to a preference scale, for example, 1 = most preferred to 5 = lease preferred. Members are then asked to rate everyone in the group except themselves in relation to a particular activity. For example, children in a residential treatment center might be asked, "If we were going on a day trip together, who would you like to sit next to during the bus trip?" and "Who would be your second choice?"

An index of preferences can be calculated for each member by dividing the total score a member receives from all group members by the highest possible score the member could receive. Members of attractive, cohesive groups have higher mean preference scores than members of groups that are less cohesive and attractive. Another way of presenting sociometric data is through a sociogram. As shown in Figure 7–4, solid lines represent attraction, dotted lines represent indifference, broken lines represent repulsion, and arrows represent the direction of preferences that are not reciprocal. For research purposes, sociometric data can be analyzed by more complicated methods, such as multidimensional scaling (see, for example, Gazda and Mobley, 1981).

## Measuring Social Controls and Group Culture

The most fully developed method for assessing the dimensions of a group as a whole is Bales' Systematic Multiple Level Observation of Groups (SYMLOG). Although it has received little attention since its development (Bales, 1980; Bales, Cohen, and Williamson, 1979), SYMLOG is the most comprehensive method now available to assess the functioning of groups. It is useful in the training of novice group workers in connection with processing lab group experiences. SYMLOG can be used as a self-report method in which members rate each other in relation to twenty-six behavioral descriptors, such as, "dominant, talks a lot." Each descriptor is used to rate each member on a three-point scale from 0 = not often to 2 = often, or it can be used as an observational measure in which independent raters assess group functioning. The product of a SYMLOG analysis of group functioning is a three-dimensional pictorial representation of group members' relationships to one another, called a SYMLOG field diagram.

Figure 7–5 is a SYMLOG field diagram made by Sharon, a member of a educational group for students learning how to lead treatment groups. The horizontal axis of Figure 7–5 represents the dimension friendly versus unfriendly, and the vertical axis represents the dimension instrumental versus emotionally expressive. The third dimension, dominant versus submissive, is represented by the size of the circles shown in Figure 7–5. Larger circles represent greater dominance, and conversely, smaller circles represent greater submissiveness. For example, as shown in Figure 7–5, Sharon perceives that Ann is the most dominant group member and Ed is the most friendly and emotionally expressive member.

Each member rates all other members as well as themselves in relation

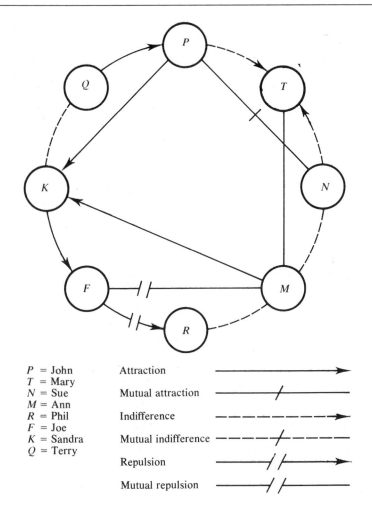

| | | |
|---|---|---|
| *P* = John | Attraction | |
| *T* = Mary | | |
| *N* = Sue | Mutual attraction | |
| *M* = Ann | | |
| *R* = Phil | Indifference | |
| *F* = Joe | | |
| *K* = Sandra | Mutual indifference | |
| *Q* = Terry | | |
| | Repulsion | |
| | Mutual repulsion | |

**Figure 7–4** A Sociogram

to the three-dimensional SYMLOG space. In addition to rating overt behaviors, members can rate their values by evaluating which behavior they
would "avoid," "reject," "wish to perform," and "ought to perform" (see
the circles marked avoid, reject, wish, and ought in Figure 7–5).

SYMLOG field diagrams can be used for assessment in a variety of
ways. One of the most basic ways is for members to compare their field
diagrams. Are members' perceptions of the relationships among group
members similar? Do individual members place themselves in the same position that other members place them?

A composite of group field diagrams can be made from the field diagrams
of individual members. The resulting composite field diagram can be used to
analyze the functioning of the group as a whole. For example, who is the
most dominant group members? Which members are included in the domin-

ant subgroup (in Bales' terminology, "dominant triangle" as illustrated in Figure 7–5)? Which members are similar (spatially close), and which members appear to be dissimilar (spatially distant)? Who is the task (instrumental) leader and who is the socioemotional (emotionally expressive) leader? In this way, the SYMLOG procedure can be used to help members gain an understanding of how they are perceived within the group.

Particular roles of individual group members can also be identified. For example, in Figure 7–5, Bill is isolated in the unfriendly, instrumental quadrant of the field diagram. Is he an isolate or perhaps a scapegoat? A number of more complicated and more sophisticated ways of interpreting field diagrams have been developed. For a detailed discussion of these methods, see Bales, Cohen, and Williamson (1979) and Bales (1980).

Despite its advantages as a comprehensive assessment method, the SYMLOG method has two major limitations. One limitation is that the method is complex and takes several hours to learn before it can be used effectively. A more serious limitation is that a SYMLOG self-study takes about three hours to complete. Although this amount of time may be warranted for a team that functions together on a daily basis over a long period of time, it may not be justifiable for a short-term treatment group that is meeting for a total of eight one-and-a-half-hour sessions.

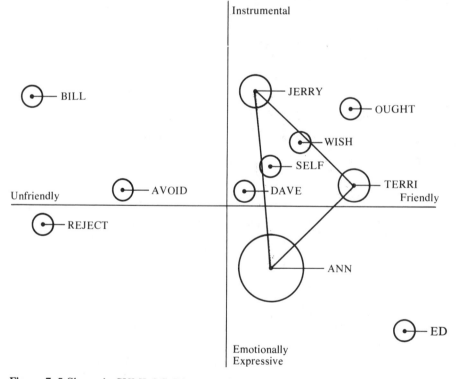

**Figure 7–5** Sharon's SYMLOG Diagram of the Group

## Other Methods of Assessing the Group as a Whole

Several other methods, including the Hemphill Index of Group Dimensions (Hemphill, 1956); the Hill Interaction Matrix (Hill, 1977), a process analysis adaptation of the Hill Interaction Matrix (Piper, Montvila, and McGihon, 1979); and Seashore's Group Cohesiveness Index (Seashore, 1954) can be used to assess the functioning of the group as a whole. Because these measures are more frequently used for research than for assessing the functioning of ongoing groups, they are described in Chapter 10 in relation to the evaluation of group outcomes.

## ASSESSING THE GROUP'S ENVIRONMENT

The worker's assessment of the environment's influence on the functioning of the entire group should be distinguished from the worker's assessment of environmental factors that affect individual group members. In both cases, however, the environment in which group members and the group as a whole function has an important impact on group work practice. When assessing the influence of the environment on the group, the worker focuses on (1) the agency or other sponsor that sanctions the group work effect; (2) the interagency environment; and (3) the community environment. The emphasis on the influence of the environment is a distinctive aspect of social work practice and is not found to any great extent in the writing of group workers from other professional disciplines (see, for example, Yalom, 1975; Dinkmeyer and Muro, 1979; Corey and Corey, 1977).

### The Agency Environment

When assessing the influence of an agency on the group, the worker examines how the group's purposes are influenced by the agency, what resources are allocated for the group's efforts, what status the worker has vis-a-vis others who work for the agency, and how the agency's attitudes about service delivery influence the group work endeavor. Taken together, these factors can have a profound influence on the way the group functions.

As Garvin (1981) points out, an agency always has a purpose for sanctioning a group work effort. The agency's purpose may be stated explicitly or may be implied in the overall program objectives. The agency administration's purpose for encouraging the development of a group may not correspond to the worker's or the group members' ideas about a group's purpose. The extent to which the agency, the worker, and the group members can agree on a common purpose for the group will determine, in part, the extent to which the group will receive the support it needs to function effectively and the extent to which the group experience will be judged as beneficial by all concerned.

It is helpful for the worker to clarify the agency's purpose for sponsoring the group. A written group proposal, such as the one described in Chapter 5, can be helpful because it serves to clarify the worker's intentions and to provide the agency administration with an opportunity to react to a written document.

During the process of clarifying the agency's purposes for the group, the worker can help to shape the purposes proposed for the group. For example, a nursing home decides to sponsor a group for residents with the purpose of helping the residents become more compliant with the nursing homes rigid schedule of bathing, feeding and housekeeping. The worker should help the nursing home staff and residents to reformulate the group's purpose. The purpose might be reformulated as improving the relationship between residents and staff.

An agency can also influence a group by its allocation of resources (Wolfe and Proshansky, 1974). As mentioned in the planning chapter, the worker should identify as early as possible the resources the group will need to function effectively. Once this is done, the worker can assess the likelihood that the agency will be able to allocate sufficient resources, and plan the best strategy to obtain any that may be needed. The worker's assessment may also include the extent to which resources, for example, a meeting room, or some refreshments, can be obtained from alternative sponsors.

The worker's status in a sponsoring agency can also influence the group. If the worker is a low-status member of the sponsoring agency, he or she is likely to have difficulty obtaining resources for the group, convincing the sponsor that the group worker endeavor is a good use of his or her time, and demonstrating that the group's purposes are consistent with the overall objectives of the agency. The worker may want to consult with trusted colleagues who can give the worker some feedback about the feasibility of the group worker endeavor vis-a-vis the worker's status within the agency.

The attitudes and practices of the sponsoring agency in regard to service delivery can also influence the group work endeavor. The worker should assess whether or not the agency stresses individual or group work services. In an agency in which individual services are given priority, the worker must spend considerable time in developing the rationale for the group and in convincing the agency it is important to undertake such an endeavor (Hasenfeld, 1974).

Another aspect of an agency's service delivery system that affects the group is its policies regarding recruitment and intake of potential members. The worker should assess whether the clients are receiving services voluntarily or whether they have been mandated to attend the group. Mandated clients are likely to be hostile or apathetic about becoming members of the group. The worker should also assess the members' attitudes about coming to the agency, their attitudes about receiving group work service, and the extent to which they are prepared by intake workers to receive services. This helps prepare the worker to deal with members' reactions.

The agency's commitment to a particular service technology, such as practice theories, ideologies, and intervention techniques, may also influence the group work endeavor. For example, if the agency is committed to a long-term, psychodynamic treatment model, it may oppose the development of a short-term, behaviorally oriented group. When the service technology planned for a particular group runs counter to an agency's preferred service technology, the worker should develop a convincing rationale for the particular service technology he or she plans to use. For a treatment group, the rationale might include the effectiveness and efficiency of a particular method for treating a problem, whereas in the case of a task group, the rationale might include the effectiveness or efficiency of a particular method for generating ideas or making decisions about alternative proposals.

## The Interagency Environment

In assessing the group's environment, the worker should also become aware of what is happening in other agencies that may be relevant for the worker's own group. The worker can make an assessment of the interagency environment by discovering the answers to a number of questions. For example, are other agencies offering similar groups? Do workers in other agencies perceive needs similar to those that formed the basis for establishing the group in the worker's own agency? Do other agencies offer services or programs that may be useful to members of the group? Would any benefit be gained by linking with groups in other agencies to lobby for changes in social service benefits?

Unless the worker or others in the agency are already familiar with what is being offered by all other agencies in the community, the worker's primary task in making an interagency assessment is to contact other agencies to let them know about the group offering. In addition to generating referrals and making other agencies aware of the group, the assessment may uncover needless duplication of service or, conversely, a widespread need that is either not being met or is being met by uncoordinated individual efforts within separate agencies.

An example of a recent practice experience illustrates the importance of interagency assessments. An executive director of a small agency, who led weekly staff meetings, decided to do an interagency assessment after problems encountered in serving homeless persons were raised several times in meetings of the group. The worker discovered a lack of sufficient space in shelters and a general lack of community interest in the welfare of homeless persons. The worker called a meeting of professionals from a number of agencies to see what could be done. This interagency group contacted a local planning agency. In cooperation with the planning agency, the interagency group sought federal, state, local, and private funding to address the needs of the homeless. After much work, a social service program for homeless persons was founded with a combination of federal, state, and local funding, and a new community shelter was opened.

## The Community Environment

The worker should also assess the impact of the community environment on the group. In doing this, the worker focuses on the attitude of the community concerning the problems or issues being addressed by the group. In treatment groups, if the problem is one that violates basic community values, members of the group are likely to be stigmatized. Lack of community acceptance and the resulting stigma attached to the problem may have other consequences such as discouraging potential members from identifying themselves and reaching out for help. It may also increase the level of confidentiality of group meetings and may affect procedures used to recruit new members. For example, because of the stigma attached to those who abuse their children, Parents Anonymous groups generally have confidential meetings, and the recruitment process occurs on a first-name basis to protect members from those who may be more interested in finding out their identity than in attending meetings. Similar recruitment procedures are used in other groups that deal with socially stigmatized problems, such as groups for spouse abuse, alcoholism, and compulsive gambling.

After determining the level of acceptance of a particular problem within a community, the worker can then make an assessment of who in the community might be supportive of the group endeavor. For example, ministers, priests, and rabbis might be receptive to a group for abusive or neglecting parents, alcoholics, or spouse abusers. The worker can then work with these persons to obtain referrals or to obtain a meeting room such as a church basement.

A worker's assessment of the community environment may lead to a coalition of community forces to resolve a concern. For example, a community assessment indicated that police officers were asked increasingly to handle family disturbances. With the cooperation of the police force and local community leaders, a community agency decided to reach out to those experiencing family disturbances. In addition to casework service, these efforts resulted in the development of several treatment groups, such as a couples' communication group, a parenting group, and a recreational group for adolescents. It also resulted in a task force of community leaders to work on issues of concern to families in the community. For additional methods for assessing community environments, see Warren, 1977; Lauffer, 1978, and Cox and others, 1974, 1977.

## LINKING ASSESSMENT TO INTERVENTION

In preparation for treatment planning, which will be discussed in Chapter 8, workers should consider how they will use the data they collect during assessments to plan effective interventions. This chapter has suggested that the worker assess three areas of the functioning of individual group members, four areas of the functioning of the group as a whole, and three areas of the environment in which the group functions. Chapter 8 describes a number of interventions that the worker can use when an assessment indicates an intervention is warranted.

Few texts in group work or casework practice have addressed linking assessment to intervention. This may, in part, account for findings from practice studies suggesting that there is little correlation between workers' assessments or diagnoses and the interventions that are selected (see, for example, Mullen, 1969; Stuart, 1970, pp. 80–83). Without guidelines about the interventions that are most appropriate for particular problems, workers

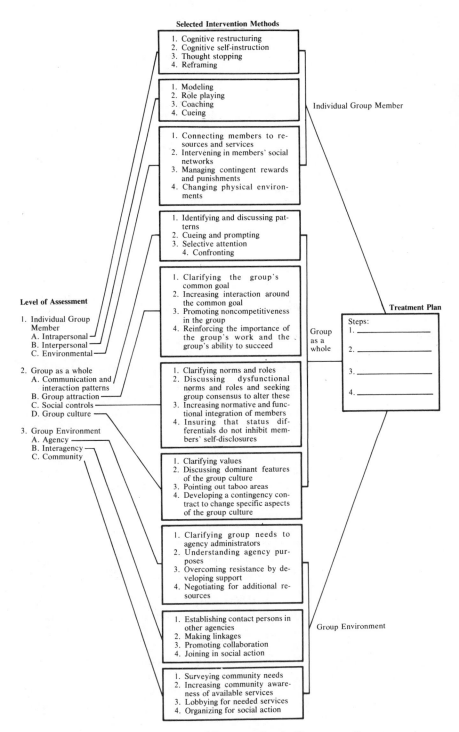

**Selected Intervention Methods**

1. Cognitive restructuring
2. Cognitive self-instruction
3. Thought stopping
4. Reframing

1. Modeling
2. Role playing
3. Coaching
4. Cueing

1. Connecting members to resources and services
2. Intervening in members' social networks
3. Managing contingent rewards and punishments
4. Changing physical environments

1. Identifying and discussing patterns
2. Cueing and prompting
3. Selective attention
4. Confronting

1. Clarifying the group's common goal
2. Increasing interaction around the common goal
3. Promoting noncompetitiveness in the group
4. Reinforcing the importance of the group's work and the group's ability to succeed

1. Clarifying norms and roles
2. Discussing dysfunctional norms and roles and seeking group consensus to alter these
3. Increasing normative and functional integration of members
4. Insuring that status differentials do not inhibit members' self-disclosures

1. Clarifying values
2. Discussing dominant features of the group culture
3. Pointing out taboo areas
4. Developing a contingency contract to change specific aspects of the group culture

1. Clarifying group needs to agency administrators
2. Understanding agency purposes
3. Overcoming resistance by developing support
4. Negotiating for additional resources

1. Establishing contact persons in other agencies
2. Making linkages
3. Promoting collaboration
4. Joining in social action

1. Surveying community needs
2. Increasing community awareness of available services
3. Lobbying for needed services
4. Organizing for social action

Individual Group Member

**Level of Assessment**

1. Individual Group Member
   A. Intrapersonal
   B. Interpersonal
   C. Environmental

2. Group as a whole
   A. Communication and interaction patterns
   B. Group attraction
   C. Social controls
   D. Group culture

3. Group Environment
   A. Agency
   B. Interagency
   C. Community

Group as a whole

**Treatment Plan**

Steps:
1. _____
2. _____
3. _____
4. _____

Group Environment

**Figure 7–6** Linking Assessment and Intervention in Treatment Groups

187

will rely on interventions with which they are most familiar, regardless of their assessment of the group or its members.

Figure 7–6 illustrates a framework for selecting appropriate intervention methods. Because problems are often multidimensional, a number of different interventions may be selected to become part of a comprehensive treatment plan. For example, in a couples group, the worker develops individualized intervention plans to meet each member's needs. At the same time, the worker intervenes to change the interaction patterns in the group. Between meetings, the worker reports the group's progress to her supervisor to help assure continued agency support for the group.

## SUMMARY

This chapter examined the process of assessment. Although assessments are made throughout the stages of a group's development, they are often concentrated in the latter portions of the beginning stage and the initial portions of the middle stage of a group's development. These are when the worker and the group members are planning intervention strategies to achieve the goals they have agreed upon in the planning and beginning stages of the group.

In making assessments, the worker examines the functioning of individual group members, the group as a whole, and the group's environment. When assessing individual members, the worker examines intrapersonal, interpersonal, and environmental areas of each member's functioning. In addition, the worker examines each member's functioning in relation to what they can contribute to the group, what needs they bring to the group, and what intervention plans are most likely to be successful in helping them alleviate their concerns and problems. A number of methods that can be used separately or in combination were suggested for assessing the functioning of individual members.

To assess the group as a whole, the worker focuses on the four areas of group dynamics described in Chapter 3. These include (1) interaction and communication patterns, (2) the attractions of the group for its members, (3) social controls such as roles, norms, and status hierarchies, and (4) the group's culture. A number of methods for assessing the group as a whole were discussed.

Because group work practice occurs within the context of a larger service delivery system, it is important to consider the impact of the group's environment on its functioning. To make a thorough assessment of the group's environment, it was suggested that the worker should assess the agency environment, the interagency environment, and the larger community environment in which the group functions. After a brief discussion of the potential effects of each of these aspects of the environment on the group, the chapter described the linkage between assessment and intervention.

# PART IV
# The Middle Phase

# 8

# The Middle Phase: Treatment Groups

This chapter focuses on leading treatment groups during the middle stage of their development. It is assumed that workers leading groups at this stage have already discussed the group's purposes, developed a group contract concerning confidentiality, attendance, and number of sessions, and developed individual contracts specifying particular treatment goals for each member. It is also assumed that the group as a whole has developed an initial set of dynamics, including a pattern of communication and interaction, a beginning level of interpersonal attraction and group cohesion, tentative social controls, and a group climate.

The typology of treatment groups in Chapter 1 and the history of group work presented in Chapter 2 both suggest that treatment groups can be used for many purposes. Treatment groups are often associated with remediating social and psychological impairments but they are often used for other purposes. For example, group treatment can be used to educate, to promote psychological and social growth and development, to maintain and enhance coping skills, to provide support or to advocate for changes in social systems. A narrow conception of group work focused solely on remediation unnecessarily limits the scope of a very versatile treatment modality.

This chapter is divided into two sections to examine both the common base of group work practice and the differential use of specialized interventions for particular treatment problems. The first section describes a number of activities workers commonly perform when leading treatment groups during the middle stage. This section also illustrates commonalities in group work practice across different types of treatment groups. The second section focuses on specific interventions that are useful in particular planned change efforts for individual group members, the group as a whole, and the group's external environment.

# LEADING TREATMENT GROUPS

The middle stage of treatment groups is characterized by an initial period of testing, conflict, and adjustment as members work out their relationships with one another and the larger group. During this period, contracts are negotiated and renegotiated, members establish their positions in relation to one another, and the group develops a niche for itself within the sponsoring organization.

After this initial period of adjustment, the middle stage focuses on goal achievement. Members work together to achieve the goals expressed in the contracts they have made with the group's leader, other group members, and the group as a whole. Workers are aware of how the group has been planned and what has been accomplished during the beginning stage. During the middle stage, they make modifications in relation to their assessment of the group's development, the changing needs of members, and the changing demands of the social environment in which the group functions.

Although every group has a unique developmental pattern that calls for different leadership skills, workers are expected to perform four broad activities during the middle stage of all treatment groups. These worker activities are:

1. Preparing for group meetings.
2. Structuring the group's work.
3. Helping members achieve their goals.
4. Monitoring and evaluating the group's progress.

## Preparing for Group Meetings

During the middle stage, the worker should continuously assess the needs of the group and its members and plan to meet identified needs in subsequent meetings. The continuous cycle of assessment, modification, and reassessment is the method by which the leader ensures continued progress toward contract goals. The effective group worker uses the time between group meetings to prepare for the next group meeting.

In structured, time-limited groups, the worker spends a considerable amount of time preparing the agenda for the next group meeting. For example, for the fourth session of an educational group for prospective foster parents, a worker prepares: (1) material on helping children develop values, (2) a brief handout on value clarification to be distributed to parents, (3) an exercise to illustrate some concepts about helping children develop their own value system, and (4) questions that will help to organize the group's discussion of values. In preparing for the meeting, the worker selects material that will lead to a stimulating and interesting discussion. The worker also estimates the time needed to cover the material in relation to the time available for the meeting.

Less structured process-oriented groups also require the worker to prepare for future meetings. A worker leading a group for the residents of a cottage in an adolescent residential treatment center prepares for the next meeting according to her assessment of the efficacy of previous group meetings and the current functioning of each group member discussed in weekly treatment review meetings. After discussion with members, the worker decides to focus the next meeting on helping members to improve the way they express anger. In preparing for the group, the worker gathers examples of how anger has been expressed in the past by members living in the cottage, and uses these examples to prepare role play exercises designed to improve the way members express anger. The worker plans to model more appropriate methods of expressing anger and to help members try out the new methods that have been modeled.

Preparation is also required when workers use program materials to achieve group goals. As Middleman (1980) points out, the use of program materials has had an important place in the history of group work. *Program materials* refers to activities, games, and exercises that are designed to provide fun-filled, interesting experiences for members while achieving particular goals. Workers sometimes make the mistake of thinking that program activities such as arts and crafts or preparing for a dance are not appropriate group work activities because they are not solely focused on therapeutic verbal interactions. However, when carefully selected, program activities can be very therapeutic.

Program activities provide a medium through which the functioning of members can be assessed in such areas as interpersonal skills, ability to perform activities of daily living, motor coordination, attention span, and ability to work cooperatively. Program activities can also be used as a part of specific treatment interventions. In addition to achieving specific goals such as improving skills in interpersonal functioning, leadership, problem solving, and activities of daily living, program activities help build group cohesion, prosocial group norms, and a group culture that fosters continued member participation. Program activities can also be used to make the group more attractive for its members. For example, in a children's group, the worker may place program activities in between group discussions to maintain members' interest. In a group for chronic schizophrenics the worker may stimulate members' interest by offering them coffee and donuts between exercises or discussions.

Choosing appropriate program activities can be a demanding task that requires a careful assessment of the needs of group members. Characteristics of members should be matched with the characteristics of potential program activities. Vinter (1974b) has developed a scheme for rating program activities on their prescriptiveness, control, movement, rewards, competence, and interaction. Similarly, Middleman (1968) has attempted to point out some of the particular benefits of more than 100 program activities and Henry (1981) has attempted to categorize program media that are especially useful for members at different stages of a group's development.

Because of the great number of possible program activities for children, adolescents, adults and older persons, workers should keep a resource file of catalogued activities that may become useful as workers are called upon to work with different types of groups. Such a resource file can be an asset in selecting specific program activities during the life of a group. Appendix F lists a variety of sources that contain program activities workers may find useful.

Figure 8–1 presents a procedure for evaluating the suitability of program activities for specific group needs. The selection should be based on the (1) objectives of the program activity, (2) purposes and goals of the group, (3) facilities, resources, and time available for the activity, (4) characteristics of the group members, and (5) characteristics of particular program activities.

The procedure suggested in Figure 8–1 can be used to help workers select program activities for any type of treatment group. For example, when selecting program activities for an inpatient group whose purpose is to help remotivate members and prepare them for community living, the worker should consider activities that stimulate members' interest in the outside world. In addition to a group's purpose and the objectives of particular program activities, the worker should consider the other factors shown in Figure 8–1. For example, the inpatient group mentioned previously meets in an occupational therapy room, equipped with kitchen facilities, tables, blackboards, arts and crafts, and toys. All members are above 70 years old and their physical and mental health is poor. Their interests include gardening, nature, travel, and cooking. The worker wants to select a program activity that stimulates members physically as well as socially to prepare them for living in a community residence.

On the basis of Figure 8–1, the worker ruled out activities such as a bus trip or a discussion of current events in foreign countries, and selected an activity in which each member helped to prepare a meal to be shared by all. After the program activity, the worker reconvened the group around the meal and asked members to share their feelings. Questions such as "Did the activity remind you of when you lived at home?" and "How do you feel about living on your own and having to prepare meals?" were used to stimulate a therapeutic discussion based on the program activity.

The therapeutic benefit of any program activity is determined by how it is used by the worker. Activities provide little benefit when careful attention is not given to making sure they are directed toward therapeutic purposes. For example, the program activity of preparing the meal stimulated the sensory awareness of members. During the activity, the worker encouraged social and physical interactions among members. At the end of the meal, a discussion of the thoughts, feelings, and behaviors that members experienced during the activity was used to stimulate members' interest and desire to return to the community.

In order to prepare for meetings, workers should also review recordings of previous meetings and any data from other monitoring devices. Making effective use of feedback about the progress of a group is essential during the middle stage. The worker can use observations collected in summary recordings, for example, as the basis for determining that the interaction pattern of the previously described remotivation group should be changed to encourage participation from several members who have not been active in group discussions. In another case, data about members' satisfaction with the previous meeting of a single parents support group suggested that information about educational opportunities for adult students should be included in future meetings.

Preparation for the next group meeting may also include visualizing how it will be conducted and, if necessary, rehearsing intervention procedures or techniques. This is particularly important when a worker is using a new or unfamiliar procedure or exercise in the next meeting. Co-leaders can be particularly valuable when discussing future group meetings or rehearsing new procedures.

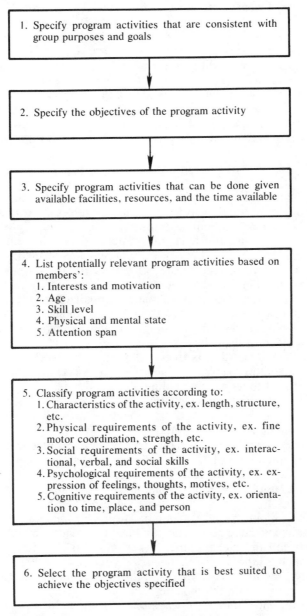

Figure 8–1 A Procedure for Selecting Program Activities

Workers must be fully cognizant of the history of the group's development as well as its needs when preparing for meetings during the middle stage. Preparing agendas, developing role play exercises, selecting program activities, reviewing and assessing the last group meeting, and visualizing and rehearsing aspects of future meetings are some of the many ways effective workers prepare for meetings. In recent years, an increased awareness of the benefits of clear contracts and specific goal statements has highlighted the need for careful preparation between meetings. For example, Rose (1977) suggests that specific written agendas be distributed at the beginning of each meeting. Specific written agendas are appropriate for structured short-term groups that are focused on a single concern or problem. Other treatment groups may have broader concerns that are not easily anticipated or addressed by a written agenda prepared before each meeting. However, whether or not a written agenda is distributed at the beginning of a meeting, workers should be sufficiently prepared so they are clear about their objectives for each meeting and their plans for achieving those objectives.

## Structuring the Group's Work

A primary activity of group workers during the middle stage of treatment groups is to structure and focus them. *Structure* refers to the degree to which planned, systematic, time-limited interventions are used to help clients change in desired directions. Highly structured interventions rely on the guidance and direction of the worker, whereas less structured approaches encourage members to take full responsibility for the purpose, goals, and interventions used in the group. A worker may structure group processes to enable the group as a whole to help members change. Structure may be used by intervening with individual members to help them plan how to achieve their goals, or by intervening in the group and its environment to help all members achieve their goals.

During the middle stage of treatment groups, the worker should perform a variety of activities to structure the group's work. One of the most basic of these activities is to let members know that each meeting will begin and end on time. Except for the first meeting, openings should not be delayed in anticipation of late members. Starting meetings late only serves to reinforce members' coming late in the future.

The worker should also structure the end of a meeting to summarize and conclude interactions rather than to begin new agenda items. New items should not be introduced near the end of a session. Sometimes a group member waits until the end of the meeting to disclose an important piece of information or to voice an important concern. These "door knob" communications (Shulman, 1979) can't be dealt with adequately in the short period of time available at the end of a meeting. When a member introduces new material late in a meeting, the worker should ask the member to hold the new material until the following meeting. When the member's concerns can not wait until the next group meeting, the worker may want to schedule an individual meeting with the member.

One of the most important ways that a worker can structure a group's time is by setting agendas (Shulman, 1979). Whether verbal or written, a clear agenda helps to focus attention on what will be covered during the meeting and make members aware of how much time is available for exercises, role plays, presentations, and discussions. When preparing and presenting agendas, workers should encourage members to share their ideas about what direction the group should take.

The worker also structures a group by establishing and maintaining orderly communication and interaction patterns. The structure of the interaction process should allow all members to have an opportunity to participate. Some members, however, may receive more attention in one meeting and less attention in others. For example, in a remedial group where members have individualized treatment contracts, the worker may decide to focus on one member at a time, helping that member to work on his or her treatment contract for an extended period of time. In other situations, such as an educational group, the worker may decide to present some didactic material and then encourage all members to discuss the material. The worker decides to structure the discussion so that each member is encouraged to participate and no member is allowed to talk for longer than several minutes at one time. In either case, the worker has made a planned effort to structure the way communication and interaction patterns are used in the group.

The worker structures a group's communication and interaction patterns by determining the amount of time spent on a particular issue or problem and by directing members in role plays, exercises, and other group activities. In these efforts, the worker balances the socioemotional needs of individual members and the needs of the group as a whole to accomplish specific goals. During the middle stage of groups, the worker struggles to maintain a proper balance between socioemotional and task needs.

Sometimes workers are reluctant to assert themselves and move the group from a discussion of one issue to another or to direct role plays or exercises. However, group members look to the worker for direction. The worker has professional knowledge and skills for guiding members' progress toward specific goals. When the worker is unsure about whether or not the group needs more time to work on an issue or an exercise, the worker should ask members a direct question about their needs. When guiding group activities, the worker should ensure that the transition from one activity to another is as smooth as possible. This can be done by summarizing what has been said, by recommending how the group might pursue unresolved issues, and by suggesting that the group move along to pursue remaining issues.

Focusing a group's work is another way to structure its work. In any treatment group, the focus of an intervention, sometimes referred to as the level of an intervention, can be either the individual member, the group itself, or the group's external environment. The focus of the group should change with the changing needs of the group. For example, a worker leading a group for men who have battered their wives makes an assessment that the group fails to encourage members to express feelings of anger. This, in turn, inhibits the group from achieving its objective of preventing further domestic violence. The worker decides to select the group as the target of an intervention designed to help members talk about feelings. The worker has each member express two'feelings that he has about being a member of the group. Other exercises are used in later group sessions to help members learn to identify their feelings of anger and to intervene before they escalate into violent outbursts. (See, for example, Edleson, Miller, and Stone, 1983; Novaco, 1975; Rahaim, Lefebvre, and Jenkins, 1980). However, at the end of the first exercise, the group leader changes the focus of the group and concentrates on helping an individual member work on a particular treatment plan. By changing the focus, the worker structures the group's process and affects the type of work that is done in the group.

*Degree of Structure.* Treatment contracts may suggest the need for a structure that encourages members to use their own resources when carrying out intervention plans. A group for parents of Down's Syndrome children, for example, may be most successful if the worker acts as a facilitator of group discussions in which members are encouraged to share their mutual concerns and their diverse efforts at being effective parents for their handicapped children. Such a structure encourages the formation of a mutual support network among the parents.

In other cases, it may be best if interventions are highly structured by the worker. For example, a worker leading a group to teach children to resolve conflict may have a specific outline for each group session that includes didactic material about resolving conflict, reviewing homework assignments, role playing, observing and recording observations about the role play, making suggestions and giving feedback about the role play, modeling a new response, reviewing the new response, and assigning tasks to be done before the next session (see, for example, Edleson, 1981).

In both the parents' group and the children's group, the worker is clear about how the structure of the group has contributed to goal achievement. The worker has selected an intervention method by assessing the specific problems facing members and the needs of the group as a whole. The worker has not blindly applied a familiar intervention plan regardless of the particular situation.

Structure encourages rapid learning of new responses. Therefore, one of the advantages of structured groups is that they provide an efficient means for members to learn new skills. The appeal of the Minnesota Couples Communication Program (Miller, Nunally and Wackman, 1972), Parent Effectiveness Training (Gordon, 1975), Systematic Training in Effective Parenting (Dinkmeyer and McKay, 1982), and similar approaches testifies to the popularity of structured group programming for certain types of problems.

Structure is essential in multicomponent treatment programs in which interventions occur on several different levels. For example, an assertion training group treatment program includes group discussion, role playing, modeling, rehearsal, reinforcement, and cognitive interventions all designed to help members become more assertive. Interventions in this treatment program focus primarily on intrapersonal and interpersonal changes. Other multicomponent treatment programs may focus on societal changes as well. As the number of treatment components becomes greater, the need for careful structuring of the entire intervention program increases.

Structure has been recognized as a necessary ingredient of social work treatment for many years (see especially, Ryder, 1976; Perlman, 1970; Reid, 1978; and Reid and Epstein, 1972), but in recent years it has been given increasing attention. Reviews of the effectiveness of social work interventions (Fisher, 1978; Mullen, 1981; and Reid and Hanrahan, 1982) indicate that structured interventions are effective in helping clients to achieve treatment goals. Fisher (1978), for example, suggests that the use of structure is a critical element of social work practice. Melnick (1974) suggests that lack of structure tends to increase members' fears and anxieties. Similarly, Reid and Shyne (1969), Goldstein (1973), and Kanfer and Goldstein (1975) all indicate that structured interventions are more effective than unstructured interventions.

Despite findings suggesting that structure is an essential ingredient of social work practice, considerable controversy exists about how much structure is useful for treatment groups. It has been argued, for example, that a great deal of structure may not be beneficial because it prevents members from exercising their own initiative (Egan, 1976). Too much structure may decrease members' commitment to the group because they may feel that structure has been imposed on them rather than selected by them to help them achieve their own self-monitored goals. Lieberman, Yalom, and Miles (1973) found that structured exercises did not facilitate group development or successful outcomes in the groups they observed.

Although much of the available evidence indicates that structured interventions are at least as effective as less structured interventions (Mullen, 1981; Lazarus, 1971; and Fisher, 1978), highly structured interventions may be more appropriate for certain problems than for others. For example, although a highly structured multicomponent group treatment program was found to be more effective than a less structured group treatment program for helping older people increase their social skills (Toseland and Rose, 1978), a less structured process-oriented approach, focused on facilitating group members' determination of their own purposes and goals, was found to be more effective than a structured approach in developing mutual support groups for older people (Toseland, Sherman, and Bliven, 1981).

Another way of structuring a group is by setting time limits. Brief time limits are often associated with a greater degree of structure. Although Drum and Knott (1977) suggest that short-term structured group treatment can be helpful for facilitating members' growth and development, the popularity of long-term, open-ended, less structured self-help groups suggests that support through life transitions, life crises, and in alternative life-styles may be best provided in this type of group (Toseland and Hacker, 1982). It may also be preferable to treat other types of problems in groups that do not emphasize a time-limited structured format. For example, when members seek help in changing established personality characteristics, long-term rather than short-term group treatment approaches are often used. In his recent work on existential psychotherapy, Yalom (1975) points out that issues about the meaning of life and death are most effectively dealt with by long-term intervention methods.

Work with antisocial adolescents, clients in residential treatment centers, severely impaired psychiatric patients and street gangs often occurs in long-term groups. This is because these groups focus on specific, narrowly defined concerns and objectives only in the context of broader, long-term objectives and goals. For example, a short-term goal for a group of psychiatric inpatients is for them to learn some basic social skills. The long-term goal for the group is for each member to live independently in the community. Short-term structured approaches such as the task centered approach seem to recognize long-term treatment needs when suggesting that successive short-term contracts can be developed for certain clients, such as antisocial adolescents, who may need long-term treatment (Larsen and Mitchell, 1980; Reid, 1978).

Short-term highly structured approaches may not be best for clients who are mandated to attend group treatment. These clients take time to develop relationships and to build trust in workers' efforts to help them. On the other hand, clients who are "in crisis" may need less time to build relationships with the worker and other members and therefore can profit from short-term treatment.

These findings suggest that the worker should make a careful assessment of the problem before deciding on how to structure a particular group. Although additional research is needed, it appears that specific, relatively circumscribed problems and goals, such as becoming more assertive or losing weight, can be treated in short-term, highly structured, multicomponent treatment group at least as effectively, and more efficiently, than in less structured long-term groups. For other problems, however, group members may benefit most by developing their own structure for a group. Such an approach often requires more time and greater flexibility on the part of the worker as he or she facilitates members' efforts to develop their own structure and goals for a group.

## Helping Members Achieve Their Goals

A third activity that workers engage in while leading treatment groups during the middle stage of their development is helping members achieve their goals. Contracting for treatment goals is an evolving process. A tentative agreement or contract is usually discussed while interviewing potential members during the planning stage of a group. It is reaffirmed and made more concrete and specific during the beginning stage of the group as members have the opportunity of interacting with one another for the first time. Although much of a treatment group's work during the middle stage is devoted to carrying out contracts developed during the beginning stage of a group, contracts continue to evolve as the group progresses during the middle stage.

As Croxton (1974) notes, secondary contracts may be developed to refine initial contracts. For example, the individual contract of a member of a group for recently separated persons is to reduce her angry feelings and violent outbursts towards her former spouse when he comes to pick up their children. A secondary contract is for the member to discuss her feelings of anger with a member outside of the group and to report back to the group what she has learned from the other group member about ways to handle angry feelings. A variety of different secondary contracts can be used to help this member achieve the goals specified in her primary contract. Thus, secondary contracts evolve as group members progress toward their treatment goals.

Although a portion of a treatment group's work should be devoted to maintaining a group's optimal functioning, most of an effective treatment group's time during the middle stage should be focused on helping members achieve their goals. This can be accomplished by helping members to (1) maintain their awareness of their goals, (2) develop specific treatment plans, (3) work on treatment plans, and (4) carry out treatment plans.

*Awareness of Goals.*    The first step in helping members to achieve their goals is to maintain their awareness of the goals they identified and agreed to work on in earlier group meetings. Workers should not assume that members continue to be aware of these goals as the group progresses. Reminding members of the goals they have decided upon serves several purposes. It lets them know that the worker remains interested in the progress they make toward their goals. It checks for a continued mutual understanding of the contract. It helps to ensure that the worker and member remain focused on the same issues. Confirming goals also helps to avoid confusion and promote members' organized and systematic efforts to work on contracts.

In treatment groups in which a group contract for all members is emphasized, and individualized treatment contracts between each member and the worker are de-emphasized, periodically confirming goals gives the worker an opportunity to check as to whether any changes need to be made as the group develops. It also gives members a chance to share their feelings and thoughts about how to improve their treatment contract. For example, the contract for a group of parents waiting to adopt children includes attending group meetings on (1) child development, (2) legal proceedings for adoption, (3) special issues and concerns of adopted children, and (4) supportive resources and services available for adoptive parents and their children. During each meeting the worker asks members if the content of the meeting is useful. Members are given the opportunity to express their reactions to what has occurred, making suggestions for improving future meetings or continuing them as planned.

Maintaining members' awareness of contract goals is also essential in treatment groups that focus their work on individual contracts. Garvin, Reid, and Epstein (1976) recommend that during each meeting the worker go around the group helping each member to work in turn. At times, the worker may spend a considerable amount of time helping a member work toward a particular goal. For example, in a group for alcoholics, the worker spends forty minutes working with one member in relation to a secondary contract to help the member improve his methods of expressing anger. During the two-hour group meeting, the worker has the opportunity of working intensively with only three members. When this occurs, it is particularly important to generalize work with an individual member to other members so that everyone feels involved in the group. For example, members can be asked if they use similar ways of coping with stressful situations to those described by the member currently being given the group's attention. The worker can also encourage other members to share experiences that may be helpful to the member. Such interventions help to establish a norm for mutual helping among members.

If extensive time is spent with several members during one meeting, the worker should spend a brief period of time checking on other members' progress. Members who did not have an extensive opportunity to participate in a meeting should be encouraged to do so during the next one. This helps to prevent repeated and prolonged attention to a few members and reduces the possibilities that some members will avoid working on their contracts.

During the middle stage the worker should also help members to develop a process for reviewing their treatment goals and contracts. Although the review process may be idiosyncratic to the needs of a particular group, the worker should avoid haphazard or constantly changing review procedures. Without a clearly defined process that all members come to expect, there will be an ambiguous demand for work in which some members' progress is carefully monitored and that of others is not. When monitoring is haphazard, those who are assertive and highly involved will have their progress toward treatment goals monitored, whereas those who are less assertive and those who are resistant will not receive the attention they require.

With unsystematic monitoring procedures, tasks that are to be completed between meetings do not receive proper follow-up. There is nothing more frustrating and disconcerting for members than to complete a task between meetings and then not be given the opportunity to report the results during the next meeting. In addition to creating an ambiguous demand for work, failure to follow up on tasks often gives members the impression that the worker is disorganized and that the group does not function smoothly from one meeting to the next.

Once a systematic procedure for monitoring is established, the worker rarely needs to remind members to report their progress to the group. The expectation of weekly progress reports helps to maintain members' motivation to work toward contract goals between sessions and reduces the necessity of reminding members of their contract agreements. It also helps members gain a sense of independence and a sense of self-accomplishment as they assume responsibility for reporting their own progress.

*Developing Treatment Plans.*   A second way to help members achieve contract goals is by facilitating the development of specific goal-oriented treatment plans. When all members are working on the same contract goal, the worker develops and implements plans with the group as a whole. For example, in a weight loss group, a medical social worker helps members to prepare a method for monitoring their daily caloric intake, presents material on good nutrition, and introduces methods for modifying eating habits. The worker may then help individual members discuss the special needs inherent in their particular situations, helping them to modify what has been presented to fit specific circumstances.

When helping a member develop and implement an individual intervention plan, the worker should enlist the support of all group members. The worker should use every available opportunity to make connections between members, to point out parallel issues and concerns among members' situations, and to encourage all members to participate. As members become involved as helpers, the group's cohesion increases and members feel satisfied that they have had something to contribute. Known as the helper-therapy principle (Lieberman and Borman, 1979), this strategy works in such a way that members who help others often benefit as much as those who are helped.

The worker helps members to develop treatment plans in several ways. Before deciding on a plan, the worker helps members to explore and gather facts about their situation. A guided group discussion on the specifics of a situation, the alternatives that have been tried, and the possibilities that have not been explored is often sufficient to help members develop intervention plans. Sometimes, however, members will try to grab at potential solutions without exploring alternatives. This is particularly true when members are experiencing a great deal of stress or psychic pain from their problems. The worker should encourage members to explore alternatives thoroughly before deciding on an action plan.

An exploration of the situation may reveal a need for additional information. The member, with or without the help of the worker, is asked to spend time between sessions gathering data. The process of members' monitoring their own behavior and gathering additional facts about their situation is essential if effective treatment plans are to be developed. Effective action plans can not be developed without sufficient information. When a member is severely impaired, unwilling or unable to collect needed information, the worker may have to share the responsibility for collecting additional information about a member's situation to use in treatment planning during the next meeting.

An intervention plan may become readily apparent as the group explores a particular situation. For example, data gathered by a severely depressed member of an outpatient psychotherapy group suggests that negative and self-deprecating thoughts and self-statements are maintaining his depression. These thoughts and self-statements persist despite the member's adequate performance in job- and family-related responsibilities.

The intervention plan helps the member to replace negative thoughts and deprecating self-statements with realistic thoughts and self-statements about his abilities, accomplishments, and positive qualities. This is done by having the member make a list of positive self-statements to be repeated each time an obtrusive, negative, self-statement occurs. Secondary contracts, such as having the member ask other group members to describe how they perceive him during interactions in the group and having the member get positive feedback from significant others are also used to help him overcome his depression.

Sometimes, exploration of the problem may not immediately lead to a clear plan of action. The worker should help members consider alternatives before deciding on a final plan of action. Because of workers' professional training and knowledge, they are often the primary generators of alternative intervention plans. Although the intervention plan that is selected may have been originally generated by the worker or another group member, members should be encouraged to refine alternatives and select the most appropriate plans for their own needs. They should not experience a plan as imposed on them by someone else. Members who experience their action plans as self-selected are more likely to follow through on them.

Treatment plans can be quite complex. A treatment plan may involve a sequence of actions suggested by different members of the group. These different sequences of actions occur simultaneously. A complex plan should be divided into a series of discrete steps that are defined as clearly and specifically as possible. For example, in order to become more assertive, a member might (1) clarify the difference between aggressiveness and assertiveness through group discussion and reading a book on assertiveness, (2) decide in what situations to become more assertive, (3) practice being more assertive in the group during role plays and group discussion, (4) practice being assertive outside of the group with family members or a friend, and (5) practice being assertive in a real life situation.

Ideally, each step of the treatment plan should specify (1) who, (2) does what, (3) when, (4) where, (5) how often, and (6) under what conditions (Maple, 1977). It is especially important to be clear and specific when there are several persons responsible for different aspects of a comprehensive treatment plan. Treatment plans often require the involvement of the worker, the client, other agency personnel, and the client's family. The effective worker should make sure that all those who are a part of the treatment plan are clear about their roles, their responsibilities, and their expected contributions.

In some groups, all work is completed during meetings, but we have found that it is often helpful to encourage members to complete tasks between meetings. Many different tasks can be developed to help accomplish treatment plans between meetings. According to Wells (1982), there are (1) observational or monitoring tasks to gather information or to increase awareness of behaviors, emotions, or beliefs; (2) experiential tasks to arouse emotion, to challenge beliefs or attitudes; and (3) incremental change tasks to stimulate change in a step-by-step manner. Other types of tasks include mental or cognitive tasks to help group members change cognitions and belief systems (Reid, 1978) and paradoxical or two-sided tasks that result in changes no matter how they are carried out. For example, the treatment plan of a nonassertive group member includes the paradoxical task of having the member assert her right in a situation where she would normally remain passive. If the member does the task, she is learning to be more assertive. If she does not do it, then she is showing that she can assert herself in reference to her treatment plan.

According to Reid (1978), tasks can be individual, reciprocal, or shared. For example, an individual task for a member in a smoking cessation group may be to keep a log of the number of cigarettes smoked each day. Workers may also agree to perform individual tasks. For example, a worker in a rural county welfare agency agrees to find out if there are any transportation services available to enable teenage parents to attend a parenting skills group.

In a reciprocal task, if one person does something, another person will also do something. For example, if a member of an adolescent group does his assigned chore in the cottage each day for one week, the worker will help the member to obtain a pass to see his parents the following weekend. A third type of task is shared by two or more people. For example, members of the group may form a buddy system (Rose, 1977), also referred to as consulting pairs (Garvin, Reid, and Epstein, 1976), where each member is expected to remind his or her buddy to work on a specific task between group meetings.

In developing treatment plans and specific tasks, the worker should proceed by making sure that members are able to carry out each step successfully. It is especially important for members to have a successful experience in carrying out the first task they agree to accomplish. If they are successful in completing their first task, they are much more likely to successfully complete a second task (Stotland, 1969; D'Zurrilla and Goldfried, 1971). Successfully completing an initial task gives members a sense that their particular goals are reachable. It also helps build self-confidence, feelings of self-efficacy, and a sense of control and mastery over the problem or concern the member is attempting to alleviate. As members begin to feel self-efficacious, they are more likely to persist in their attempts at solving problems and concerns and are therefore more likely to be successful than when feelings of inadequacy limit their attempts to solve problems (Bandura, 1977b).

In developing treatment plans, the worker should assess a member's competencies and work with the member to plan an initial task that can be accomplished without an extraordinary amount of effort. Novice workers often develop treatment plans with too few steps. Members may agree to tasks in order to please a worker, or another group member, only to find that they are not sufficiently prepared to undertake the tasks they have agreed to perform. The worker should also attempt to ensure that tasks are timed and paced appropriately so that they become progressively more difficult as the member gains confidence and skill.

The worker can intervene to reduce the possibility that a member might have a great deal of difficulty completing a task. Simulations, role plays, and other exercises can be performed in the group before the member agrees to perform a task at home, in the community or in any other less hospitable environment. Rose (1977) suggests that members can be prepared for unreceptive or hostile environments by simulating these conditions in the group. One of the advantages of group treatment is that members have the opportunity to practice with other members of the group before they attempt to perform a task in the natural environment. Acting out roles also helps members become more aware of their own roles in a situation. An entire treatment method known as *psychodrama* is based on the benefits of acting out life experiences with others. (See, for example, Blatner, 1973.)

Members should be encouraged to tackle only one task at a time. In treatment planning, it is surprising to find how many underorganized, multi-problem clients will suggest working on several different problems and their resulting tasks simultaneously. Although members often have good intentions when they are taking part in a group session, when they return home they have less motivation to follow through on the multiple tasks they have agreed to accomplish. It is better to start with one or two concrete tasks that are planned carefully than to encourage a member to work on a variety of tasks simultaneously. When a member has completed initial tasks, he or she can then take on more difficult ones. If a member does not perform a task satisfactorily, the worker should help the member to view this as a learning experience rather than as a failure experience. A task should then be planned that can be completed on the basis of the information and feedback gained from the initial experience.

At the end of a session, the worker should ask members to review the tasks that were agreed upon during the session. It is not uncommon for members or the worker to forget tasks that were agreed to one or two hours earlier in the midst of an active and interesting group session. A review can help to eliminate confusion, misconceptions, or discrepancies about specific tasks. At this time, members should also be encouraged to remind each other of any tasks or portions of tasks that have not been mentioned. This ensures that everyone leaves the group with a clear notion of what has to be done before the next meeting. A recording form such as that shown in Figure 8 –2 can also be used to help the worker and the group members keep track of the tasks they have agreed to complete.

*Helping Members to Work.*   A third way to help members achieve their goals is by increasing their willingness to work on the concerns, problems, and issues that confront them. Members need help to work on their goals because they often find it difficult to make changes in their lives. For example, a member of a psychotherapy group who has contracted to stop drinking alcohol begins drinking again after only two days of abstinence. In a different group, a member, who has contracted to become independent of her parents, makes excuses about why she has not had time to explore alternative living arrangements.

In both cases, members have encountered obstacles to achieving their goals. First, the worker should check with the member to find out if the member also acknowledges that he or she has encountered an obstacle. Shulman (1979) suggests that the worker should also make a clear and specific "demand for work." The initial demand for work is a gentle reminder to the member that the worker and the other group members are interested in helping that member achieve his or her goals. The "demand for work" should be accompanied by an offer to help the member overcome obstacles that are impeding him or her.

With a member's agreement, the worker can take several steps to facilitate a return to goal-directed work. The first step is to encourage a member to explore what has been happening to prevent or block him or her from working on treatment goals. The worker can involve the group as a whole by having members participate in the analysis of factors that may be inhibiting a member's goal achievement. This can be helpful both for the member who is having difficulty following through on a treatment contract and for other members who can obtain practice in overcoming ambivalence and resistance concerning their own planned change efforts.

In helping members to overcome obstacles, workers should not ask

Date: _____
Session #: _____
Group _____

| Member's Name | Task | When | Where | How Often | Under What Circumstances |
|---|---|---|---|---|---|
| | | | | | |
| | | | | | |
| | | | | | |
| | | | | | |
| | | | | | |
| | | | | | |
| | | | | | |
| | | | | | |
| | | | | | |
| | | | | | |
| | | | | | |
| | | | | | |

**Figure 8–2** A Group Task Recording Form

"why" questions because these have been found to be unproductive in helping members work toward treatment goals (Flowers, 1979). Group members often do not have the answers to "why" questions, and if they do, their explanation may attribute causes to incorrect sources, further complicating their problem. Instead of asking "why" questions, the worker should ask members "how" or "what" questions that help them to describe cognitive, affective, behavioral, or environmental circumstances that may be diminishing their ability to work on treatment goals.

"How" questions and "what" questions keep members focused on current behaviors that lead to or exacerbate existing problems. Thus, for example, the worker might ask "what occurred just before you became angry" or "how did you feel when _____ happened?" "What" and "how" questions tend to elicit actual behavior and events, whereas "why" questions tend to elicit the opinion or judgments of members on the basis of their interpretations of information. This makes it difficult for the worker and other members to form their own opinions. It also makes it more difficult for the worker to suggest ways in which a member's current thoughts, feelings, behaviors, and environmental situation could be changed to alleviate a particular problem.

For example, in response to a "why" question, a member who is depressed indicates that her depression is a result of her low self-esteem, which she attributes to her relationship with her now deceased mother. In response to a "how" question, the member responds that she constantly repeats phrases to herself, such as "you can't do that," which she first heard from her mother when she was a young girl. Although the response to the "why" question may produce some insight into the origins of the member's depression, insight by itself often produces little behavior change. The response to the "how" question, however, leads directly to helping the member change her cognitive self-statements that are maintaining her depression. Thus, "how" questions are more likely than "why" questions to elicit information that will help members make active behavior changes to achieve their treatment goals.

Obstacles interfering with members' ability to work toward treatment goals may be the result of an inappropriate contract. A careful analysis of the contract may indicate that it was poorly designed and should be renegotiated. A contract can be inappropriate for several reasons, including:

1. Goals specified in the contract may be vaguely defined or too global to be achieved.
2. Goals may be too difficult to achieve at a particular stage in treatment.
3. The worker and the member focused on long-term goals rather than on more immediate, short-term goals that have a higher probability of being accomplished in a shorter period of time.
4. There may be a misunderstanding between the client and the worker about the nature of specific contract goals.
5. Inappropriate goals may have been set without careful assessment of the member's situation.

6. Changing problems and situations may necessitate modifications in the treatment goals developed for a contract made earlier in the group's development.

For all these reasons, helping members to work toward treatment goals often necessitates that the worker help members clarify, redefine, or renegotiate contracts to make them more appropriate for a member's particular needs.

The second step in working toward treatment goals is to increase members' motivation to take action to overcome the obstacles they have encountered. If a member agrees that action is important, the worker's task is to help the member believe that change is possible. Many group members are willing to act, but refuse to do so because they do not believe in their own ability to do something to change their situation. In such cases, self-instructional training (Meichenbaum, 1977), discussed in the next section of this chapter, may be useful in increasing a member's willingness to attempt a new behavior. When the lack of motivation is severe, the worker should consider renegotiating a contract, focusing the new contract on helping the member increase his or her motivation to work on a specific issue or concern rather than to work on the specific concern itself. Such a contract may involve helping members to examine factors that affect their motivation to work on a particular goal and to examine any consequences that may result from not working toward a goal.

The final step is to help members decide on what actions to take so as to overcome obstacles and renew their progress toward treatment goals. In making the plan, the worker helps members to get support for their efforts from as many sources as possible. For example, the worker instructs the member who returned to drinking after two days to go around the group and tell each of the other group members that he will not drink until the next group meeting. Members are encouraged to support this member by making replies such as "I'm happy for you—I admire your determination to work on your problem." Group members also help the member by suggesting interventions such as changing his cognitive self-statements and modifying his home environment by removing all liquor from his house. The worker asks several members to give the member a call during the week to help him follow through on his verbal commitment. In order to enlist the help of his family and friends, the worker asks the members' permission to contact them to gain their support and encouragement for the member's decision not to drink. To provide continued support during evening hours, the member is referred to an Alcoholics Anonymous group. In this way, the member receives support for working toward contract goals from a variety of sources within and outside of the group.

In summary, helping members to work toward treatment goals is an important activity for any worker who plans to lead effective treatment groups. All treatment groups require effort from members if they are to be successful in achieving their goals. The worker's task is to help members mobilize their resources and maximize their use of the group to help them accomplish their goals. The worker should be constantly vigilant, pointing out inertia, ambivalence, and other psychological, social, and environmental barriers that block members' progress in the group.

*Helping Members Carry Out Treatment Plans.*   There are five interventive
roles that workers can use to help members carry out their treatment plans.
These include the roles of (1) enabler, (2) broker, (3) mediator, (4) advocate,
and (5) educator. Although other roles have been identified as appropriate
for helping members to carry out their treatment plans (for example, om-
budsman and lobbyist), these five roles are the most important and most
frequently assumed by workers leading various types of treatment groups.

    ENABLER ROLE.   The enabler role is the most basic of all intervention
roles. As Shulman (1979) points out, the enabler reaches out to members,
letting them know that their ideas, opinions, and feelings are valued. As an
enabler, the worker encourages members to express their concerns and
feelings regarding their treatment plans. The worker monitors members'
reactions to the work occurring in the group and encourages those who
appear to have something to contribute to share their thoughts with the
group. As obstacles are encountered, the difficulty of making changes in
established behavior patterns is acknowledged. In this way, the worker
shows empathy for members who are confronted with difficult life situations. At the same time, the worker helps members to use their own skills to
identify, confront, and remove obstacles that detract from their ability to
carry out treatment plans.

    As the group progresses, members are praised for their contributions
and encouraged to continue their participation. The worker helps the group
develop a supportive culture in which members can count on one another for
mutual aid in overcoming difficult problems. As an enabler, the worker helps
members to revitalize and mobilize their own strengths and resources to
cope with difficult problems (Compton and Galaway, 1979).

    BROKER ROLE.   In the broker role, the worker identifies community
resources that may be helpful to clients in carrying out their treatment plans.
In most communities throughout the United States, there is an extremely
complex and often confusing network of community services and resources
that group members may know little about. As a broker, the worker helps
members to become aware of appropriate services, eligibility criteria, and
other conditions for using a service. For example, a member of a group
experiences great distress in caring for her aged mother. As part of a plan to
help reduce some of this distress, the worker suggests that the member
contact a local home health care agency. Before helping the member contact
the home health care agency, the worker discusses eligibility criteria for
receiving home health aid, the availability of third-party reimbursement for
this care, the duration and the extent to which services can be expected, and
whether services are available twenty-four hours a day. After this discussion, the worker refers the member to a specific contact person in the home
health care agency. In order to avoid frustration, disappointment, and unmet
expectations, the worker also prepares the member for possible barriers that
may be encountered, such as a one-month delay in processing reimbursement claims for home health care services.

    To help workers perform broker functions adequately, agencies should
keep an up-to-date listing of community resources, with brief, pertinent
information about contact persons, access points, eligibility requirements,

and other miscellaneous requirements for receiving services. In some communities, this listing is prepared by a planning agency and made available to all local agencies. Workers who may not be thoroughly familiar with all community services that are available in the area served by their agency can refer to this listing for information needed by members of a group they are leading.

MEDIATOR ROLE.   As a mediator, the worker helps to resolve disputes, conflicts, or opposing points of view within the group or between a member and some other person or organization. For example, in a group for adolescents in a residential treatment center, the worker helps two members resolve a conflict they have been having about their participation in a recreational activity. In another group, the worker helps a member to resolve a conflict with a child care worker.

In order to serve as an effective mediator, Compton and Galaway (1979) suggest that a worker should help members in conflict recognize the legitimacy of each others' interests. The worker identifies and works toward common values and interests, helps the members avoid a situation in which winning and losing are paramount, attempts to get at the specifics of the conflict, and helps the members to recognize that their ongoing relationship is more important than winning or losing a specific conflict. As a mediator, the worker acts to resolve disputes by helping members arrive at a settlement or an agreement that is mutually acceptable.

ADVOCATE ROLE.   In some cases, a worker's efforts to act as a broker and refer members to needed services and resources may not succeed. The referral source may not be sympathetic to members' needs or there may be no appropriate services or resources available to meet members' needs. In these situations, the worker advocates on behalf of group members to help them obtain services or resources. As an advocate, the worker represents members' interests and needs.

The worker can negotiate to obtain needed services on behalf of one or more group members. For example, in negotiating with a community service center to plan more activities for adolescents a worker might offer to supervise the youth worker or volunteer who is to lead one of the new activities. In other cases, the worker uses persuasion to obtain voluntary acceptance of a change. According to Pincus and Minahan (1973), voluntary acceptance of a change comes about because the target of the change realizes that the worker's request is correct, just, and legitimate and recognizes and accepts the worker's professional expertise and judgment.

In attempting to gain what is needed for members of a group, the worker may also assume an adversarial role. As an adversary, the worker challenges the validity of the status quo. The worker may appeal a ruling, lobby for a change in rules, organize a rally, or in countless other ways work for changes in systems that affect members of the group. For example, in a group for nursing home residents, one member's treatment plan includes having her take part in a regularly sheduled activities program. The member missed the program several times because a clock in her room was stolen, and the activities director had a policy that residents must be responsible for getting to the program by themselves. The worker advocated for the member by speaking to the activity director, explaining the situation, and working out a plan whereby the member was notified by the activity director one hour before the program began. In the same group, the worker also advocated for members by requesting that nurse's aides change their order of serving dinner so that residents who took part in the group did not have to eat cold dinners.

When services or resources to address particular needs are not available, advocacy efforts include making others aware of the unmet needs and establishing services to address them. For example, in the nursing home activities group, members expressed a variety of concerns about their lack of control over their living conditions in the nursing facility. The worker met with the nursing home director to advocate for patients' rights to self-determination. Through these efforts, the worker obtained the permission of the director to form a residents' council to advise the administrative staff on issues affecting residents. Members of the activity group served as the nucleus for beginning the residents' council, which continued after the twelve-week time-limited group that the worker led had ended.

The worker's advocacy efforts may, therefore, also include helping to develop new services and resources. The worker acts as an advocate by helping others to understand the importance, the intensity, and the extent of a particular problem. By demonstrating how a need is relevant to the objectives and goals of an agency and by making their own expertise and knowledge available, workers can actively participate in developing new services for group members.

EDUCATOR ROLE.   One of the most important roles assumed by workers in helping members to achieve their treatment goals is that of the educator. As an educator, the worker presents new information to help resolve members' concerns, demonstrates and models new or improved behaviors, and suggests role plays, simulations, and in-vivo activities to help members practice new or different ways of behaving in problematic situations. Unlike the enabler role in which the worker helps members use their own resources, as an educator the worker utilizes professional expertise about how to change or modify behavior patterns and adds to members' existing knowledge and skills.

In educating group members, it is often helpful to use visual and motor modes of teaching, as well as the more common didactic mode. Learning can often be enhanced, for example, by visual displays on newsprint and by graphs, charts, or other media. Video tape and audio tape recordings can also be helpful in providing members with feedback about their behavior in a group.

Motor modes of learning are best suited for teaching new skills (Bandura, 1977a). Novice workers sometimes assume that mentioning a new piece of information or discussing how to perform a new behavior is sufficient to help a member learn it. Despite members' indications that they understand explanations about how to perform a behavior, our experience suggests that they are frequently unable to perform behaviors described verbally. Therefore, it is important to have members rehearse new behaviors before trying to perform them in real life situations. This is particularly true when helping members learn complex skills. Sometimes a series of steps involving modeling, rehearsing, feedback, coaching, and further rehearsing is necessary to help a member perfect a new skill.

## Monitoring and Evaluating

Like preparing for group meetings, structuring the group's work, and helping members achieve their goals, monitoring and evaluating are also important tasks for workers during the middle stage of treatment groups. Monitoring and evaluating provide feedback for workers and members. This feedback is useful in developing, modifying, and changing treatment plans and in maintaining the functioning of the group as a whole. Monitoring and evaluating are important ongoing processes that should occur throughout the life of a group.

One of the most common methods of obtaining feedback from members during the middle stage of a group's development is to give members a session evaluation form, such as that shown in Chapter 10 (Figure 10–3), at the end of each group session. Although the format of session evaluation questions (close ended Likert-type questions and open-ended questions) remains fairly standard from group to group, the content of questions varies with the type of group. Changing the content of questions provides workers with the specific information they need about a particular group's work.

How frequently should session evaluation forms be administered? In some groups, they can be used at the end of each session. Workers who are not familiar with using session evaluation forms sometimes wonder how they will be received by members, but brief forms that take only a few minutes to fill out are not a burden for members to complete. Members often enjoy the opportunity of letting the worker know what they like and don't like about the group.

In other groups, workers may prefer to evaluate the group's progress after every second or third session. The exact frequency of monitoring and evaluating ultimately depends on the need for ongoing feedback about the group's development. Verbal evaluations are often used as a substitute for written evaluations, but written evaluations may prove better quality feedback because when they are returned without members' names they offer a measure of confidentiality not available through verbal evaluations.

Other frequently used methods of monitoring and evaluating progress during the middle stage of a group's development include having members self-monitor their own behaviors and having others who are familiar with members' concerns (such as other workers or family members) report progress to the worker. These and other monitoring and evaluation methods are described in Chapters 7 and 10. The actual methods selected for obtaining feedback are, however, not as important as whether or not feedback is systematically solicited, collected, and acted upon. Obraining feedback allows workers to fine-tune a group as it progresses through its middle stage. It also serves as a signal to members that their opinions are valued and that their ideas and concerns will be analyzed and acted upon as attempts are made to achieve the group's work. For these reasons, monitoring and evaluating a group's progress is an essential worker activity during the middle stage of group development.

## INTERVENTION METHODS IN TREATMENT GROUPS

The first section of this chapter described a number of worker activities frequently performed during the middle stage of treatment groups. This section focuses on specific interventions for alleviating the problems and concerns commonly experienced by members of treatment groups.

Workers may focus their interventions at the level of (1) the group member, (2) the group as a whole, or (3) the environment in which the group functions. The selection of a particular focus is based on the needs of the group and its members. The worker changes interventive levels as the needs of the group change. For example, in beginning the fourth session of a psychotherapy group, the worker intervenes in the group as a whole to increase member-to-member communication. The worker then focuses attention on the concerns of an individual member while helping the group to continue a high level of member-to-member communication. Interventions at one level affect other levels (Garvin, 1981). Thus, the worker often moves back and forth among interventive levels as the group progresses. In most treatment groups, the worker spends some time intervening at all three levels, combining interventions in order to alleviate members' problems and help them reach their treatment goals.

## INTERVENING WITH GROUP MEMBERS

When intervening with individual group members, the worker may select from (1) intrapersonal, (2) interpersonal, or (3) environmental interventions. Intrapersonal interventions are focused on members' cognitions and affects, that is, their thoughts, beliefs, values, feelings, sensations, and emotions. They are particularly appropriate when an assessment has determined that a member's psychosocial development may have helped to contribute to dysfunctional or irrational belief systems. Interpersonal interventions focus on members' relationships with others within and outside the group. These are particularly useful when an assessment has determined that a member lacks interpersonal skills. Environmental interventions seek to change or to modify the psychosocial and physical space in which members function in order to help them achieve their treatment goals. They are particularly useful when an assessment determines that a member lacks material resources to ameliorate a problem.

In keeping with the eclectic approach of this text, the interventions selected for inclusion in this section were drawn from a number of different approaches to practice. Workers using some approaches rely exclusively on the skills mentioned in Chapter 4, but we have included specialized intervention techniques in this chapter because we have found them to be effective for particular types of problems that we have encountered in leading treatment groups. Many specialized interventive methods have not been included in the following sections. We encourage readers to add to the intervention methods described here as they become familiar with those that are grounded in practice models and theories that they find particularly useful.

## Intrapersonal Interventions

Since the beginnings of group work practice, workers with psychodynamic orientations have focused most of their interventions in treatment groups on the intrapersonal aspects of group members' behavior. In recent years, there has also been a growing interest in techniques to intervene in the covert, intrapersonal lives of group members within behavioral approaches to practice. Perhaps this is the result of the accumulating evidence suggesting that what people think and feel has a direct bearing on how they behave (Meichenbaum, 1977; Mahoney, 1974). Increased interest in covert, intrapersonal events has led to an explosion in the number of techniques designed to alter cognitive and affective development.

Before using specific techniques, group workers should be aware of the overall process of helping members to make intrapersonal changes. This process includes helping members to (1) identify and discriminate among thoughts, feelings, and behaviors; (2) recognize associations between specific thoughts, feelings, and behaviors; (3) analyze the rationality of thoughts and beliefs; and (4) change distorted or irrational thoughts and beliefs.

*Identifying and Discriminating.*   The first step in any intrapersonal intervention is to help members accurately identify thoughts, feelings, and behaviors and to discriminate among them. Some members have great difficulty putting their subjective thoughts and feelings into words. But without clearly identifying a member's internal thoughts and feelings for the rest of the group, it is not possible to help members cope with or change these covert processes.

In helping members to identify and discriminate behavior from thoughts and feelings, members should describe their behavior as if a camera were taking a picture of the event and the member were a bystander observing the behavior. (See, for example, Maultsby, 1975, and Maultsby and Carpenter, 1980.) This technique also helps members to describe events in specific, observable terms.

Some people have a difficult time describing feelings. It is common for group members to respond to a question about what they are feeling with a description of a behavior or a thought. This is particularly true of men, who are taught as they are growing up that expressing feelings is a feminine, not a masculine, trait. For example, in response to a question about what he was feeling, an obviously angry group member stated, "I'm not feeling anything." When the worker stated that we are always feeling something, no matter how slight, the member stated, "I'm feeling that your interpretation of my behavior is not correct." This statement, of course, is a thought and not a feeling, and from this group member such responses were quite common.

To help members who have difficulty discriminating feelings from thoughts, the worker can have the member get feedback from the group. In the previously described situation, the member went around the group asking other members if they had an idea of how he was feeling. As the members expressed that he appeared to be angry, the member gradually became aware that he was not in touch with his feelings. Sometimes it is necessary to have members practice discriminating thoughts from feelings in a number of situations inside and outside the group before they are able to correctly identify and separate them.

*Recognizing Associations.*   The second step in intrapersonal interventions is to help members recognize that there is an association between thoughts, feelings, and behaviors. For example, if a man thinks that someone is deliberately following him as he is walking home one evening, he is likely to feel apprehensive and to behave accordingly. He may look over his shoulder or walk on the well-lighted side of a street. Similarly, if a woman thinks that she is not skillful at a particular task, she is likely to feel incompetent and is less likely to continue to work on the task if she encounters difficulty than if she thinks that she can perform the task adequately.

For members to alter associations between thoughts, feelings, and behaviors, they must be aware of their existence. Awareness can be accomplished through a self-monitoring process. Members are asked to monitor particular thoughts as well as the feelings and behaviors that occur immediately following them. The group helps members to look for patterns of association among particular thoughts, feelings, and behaviors. Sometimes members may clearly remember specific thoughts and their associated feelings and behaviors, and it may not be necessary to spend time monitoring them before reporting them to the group. This is often the case with automatic thoughts that constantly reoccur to members (Beck, 1976).

Data about thoughts, feelings, and behaviors collected either prospectively or retrospectively, are discussed in the group. Such a discussion usually reveals that specific thoughts are exacerbating or maintaining unwanted feeling states and behavior patterns. For example, the anxious group member found that her thoughts were focused on her "inability to do anything right" and thoughts that she "would not be able to complete her work assignments on time." As her thoughts were discussed in the group, it became clear that they led to her fears and her anxiety about her performance on the job. These feelings, in turn, tended to distract her from her work and often led to migraine headaches. Both of these consequences only served to further reinforce her beliefs that she would not complete her assignments, that she couldn't do anything right, and that she was a failure.

The previous example suggests that thoughts lead to feelings and behavior, but it is also possible that particular cues or signals can lead to thoughts, which can in turn, lead to feelings and behavior. For example, a cue for an anxiety-producing thought might be the approach of a person of the opposite sex in a singles bar. The approach cues or signals the person who begins to think anxiety-producing thoughts, such as, "I hope he doesn't come over here" and "I won't know what to say." These thoughts can then lead to feelings of anxiety and to avoidance behavior. Such a sequence of events can become habituated, and a particular cue, or even the thought of the particular cue, can lead to the entire sequence of dysfunctional thoughts, feelings, and behaviors.

The second step in the process of intrapersonal interventions, therefore, also includes helping members become aware of internal cues such as muscle tension or "butterflies" in the stomach and external cues, such as the approach of a person, that trigger a sequence of events. In long-time treatment focused on personality change, workers may want to help members gain insight into the historical determinants of these cues. Once members are aware of the cues that trigger an association between thoughts, feelings, and behavior, they are ready to move on to the next step in the process.

*Analyzing the Rationality of Thoughts and Beliefs.*    The third step in intervening intrapersonally is to help members analyze the rationality of the thoughts and beliefs that maintain or exacerbate dysfunctional feelings and behavior patterns. As Epictetus wrote in *The Enchiridion*, "Men are not disturbed by things but by the views taken of them." According to many cognitive psychologists (Beck and others, 1979; Ellis, 1962; Meichenbaum, 1977; Mahoney, 1974), dysfunctional and irrational thoughts and beliefs arise from erroneous or misleading interpretations of events. Group members may (1) overgeneralize from an event, (2) selectively focus on portions of an event, (3) take too much responsibility for events that are beyond their control, (4) think of the worst possible consequence of future events, (5) engage in either/or dichotomous thinking, and (6) assume that because certain events have led to particular consequences in the past they will automatically lead to the same consequences if they reoccur in the future.

Sometimes corrective information and feedback are sufficient to change thoughts and beliefs based on incomplete or incorrect information. For example, some teenage girls believe that they won't get pregnant if they have sexual intercourse only once or twice. With proper information, beliefs about the results of sexual activity can be changed.

Ellis (1962) suggests that faulty interpretations occur because of irrational beliefs and ideas people have about the way things should operate in their world. For example, members may believe that they must be thoroughly "competent, adequate, and achieving in all possible respects if they are to consider themselves worthwhile" (Ellis, 1962, p. 63). Ellis lists eleven common irrational ideas that affect members' interpretations of events. These irrational beliefs are usually based on absolutist thinking rather than on well-reasoned, logical interpretations or elaborations from factual evidence. Words such as *should, ought,* and *must* are cues to the existence of absolutist thinking, which may lead to irrational or erroneous interpretations of events. For example, a group member believes that in order to consider himself worthwhile he must be competent in all possible respects. In those instances where his performance falls short of his unrealistically high standards he becomes depressed.

*Changing Thoughts, Beliefs, and Feeling States.*   The fourth step in intrapersonal interventions is to help members change irrational or distorted thoughts and beliefs and associated feeling states. A number of techniques that have been developed for this purpose are listed here along with a brief description of their use in group treatment.

COGNITIVE RESTRUCTURING.   Cognitive restructuring is a term used by Mahoney (1974) to refer to a group of techniques such as rational emotive therapy and reattribution therapy. These techniques are designed to expose faulty logic in group members' thought patterns and to help them replace these irrational thought processes with logical, rational patterns of thought. The worker can help members to change their faulty logic by:

1. Having members examine the assumptions on which thoughts and beliefs are based.
2. Helping members generate alternative assumptions.
3. Helping members test assumptions by taking actions to verify them in situations outside of the group.
4. Helping members to get feedback from other group members about the logic of their assumptions.

Through a combination of group discussion, rational analysis, and action, members help each other to change their attributions concerning previous events and to replace the cognitions that result from these attributions with thoughts and beliefs that are more functional for coping with events in their daily lives.

COGNITIVE SELF-INSTRUCTION.   The cognitive self-instruction technique, described by Meichenbaum (1977), refers to helping members use internal dialogs and covert self-statements for solving problems and coping with difficult life events. Children and adults can use the technique to replace dysfunctional internal dialogs with self-statements that help them to solve a problem. For example, instead of a member saying to himself or herself, "I can't do this," the member can be trained to say, "I'll try to do it the best I can," or "I'll bet my answer is as good or better than anyone else's," and "first I'll examine all the data and then I'll think of the possible solutions." Cognitive self-instructions can be used to prepare for a particular situation or to help a member perform effectively while in a situation. For example, to prepare for a particular situation, a member might say, "What I will do when I talk to Sally is tell her directly that I can't do it. If she tries to persuade me I'll just repeat that I've decided not to do it." While in a particular situation, a member might say, "I'm in control" or "I can do this."

It has been found by Meichenbaum (1977) and D'Zurilla and Goldfried (1971) that internal dialogs are important mediators of effective problem solving. Poor problem solvers tend to repeat dysfunctional self-statements, which make them give up more quickly and get blocked more easily in problem-solving efforts than those whose self-statements encourage active problem-solving efforts. Research evidence presented by Meichenbaum (1977) and Mahoney (1974) confirms that this procedure is an effective intrapersonal intervention for members who engage in dysfunctional internal dialogs.

THOUGHT STOPPING. Some group members have difficulty controlling maladaptive or self-defeating thoughts and internal dialogs. The thought-stopping technique is a way to help them reduce these thoughts (Upper and Cautela, 1982; Wolpe, 1973). While the member is concentrating on a thought, the worker suddenly and emphatically says, "stop." This procedure is repeated several times. The member gradually begins to think "stop" and to hear the worker's voice saying "stop" to himself or herself whenever the obtrusive thought occurs. Variations of the technique include having members pinch themselves when obtrusive thoughts occur, having them replace obtrusive thoughts with covert dialogs and images that are not self-defeating, and having members meditate on a particular scene or phrase when obtrusive thoughts occur.

REFRAMING. Reframing is a cognitive technique used to help group members see situations or problems from another point of view. Reframing "means to change the conceptual and/or emotional setting or viewpoint in relation to which the situation is experienced and to place it in another frame which fits the facts of the same concrete situation equally well or even better, and thereby changes its entire meaning" (Watzlawick, Weakland, and Fisch, 1974, p. 95). For example, a member who complains that he is afraid to ask a co-worker to dinner might be helped to reframe the situation as one where he is sparing himself and his co-worker from possible romantic entanglements that may interfere with job performance. In another case, a single parent who is angry at her former husband for encouraging their child to fight back when teased may be helped to reframe the situation as one in which her former husband is helping the child develop and maintain a male identity.

Once a member experiences a problem from a new perspective, the positive aspects of the situation are highlighted and the negative aspects of the situation have a better chance of being changed. The woman, for example, thanked her former husband for staying involved with their child and suggested some other ways that the husband might help the child, such as how to settle disputes without fighting. The male group member developed a platonic friendship with his co-worker.

Reframing can also be used to help a member to experience a problem or concern as an asset (Haley, 1973). For example, a member's spouse does not want to have sexual relations. This problem can be viewed as a helpful sign that something is wrong in their relationship. The member will know when this problem is worked out when the couple begins to have sexual relations regularly again.

COGNITIVE IMAGERY TECHNIQUES. Flooding and implosion are two cognitive imagery techniques that are useful for extinguishing excessive and unproductive reactions to feared or anxiety-provoking events (Shipley and Boudewyns, 1980; Rimm and Masters, 1974). In implosion, the member is asked to imagine the most extreme version of a feared event or stimulus within the protected environment of the group. Thus, if a group member experiences anxiety when thinking about asking someone for a date, the member would be asked to imagine that person saying no and making a disparaging remark such as, "I wouldn't go out with someone like you" or, "You're not sophisticated enough for me." Because the member will not experience any horrible consequences from such a rebuff, he or she will overcome the fear associated with the possible consequences of asking for a date. Members' reactions to the use of this technique are often comments such as "that wasn't so bad" or "I didn't like the reaction I received, but I learned that I could live with it. I won't be so afraid of the consequences the next time."

Flooding is a procedure similar to implosion except that the member is asked to imagine the actual feared event rather than any extreme or exaggerated version of it. Feedback from other group members can be used to help the member see that although reactions may, at times, be unpleasant, they can be handled without great difficulty. The member learns how others cope with unpleasant reactions and develops his or her own methods for coping.

Research evidence on flooding and implosion suggests that in-vivo exposure to the situation or event is more successful than imagined exposure (Rimm and Masters, 1974). In group treatment, a role play exercise may be used to expose a member to the feared situation. When the member practices handling the situation in the group, the member can then be assigned the task of experiencing the situation outside the group. Because duration of exposure is also associated with treatment outcome, the member should be encouraged to practice coping with the situation several times inside and outside the group.

A variety of other cognitive imagery techniques can be used effectively in groups. Lazarus (1971) suggests that rational imagery can be used effectively to help members challenge irrational beliefs and assumptions and to act effectively in anxiety-producing situations. For example, in practicing to be more effective in a situation in which a member would routinely begin irrational self-talk, the member could use rational imagery including a covert dialog that challenges irrational self-talk and replaces it with rational statements. Other cognitive imagery techniques include imagining pleasant events occurring while being in anxiety-producing, feared situations. For example, in a group for agoraphobics, members could be asked to imagine themselves walking in a beautiful outdoor setting on a sunny, autumn day.

When using imagery techniques, the worker should ensure that members remain in a relaxed state and that they are able to vividly imagine the situation. Members should be instructed to signal the worker immediately if their anxiety increases or if the cognitive image they are visualizing fades. To help produce vivid imagery, the worker should recite a richly detailed image while members close their eyes and are in a relaxed state.

PROGRESSIVE MUSCLE RELAXATION. Progressive muscle relaxation combines cognitive instructions with physical activities to relieve stress and help group members overcome anxiety. The basic premise is that muscle tension is related to anxiety and stress. Helping members to reduce muscle tension will therefore help to relieve anxiety.

With members either seated in comfortable chairs or reclining on the floor, the worker explains the entire procedure to them. Members should be as comfortable as possible throughout the procedure. In a soft, calm, hypnotic voice, the worker (or an audio-taped voice) repeats the relaxation instructions, which include tensing and relaxing each of the major muscle groups in the body. For example, the worker might say, "stretch your arms out next to you (or on your lap, if seated). Make a fist with both hands as hard as you can. Feel the tension and tightness in your hand. Keep your hands clenched (ten seconds). Now relax. Just let your hand rest against the floor (or on your lap, if seated). Notice how the tension and tightness are leaving your hands. Notice how the feelings of tension are being replaced by a warm feeling of relaxation and comfort. Notice how your hands feel now as compared to when you were tensing them."

In this manner each of the muscle groups are tensed and relaxed. Instructions for the entire procedure will not be given here since several other excellent sources exist (see, for example, Bernstein and Borkovec, 1973; Wolpe, 1973; or Rimm and Masters, 1974, for complete instructions about the progressive muscle relaxation procedure). Records and audio-tape cassettes are also available with a complete set of instructions (Bernstein and Borkovec, 1973).

Although progressive muscle relaxation is most often conducted in individual treatment, it can be used effectively in group treatment (Rose, 1977, Wolpe, 1973). Some research has shown that group desensitization is more effective than individual desensitization (see Rose, p. 124–125). The major drawbacks in using this technique in group treatment is that it requires cooperation from every member. A single member who distracts the group can ruin the effect of the procedure for everyone else. Sometimes the distraction may be unintentional such as when a member falls asleep and begins to snore. In other situations, the distraction may be intentional. For example, a member who is not motivated may laugh or joke during the first tension release cycle, thereby distracting other group members.

In order to use relaxation effectively, the entire procedure should be explained before beginning. To reduce intentional distractions, members should have the opportunity to voice any questions or any reluctance about using the procedure before beginning. To reduce unintentional distractions, members should be given a signal to let the group leader know if they are having a problem. For example, a member might not be able to relax or in rare cases may become more tense. The member can signal the worker and the worker can give that member individual attention.

The relaxing nature of the procedure, dim lights, and comfortable position sometimes cause members to fall asleep. However, the regular breathing or snoring of a sleeping member can be distracting to other group members. Such unintentional distractions can be reduced if the worker explains that sleeping members will be awakened by a touch on the hand or arm.

Other relaxation procedures can be used as a substitute for progressive muscle relaxation. For example, some workers prefer mediation, bioenergetics, hypnosis, rolfing (deep muscle massage), or jogging. Although each of these procedures was developed from differing theoretical orientations, they may be used as alternatives for achieving a similar result, a relaxed group member.

SYSTEMATIC DESENSITIZATION.   The technique of systematic desensitization can be particularly effective for treatment groups composed of members with phobias. In systematic desensitization, the worker helps members to construct a hierarchy of situations or scenes that are feared. Starting with the least feared situations and progressing to the most feared situation, members are asked to imagine each situation while they are in a state of deep muscle relaxation induced by progressive muscle relaxation.

A hierarchy of situations should consist of at least ten scenes in which the member experiences gradually increasing levels of anxiety. For example, a hierarchy for a member who has been too fearful to date consists of (1) thinking about a prospective dating partner, (2) considering asking a particular person for a date, (3) planning where to go on the date, (4) planning how to ask the person for a date, (5) approaching the person to ask for a date, (6) opening the conversation with the person, (7) asking the person for a date, (8) driving to the person's house for the date, (9) walking up to the person's home, and (10) going out together. Depending on the extent and the intensity of the anxiety, hierarchies may contain many more scenes. Scenes should not jump too quickly from a low to a high level of anxiety. For very fearful members, it is necessary to construct hierarchies with as many as twenty or thirty scenes.

Once the members are helped to construct their own hierarchies (even if each member has the same phobia, individual hierarchies will differ), the progressive muscle relaxation technique is used to induce a state of relaxation. The members are then asked to imagine the first scene on their hierarchy as if they were actually involved in it for approximately ten seconds (Wolpe, 1973). If members experience anxiety, they are instructed to signal by raising a finger. Members experiencing anxiety are told to stop imagining the scene and are helped to return to their former state of relaxation. When they are fully relaxed, they can imagine the scene again.

At this point, desensitization proceeds at the pace of the slowest group member (Fisher, 1978), unless some provision is made for members to complete their hierarchies at their own pace. One method to overcome this problem is to have members work in pairs, helping each other work through the hierarchy each has developed (Rose, 1977). The worker should not allow members to work on their hierarchies for more than thirty minutes, because the desensitization procedure is quite demanding, both in terms of continuously visualizing scenes and in remaining in a deeply relaxed state. If members do not complete their hierarchies during one meeting, they can begin the next meeting with the next to last scene they had completed successfully in the previous meeting.

## Interpersonal Interventions

Group work is an especially appropriate modality for working with interpersonal problems. Used effectively, the group can become a natural laboratory for examining and improving the relationships members have with one another. Unlike individual treatment, a group offers members the opportunity to demonstrate their interpersonal skills and to receive feedback from a variety of different people. Members can serve as models for each other of particular interpersonal skills and can play various roles in situations acted out in the group.

Interpersonal behaviors can be learned in three ways: (1) indirectly, by listening to others describe how to behave in a situation, (2) vicariously, by watching what other people do or say, and (3) directly, by repeating and practicing new behaviors. When learned directly, a new behavior is usually performed on a trial-and-error basis until it is performed appropriately.

Because learning a new behavior by hearing it described by another group member or the worker is often imprecise and fraught with potential misinterpretation, teaching behavior is most adequately accomplished by having a member watch someone else perform a behavior correctly, and by having the member practice the new behavior in a role play exercise. Many novice and experienced workers allow the group to spend too much time discussing how to behave without actually helping members to practice new behaviors. Perhaps this is because of the contrived nature of role play situations, the initial resistance of some members to role playing, and the extra instructions and direction the worker must provide to make a role play successful. The learning that occurs from watching a model and rehearsing a new behavior, as compared to merely talking about how to perform a new behavior, suggests that both modeling and role play techniques should be used more frequently by workers when helping members learn new or improved interpersonal behaviors.

*Learning by Observing Models.* A number of factors affect the extent to which behaviors are learned by observing others (Bandura, 1977b). It is important for workers to understand the process underlying observational learning so that they can use modeling to help members solve interpersonal problems and learn new interpersonal skills.

Figure 8–3 illustrates the major components of observational learning. As can be seen, performance of the modeled behavior depends on (1) the level of attention or awareness of the observer, (2) the extent to which the observer retains what is observed, (3) the observer's abilities to perform the observed behavior, and (4) the extent to which the observer is motivated to perform the behavior (Bandura, 1977b).

The attention of a member who observes a model is important, because although behavior may be learned without one's awareness, attention is always selective and it is greatly facilitated by focusing awareness on what is being observed. The worker can help to focus awareness by calling members' attention to particular aspects of a model's behavior. For example, a member who is learning to be more assertive may be asked to pay particular

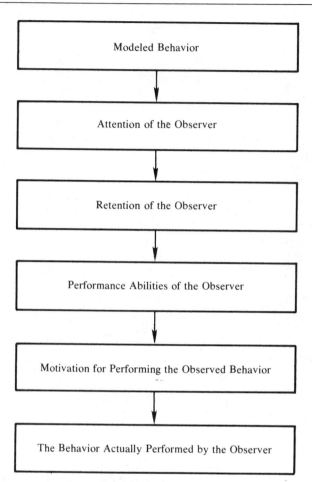

**Figure 8–3** The Process of Observational Learning

attention to the facial expressions, body positions, and voice tones of a member who is modeling an assertive response. Attentional processes are also enhanced by the attractiveness of a model. For example, a member is more likely to pay attention to a group member who is held in high regard than to a member who has little status within the group.

Members find models most attractive when they are similar to themselves. Thus, workers should try to match the demographic characteristics of models to the members who are observing them.

Retentional processes are also important in learning an observed behavior. In addition to developing images of the behavior to be learned that can be easily retreived from a member's memory, retention is often facilitated if the model explains the covert and overt processes he or she goes through before performing a behavior. These explanations help the member develop a cognitive structure in which to organize perceptual images. When modeling an assertive behavior, the worker may, for example, explain the cognitive process occurring before the assertive response. Internal dialogs such as, "I say to myself, I have a right to tell that person _____ _____ _____" can be helpful to members observing someone modeling a behavior. The model may also explain general principles. For example, in making an assertive response, the member modeling the behavior might explain, "In general, I am always direct—I explain my needs to the person and I make a direct request for him to change his behavior." Explaining general principles also provides an organizing framework that the member can use in a variety of different situations encountered in the future.

The member's ability to perform the modeled response is a critical component of observational learning. The member may pay careful attention to the way a model performs a behavior and retain details of the performance but may not be able to respond in a similar fashion. The best way to ensure that a member is able to perform a behavior correctly is to have the member perform the behavior in the group and receive feedback about the performance. If it is available, videotape feedback of the member's performance can also be effective in helping to learn new interpersonal behaviors.

Group members may know how to behave in interpersonal situations but may not do so because they lack motivation. What factors increase motivation? According to Bandura (1977b), behaviors are more likely to occur if the observer sees others being rewarded for similar performances. Conversely, if an observer sees others being sanctioned for performing a given behavior, the observer is less likely to reproduce a response that may also result in similar sanctions. A member, however, may not have to observe someone being sanctioned in order not to perform a new behavior. New behaviors are often difficult to perform until they are well learned. Difficulties associated with learning a new behavior, along with the absence of strong incentives, are frequently a sufficient disincentive for members considering performing new behaviors. Therefore, observational learning is selective. In daily living we often do not repeat a new behavior that we see performed by someone else.

In order to ensure that group members learn new behaviors by observing the worker or other members, several factors should be present. Members' attention should be carefully focused on how the behavior is being performed. Members should be helped to retain cognitive images of observed behavior by developing a set of organizing principles, a cognitive framework, which explains why a model responded in a particular manner. In order to build members' capacity to respond, they should practice responses and receive feedback about the quality of their performances. Members' motivation for performing observed behaviors can be increased by demonstrating to them that the incentives sufficiently outweigh the disincentives for performing a particular behavior.

*Learning by Role Playing.* Role playing has been defined as a realistic enactment of a social role in an imagined social situation (Shaw and others, 1980, p. 11). It is a frequently used procedure in group work. The first reported therapeutic use of role playing was by Moreno (1946), who developed psychodrama and sociodrama procedures in the 1930s. Kelly (1955) also reported early uses of role playing procedures in the development of fixed role and exaggerated role therapies. Since that time, many books have been written about role playing from a variety of theoretical orientations (see, for example, Klein, 1956; Corsini, 1966; Blatner, 1973; Maier, Solem, and Maier, 1975; Shaw and others, 1980).

There are at least five uses of role playing in group work, including (1) assessment, (2) stimulation, (3) understanding, (4) decision making, and (5) behavior change (Etcheverry, Siporin, and Toseland, in press). Role playing is a powerful tool for any of these purposes. As shown in Table 8–1, role playing techniques increase members' awareness and understanding of their interpersonal skills, and produce behavior changes by providing members with corrective feedback and the opportunity to practice improved responses in the sheltered environment of the group.

Different types of role playing techniques available for use by group workers can be divided into structured and unstructured procedures. Structured procedures use predetermined scripts or vignettes developed by the leader. Members are called upon to act out prescribed roles and in this way learn to handle specific situations believed to be important by the leader. For example, in an assertiveness training program group members may be asked to role play a number of common situations requiring assertive responses such as someone getting ahead in a line, returning damaged merchandise, or turning down a request to borrow an item. Structured role plays are not spontaneous, but they have the advantage of ensuring that the worker is ready with an effective response.

Different unstructured role play procedures are listed in Table 8–1. According to Shaw and others (1980), these procedures are developmental and open-ended. They allow for spontaneous, emerging processes of learning and problem solving. Unstructured role play procedures can be further divided into primary and secondary procedures. Primary role play procedures can be used alone to accomplish particular purposes, whereas secondary procedures are used in conjunction with primary procedures to extend their impact and widen their scope (Etcheverry, Siporin, and Toseland, in press).

### Primary Role Play Procedures

OWN ROLE.    In the own role procedure, a member uses his or her experiences and plays the protagonist. Other roles are played by auxiliaries who are other group members or the worker. Auxiliaries may represent persons, feeling states, thoughts, or objects. The own role technique is particularly useful in assessing a member's interpersonal skills, because it allows the worker and other group members to observe how the protagonist acts in a particular situation. The own role procedure is also helpful as a means for members to practice new behaviors. Supportive procedures such as the soliloquy, on-the-spot interview, or doubling can be used to increase a member's awareness of his or her behavior as he or she performs the role of protagonist.

ROLE REVERSAL.    In role reversal, a group member acts as the protagonist by taking on the role of another person. For example, a member may act in the role of his spouse. The procedure enables a member to experience a situation from another's point of view. It is particularly useful for teaching empathy, especially if it is used with doubling or soliloquy. It helps to clarify situations and it increases members' self-awareness. As Shaw and others (1980) point out, role reversal also increases spontaneity, flexibility, and openness of the member playing the protagonist's role. Variations of this procedure include substitute role playing (playing a symbolic, substitute role) and role distance (playing an emotionally distant role).

AUTODRAMA, MONODRAMA, AND CHAIRING.   A procedure in which a group member plays multiple roles is variously called autodrama, monodrama, and chairing (Blatner, 1973). The multiple roles a member plays represent the different ways the member views himself or herself or the different ways others view the member. The procedure is usually conducted using one or more empty chairs, each representing a role, a character part, or a personality aspect. The member switches from one chair to another as he or she changes roles. When occupying each chair, the person initiates and maintains a dialog with the other chairs, which represent other aspects of the person's self.

The technique is particularly useful in helping members become aware of the various roles they play and their impact on each other. It is also useful in helping members assess internal dialogs and self-talk, including irrational beliefs and devaluating self-statements. Therefore, the procedure can be used effectively in cooperation with cognitive restructuring procedures to practice adaptive self-statements and self-instructions that aid effective problem solving. Self-role and double chairing are other names for this procedure.

SCULPTING AND CHOREOGRAPHY.   Also called action sociogram, variations of the sculpting and choreography technique are psychodrama and sociodrama (Moreno, 1946; Blatner, 1973). In this procedure, a member, as protagonist, is directed to sculpt or position himself or herself and other group members in a drama that represents a symbolic or real situation in the member's life. The protagonist explains each person's role and the worker acts as leader, directing the action, which may last for an extended period of time.

The dramatic enactment is designed to expose intense feelings and conflicts in a member's life. Because of this, it can be used as an assessment device by the worker. Another benefit of the technique is that it immerses the whole group in intense participatory involvement leading to in-depth self-disclosure and enactment of crucial concerns and issues. In addition to the self-awareness this produces, the procedure helps the protagonist understand the importance of others in his or her own life situations. Although there is little empirical evidence for the efficacy of the technique, clinical reports and our own experience suggest that the cathartic experience and heightened awareness that result from participating in a dramatic enactment can lead to changes in members' thoughts, feelings, behaviors, attitudes, and interaction patterns. The psychodrama variation of the technique focuses on the internal, psychological status of the actors. The sociodrama variation emphasizes the social and environmental aspects of the protagonist's situa-

*Table 8-1*

## USES OF UNSTRUCTURED ROLE PLAY PROCEDURES

| Procedure | Awareness/Understanding | Behavior Change |
|---|---|---|
| A. Primary Role Play Procedures | | |
| 1. Own role | Demonstrates and clarifies members' behavior, their role in interpersonal interactions, and their concerns and problems | Allows members to try out and practice new behaviors |
| | Facilitates members' insight into their own feelings, thoughts, and behaviors | Reduces members' performance anxiety |
| | Identifies situational cues to facilitate differential responses | Prepares members for obstacles and setbacks |
| | Identifies members' problems and concerns | |
| 2. Role reversal | Stimulates empathy for another person whose role is being enacted by the protagonist | Encourages spontaneity and participation |
| | Increases members' awareness of cognitive and affective aspects of their own behavior in a role, including the expectations of other people | Facilitates changes in members' expectations of others |
| | Objectifies and clarifies the situational context of members' own behaviors | Facilitates change in members' behavior |
| | | Improves empathic skills |
| 3. Autodrama/monodrama/ chairing | Same as for own role and role reversal procedures | Same as for own role and role reversal procedures |
| | Identifies and clarifies members' own feelings at deeper levels than own role or role reversal procedures | Facilitates learning of adaptive "self-talk" |
| | Increases members' awareness of their own "self-talk" | Enables changes on deeper, more complex levels than own role or role reversal procedures |
| 4. Sculpting/choreography (Action sociogram) | Stimulates members' awareness and discussion of their own behavior and the group's interaction patterns | Facilitates changes in members' attitudes, behaviors, and interaction patterns |

| Procedure | Awareness/Understanding | Behavior Change |
|---|---|---|
| B. Supportive Role Play Procedures | | |
| 1. On-the-spot interview | Identifies and clarifies members' thoughts and feelings while they are in a role | Provides practice in self-awareness and self-talk |
| | Connects thinking and feeling to behaviors in a role | |
| 2. Soliloquy | Same as on-the-spot interview procedure but less structured | Same as on-the-spot interview procedure |
| 3. Doubling | Same as on-the-spot interview procedure | Same as on-the-spot interview procedure |
| | Helps members to verbalize and express covert thoughts, feelings, and behaviors | Gives permission and support for members' "owning" their own thoughts, feelings, and behaviors |
| | Identifies new behaviors for acquisition | Facilitates expression of feelings |
| | | Promotes members' skill in using feelings as cues for appropriate responses |
| | | Allows members to practice their self-expression skills |
| 4. Mirror | Promotes members' knowledge of the consequences of their own behavior upon others | Provides members the opportunity to practice new behaviors |
| | Enables self-confrontation | Enables feedback and reinforcement when learning new behaviors |
| 5. Sharing | Universalizes members' experiences | Provides support and confirmation of members' experiences, abilities, etc. |
| | Provides a model of and experience with others' self-disclosure | Facilitates learning of self-disclosure skills |

tion. For an excellent, in-depth explanation of these procedures, see Blatner (1973).

### Supplementary Role Play Procedures

ON-THE-SPOT INTERVIEW.   The on-the-spot interview involves stopping the role play action before it is finished and interviewing one or more of the actors. The worker asks specific, detailed questions designed to elicit particular thoughts and feelings at that point in the role play. The procedure is designed to increase an actor's awareness of cognitive, affective, and behavioral aspects of a role performance. It identifies self-statements and self-talk that is dysfunctional and self-devaluating. It also teaches self-observation and enhances self-awareness.

SOLILOQUY.   The soliloquy procedure involves stopping the role play action and asking an actor to disclose what he or she is thinking or feeling. Unlike the on-the-spot interview in which an actor is asked specific close-ended questions, in the soliloquy the questions that are asked are open-ended, encouraging the member to engage in a monolog that discloses in-depth thoughts and feelings. The procedure is particularly useful for increasing a member's self-awareness.

DOUBLING.   The doubling procedure uses an auxiliary group member to act as the alter-ego or inner voice of the protagonist. To emphasize the identification with the protagonist, the double is required to speak in the first person, for example, saying, "I feel _____ _____ _____" or, "I think _____ _____ _____." Variations on the procedure are the "divided double" and the "multiple double." In the divided double, the alter ego speaks for different parts of the protagonist's inner self. The multiple double calls for two or more actors to speak for different aspects of the protagonist's self. To validate the truth of a double's statements in offering inferences, interpretations, or alternative reactions, the protagonist is sometimes asked to repeat and to accept or reject the double's statements.

The doubling procedure can serve several important functions. It helps to make role plays more dramatic and in-depth experiences. It facilitates understanding and self-awareness of the protagonist's behavior. In addition to fostering insight, it gives permission for the protagonist to acknowledge repressed or taboo thoughts and feelings. It also increases the emotional sensitivity and self-expression of the protagonist. The procedure is often used in conjunction with own role, chairing, and sculpting procedures.

MIRROR.   In the mirror procedure, a group member re-enacts a role played performance to demonstrate the performance to the protagonist. Other members can verify the accuracy of the replay. The procedure may also be used in an exaggerated, amplified, and stereotypical manner in order to emphasize particular aspects of the protagonist's behavior.

The procedure is useful as a confrontational technique to help the protagonist gain awareness of his or her behavior. It is an excellent substitute for videotape feedback when videotape equipment is unavailable. The procedure is particularly useful in conjunction with modeling, coaching, and prompting to provide feedback to a member who is attempting to learn a new behavior. It is also a way of involving other group members in a member's situation, facilitating their empathy and their skills in self-expression.

SHARING. The sharing procedure is often used at the close of role play action. Group members give the protagonist and the other actors feedback about their performances. They may also share similar experiences and self-disclose their own reactions and feelings regarding the role play. The procedure is designed to provide supportive feedback to the member who risked himself or herself in revealing a difficult situation by acting as the protagonist in the role play. It also facilitates the learning of self-disclosure skills.

## Environmental Interventions

A third way for workers to intervene is by helping members to modify or change the psychosocial and physical situations in which they live. Environmental modification is an important but often neglected aspect of social work practice (Grinnell, 1973). Environmental interventions consist of (1) connecting members to concrete resources, (2) expanding members' social networks, (3) modifying the contingencies that result when members perform desired behaviors, and (4) planning physical environments to facilitate members' goal achievement. The roles of enabler, broker, and advocate, discussed previously, are particularly useful when making environmental interventions.

*Connecting Members to Concrete Resources.* To connect clients to concrete resources, the worker first identifies the member's need for a particular resource and then assesses the member's ability and motivation to follow through and obtain the resource. For highly motivated, well-functioning group members, the worker may be able to act as a broker, identifying a contact person at the appropriate resource and giving the member general information about what to expect when contacting the resource. The worker verifies that the member has obtained the needed resource during the next group session.

In some treatment groups, for example, those composed of severely impaired psychiatric patients or older persons with organic brain disorders, workers may have to take additional steps to ensure that members obtain the resources they need. It may, for example, take some time to prepare members for a referral because of their lack of motivation or their failure to recognize their need for services. It may also be necessary to contact family members or guardians to help prepare them for a referral. Members' impairments may limit or prevent them from contacting resources without assistance. Transportation may have to be arranged and, in some cases, the worker, an aide, or a volunteer may have to accompany the member to the resource. It may also be necessary to teach members the skills necessary to obtain a needed resource. For example, it was necessary to teach an unem-

ployed group member interviewing and resumé writing skills, before suggesting that he renew his search for a job.

*Expanding Members' Social Networks.*    Another type of environmental intervention consists of helping socially isolated members to expand their social
networks. In recent years, social network interventions have received growing attention (see, for example, Toseland, Decker, and Bliesner, 1979; Collins and Pancoast, 1970). The first step in expanding a member's social
network is to analyze the member's current social relationships. Figure 8–4
is an illustration of the social network of Tom, a socially isolated member of
a support group for recently separated persons. The diagram indicates that
Tom has only two active social relationships. Tom's other network relationships shown in Figure 8–4 are inactive. Tom no longer plays with the softball
team. He no longer sees Jean or Bob, with whom he used to be quite friendly.
His brother lives nearly 1,000 miles away, and they rarely see one another.

Diagramming a member's social network on newsprint or some other
media stimulates group discussion about ways to expand it. For example,
after examining Figure 8–4, several group members suggested that Tom
renew former network relationships that were not actively pursued after he
got married three years ago. In order to do this, Tom rejoined the softball
team. He also renewed his friendships with Jean and Bob. In addition to
reactivating existing network relationships. Tom was encouraged to join
Parents Without Partners, a self-help group, which sponsors many social,
recreational, and educational events in the community where he lives.

Analyzing one group member's social network can stimulate other
members to consider their own social networks. In the group described,
several other members became aware that they could also benefit from
expanding their own social relationships. After confirming that group members wanted to become more actively involved with one another, the worker
suggested that members exchange telephone numbers and choose one person to call during the week. By holding one meeting at a member's home and
by supporting members' suggestions that they get together informally with
each other after the meeting, the worker encouraged members to form a
supportive social network for one another. Child care responsibilities limited
many of the members' abilities to socialize and so five members who had
children decided to help each other with child care responsibilities, thereby
increasing each others' opportunity to engage in social activities without
having to spend limited resources on child care. Thus, through a worker's
interventive efforts and the mutual aid properties of the group, members'
social networks were expanded.

*Contingency Management Procedures.*    In order that members can maintain
the gains they make in treatment outside of the group, it is often necessary to
modify or change the rewards and punishments they receive for behaving in
ways that are not consistent with their treatment goals. This procedure is
sometimes called contingency management, because the rewards or
punishments that are contingent on the performance of a behavior are mod-

ified to increase or decrease the probability that a behavior will be performed in the future.

Contingencies that increase the probability that a member will perform a behavior are defined as reinforcers. Typical positive reinforcers include social rewards that are verbal, such as praise, and non-verbal, such as a smile. a pat on the back, and similar signs of approval. They also include tangible rewards such as money and food.

Negative reinforcers also increase behaviors. But unlike positive reinforcers that increase behavior through rewards, negative reinforcers increase behavior through aversive means. Negative reinforcers include yelling, nagging, and "silent treatment." When workers help members modify contingencies so that desired behaviors are maintained and increased, they should emphasize the use of positive reinforcers that members enjoy receiving rather than negative reinforcers that are unpleasant and often result in deleterious side effects such as anger.

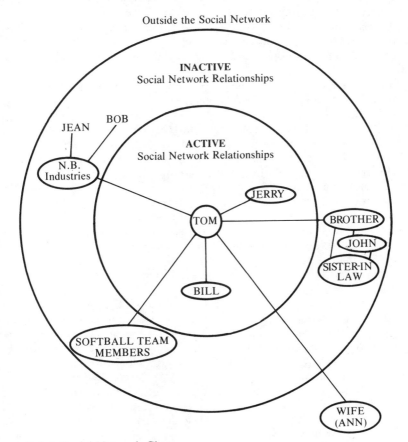

**Figure 8-4** A Social Network Chart

Unless a behavior is self-reinforcing, it will decrease if rewards are not received for performing it. Therefore, ignoring a behavior will tend to extinguish it if the behavior is not self-reinforcing to the member. Social disapproval, taking tangible rewards away from a person, and physical punishment will also decrease behaviors.

In general, workers should encourage the use of positive reinforcers and extinction procedures rather than negative reinforcers or punishment procedures. Often, it is sufficient to reward a desired behavior and ignore an undesirable behavior. Although it is better to use positive reinforcers whenever possible, in some circumstances punishments may be imposed for failure to comply with group rules. For example, the members of a children's group decided that those who came late to group meetings would clean up after snacks were served.

As Rose (1977) points out, the undesirable side effects of punishment procedures are avoided when members impose their own punishments, sometimes referred to as "response costs." Thus, when punishment procedures are used, they should not be imposed unilaterally by the worker. The group as a whole should decide on a policy, that is, the type of punishment, social disapproval, or removal from the group, and the circumstances in which particular sanctions will be applied. The resulting policy should be applied uniformly.

The worker should help the group develop a realistic policy that is not too severe. Sometimes members develop unrealistically harsh rules to govern behavior in the group. It is common for members of children's groups to develop group rules which, left unchallenged, would lead to severe punishment. For example, in one group, members decided that anyone "caught laughing" should be thrown out of the group. In such cases, the worker should intervene and help the group develop less severe sanctions for misbehavior. William Golding's novel *Lord of the Flies* is an excellent literary example of how groups can decide on punishments that are too severe.

When using contingency management procedures, the worker should begin by helping members to identify the rewards and punishments that they receive for performing desired behaviors. These contingencies are identified by monitoring the consequences resulting from the performance of a particular behavior. If contingencies do not act to increase desired behavior and decrease undesired behavior, the worker can help the member modify them. Sometimes members may be able to administer their own rewards and punishments. For example, members may be encouraged to praise themselves for performing a certain behavior, to take themselves out for a good meal, or to buy a new piece of clothing. Such self-reinforcement procedures have been shown to be effective in helping members to control their own behaviors (see Thoreson and Mahoney, 1974; Stuart, 1977).

It can also be helpful to involve other group members or significant others in members' lives in modifying the contingent rewards and punishments members receive for performing desired behaviors. Family members and friends can be helpful in providing an environment that promotes therapeutic goals. For example, a wife or husband may compliment his or her spouse for positive changes. A mother or father may praise their daughter for helping her little brother with his homework.

In order to formalize agreement about what behaviors to reinforce, a contingency contract can be developed. According to Rose (1977, p. 92), "contingency contracts are written agreements between two or more persons in which consequences following the performance of specified behaviors are administered by another party." For example, the father of an adolescent group member may agree to take his son on a fishing trip if his son agrees to attend classes without misbehaving for two weeks.

There are many different types of contingency contracts. As mentioned, members may administer their own rewards and punishments in self-administered contingency contracts. Contracts may be made between the group member and significant others, between two group members, or between all group members and the worker. Contracts may also be reciprocal, that is, parties to the contract reward each other for performing desired behaviors. Reciprocal contracts are particularly useful in couples groups where spouses can reinforce each other for performing desired behaviors.

By using contingency management procedures, the worker helps members to perform desired behaviors by changing the environmental consequences that result when a behavior is performed. Too often, workers intervene effectively in the group to help members reach desired goals but fail to pay any attention to what will happen when members try to perform desired behaviors outside the group. Contingency management procedures are a useful way to extend therapeutic interventions beyond the boundaries of group sessions.

*Planning Physical Environments.*   Helping members to modify the physical environments in which they live is another type of environmental intervention. Although it is often given little consideration, the physical environment has a profound impact on the problems and concerns members experience. Environmental stimuli can make it easier or more difficult for a member to accomplish treatment goals. For example, members of a weight loss group find that it is more difficult to lose weight if their refrigerators are stocked with fattening foods than if their refrigerators contain only those items that are a part of the diet that members agreed upon. Similarly, it is difficult for a member of an inpatient psychotherapy group who is about to be discharged to learn independent living skills in an institutional environment that does not allow him or her to cook, clean, or shop.

To the extent possible, workers should help members modify physical environments so they promote goal achievement. In general, physical environments should give members the opportunity to practice the skills they are learning in the group. For example, members who are learning skills for independent living should have the opportunity to practice as many of these skills as feasible in the institutional setting in which they live. Physical environments should reduce barriers that are likely to impede a member's attempts to accomplish a goal. For example, a member who is attempting to stop drinking should remove all alcohol from his home.

Environmental interventions should be proactive as well as reactive. That is, in addition to ensuring that an environment does not provide unwanted stimuli, the worker should help members modify environments so that they encourage goal-directed behavior. A member who is attempting to lose weight may, for example, place a calorie chart on his refrigerator door to help him plan meals. A member of a parenting group may place a monitoring chart in her child's room. Each time the child behaves correctly, gold stars are placed on the chart, When a certain number of stars accumulate, they can be redeemed for a trip to the zoo or extra play time with Mom or Dad. In both cases, modifications of the environment stimulate efforts toward goal achievement.

## INTERVENING IN THE GROUP AS A WHOLE

Workers select the group as a whole as the focus of interventions when they decide that the group process should be altered to help members achieve their goals. In this way, the group becomes the means as well as the context of treatment. As discussed in Chapter 3, four areas are critical to the effective functioning of any group, including (1) communication and interaction patterns, (2) attraction, (3) social controls, and (4) culture. These are the primary areas in which the worker intervenes when selecting the group as a whole as the focus of interventions.

Group dynamics have already developed before the middle stage of a treatment group's development. The worker's task in the middle stages is to maintain and enhance those dynamics that are contributing to the group's success and intervene to change those dynamics that are interfering with the group's development.

Experienced workers realize the power that group dynamics have in leading to successful group outcomes. In comparing ten different methods of leading encounter groups, Lieberman, Yalom, and Miles (1973) found that "group characteristics" such as norms, cohesiveness, and climate had an important impact both on members' satisfaction with their experience in different groups and on the overall outcomes achieved by the groups. In a study comparing methods of working with antisocial boys in groups, Feldman, Kaplinger, and Wodarski (1983) also found that group dynamics had a powerful mediating effect on outcome, regardless of the type of treatment modality used.

With these notable exceptions, studies about how specific group dynamics influence the outcome of treatment groups are rare. Evaluation of the effects of group processes on treatment outcomes are difficult to conduct because it is a complex task to sort out the separate effects of such factors as norms and cohesiveness from the effects of leadership and specific intervention procedures. A review of process studies in group treatment suggests that most are methodologically flawed (Bednar and Kaul, 1978). Therefore, recommendations about what dynamics workers should try to increase or to decrease in particular situations should be viewed cautiously. They are based largely on clinical, impressionistic data and data from secondary analyses of studies designed for other purposes.

## Changing Communication and Interaction Patterns

The worker may intervene to change the frequency, duration, distribution, or content of the communication and interaction patterns occurring in a treatment group. The frequency of interactions a member initiates in a group is important because it is difficult, if not impossible, to assess and treat a member who remains relatively silent throughout the group. Members must actively participate if they are to benefit from group treatment.

Usually, two relatively simple methods can be used to increase a member's participation. One method is to point out that a member is communicating infrequently. Although members usually respond well to such feedback, sometimes it is helpful for the worker or the member to use one of the instruments discussed in Chapter 7 to obtain objective feedback about the frequency of a member's participation. Shulman (1979) points out that what silent members really fear is being confronted with their silence. Therefore, in some cases, it may be more helpful to prompt such members to speak by such statements as, "What do you think about what _____ is saying?" or "You have some experience with this _____, what do you think?" rather than to confront them with data that suggest they are not participating frequently enough.

Another way to increase participation is to praise members when they add to the group's discussion. Positive comments such as, "that was really helpful" or, "I see that you really understand what _____ is saying" can be used to show quiet group members that their contributions are valued. Positive reinforcement procedures have been proven to be effective in increasing a member's participation in a number of studies (Rose, 1977). Other techniques to increase the frequency of a member's communication include asking the member to lead the group's discussion on a certain topic or going around the group and eliciting each member's thoughts and comments on a particular topic.

Workers may wish to change the duration of a member's communications in the group. This is particularly true with verbose members who dominate the group's discussions. Sometimes simply pointing out that other members of the group need time to participate is sufficient to limit the member's communications. For others, it is necessary to develop a contingency contract in which members agree to ignore the talkative member when he or she talks for more than a specified length of time. Alternatives to this procedure include interrupting the member after he or she talks for a certain amount of time or reminding the member with a nonverbal cue that he or she is talking too much.

Workers may also want to change the distribution of communication and interaction patterns. What distributions might workers find problematic? Ideally, each member of the group should have an opportunity to participate. Although some group members may be more involved in a particular discussion than other members, communications should be distributed fairly evenly among all members over the course of several meetings. Workers should prevent situations in which they are doing most of the communicating or situations in which members direct most of their comments to the worker rather than to each other. Workers may also want to intervene when members of subgroups interact primarily with one another rather than with all group members.

As in efforts to change the frequency and duration of members' communication patterns, the most successful interventions for changing the distribution of communication patterns include cues to help members remain aware of their inappropriate communications, accompanied by prompts and positive reinforcement to help them change these patterns. For example, Toseland, Krebs, and Vahsen (1978) reported that an intervention consisting of cues, verbal prompts, and reinforcement was successful in reducing the number of member-to-leader communications and increasing the number of member-to-member communications.

The content of the messages sent and received in the group is just as important as the frequency, duration, and distribution of group members' communications. Workers should be particularly concerned about the task orientation and the tone of the messages communicated in the group. Workers should intervene when most communications are not task-relevant or when they are excessively negative. Of course, some group discussion will not be task-relevant. Joking, "small talk," and interesting but irrelevant stories often help to make the group more attractive for its members. Members have a need to express their own identity in the gruop. However, task-irrelevant discussions should not be allowed to take a great deal of the group's time. Members come to treatment groups for particular purposes and too much irrelevant conversation interferes with their ability to achieve goals, ultimately leading to their dissatisfaction with the group.

Usually, it is sufficient to point out excessive digressions to the group, calling the group's attention back to the session agenda and the goals that should have been briefly mentioned at the beginning of the meeting. In some cases, however, such an intervention may not be sufficient to help the group return to a task-centered discussion. The group's digression may signify a test or a challenge to the worker's authority, dissatisfaction with the content outlined in the session agenda, or an indication that group members are too fearful or anxious to discuss a particular topic. In such cases, it is helpful for the worker to point out his or her hypothesis about the reasons for the group's digression. Through discussion and feedback, the worker can help members to decide on how best to renew their focus on the group's goals. This may, for example, make members aware that they are avoiding a difficult issue that they need to discuss. In other cases, it may lead to changes in the worker's style or the session agenda.

Workers should also be concerned about the tone of the messages conveyed in the group. Frequent "put downs," excessive negative comments without suggestions of ways to improve, and infrequent supportive, warm, or reinforcing comments make the group unattractive for its members. To change the tone of messages being communicated in the group, workers can act as models, making supportive, warm, reinforcing comments whenever possible. Workers can also show their disapproval of negative comments by ignoring them or by suggesting that the member who makes the negative comment accompany it with a positive comment. Exercises designed to help members give positive feedback can also be helpful. For example, a worker might say, "I've noticed we make a lot of comments about what a person does wrong during our role plays. How about for the next role play, each member tries to identify at least one thing that the person doing the role play does well."

### Changing the Group's Attraction for Its Members

There is a general consensus in the group work literature that workers should help their groups become cohesive and attractive units. In his classic text on group psychotherapy, Yalom (1975) points out the benefits that cohesive groups have on members' self-esteem, their willingness to listen to and be influenced by others, and their continued attendance and participation in group meetings.

Liberman (1971) and Rose (1977) both suggest that cohesion and interpersonal attraction can be increased by rewarding members for their participation in the group. Groups also tend to be more cohesive and attractive when they are relatively small and there is plenty of interaction that is distributed fairly evenly throughout the group. In small groups where there is a good deal of interaction, members have the feeling that their ideas are being heard and considered, whereas in large groups and groups with poorly distributed communication patterns, members who are not a part of the "inner circle" of decision makers often feel that their ideas and suggestions are not being given sufficient attention. Suggestions made in the previous section for redistributing communication patterns can be used to help groups become more attractive for their members. For large groups, procedures such as Phillips 66 (described in Chapter 9) can also be useful in maintaining the group's attractiveness for its members.

Refreshments such as coffee and donuts often make groups more attractive for members. Socializing over coffee during a break in a long session or immediately following a short session helps to reduce the exclusive problem focus of groups and allows members to get to know each other as "ordinary" people rather than as "clients." For some group members, such as children and psychiatric inpatients, whose access to donuts, coffee, or soda is limited, refreshments can serve as particularly strong incentives for participating in the group. Other ways to increase the attractiveness of groups include the dispensing of rewards such as a weekend pass as an incentive for participation in a group, planning interesting program activities and outings for the agenda of future group meetings, encouraging members to select topics for group discussion, and ensuring that members continue to make progress toward their treatment goals.

Are there times when a worker would not want to increase a group's cohesion? Cohesion should not be increased in groups in which antitherapeutic norms have been established. Research by Feldman, Kaplinger, and Wodarski (1983), for example, has found that in groups composed solely of antisocial boys, interpersonal integration, defined as the reciprocal liking of the boys in a group for one another, was negatively associated with treatment outcomes. Apparently, in these groups cohesion resulted in peer pressure to conform to antitherapeutic group norms. Thus, antisocial behaviors were reinforced rather than extinguished by group treatment. Similarly, in work with street gangs, the more cohesive a gang is, the more difficult it is for the worker to influence the group.

## Using Social Controls Effectively

The social controls exerted in a group can enhance the functioning of the group as a whole or they can lead to the demise of the group. Social controls exerted through norms, roles, status hierarchies, and the various power bases from which the leader draws his or her authority are important forces within the group. As mentioned in Chapter 3, without social controls, group interaction would become chaotic and unpredictable, and the group would soon cease functioning. But in groups in which social controls are too strong, members soon feel restricted and coerced. They tend to rebel against the control or refuse to attend future meetings.

During the middle stage of treatment groups, the effective worker helps the group develop social controls to integrate members' activities for goal achievement. Both normative integration (members' acceptance of group norms) and functional integration (members' assuming roles and activities that contribute to the group's work) are positively associated with beneficial group outcomes (see, for example, Feldman, Kaplinger, and Wodarski, 1983).

Workers should help members to become normatively and functionally integrated into a group. Workers should prevent the domination of a group by one or more members who have a great deal of social power. It has been found that group members who are socially powerful (able to exert a great deal of influence over the group) are likely to resist change efforts (Feldman, Kaplinger, and Wodarski, 1983).

Effective workers are potent leaders who command the respect and admiration of group members. Their interventions have considerable influence over the way a group conducts its business.[1] When workers are potent, they exert social control over the group without dominating it and without the need to apply social sanctions to control deviant members.

Why are some leaders more potent than others? Although there is no clear answer to this question, some indicators of potency can be readily identified. Potent leaders are self-confident, but they are able to admit mistakes. They have the knowledge and the practical experience to help members with their problems and concerns. They are emphatic, yet they are able to remain calm and collected in difficult situations. They tend to ignore

---

[1]For some brief, but fascinating descriptions of differences among more potent and less potent group workers, see the profiles of the encounter groups in Lieberman, M., Yalom, I., and Miles, M. *Encounter groups: First facts.* (New York: Basic Books, 1973).

rather than to sanction deviant behavior exhibited by group members, preferring to praise and encourage members for positive contributions to the group. In general, potent workers possess characteristics that members would like to achieve.

In facilitating the development of social controls that will help the group function effectively, potent workers help members adhere to therapeutic group norms and change norms that are interfering with the group accomplishing its goals. In groups that have developed therapeutic norms, the worker should help members become normatively integrated in the group by helping those who are deviating from group norms to accept and abide by them. For example, in a group that has developed a norm that members are not to be verbally abusive with one another, a member who becomes verbally abusive may be asked to leave the group until he or she can regain control.

In other cases, the worker may encourage and protect members who are deviating from antitherapeutic group norms. For example, a worker supports and encourages a member of a couples group who begins to describe problems in the couple's sexual relations, a topic that has not been previously discussed by group members. In another group, the worker encourages a member to talk about the scapegoating of a member who is intensely disliked by other group members.

Workers should also help members to become functionally integrated in the group. As mentioned in Chapter 7, some members take on deviant group roles such as the "group jester" or the "isolate." It is the worker's responsibility to either help the member assume a more functional role or, in some cases, to help the group modify its processes so as to find a useful role for the member. For example, the "group jester" is encouraged to take on a more functional role, such as helping members to express feelings and concerns about a particular problem.

## Changing Group Culture

Another aspect of group dynamics that workers should consider during the middle stage of treatment groups is the culture that has developed in the group. Does the culture help the group achieve its goals? One way to change a group's culture is to challenge commonly accepted beliefs and ideas held by members. For example, in a group for abusive parents, the worker wanted to change a group culture that discouraged the expression of intense feelings and emotions. First, the worker pointed out to the group that feelings were rarely expressed during group sessions. Next, the worker invited the group to discuss his observation. Several members indicated that if they showed their feelings they were afraid they might lose control of their actions. In order to help members learn that they could express feelings without losing control, the worker suggested a series of role play exercises designed to help the members gradually express more intense emotions. The exercises taught members new ways to express emotions and at the same time helped them to realize that they could express their emotions without losing control of their actions. As the group progressed, members acknowledged that allowing feelings to build up inside of them until they exploded was much less healthy for themselves and their families than learning to express their feelings in appropriate ways as they experienced them.

Another way to help members change the existing group culture is to point out its dominant features as well as those areas that appear to be "taboo" or not able to be discussed. When this is done, members often indicate that they had wanted to discuss "taboo" areas in previous group meetings but did not do so because they thought the group would not have been receptive. These members can then be encouraged to express their thoughts and feelings on the "taboo" subject. In other instances, role play exercises can be used to stimulate the group's consideration of an area that was formerly "taboo."

A third way to change the culture established in a group is for the worker to develop a contingency contract with members. This procedure was used successfully in working with adolescents in a group home. The contract specified that if a member was supportive and helpful to other members who disclosed personal problems and concerns during three out of five group meetings each week, the member would have access to special rewards such as a trip to a sports event or tickets to a favorite movie. The contract helped to change the group culture from one in which members were laughed at and ridiculed for expressing personal issues to one in which members supported and encouraged personal disclosures. A similar procedure was used in a children's group. Peer pressure created an environment in which members were teased for participating in role play and program activities. The worker developed a contingency contract about participating that utilized a point system. Points accumulated for participating in role plays could be used at the end of the group meeting to obtain special refreshments, games, or small toys. The incentive system was effective in encouraging the children to participate in role play exercises designed to teach them problem-solving skills.

## CHANGING ENVIRONMENTS IN WHICH GROUPS FUNCTION

Groups do not exist in a vacuum. Usually, group treatment is offered as one component of the clinical services of a social service agency. Hansenfeld (1974) points out the tremendous influence that agencies have on the groups they sponsor. In addition to the material resources provided for group work services, the types of clients treated by an agency and the service technologies and ideologies endorsed by the agency all have a bearing on the services which the group worker offers.

Group services are also influenced by interagency linkages and by the community's response to the problems and concerns of those who seek group treatment. Despite the impact of agency, interagency, and community environments on group work services, relatively little has been written about this subject in the group work literature. Those writers who have pointed out the influence of the environment in which groups function have made few suggestions about how workers might intervene to improve support for group work services (see, for example, Hasenfeld, 1974; Peterson, 1974; Hirschowitz, 1974; and Shulman, 1979). In this section, suggestions are made about ways to (1) increase social service agency support for group work services, (2) develop linkages to interagency networks, and (3) increase community awareness of social problems that could be treated through group work services.

## Increasing Agency Support for Group Work Services

Before intervening to increase support for group work services, workers must first have a thorough understanding of their agencies. Like people, agencies have unique histories that influence their continued growth and development. It is often helpful to gain a historical perspective concerning the development of clinical services within an agency, including an understanding of the changes and innovations that have taken place over time. This can help the worker to understand the rationale for current clinical services, the agency's responsiveness to proposals for change, and the ways in which previous proposals for change were incorporated into the agency's structure. A historical perspective helps the worker avoid making a proposal for increased support for group work services based on a rationale that has been rejected in the past. It also helps to give the worker an understanding of the long-term development of the agency, an understanding that is likely to be shared by administrators whose support for innovations in clinical programing is essential.

To propose an increase in support for group work services, it is also important for the worker to have a sound grasp of the current needs and future development plans of the agency. A proposal for group work services should be structured in such a way that it clearly shows how new or increased services will meet the current needs and future developments anticipated by the agency's administrators and board members. The proposal should emphasize the distinct advantages of group work services. For example, it may be possible to show that treatment groups are a cost-effective alternative to individual treatment services (see, for example, the cost benefit analysis example in Chapter 10). Because most agencies are interested in maximizing their resources by serving as many clients as possible for as little cost as possible, group treatment services may be demonstrated to be an attractive alternative to individual treatment services.

A well-thought-out proposal is not sufficient to guarantee that an agency will increase its support for group work services. Workers should know how to proceed within their agencies to get proposed changes accepted. Patti (1974) suggests that workers should be aware of several organizational factors that help to predict the degree of resistance that can be expected to a change proposal. These include (1) the extent of the proposed change, (2) the value orientation and decision-making style of the administrator responsible for deciding whether or not to accept the proposal, (3) the administrative distance between the practitioner and the decision maker, and (4) the agency's investment in the status quo. The worker can, for example, anticipate greater resistance to a proposal for a basic change in the agency's services, such as a change from individual treatment to group treatment in all clinical programs, than to a modest proposal for group services to a specific client group.

The rationale for a proposal is also important in terms of the resistance it will encounter. An administrator who is concerned about saving money will, for example, be less inclined to accept a proposal that requires new funding than a proposal that is expected to reduce costs. Whenever possible, workers should try to present multiple rationales for group work services, including at least one that is likely to gain the support of those who are responsible for making the decision about the proposal.

The more levels of approval, that is, the further a proposal must go from the originator to the level of final administrative approval, the greater the likelihood of resistance. If a group worker's proposal requires approval from administrators who are at a much higher level in the bureaucratic structure, he or she will have to elicit the support of supervisors who can argue for the proposal when it reaches higher levels of review. Even with support from supervisors, proposals are likely to be altered the farther they move up the bureaucratic hierarchy.

Resistance may also be encountered if the worker is proposing changes that reverse or negate program components or services that have received a great deal of support in the past. Agencies are not likely to abandon already funded commitments so as to approve a new proposal unless it can be proved to be quite exceptional.

Once the worker has anticipated the resistance a proposal may encounter, he or she is ready to develop sufficient support to overcome this resistance. Brager and Holloway (1978) suggest that resistance can often be reduced by involving resistant co-workers in the proposal's development. Because they have had a hand in shaping the proposal, initially resistant co-workers can usually be counted on for support in later negotiations. It is especially important to allow administrators who will be deciding whether or not to accept the proposal and those who will be responsible for carrying out the proposal to have input into its development. During its development, a proposal may be revised several times in order to gain the support of those who have reservations about the proposed changes. By the time it is ready for final consideration, the proposal should have gone through several levels of review, in which important actors have become sensitized to its benefits and have had a chance to have any of their own questions or concerns about the proposal addressed. See Chapter 5 for more information about developing a written proposal for a group.

## Linkages with Interagency Networks

Interventions in a group's environment also include establishing linkages between agencies. Interagency linkages can be established by identifying and making contact with workers in other agencies who work with similar populations or deal with similar social service problems. After informal telephone discussions are initiated, a planning meeting should be held. Because workers are often extremely busy, meetings do not have to occur frequently (monthly or quarterly is usually sufficient), but they should be held on a regularly scheduled basis so that time can be set aside to attend before workers' schedules become filled with other appointments.

Interagency linkages can have several benefits. When other agencies are aware of particular types of group services offered by an agency, they may refer clients for treatment. For example, if a worker at a community agency is aware that a battered women's shelter offers support groups for women, the worker can refer women, who would otherwise not receive services, to this agency.

Agency networks help to identify needs for particular services. In a meeting of workers from several agencies, for example, it became apparent to a group worker from a family service agency that no services existed for treating men who battered their wives. After carefully documenting the need in other agencies, a group work service was established for this population by the family service agency.

Interagency networks can also help to avoid duplication of services. Competition between agencies can be avoided by preventing the development of duplicate services existing elsewhere in the community and by facilitating the development of services when gaps in service delivery exist. Workers who cultivate interagency linkages can share the knowledge and practice experience they have gained from working with specific client groups and learn from the experiences of group workers in other agencies. In this way, knowledge can be pooled and mistakes made by one worker can be avoided by others.

Interagency networks are also useful in lobbying for new group work services. For example, in a meeting of workers from a number of community agencies, it became apparent that additional services were needed to prevent criminal activity among unemployed youths. Although none of the workers was able to do anything about this problem by themselves, together they were able to put enough pressure on the city's youth services program to obtain funding for a half-time group worker for the local community center.

## Increasing Community Awareness

Ultimately, group work services depend on the support of local community residents. Their awareness of the social problems that exist in their communities and their belief that group work services can help to maintain adequate social functioning and alleviate social problems are essential. Group workers have a responsibility to bring community problems to the attention of local officials and civic organizations and to make them aware of how group work services can help to alleviate their problems.

A variety of methods can be used to increase a community's awareness of social problems and increase their commitment to group work services. Needs assessments (see Chapter 10) are especially effective for documenting the need for additional services. Agency statistics about the number of clients not served because of a lack of resources or a lack of available services can also be useful to document needs. To call attention to community problems, workers can testify at legislative hearings. They can become members of local planning bodies or they can help to elect local officials who are supportive of the community's social service needs. Only through such efforts will group work services remain available to those who need them.

A group worker's skills can also be used to organize clients so that they may lobby for needed services on their own behalf. For example, an after-care group (for those who had been in a state mental hospital) at a community mental health center in a poor urban area was composed entirely of women who were receiving ADC benefits. It became apparent that many of these women's problems were tied to the subsistence level benefits they received, as well as to the environmental conditions in which they lived. The worker informed these women of a national welfare rights coalition and helped them to form their own local welfare rights group. Although this effort did not make a tremendous or immediate change in their life circumstances, it did give them a constructive way to voice their complaints and to lobby for changes in their community. It helped them to overcome what Seligman (1975) has called "learned helplessness."

## SUMMARY

The middle phase of treatment groups is the period in which most of a group's work is accomplished. In order to include all of the skills necessary for leading treatment groups during this phase, this chapter was divided into two sections. Section one examined the generic activities that all workers perform while leading treatment groups. Because workers may lead many different types of treatment groups for a variety of different purposes, section two focused on specific interventions that can be used differentially to meet needs encountered in differing groups.

Workers perform four generic activities during the middle phase of treatment groups. These include (1) preparing for group meetings, (2) structuring the group's work, (3) helping members to achieve contract goals, (4) monitoring and evaluating the group's progress. In describing each of these activities, emphasis was placed in the skills and the procedures workers should use to lead effective treatment group sessions.

Section two focused on some of the major intervention methods used in treatment groups. These methods are commonly used to intervene at the level of the (1) group member, (2) group as a whole, and the (3) environment in which the group functions. Because of the extent to which the group treatment literature has focused on individual change in small groups, much of the second section was devoted to interventions at this level. These interventions were subdivided into those that dealt with (1) intrapersonal, (2) interpersonal, and (3) environmental concerns.

Interventions in the group as a whole were divided into those that focused on each of the four major areas of group dynamics described in Chapter 3. These include changing the group's (1) communication and interaction patterns, (2) attraction for its members, (3) social control mechanisms, and (4) culture.

The chapter concluded with an examination of interventions to change the environment in which a group functions. This is an important, but often neglected, area of group work practice. Discussion of interventions in this portion of the chapter included ways to (1) increase agency support for group work services, (2) develop linkages to interagency networks, and (3) increase community awareness of social service problems that could be effectively alleviated by group treatment.

# 9
# The Middle Phase: Task Groups

It has been said that Americans are involved in committees and other task groups more than any other people (Tropman, Johnson, and Tropman, 1979). Participation in the decisions that affect our lives is characteristic of our democratic society. Every day millions of meetings take place throughout the United States. Social service agencies could not function without meetings of committees, treatment conferences, teams, boards, and other work groups.

Social workers and other helping professionals are often called upon to chair committees, teams, and other task groups. For example, the social worker is frequently designated as the team leader in interdisciplinary health care settings, because social work functions include coordination, case management, and concern for the biopsychosocial functioning of the whole person (Kane, 1975, 1976; Wise, 1974; Siporin, 1980a). Workers also are asked to "staff" task groups (Tropman, Johnson, and Tropman, 1979). In general, the staff person plays a supportive role, helping the group to clarify its goals and to carry out its work. Acting under the direction of the task group's leader, the staff person reports directly to the group. The duties and roles of a staff person are quite varied, and they include serving as a resource person, consultant, enabler, analyst, implementer, tactician, catalyst, and technical advisor (Tropman, Johnson, and Tropman, 1979).

Despite the importance and the widespread use of task groups in social service agencies, relatively little has been written about how to lead or staff them. Brill (1976) and Trecker (1946) point out that teams and other task groups have great potential for helping clients receive effective services. Yet, with a few notable exceptions (see, for example, Brill, 1976; Bradford, 1976; Delbecq, Van de Ven, and Gustafson, 1975; Napier and Gershenfeld, 1981), the human services have paid little attention to how task groups work.

Although task groups can be useful, they can be a source of frustration for their participants when they function ineffectively. For example, Napier and Gershenfeld (1981, pp. 310–349) describe the "incredible meeting trap" in which little is accomplished and members leave feeling frustrated by the group process. In one of the few articles published in a social work journal about leading task group meetings, Edson (1977) suggests unorthodox methods that can be used to guard against the irrational and manipulative strategies used by "narrowminded, pigheaded, sly, opinionated, bigoted manipulators" who often dominate committee meetings (Edson, 1977, p. 224).

Edson's (1977) comments are rather strongly stated, but they make the important point that many workers are dissatisfied with task group meetings and indifferent or suspicious about their outcomes. Meetings that are not well run are boring and dissatisfying to members. They suffer from a lack of participation and corrective feedback from members, who lose interest.

Although task group meetings are often seen as a chore to be endured by members for the good of the organization, meetings that are well run can be a positive experience. They help draw people together, creating effective teamwork in which ideas are shared, feelings are expressed, and support is developed for group members, as well as for the decisions made by the group. There are few experiences in the workplace that equal the feelings of cohesion, commitment, and satisfaction that members feel when their ideas have been heard, appreciated, and used in resolving a difficult issue and arriving at a mutually agreed upon decision.[1]

This chapter is divided into three sections. All focus on the skills, procedures, and methods that workers will find useful when staffing or leading task group meetings during the middle phase of group work. The first section describes some generic skills in conducting task group meetings during the middle phase. This section also includes a discussion of some of the most common functions of task groups and the generic practice principles that are helpful in carrying out each function. Because effective problem solving is basic to many task group efforts, the second section of this chapter describes a six-step model for effective problem solving in groups. The model includes a discussion of the practice skills group workers use during each step. The final section of this chapter explicates different methods and techniques for problem solving in task groups that have been used successfully in social service agencies as well as in business and industry. The advantages and disadvantages of these methods for leading effective task group meetings are discussed.

## CONDUCTING MEETINGS

The middle stages of task groups are characterized by repetition and by diversity. Repetition occurs because meetings generally follow a similar pattern: an opening portion for warming up, a middle portion for working, and a

---

[1]See the film *Meeting in Progress*, Round Table Films, 113 North San Vincente Blvd., Beverly Hills, California 90211, for a vivid example of task group members who are ready to end a meeting as soon as a decision is reached.

closing portion for summarizing and ending. At the same time, there can be great diversity among task groups during the middle stage of their development. Diversity is fostered by the wide range of functions and the great variety of procedures that can be used to help task groups conduct their business.

During the middle stage, work is accomplished between meetings as well as during the beginning, middle, and end of each meeting. The following sections include a brief discussion of the ways that workers can help groups to accomplish their tasks during each of these periods.

## Between Meetings

Between meetings, the worker has two major tasks: seeing that decisions and tasks decided upon at the previous meetings are carried out, and preparing for the next group meeting. The worker can prepare for the first task by reading the minutes of the meeting. Properly kept minutes should include a summary of the actions taken, tasks that were assigned, and the time frame for reporting back to the group. It is also helpful for the worker to make brief notes during a meeting or soon after the meeting ends about decisions made by the group, which need to be followed up prior to the next meeting.

In seeing that the decisions decided upon by the group are carried out between meetings, Tropman (1980) suggests that a worker should become "a bit of a nag." The worker ensures that members work on and complete reports and other assignments that are necessary for the next group meeting. This does not mean that the worker takes over these tasks. The worker's function is to encourage and to facilitate the progress of those whose responsibility is to carry out a task.

Between meetings the worker might meet with subcommittees of the larger group to provide information or guidance as they carry out the functions assigned to them in the larger group. During this time, the worker may also develop contacts that will be helpful to the group in accomplishing its purpose. This includes maintaining close contacts with administrative staff, governing bodies, and the constituencies that may be affected by the group's work. As spokesperson for the group, a worker should keep in mind that he or she represents the group's public image. A worker should express the officially accepted opinions of the committee rather than his or her own personal views. The worker should not enter into private agreements, which commit the group to decisions or positions that have not been deliberated on and accepted by the group. In all but emergency situations, the worker should convene the group and consult with it before making decisions. The only exception to this rule is when the group, the agency, or a regulatory body has clearly empowered the worker to act independently without first consulting with the group.

The second major task of the worker in between meetings is to prepare for the next group meeting. When there is a written agenda for each meeting, the worker or the member designated as the group's secretary should send a memo to each group member soon after a meeting to request agenda items well ahead of the next meeting. This allows enough time for agenda items and background or position papers to be completed and sent to group members so they can be read before the next meeting. Meeting agendas should be established to facilitate discussion. One effective framework is to:

1. Examine and approve (with any corrections) brief, relevant minutes from the last meeting.
2. Make informational announcements.
3. Vote to include special agenda items.
4. Work on less controversial, easier items.
5. Work on difficult items.
6. Break.
7. Work on "for discussion only" items.
8. Consider any special agenda items if there is sufficient time.
9. Summarize.
10. Adjourn.

In preparing for the next meeting, the worker should also organize opening remarks and administrative summaries that he or she will present during the meeting. Special care should be taken in preparing for meetings that do not have a written agenda. In such instances, the worker should be clear about how to direct the meeting, what tasks the group will work on, and what goals are to be achieved.

As a part of the worker's responsibility in preparing for a meeting, he or she should assess the group's functioning. Questions such as "What is the group's relationship with its outside environment?"; "Has the group been functioning smoothly?"; "What norms, roles, and interaction patterns have developed in the group?" can stimulate the worker to consider how he or she can best prepare for the next meeting.

In many task groups, the worker acts as both the leader and staff person. However, if a separate staff person is available to a task group, he or she should be used. A staff person can be a valuable asset to a group's leader and to the group as a whole. A staff person can prepare background reports and memos that analyze the group's options, develop resources, set up the meeting arrangements, and, in general, service the group's needs.

## During Meetings

*Beginning.* At the beginning of a meeting, the worker is responsible for several tasks. The worker begins by introducing new members and distributing additional handouts not included with the material distributed before the meeting. Before working on agenda items, the worker should make a brief opening statement about the purpose of the meeting. In this statement, the worker may want to call members' attention to previous meetings and to the mandate of the group as a way to indicate that the meeting will undertake a necessary and important function. Making members aware of the salience of the particular agenda items they will consider is important for maintaining members' interest and willingness to work during the group meeting.

The worker should seek members' approval of written minutes that were distributed before the meeting and request that members raise any questions, changes or amendments they would like to enter into the minutes. After the minutes are approved, the worker makes announcements and calls upon group members to make designated reports. Reports should be kept brief and to the point. Members should verbally summarize written reports that have been circulated with the agenda rather than reading them verbatim. Reading lengthy reports can be boring and can result in the loss of interest and attention of other members.

*Middle.*   During the middle portion of meetings, the worker's task is to help the group follow its planned agenda. Whatever the particular purpose of a specific meeting, the middle portion is the time when the group accomplishes much of its most difficult work. To avoid getting stuck on one item of business in meetings that have extensive agendas, details of a particular item should be worked out prior to the meeting. If this is not possible, Tropman (1980) points out, the group can agree "in principle" on overall objectives and goals about a particular task and a subcommittee or an individual group member can be charged with working out the details and bringing these back to the group at a later date.

The worker should model the behavior that is expected of all members. A worker who shows respect, interest, integrity, and responsibility will convey these feelings to members. By encouraging equitable participation, the expression of minority group opinions, and an appreciation of all sincere contributions to the group's work, the worker sets a positive example for group members to follow.

Jay (1977) suggests that the worker should act more as a servant of the interests of the group as a whole rather than as a master who imposes his or her will upon the group. According to Jay (1977, p. 263), the worker's self-indulgence is the "greatest single barrier to the success of a meeting." By demonstrating that he or she has the good of the group as a whole in mind in conducting the group's business, the worker gains the respect of members. Authority, control, and discipline should be used only to reduce threats to the group's effective functioning rather than to impose the worker's wishes on the group. As members perceive that the worker is committed to accomplishing the group's common objective, he or she will gain the cooperation and the admiration of group members.

*Ending.*   The worker should ensure that the pace of the meeting leaves enough time at the end to accomplish the items specified in the agenda. Task groups can make serious mistakes when they rush through important decisions because they are pressed for time at the end of a meeting. Members also become frustrated when they are expected to present or to discuss ideas but have no time to do so, because the group has spent too much time discussing earlier items on the agenda. Part of the responsibility of an effective worker in preparing for a meeting is making sure that the number of agenda items is manageable and can be accomplished in the available time. Items sometimes take longer to discuss than anticipated, so it is a good practice to plan some extra time into an agenda. When too many agenda items are submitted for a meeting, items should be prioritized by the worker. Items that are assigned a low priority should be postponed to a later meeting.

Before adjourning, the worker should summarize the meeting's accomplishments, identity issues and agenda items that need further attention, and mention major topics for the next group meeting. When the group is working on a large task, the worker should also mention where the meeting has placed the group in terms of its overall schedule. At this time, the worker should also summarize as clearly as possible the tasks that members agreed to accomplish before the next meeting. This avoids confusion, clarifies responsibilities, and reduces the possibility that members might forget assignments that were agreed to during earlier portions of the group's discussion. For more information about ending meetings, see Chapter 11.

## FUNCTIONS OF TASK GROUPS

Whereas the main focus of treatment groups is on the functioning and the socioemotional needs of individual group members, task groups are focused on the projects and results that the group as a whole produces. Task groups, of course, are also concerned with individual members. Attention to members' satisfaction, comfort, motivation, and skills are essential if the group as a whole is to accomplish its tasks. However, unlike treatment groups, the primary concern of task groups is not to change members. Task groups are created to accomplish work that will meet evaluative criteria set both from within and from outside of the group.

Many important functions of task groups are similar to those of treatment groups. Despite this overlap, the differing foci of task and treatment groups are evident in their respective functions. Task groups, for example, are more concerned with creating new ideas, developing plans and programs, solving problems that are external to the group, and making decisions about the organizational environment than are treatment groups.

In order to work effectively with task groups, the first step is to determine what purposes and functions the group is expected to accomplish. In his classic text on leading task groups, Maier (1963) suggests that the primary functions of task groups are problem solving and decision making. Maier (1963) goes on to describe methods designed to increase task groups' problem-solving and decision-making abilities.

Although problem solving and decision making are important functions, several others have been identified in the literature (see, for example, Scheidel and Crowell, 1979; Napier and Gershenfeld, 1981; Bradford, 1976). Functions that govern the work of task groups during their middle phase include:

1. Sharing information, thoughts, and feelings about common concerns and issues that workers encounter as they function in their assigned roles within an agency.
2. Helping members feel involved and committed to the group and the agency in which they work.

3. Developing facts and information about particular issues, concerns, and problems facing the group.
4. Making effective decisions.
5. Monitoring and evaluating decisions and program components for which the task group is responsible.
6. Problem solving.

Sometimes, task groups perform only one of the functions described. Usually, however, task groups attempt to perform several functions simultaneously. Task groups often develop primary and secondary functions. For example, in a community agency serving homebound older persons, paraprofessional outreach workers meet together with their supervisor on a weekly basis to discuss common problems which they confront in obtaining psychological, social and medical services for their clients. Because they spend so much time out of the office, a secondary function of the group is to help workers identify with the organization for which they work. In the following pages, task group functions are described separately to illustrate particular group work skills, but in practice they are frequently combined so that several purposes can be accomplished simultaneously.

## Sharing Information

Perhaps the most common function of task groups is to help members share information, thoughts, and feelings with one another. Teams, committees, delegate councils, and boards use group meetings as a means for members to share their concerns, their experiences, their perspectives, and their expertise with one another. This is an important function because, as a result of highly differentiated work roles, there is infrequent contact among workers in many agencies. Job assignments such as individual treatment sessions and home visits limit opportunities for communication among workers.

Social issues and problems often have an interagency impact, and task groups serve as the vehicle for bringing workers from different agencies together. A group meeting is a convenient way for workers from different agencies to share unique viewpoints and differing perspectives on issues, problems, or concerns they face in their own agencies. By providing a forum for sharing knowledge and resources, interagency task groups encourage cooperative and coordinated problem solving.

Open communication and unimpeded sharing of information are prerequisites for other functions of task groups. Brill (1976), for example, suggests that the communication network that is established in a group is the key to effective work in teams and other task groups. Empirical findings regarding group productivity and group process confirm that the way information is communicated and used in a group has an important effect on the quality and the quantity of a group's productivity (Hackman and Morris 1975, Steiner, 1972).

Task group participants make differential use of the information and resources possessed by various group members, depending on how members' expertise relate to the issues and tasks facing the group. During the middle phase of group work, the worker's task is to help the group develop open channels of communication that can be used appropriately as members have contributions to make during the meeting.

What steps can be taken to aid effective communication and open sharing of information in task groups? The first step is to ensure that all members have a clear understanding of the topic being discussed and the task facing the group. In order to stimulate all members' participation in the discussion, the topic must be relevant. If members have little interest in the topic and no stake in the outcome, there is little reason for them to participate. In many groups, members become bored, disinterested, and dissatisfied because they do not understand the importance of a particular topic. It is important for the task group's leader to help each member see the relevance and importance of issues as they are brought before the group. When it is clear that a discussion topic is relevant to only a subset of members of a task group, the worker should consider forming a subgroup to meet separately from the larger group. The subgroup can provide a brief report of its deliberations and recommendations at a later meeting of the entire group.

In order to focus interest, promote task-relevant discussions, and reduce confusion among members, Zander (1977), Huber (1980), and Steiner (1972) suggest developing clear procedural steps that can be followed during the discussion. Maier (1963, p. 41) refers to discussions that follow clear procedural steps as "developmental discussions." Later in this chapter, a six-step problem-solving model for conducting task group discussions is presented.

Workers also can use their leadership skills during the group meeting by summarizing frequently and by helping the group to remain task-focused. Summarizing can be used to check understanding, to review previously discussed subjects, to go back to items that were not fully discussed, to help separate a problem or issue into several parts, and to bring members' attention to a particularly important aspect of the discussion. Focusing can be accomplished by suggesting that the group discuss one issue at a time, by pointing out that the group has digressed from the discussion topic, and by making task-relevant statements. As Jay (1977) points out, effective workers often have self-imposed rules limiting their communications early in group meetings to allow members the maximum opportunity to participate in the discussion. A few brief summaries and comments that focus the discussion are all that is often needed early in the group's work.

Another method of establishing open communication channels and promoting information sharing among all group members is to ensure equitable participation in the group. Domination by a few members who have high status or who are very expressive leads to less felt freedom to participate among all members and to a reduction in the quality of group decisions (Torrance, 1957; Chung and Ferris, 1971; Delbecq, Van de Ven and Gustafson, 1975). Workers should help task groups develop mechanisms that ensure equitable participation. According to Huber (1980, p. 185), equitable participation "is the level of participation that is in keeping with the individual's information, knowledge, or other contribution to the group's effort." Inequitable participation occurs when members participate either more frequently or less frequently than their potential contribution to the group warrants.

The worker should help the group develop a standard of fairness in participation (Huber, 1980). This can be done by helping the group develop rules for participation. Members may agree to keep their comments brief, be attentive to the communication of others when they are speaking, and to encourage silent members to participate. In addition to modeling appropriate behavior, the worker can help members follow the rules that are established. For example, the worker can interrupt long speeches, ask members to summarize their comments briefly, or suggest that members give others a chance to reply. When a member presents an idea, the worker can invite participation by asking other members for feedback about the proposal. In some cases, it is helpful to structure the discussion by using a round robin procedure or the rules of parliamentary procedure.

In a round robin procedure, each member is asked to present one idea or one piece of information. Going around the group, members take turns at presenting one piece of data. This procedure is continued and each member takes as many turns as needed. Members who do not have any additional ideas or information simply pass during their turn. The cycle is completed when all ideas have been shared by all members.

The round robin procedure has several advantages over unstructured, interacting communication procedures. It does not force members to participate equally although all members have an equal opportunity to participate. Because only one idea is presented at a time, the procedure avoids the boredom that often results when one member enumerates several ideas at the same time. By continuing to go around the group until all ideas are heard and by asking members to pass if they do not have any new information to present, a norm is established for sharing as many ideas as possible.

In large task groups, round robin procedures are often too time-consuming. Unless the group is divided into subgroups, the procedure is not useful. In order to facilitate equitable participation in large groups, the worker should consider using parliamentary procedures (Gulley, 1968; Maier, 1963; Scheidel and Crowell, 1979) following *Robert's Rules of Order* (Robert, 1970). These procedures, which have been developed over the past 600 years in meetings in business, industry, and political bodies in Britain and the United States, provide for orderly and structured participation in large group meetings. Group workers should be aware that parliamentary procedures are subject to manipulation by members who are familiar with its complexities. Strauss and Strauss (1952) and Maier (1963) claim that parliamentary procedures have been used for years by a small minority of members to control large meetings. By trading favors for votes prior to a meeting, and by calling for votes with few members present, parliamentary procedures can be used to subvert majority rule. Despite these disadvantages, *Robert's Rules of Order* can be helpful in ensuring equitable participation in large meetings. A brief description of parliamentary procedures is included later in this chapter.

## Getting Members Involved

A second function of task groups is to help members feel that they are a vital part of the agency for which they work. Because much of any organization's work is done by individuals, there is a danger that staff can become isolated and alienated from an organization. Task groups provide support for their members and a sense of belongingness that reduces alienation. For example, an individual worker in an agency for disabled children spends much of her time helping new parents with the trauma associated with giving birth to physically and mentally handicapped children. Weekly team meetings with other professionals who work with the infants in a pre-school program provide support and recognition for the worker who is faced with the difficult, often emotionally charged, task of helping parents become adjusted to having handicapped children.

Helping members become involved through their participation in a task group benefits the organization as well as individual workers. Task groups provide an organized means of developing, implementing, and getting members to follow the policies, procedures, and goals of the agency. They allow members an opportunity to influence the policies and procedures developed by their agency. This process helps to make the agency responsive to the needs of its workers. At the same time, by clearly delineating how a task group fits into the overall structure of an agency, that is, to whom the group reports and what authority and power the group has to develop or change agency policies, members' input can be organized and channeled appropriately. This helps to coordinate the efforts of workers performing a wide variety of tasks within an agency.

What can be done to help task group members feel that their input is vital to the agency's sound functioning? First, workers should make sure that members understand the importance of the group's work, its relationship to the agency's purpose, and how the group fits into the agency's administrative structure. This can be accomplished by making a clear statement of the group's purpose, by using flow charts to explain how the group fits into the entire agency's administrative and decision-making structure, and by clarifying the duties, responsibilities, authority and power that results from membership in the group. At first, this explanation might mean little to members. However, as work is accomplished within the group and recommendations and reports are prepared for the larger agency, members gather a more personal, first-hand experience of the governance structure of their agency.

Assigning members specific roles can also help them become actively involved in their agency. Roles that encourage members to become dependent on one another for task accomplishment and roles that place them in the position of representing the group to a larger constituency increase the attractiveness and cohesion of the group, and help members feel that they are part of a collective effort that is of vital importance for effective agency functioning (Deutsch, 1973).

A third, and extremely important, step in getting members involved in and committed to a task group and their agency is to invite their input into the agenda and the decision-making processes of the group. This can be done by encouraging members to develop and submit agenda items for future group meetings. Circulating the agenda and any background papers prior to a meeting can help members prepare their thoughts and concerns before a meeting and increase the chances that they will participate by sharing them during the meeting. It has been shown that the greater a member's effort and sacrifice in preparing for and working on a task, the more likely the member is to stay involved and committed to the group (Kiesler, 1978). Therefore, asking members to prepare for a meeting by reading background papers, collecting information, and submitting agenda items will tend to increase involvement and commitment to the group and the larger organization.

A fourth method of helping members become involved is to encourage them to participate in the decision-making process to the extent possible (Scheidel and Crowell, 1979). Shared decision making has been found to increase motivation (Kiesler, 1978), increase acceptance and understanding of decisions (Bradford, 1976), increase the information available for decision making (Huber, 1980), and help in processing complex information (Carnes, 1980). Although some writers suggest that decision making should always be shared among members (Bradford, 1976), there are potential disadvantages to giving members decision-making authority. According to Huber (1980), these include (1) the great amount of personnel time spent in group decision making, (2) the tendency for groups to produce decisions that are not acceptable to management, (3) expectations that future decisions will also be made through group participation, (4) the tendency for groups to take longer than individuals to reach decisions, and (5) the possibility that group decision making could cause conflict between group members who may have to work together on a daily basis. Thus, the decision to delegate decision making to groups should be made only after carefully considering both the advantages and disadvantages of shared decision making in the particular situation. When the advantages of group decision making are questionable, it is often possible to have the group make several recommendations but to reserve the final decision-making authority to one person.

## Developing Information

A third function of task groups is to generate information and develop creative alternatives for responding to difficult issues and problems facing the group. Although task groups are often used for this function, the available evidence suggests that ordinary interacting group discussions inhibit rather than increase the disclosure of information, ideas, and creative solutions. (See, for example, Van de Ven, 1974; Miner, 1979; Van de Ven and Delbecq, 1971; Delbecq, 1967.)

Reasons that group processes may inhibit information sharing and the development of creative ideas include:

1. Status-conscious group members feel intimidated by those with higher status (Torrance, 1957). Lower-status members will tend to share less information and will avoid making suggestions that will offend higher-status members.

2. Norms and social pressures for conformity tend to limit the expression of new and creative ideas (Van de Ven, 1974; Vroom, Grant and Cotton, 1969).
3. Groups have the advantage of the wide variety of opinions and knowledge offered by all members, but group members may censor controversial opinions.
4. Covert judgments are often made but not expressed openly in groups (Collaros and Anderson, 1969). Members, therefore, become concerned about the effects that their self-disclosures will have on future interactions with group members.
5. Interacting groups tend to reach premature solutions without considering all the available evidence (Maier and Hoffman, 1960; Van de Ven, 1974).

In order to reduce or eliminate the difficulties associated with generating information and developing creative solutions in interacting groups, several methods, such as brainstorming, the nominal group technique, and social judgment analysis, have been suggested as alternative procedures. These methods will be described later in this chapter. However, because interacting group discussions are commonly used in task groups, workers should be aware of procedures that can help to overcome the limitations often associated with them.

The worker can help in several ways to improve group members' opportunities to present new ideas, combine information, and generate creative solutions in interacting groups. First, the worker must clearly indicate to all members that their input is welcome. This means that the worker must be able to address the members' concerns about sanctions that may result from expressing sensitive or controversial ideas in the group. When the worker cannot guarantee freedom from sanctions, he or she should try to be as clear as possible about the boundaries of the discussion. For example, it might be possible for committee members to discuss new policies regarding service delivery, but it might not be acceptable for them to criticize existing supervisory staff who have to follow current policy guidelines. When sanctions are possible from individuals outside the group, the worker can encourage the group to consider making their discussions confidential. If lower-status members fear reprisals from higher-status members, the worker can discuss the use of sanctions with higher-status members prior to the group meeting and gain their cooperation in refraining from applying them. The worker can suggest that higher-status and lower-status members discuss this issue in the group.

Feedback can have a beneficial or a detrimental effect in helping the group to develop information and form creative solutions. It is commonly thought that all feedback is useful because it helps group members to detect and correct errors in information processing. (See, for example, Argyris, 1977; Bowers and Franklin, 1976; and Nadler, 1977.) This is not true in all circumstances. In the early phase of developing information and forming creative solutions, evaluative feedback can have the effect of suppressing further suggestions (Van de Ven, 1974, Nadler, 1979). Members fear that their ideas may be evaluated negatively and that this will reflect on their competence and their status in the agency. Under these circumstances, few members will risk making suggestions, giving opinions, or volunteering information that will not be readily accepted. To encourage free discussion, creative ideas, and new insights about a problem or issue, the worker should ask members to refrain from evaluating ideas early in the group's discussion.

Several other steps can also be taken to help the group develop information and creative ideas to solve a problem. The worker can encourage the group to develop norms that promote free discussion of ideas. As the meeting progresses, it is often helpful to point out group pressures that inhibit members' free discussion. By presenting creative, controversial, and thought-provoking ideas, the worker can act as a model for the group. Workers can also encourage members to continue to share unique ideas by praising those who present innovative suggestions. Since it is more difficult for lower status members to present their ideas after higher status members have expressed their opinions, lower status members should be encouraged to share their ideas as early as possible in the group's discussion. To avoid premature solutions during group discussions, the worker should help the group separate information and idea-generating steps from decision-making steps. When these suggestions are implemented, interacting groups can develop more creative solutions than they would under ordinary conditions.

## Making Effective Decisions

A fourth function of task groups is to make effective decisions. Although groups are often used to make decisions, the evidence as to their effectiveness is mixed. Groups are better than individuals in influencing opinions and obtaining commitments from members (Kelley and Thibaut, 1969; Lewin, 1948). Napier (1967) found that groups are better at integrating complex perceptual and intellectual tasks, because members can rely on one another for assistance. However, for other types of problems, groups may not be any more effective than individuals and sometimes they may be less efficient than individuals working alone (Campbell, 1968; Rotter and Portugal, 1969). In summarizing the literature that has compared the problem-solving activities of task groups with that of individuals, Hare (1976) has drawn the following conclusions:

1. Groups are superior to individuals in solving manual problems such as puzzles. This is particularly true when the problem can be subdivided so that each person can use his or her own expertise to work on a problem component. The superiority of groups has been less consistently documented when the task to be accomplished is of a more intellectual nature, such as a logic problem.
2. While groups are better than the average individual, they are not better than the best individual. Therefore, a group of novices may perform worse than one expert.
3. Groups have the advantage of the wide variety of opinions and knowledge offered by the members, but group members may censor controversial opinions.

**4.** A part of the superiority of group problem solving is due to the pooling of individual judgments to converge on a group norm. For some problems, similar accuracy may be achieved by averaging the decisions of non-interacting individuals.
**5.** When groups solve intellectual tasks, members' rational information-processing orientation may be impeded by socioemotional concerns.
**6.** Because task groups require the time of a number of members who deliberate until they reach a decision, task groups may be more costly than work done by one or more individuals working alone.

In order to improve group decision making, workers should help members to avoid the phenomenon known as "groupthink" (Janis, 1972). "Groupthink" occurs when group contagion takes over and members fail to express their own thoughts and feelings. Instead, they go along with the predominant sentiment of the group. This phenomenon has been recognized for many years by those who have written about groups. For example, over seventy years ago LeBon (1910) referred to "group mind," where members allow an emotional state generated from their participation in a group to dominate their intellectual powers. More than sixty years ago, Freud (1922) wrote about the power that the group has over an individual's ego.

Before 1960, it was generally thought that problem-solving groups made more conservative decisions than individuals. Experiments by Ziller (1957) and Stoner (1961), however, indicated that groups made riskier decisions than individuals. Stoner (1961) called this phenomenon the "risky shift." As evidence began to accumulate, it became clear that this shift may either be toward greater or lesser risk. Riskier decisions are made in groups whose members approve of risk taking (Teger and Pruitt, 1967; Wallach and Wing, 1968), when persuasive information is presented (Ebbesen and Bowers, 1974), when the responsibility for the decision is shared among group members (Myers and Arenson, 1972; Zajonc, Wolosin, and Wolosin, 1972), or when the leader approves of a risky decision (Myers and Arenson, 1972). On the other hand, in some groups risk taking is discouraged, and members are rewarded for developing solutions that result in conservative group decisions (Stoner, 1968).

Several steps can be taken to help groups avoid "group think" and "risky shifts." Norms and a group climate that encourages free and open discussion of ideas tend to discourage conformity and to decrease "group think." Procedures that clarify how a group will use information and arrive at a decision also tend to reduce conformity. Early in the decision-making process, the group should decide how to use the information it possesses in making a decision. For example, in a family service agency, a personnel committee deciding between many qualified applicants for a clinical position develops decision criteria. They are the rules and the standards that govern rational choices between alternative candidates. Criteria for making decisions should include all the factors that group members consider to be essential in making a good judgment. The personnel committee arrived at decision criteria that included the clinical competency of the applicant, the needs of the agency for a worker who could speak Spanish, a worker with skill and experience in supervision, and a worker who was familiar with the use of psychotropic medications in outpatient mental health settings.

To avoid disagreements later in the decision-making process, the worker should allow the group to discuss the rationale behind each decision criteria. To avoid confusion, it is often helpful to ask members about their understanding of each criteria and to use examples to illustrate how each criteria would be applied in rating alternative solutions. After developing and clarifying the criteria, the group should rate their relative importance so that the group can decide between alternative solutions. In the previous example, group members decided that clinical competency and supervisory experience were twice as important as the other criteria for this particular position. They then used the criteria to review each job applicant's folder in order to select the best candidate. A more detailed explanation of developing and using decision criteria in task groups is presented in the section on "Social Judgment Analysis" in this chapter.

During the decision-making process, conflict may occur between members. It is important for workers to realize that conflicts occur even in effective task groups (Scheidel and Crowell, 1979; Napier and Gershenfeld, 1981). Conflicts often occur over control of resources, values, beliefs, preferences, and the nature of the relationship between members (Deutsch, 1973). Maier (1963) and Filley (1974) suggest that disagreement between members can either lead to increased conflict and failure to accomplish a task or to the development of creative solutions. The outcome of a disagreement depends on how the worker and the members handle it (Lowe and Herranen, 1978).

In their analyses of hundreds of decision-making groups, Guetzkow and Gyr (1954) distinguished between two types of conflict, substantive conflict and affective conflict. Affective conflict is based on the emotional and interpersonal relationships among members within and outside of the group. Substantive conflict is based on members' differing opinions about ideas, information, and facts presented during the task group's work. In general, affective conflict is more difficult to resolve than substantive conflict because it is resistant to persuasive reasoning. When conflict is avoided and remains unresolved, the group may (1) decide not to decide, (2) delegate its decision-making responsibilities to others, or (3) decide on a solution that is not substantiated by accurate information (Kiesler, 1978).

Guetzkow and Gyr (1954) and Burke (1970) suggest that substantive and affective conflicts can be reduced by the following procedures:

1. Help members to recognize the conflict.
2. Help members to express the reasoning behind conflicting opinions and alternatives.
3. Develop facts and expert judgments to help resolve the conflict.
4. Emphasize those factors in the group discussion that promote consensus.
5. Follow orderly, pre-planned steps for considering alternatives and deciding on a solution.
6. Use decision criteria that are mutually agreed upon by group members.

7. Clarify and summarize the discussion frequently so that all members have a similar understanding of what is being discussed and the decision criteria that will be used.
8. Be sensitive to members' personal concerns and needs in developing solutions and arriving at a decision.
9. Remain neutral in the conflict, asking questions that seek clarification whenever possible.

To arrive at a final group decision, a procedure for choosing among alternatives is needed. Most groups make their final decisions using one of the following procedures: consensus, compromise, or majority rule (Gulley, 1968). In certain situations, each of these procedures can result in quite different decisions. To avoid the suspicion that a particular decision-making procedure is being chosen to influence a decision about a particular issue, a method of choosing among alternatives should be agreed upon as early as possible in a task group's deliberations.

Consensus is often considered the ideal way to select among alternatives because all group members commit themselves to the decision. When reviewing conditions for effective work with groups, Whitaker (1975) suggests that helping a group to achieve consensus reduces conflict within the group and helps to make the group more effective. Consensus does not, however, necessarily imply agreement on the part of all group members. As Napier and Gershenfeld (1981, p. 402) point out, consensus "simply requires that individuals must be willing to go along with the group's predominant view and carry out the implications of the decision in good faith."

Consensus is sometimes difficult to achieve in groups. Reaching consensus can be time-consuming and tension-provoking because each alternative must be discussed thoroughly along with dissenting viewpoints. Also, there is the danger that members will acquiesce and decision quality will be sacrificed in order to arrive at a solution that is acceptable to all group members (Napier and Gershenfeld, 1981). Although other decision-making procedures are quicker, reaching consensus often brings considerable support for a decision because members are more likely to cooperate in implementing decisions that they have thoroughly discussed and agreed upon.

When issues are controversial and there is much dissenting opinion, it is often possible to reach a decision by modifying original proposals. In order to develop amendments to proposals that are acceptable to all group members, the discussion of each alternative should focus on the reasoning behind members' objections to the alternative. This process helps all group members identify the acceptable and unacceptable parts of each alternative. After a discussion of all the alternatives, the acceptable parts of several alternatives can often be combined into one solution that is acceptable to most, if not all, members.

Majority rule is a frequently used procedure to decide between alternatives in task groups. It is less time-consuming than consensus or compromise procedures, and when the vote is done by secret ballot it protects the confidentiality of members. Majority rule is an excellent procedure to use when deciding about routine and relatively minor issues. However, because there can be a significant minority who may not agree with the final outcome, majority rule is a less appealing procedure when the issue is important and when the support and cooperation of the entire group is needed for successful implementation. For important decisions, a two-thirds majority vote is an alternative to simple majority rule. A two-thirds majority vote ensures substantial, if not total, support for a decision made by the group.

In recent years, simple mathematical procedures have also been recommended to achieve majority rule (Huber, 1980; Delbecq, Van de Ven and Gustafson, 1975). For example, each member of a task group can be asked to rate alternative solutions on a five-point scale from 5 = best alternative to 1 = worst alternative. The group's chairperson or staff person tabulates the vote on each alternative solution. Because this procedure is easily done without identifying member's individual ratings, it also preserves their anonymity during the decision-making process. Another mathematical procedure is to have all members rank order alternative solutions. Ranks are tallied, and the mean of the ranks is calculated for each alternative. The nominal group technique discussed later in this chapter uses this procedure for selecting among alternatives.

## Monitoring and Evaluating

Monitoring and evaluating are also important functions of task groups. Task groups may monitor and evaluate their own functioning or be called upon to monitor and evaluate the functioning of other systems. For example, the board of a social service agency is responsible for monitoring and evaluating the functioning of the agency. Because boards are ultimately responsible and legally liable for the proper conduct of social service agencies, monitoring and evaluating functions are a critical component of an effective board's work (Swanson, 1978; Houle, 1960). In another case, an alcoholism treatment team monitors and evaluates its own performance by reviewing recidivism data on all former clients at three-month "progress review" meetings.

For effective monitoring and evaluation during the middle phase, task groups must be clear about their mandate from the agency and their ethical, moral, and legal obligations, as expressed by regulatory agencies, professional societies, legislative bodies, and the larger society. At times these are clear, but it is often part of the responsibilities of the task group to develop a set of standards, rules, or guidelines that can be used to monitor and evaluate performance. For example, a large, private social service agency decided to encourage evaluations of several of its service programs. In order to ensure that the research would serve a useful purpose, protect the rights and the confidentiality of their clients, and meet state and federal rules and regulations, an institutional research review board was formed. The first meeting of this task group focused on reviewing the procedures of similar review boards at other agencies and examining state and federal regulations. The group then prepared guidelines governing its own operation and guidelines for researchers to use when preparing proposals to be reviewed by the board.

To fulfill their monitoring and evaluating function adequately, task groups develop feedback mechanisms to help them obtain information about the results of a decision and take corrective actions when necessary (Nadler, 1979). The type of feedback that is useful to a task group depends to a great extent on the group's mandate and the monitoring and evaluating that is required in the particular situation. A board, for example, may require periodic reports from the agency director, the director of clinical services, the agency executive, and the coordinator of volunteer services. In addition, the board may review program statistics, quarterly financial statements from a certified accountant and reports from funding sources about the performance of the agency. In other cases, a task group may use formal data gathering procedures to perform its monitoring and evaluation functions. For a discussion of these methods, see Chapter 10.

## Problem Solving

Problem solving has been given more consideration in the group work literature than any of the other functions of task groups. Task groups spend a great deal of time performing other functions, but problem solving is often seen as a task group's major function. Although problem solving is a separate function from sharing information, involving others, or making decisions, it incorporates many of the other functions of task groups. Problem solving is really a complex set of functions that vary with the type of problem facing the group. The next section describes a generic, six-step problem-solving model that can be used effectively in a variety of task groups.

## A MODEL FOR EFFECTIVE PROBLEM SOLVING

Problem solving can take as little as five or ten minutes or as long as several months. The length of any problem-solving process depends on a variety of factors, including the nature of the problem, the structure and function of the group, and the capabilities and willingness of the group members and group leader to solve the problem. The effectiveness of any problem-solving effort depends on the extent to which an optimal solution is developed and implemented. It also depends on how satisfied the members of the group are with the problem-solving process and the extent to which they support the decision made by the group. It is important for task group leaders to become thoroughly familiar with the problem-solving model presented here so they can apply it in a manner that will satisfy group members and gain necessary cooperation and support. There are six steps in problem solving, including:

1. Identifying a problem.
2. Developing goals.
3. Collecting data.
4. Developing plans.
5. Selecting the best plan.
6. Implementing the plan.

As can be seen in Figure 9–1, these steps are not discrete. In practice they often tend to overlap. For example, preliminary goals are often discussed during problem identification. Goals are modified and refined as data collection continues. Similarly, data collection often continues as the group begins to develop plans for problem resolution.

Problem-solving processes are often described as if they occur once. This may be true in groups convened to solve a single problem, but it is not

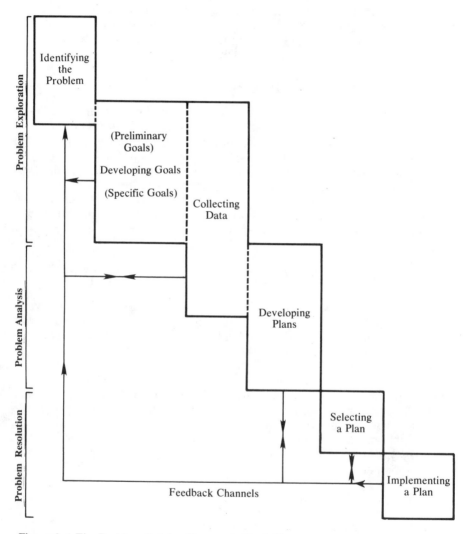

**Figure 9–1** The Problem-Solving Process in Task Groups

often the case. Problem-solving processes are generally used repeatedly by groups as they conduct their business. A task group may have to use two or more cycles of a problem-solving process to accomplish a single task. This process is represented in Figure 9–2. An adult protective service team, for example, spends three meetings developing a plan for emergency evening coverage for all clients on team members' caseloads. The plan is implemented for a two-month trial period. After the trial period, the team reconsiders aspects of the plan. Using the problem-solving process for a second time, the team decides on a modified version of the plan that proves effective in assuring adequate emergency evening coverage. Thus, over the course of several months the team is involved with two problem-solving cycles to accomplish its task.

## Identifying a Problem

How a problem is identified and defined is crucial to effective problem solving. It affects what data will be collected, what range of alternatives will be considered, and who will be called upon to work on the problem, what alternatives will be considered, and who will be affected by the problem's resolution. When they are first identified, problems are often unclear and muddled. They appear to be an unsolvable, complicated maze of tangled or disjointed components. Even when problems appear to be fairly well delineated, there is often a need for further clarification. For example, the staff of a social service agency perceives that it has a problem in serving a large group of Mexican-Americans who live in the area served by the agency. Although at first glance this appears to be a fairly clear problem, it could be defined in a number of different ways, including (1) not having Spanish-speaking workers, (2) not conducting any outreach efforts to this population, (3) having a poor public image with Mexican-Americans in the community, (4) not having the financial resources to develop programs for Mexican-Americans, or (5) providing the wrong services to meet the needs of Mexican-Americans.

Several things can be done to help a group define a problem so as to promote rather than hinder problem solving, including:

1. Clarifying the boundaries of the problem.
2. Seeking out members' perceptions of the problem and their expectations about how it will be solved.
3. Developing a problem-solving orientation.
4. Defining a solvable problem.
5. Specifying the problem as clearly as possible.

Because identifying and defining a problem adequately are critical to the effectiveness of the entire problem-solving process, each of these is described in more detail in the following sections.

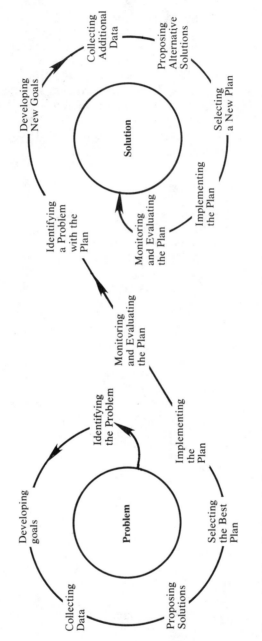

**Figure 9-2** Two Cycles of a Problem-Solving Process

*Clarifying Boundaries.* The first issue that confronts workers and members as they define the boundaries of a problem is how to handle large problems that may have several interrelated components. Groups are often confronted with large problems that seem to be unmanageable and unsolvable. In other cases, a vague concern or problem expressed by a group member may emerge as a large problem as members begin to discuss the issues that the member raises. One method of handling large problems is to partialize them. Several manageable, solvable problems should be developed from problems that are first presented as unsolvable, unmanageable issues.

When the group partializes a problem, it must decide on which aspect of the large problem to work on first. Some guidelines for selecting problems to work on first include:

1. Select a problem that is clearly under the group's legitimate authority.
2. Select a pressing problem.
3. Select a problem that is potentially under the group's control.
4. Select a problem that when resolved will have far-reaching, beneficial effects.
5. Select a meaningful problem whose solution is important to group members and other systems outside of the group.
6. Select a problem that the group has a good chance of resolving successfully.

Boundaries refer to the extent and the scope of a problem or issue facing the group. Defining clear boundaries helps problem solvers to focus and clarify their thoughts and suggestions about a problem, leading to more effective solutions (D'Zurilla and Goldfried, 1971). When setting boundaries the worker is in a delicate position. On the one hand, an effective worker does not want to hamper the group's creative problem-solving ability. The worker would like to encourage the group to consider all the relevant options for problem resolution. On the other hand, the worker is often in a better position than any other group member to recognize what is politically, economically, and organizationally feasible. For example, in a group working on ways to increase services for Mexican-Americans, it would be helpful to inform members that solutions to the problem should not commit the agency to new services that require additional funding because no new funds are available during the current fiscal year. The worker could explain that although the solution should not require new funds, the group might consider making recommendations to the agency's administrative staff about seeking additional funding during the next fiscal year.

Whenever possible, the boundaries of the problem solving process should be as broad and as flexible as possible so as not to stifle creative problem solutions. The worker should point out members' freedom within these boundaries and the importance of accomplishing the task within specified limits. The group should be given a convincing rationale for limiting the scope of a problem and the scope of the efforts used to resolve it. Without guidelines, the group may arrive at a solution that is unacceptable to those who have responsibility for its implementation. Members who spend their time and energy developing a solution that is not feasible will feel frustrated and disappointed when they realize their recommended solution is not implemented.

An example of the delicate balance the worker should strike in suggesting boundaries for problem solving occurs in the following statement by the leader of the task group addressing the needs of Mexican-Americans:

> The needs assessment we have just completed confirms our suspicions—we are not doing enough to serve Mexican-Americans in our catchment area. As we discuss the problem and decide about what to do we should keep in mind that we have just entered a new fiscal year and the agency's budget does not allow for new programming that requires additional funding. The executive director has informed me that within this constraint she will actively pursue any solutions that you suggest for improving service to this population. She is ultimately responsible for presenting solutions we suggest to the board and getting the solutions implemented in the entire agency. In discussing the problem, we should consider ways that existing services could be redirected or applied differently to the clients we serve. Eligibility requirements and other issues related to access might also be explored. We may also want to consider using regularly scheduled in-service trainings and supervision to increase our awareness of the problem and to enhance our skills in dealing with this population. What are your thoughts about tackling this problem?

This example illustrates that the worker has set some broad guidelines for problem solving and has made some tentative suggestions to the group about what aspects of the problem might be worth exploring. The worker has given the group some indication of what is feasible within the budget constraints of the agency and has clarified who is responsible for implementing potential solutions. By asking for members' thoughts about the problem the worker is inviting them to define the boundaries of the problem within these broad guidelines.

*Members' Perceptions and Experiences.*   Members' perceptions of problematic situations and their expectations about how they should be resolved determine the way they will approach a problem. If the members of a group are to be satisfied with the group's problem-solving process and committed to the solution that is decided upon by the group, the members' views about problems facing the group must be respected. There is no better way to show respect than to solicit members' views and to ensure that they are given a fair hearing by all members. Failure to clarify members' expectations and perceptions about a problem often leads to difficulties later in the group's problem-solving process. For example, hidden agendas develop, in part, because unclarified expectations are acted on by members.

Clarifying boundaries and helping members to express their perceptions and expectations of the problem solving situation can be helpful techniques in arriving at a common understanding of the problem. An open discussion usually causes a modification of all group members' perceptions and expectations. Common perceptions and expectations form the basis for mutually agreed upon goals.

Careful considerations of the views of individual group members does not mean that every opinion or bit of information should be treated as equally correct or important. Although there is a tendency to equate equality of ideas with equal treatment of group members, these concepts should not be confused (Kiesler, 1978). Members should be treated equitably in the group process, but the importance of their contribution changes as the work of the group changes.

Sometimes, one or more members may hold tenaciously to initial perceptions of a problem or to initial expectations about the ways a problem should be resolved. Group members should be invited to discuss the logic of their assessments as a means of arriving at a shared view of the problem.

When the majority of the group's members agree with the leader's assessment and ideological differences separate one or two members from the rest of the group, workers can acknowledge the conflict and help members to express minority opinions while continuing to carry out decisions made by the majority.

*Problem-Solving Orientation.*   During the process of identifying a problem it is important for the worker to help members develop a problem-solving orientation (D'Zurilla and Goldfried, 1971). A problem-solving orientation includes:

1. Minimizing irrational beliefs about problematic situations.
2. Recognizing and being willing to work on problems as they occur.
3. Inhibiting tendencies to either respond prematurely on the first impulse or to do nothing.

Irrational beliefs about "how the world should be" can inhibit members from recognizing problematic situations and can also interfere with members' ability to act on problems that need to be resolved (Ellis, 1962). Irrational beliefs can lead to primitive solutions that can have detrimental consequences for the group as a whole. It is important for the worker to encourage all members to challenge irrational beliefs and to encourage rational approaches to problem solving. Members should be helped to use evidence, logic, and sound reasoning as they identify and define a problematic situation (see, for example, Gouran, 1982; Barker, 1979; Harnack and Fest, 1964; Sattler and Miller, 1968).

An effective problem-solving orientation includes recognizing problems that need attention and being willing to work on them. It is sometimes difficult for task groups to confront and work on problems facing them. For example, a team in a psychiatric hospital avoids discussing problems in its own functioning for fear that the discussion will be viewed as an attack on individual members. In this case, the team leader can help by facilitating the development of a group climate that encourages problems to be discussed as shared concerns whose resolution will benefit all team members.

In developing a problem-solving orientation within the group, it is important to help members reduce their tendency to make immediate and automatic responses (Toseland, 1977). Frequently, members will suggest solutions without carefully considering the problem. It has been found that less effective problem solvers are impulsive, impatient, and quick to give up (Bloom and Broder, 1950). Therefore the workers should help members to stop and think about the problem and to collect data and analyze alternative solutions before deciding on what to do (Dollard and Miller, 1950).

There should be sufficient time during a meeting agenda to grapple with difficult problems. According to Tropman (1980), difficult items should be placed in the middle third of the agenda. This is when members are at the peak of their (1) psychological focus, (2) physiological awareness, (3) attention, and (4) attendance (Tropman, 1980). Easier items should be placed earlier in the agenda. Items for discussion only can be placed at the end of the agenda because they require less energy at a time when members have little energy for problem solving.

*Defining a Solvable Problem.*   Groups are sometimes blocked in their problem-solving ability because they fail to locate the problem correctly (Maier, 1963). Group members may fail to identify the correct actors, the correct systems, or the correct obstacles that comprise the problem situation. In the early stages of problem solving, the group should be tentative and flexible about its problem definition so that it is possible to modify it when new data are collected about the situation.

How problems are stated can have an effect on the entire problem-solving process. The worker can use several techniques to improve the group's ability to define a solvable problem. Maier (1963) suggests that whenever possible, problems should be stated in situational rather than personal terms. For example, a definition that attributes the problem of lack of services to Mexican-Americans to an inept director of clinical services will tend to alienate the director of clinical services, making the problem more difficult to solve. However, identifying the problem as a lack of service hours for Mexican-Americans opens possibilities for modifying service delivery patterns. Similarly, defining the problem as a lack of knowledge and expertise about Mexican-American clients suggests that the committee should consider assessing members' willingness to learn more about Mexican-Americans.

To help the group obtain a new perspective on a problem, the worker can use the reframing technique described in Chapter 8. An exercise that can help members to reframe a problem is to ask them to imagine themselves experiencing it as another might experience it. For example, members of a program committee who have some reservations about making efforts to improve services for Mexican-Americans are asked to imagine themselves going to an agency where no one speaks English and where most clients and all workers have a different cultural and ethnic background from their own. The exercise helps members to reconsider whether something should be done to improve services for Mexican-Americans.

Reframing may also be done by focusing on the positive aspects of a problem. For example, a problem that is experienced as anxiety-provoking may be reframed as one that motivates the group to improve a situation. In these ways, members' motivation to solve problems can be increased.

*Specifying the Problem.* Having a clearly defined and mutually understood problem is essential if members are to work effectively together. When problems are first expressed in a meeting, they are often stated as partially formulated concerns. For example, a committee member might say "I get a sense that some of our staff may be having difficulty with the new record keeping system." Many of the terms in this statement are vaguely defined. Terms such as "get a sense", "some of our staff" and "difficulty" can have different meanings for each member of the group.

As concerns are raised by members, the worker should help them to clarify vague or ambiguous terms. The statement mentioned previously, for example, could be clarified to indicate that three members of the community team and one member of the day treatment team expressed concerns that the new record keeping system took too long to fill out. The group should be encouraged to continue to clarify terms such as "took too long to fill out" so that it becomes clear what it is the group is being asked to consider. For example "took too long to fill out" might mean "can not complete the case record in the 15 minutes allocated for that purpose" or might mean "being asked to collect data which is not needed to work with clients." Sometimes members of the task group may find that they can't specify the problem further without collecting additional information.

After the group has clarified the problem, the worker should summarize it in a clear, brief statement. Ideally, the problem should be defined in objective terms that have similar meanings for all members. Objective terms with clear, observable referents help members to arrive at a common understanding of the situation. When summarizing, the worker should restate the boundaries of the problem and the group's authority and responsibility so that members will have a clear idea of their role in resolving it.

## Developing Goals

The second step in the problem-solving process is goal setting. Goal setting does not occur at only one time in the problem-solving process. Tentative goals are formulated soon after the problem has been identified. These tentative goals aid in data collection because they help to shape the scope of the information that is to be collected. Goals are often modified and specified during data collection as additional information is accumulated. Initial goals may sometimes be abandoned altogether and new goals may be developed on the basis of the data accumulated.

The procedures for developing goals for specific problems are quite similar to goal-setting procedures described in beginning a group. Through a process of exploration and negotiation, the worker and the members share their perspectives about what goals the group should achieve in relating to a particular problem. The emphasis should be on formulating goals that are mutually acceptable. Like problem statements, goal statements should be as clear and specific as possible. Desired changes in problem situations should be stated as objective tasks. For example, goals to increase services to Mexican Americans might include (1) providing eight hours of training for each outreach worker during the next six months, (2) increasing the number of Mexican Americans served by the agency from an average of three a month to fifteen a month by the next fiscal year, (3) translating program brochures into Spanish within three months, and (4) printing four hundred bilingual Spanish-English brochures at the beginning of the next fiscal year. Each of these goals specify tasks that can be readily understood by all members.

Group workers can utilize several other principles for developing effective goals, including:

1. Goals should be directed at the mutual concerns of all members.
2. Goals should be consistent with the group's mandate, its overall objectives, and the values which have been agreed upon by the group as a whole.
3. Goals should be attractive enough to gain the commitment, cooperation, and the investment of all group members.
4. Goals should be realistic and attainable through the resources available to the group and its members.
5. Goals should be time-limited.
6. The goal-setting process should set a supportive, encouraging climate for goal attainment.

At the end of the goal-setting process, members should be clear about the tasks they must perform in order to achieve the goals decided on by the group. It is important for the worker to summarize the goals that have been decided upon by the group and to review each member's role in goal achievement. This avoids misunderstandings about who is responsible for what during a specified time period. Members should be clear about the time frame for accomplishing goals and about the mechanisms for reporting their achievements to the group.

It is often helpful to partialize large goals into a series of smaller ones that can be more readily accomplished by the group in a short time period. This is particularly true in recently organized groups, whose members may be overwhelmed by the enormity of a task and unsure about the group's ability to accomplish it. Partializing goals gives members a sense of accomplishment as they reach subgoals. This sense of accomplishment increases the attractiveness of the group, helping to ensure highly motivated members for future problem-solving efforts.

## Collecting Data

Data collection is the third step in the problem-solving process. It begins as soon as a problem is identified by a group and continues as broad goals are defined and refined and as plans are being developed. As a process, data collection is concerned with idea generation. It should be kept separate from analyzing facts and generating solutions. Data collection relies on creative, imaginative thinking, whereas data analysis relies on evaluative thinking. Groups sometimes arrive at hasty, ill-conceived solutions because they rush to implement initial ideas without carefully exploring the situation, the obstacles to problem resolution, and the ramifications of a proposed solution.

Areas of information that are important for the group to obtain when attempting to solve any problem include (1) the history of the problem; (2) previous attempts at resolving the problem; (3) objective facts about the situation, such as who is involved in the situation, where, how, and when the problem occurred; (4) characteristics of the problem, such as its duration, intensity, scope, and importance; (5) the psychosocial context of the problem; and (6) organizational and societal rules and regulations that impinge on the problem. It is important for the group to have as much information as possible about the problem as it analyzes data and prepares alternative solutions.

Knowing the history of the problem helps the group to develop a longitudinal perspective on its development and its course. Comparing the state of affairs before and after a problem has occurred can often point to potential causes and possible solutions. While gathering data about the history of the problem, the group should become familiar with previous attempts to solve it. This can help the group avoid repeating past failures.

The worker should help members to pinpoint as many objective facts about the situation as possible. To help members separate facts from opinions and feelings, the worker should encourage members to describe the situation as if they were uninvolved observers who took a photograph of the situation. After the objective facts of the situation are described, members should be encouraged to share their unique perspectives about the problem. Scheidel and Crowell (1979) list five facilitative conditions that help to create a group climate which encourages members to share their unique perspectives. These include (1) maintaining the group's openness to speculation, (2) encouraging an open search for all pertinent data, (3) encouraging all group members to present their ideas, (4) demonstrating genuine appreciation of differences, and (5) refraining from evaluation (Scheidel and Crowell, 1979).

A supportive group climate reduces the need for members to defend their positions. Gibb (1961) points out that communications should be expressed (1) nonjudgmentally, (2) genuinely, (3) without the intent of controlling others, (4) with tentativeness rather than certainty, and (5) as an equal rather than as a superior. Facilitating this type of communication in a group increases problem exploration and contributes to high-quality solutions.

Members should be helped to become "unstuck" in the ways in which they explore and review the problem (Napier and Gershenfeld, 1981). Members should be encouraged to (1) view problem situations flexibly rather than rigidly, (2) expand rather than restrict the way information is collected and combined, (3) recognize and fill gaps in available information, (4) generate new ideas by viewing situations from alternative perspectives, and (5) use lateral as well as vertical thinking processes.

Vertical thinking processes are often associated with rational problem-solving strategies. Vertical thinking relies on inductive and deductive reasoning. Evidence and reason are used in a logical fashion until a solution is reached. Solutions are grounded in facts that are built one upon another in an orderly, systematic, and linear fashion.

Lateral thinking processes are particularly useful in problematic situations when vertical thinking processes have not yielded a creative solution. Lateral thinking helps to free ideas that have been blocked by stale, routine ways of conceptualizing a problem and its potential solutions. Instead of relying on an orderly, linear combination of facts, lateral thinking is characterized by the use of analogies, metaphors, similarities, contrasts, and paradoxes. Seemingly disparate facts, thoughts, and ideas are put together in new and creative ways. Analogies, for example, help to bring out similarities between objects or situations that were previously considered to be different. Solutions that were found to be helpful in analogous situations might, for example, be tried in the current situation. For further information about lateral thinking process, see DeBono (1968, 1971, 1972).

## Developing Plans

Whereas data collection encourages divergent thinking processes, preparing plans for problem resolution encourages convergent thinking processes (Scheidel and Crowell, 1979). The worker calls on members to organize, analyze, and synthesize facts, ideas, and perspectives generated during problem exploration. Figure 9–1 (page 266) shows that plans should be developed during the analysis portion of problem solving efforts.

The first step in analyzing the information generated during data collection is to display it so that all members can see it. It is difficult for members to keep a great deal of information in mind as they are attempting to develop alternative solutions. Displaying information on newsprint or a blackboard helps to ensure that all members are aware of the full range of information shared during a discussion.

The next step is to order and clarify the information generated by the group. Techniques that are useful for this purpose include (1) separating relevant from irrelevant facts, (2) combining similar facts, (3) identifying discrepancies, (4) looking for patterns across different facts, and (5) ordering facts from most important to least important. During the process of organizing data into a coherent whole, members should be encouraged to discuss the logic behind their reasoning rather than to discuss their particular ordering of information. Members should be encouraged to give each other a chance to explain why they see things the way they do, rather than to defend their choices. Defending choices often entrenches group members opinions, whereas a discussion of how members think information should be used often brings out commonalities and similarities in members' views of the situation.

After the information is ordered, it is helpful to redefine the problem, specifying, refining, and, if necessary, reframing it, in view of the facts, ideas, and perspectives that have been discussed. It is also helpful to reexamine the group's goals by comparing the problem situation to the outcomes the group would like to achieve by resolving the problem. Once a common definition of the problem is reached and a valued end state is specified, the group should have little trouble developing a plan to solve the problem.

Before making a decision, members should be encouraged to develop as many alternative solutions as possible. Because critical and evaluative comments tend to inhibit the production of creative ideas, workers should caution members not to criticize each other's solutions as they are presented. When members generate alternative solutions, they should also keep in mind that their strategies and plans for problem resolution must begin to specify the action system and the tasks, as well as the time, energy, and resources necessary for implementing the solution.

## Selecting the Best Plan

After all members have presented their alternatives, the group should review each one. This review has several purposes. It helps to ensure that all members understand each alternative. Misunderstandings at this point can cause conflict and reduce the chances for achieving closure in the problem solving process. Reviews can be used to clarify the objectives and goals described in each alternative plan. Objectives should clearly indicate who will be involved in problem resolution efforts and what they will be doing. Objectives should be developed in a way that allows them to be evaluated. When reviewing each alternative, members can discuss how they would overcome obstacles and challenges likely to be encountered if the alternative were implemented. For large or costly decisions, task groups sometimes recommend that one or more alternatives be tested in a pilot program before full-scale implementation.

Once this is done, members are ready to choose between alternative plans. When selecting among alternatives, members should be encouraged to consider the overall likelihood that a plan will resolve the problem in a manner that is valued by all group members (Edwards, 1961). For this purpose, it is helpful for members to develop criteria that can be used to judge each plan. Rational decision making methods based on utility theory have been developed to help members develop judgment criteria. Although much has been written about these methods (see, for example, Becker and McClintock, 1967; Shelly and Bryan, 1964; Edwards, Lindman, and Phillips, 1965), until recently they have not been widely applied in the human services (Huber, 1980; Rohrbaugh, 1979, 1981; Toseland, Rivas and Chapman, in press).

To select among alternatives, groups sometimes rely on decision criteria developed by experts. For example, a task group at HEW was charged with distributing funds for health maintenance organizations in "medically under-served" areas. By using panels of experts, the committee developed four criteria for deciding among programs that applied for funds in "medically underserved" areas. These included (1) the number of physicians per 1,000 population, (2) the percentage of families in the area served with less than $5000 annual income, (3) the infant mortality rate in the area served and (4) the percentage of the area's population over age 65 (Health Services Research Group, 1975).

At other times, groups rely on the expertise of their own members to develop decision criteria. This is frequently done by having members rate the advantages and the disadvantages of each alternative. Alternatives may be combined or modified to maximize advantages and minimize disadvantages. As members decide between alternatives they should keep in mind the group's mandate, its goals, and the ideal situation they would like to see result if the problem were resolved successfully. Members may also want to consider other factors, such as the benefits and costs of implementing alternative solutions, the comfort and ease with which particular solutions are likely to be implemented, and the political ramifications of alternative solutions. The most effective solution to a problem may not be the most desirable solution if it is costly or if it is likely to offend, inconvenience, or otherwise upset those who will be asked to implement it.

## Implementing the Plan

Excellent decisions can be worthless when task groups do little to ensure that they are implemented properly. Effective problem solving requires that a group take an active part in overseeing a plan's implementation.

Input from those who will be influential in implementing the plan should be solicited as early as possible in the problem-solving process. Once a solution is decided upon, members should begin to gain support for the decision from constituencies outside the group. Members should seek the support of those with authority to implement the decision and those who will be held accountable for the decision. For example, the committee that decided to improve outreach efforts to Mexican-Americans by training staff and publicizing agency programs in the Mexican-American community sought the cooperation of the board of directors, the agency's executive director, the directors of programs who are responsible for implementing staff training and publicity campaigns, all direct service staff who were going to be involved in the program, and leaders of the Mexican-American community.

When seeking the support of others, members may have to educate people to the value of a new approach to a problem. Motivating people to cooperate with the implementation of a decision is not an easy task. However, motivation is important because passivity during the implementation phase of problem solving can often mean the demise of a promising solution. In gaining cooperation, individual members or the group as a whole may also have to use some leverage to gain the support of others (Cox, Erlich, Rothman, and Tropman, 1974). This leverage may include persuasion by those with prestige and power or lobbying by those who will benefit by the solution.

Once the receptivity of those responsible for implementing the decision is ensured, the group can begin to organize and supervise the plan's implementation. When a group is responsible for the implementation of a large plan, a division of labor is often helpful. Each member may be assigned specific responsibilities in overseeing the plan's implementation. There may also be a need for training to educate those who will implement the plan.

It is often helpful to delineate steps in the implementation sequence. Objectives can be specified for each step, allowing the group to obtain periodic feedback about the plan's implementation. A time line can be attached to the implementation sequence. This helps to clarify how much time is available for each step during the implementation phase. During this process, members often experience surprise and even shock at how long a plan will take to become fully operational.

Implementing the proposed solution also includes identifying, contacting, and utilizing available resources. A heterogeneous group can be advantageous in the process because of the diversity of resources that members have available. Members can also help the group to prepare for opposition. Obstacles might include inertia, passive resistance, and perceived or actual conflicts of interest that can lead to attempts to block implementation of a plan.

As Figure 9–1 (page 266), shows feedback is essential in the problem-solving process. When planning for the implementation of a decision, group members should establish feedback channels. Access to feedback can keep the group apprised of a solution's utility in terms of its expected outcome. Feedback can be used to overcome obstacles, to stabilize change, and to meet the challenges of a continually changing environment.

## OTHER PROBLEM-SOLVING METHODS

Versions of the problem-solving model presented here are used in most task groups, but keen interest in improving the problem-solving and decision-making ability of groups has led to the development of other problem-solving methods. Some of these methods were developed to improve specific steps of the problem-solving process. For example, brainstorming was developed specifically for generating ideas and social judgment analysis was developed to improve decision making. Others, such as the Nominal Group Technique, are complete problem-solving methods.

Many of the methods require similar leadership skills. For example, both the nominal group technique and brainstorming rely on guided group discussion. The difference between methods is one of emphasis. The nominal group technique encourages discussion after a period of silent idea generation, whereas brainstorming encourages members to continue to communicate throughout the process.

Differences among the methods have occurred, in part, because each was developed to meet different needs. Brainstorming, for example, is primarily aimed at improving the creativity of a group's solutions. Social judgment analysis aims at fostering consensus when members choose between different solutions to a problem. The particular benefits and the limitations of each method will be presented after each is described (for more information about the comparative benefits of these methods, see Toseland and Rivas, in press). With these guidelines, workers may pick and choose among methods, depending on the particular needs of task groups in specific situations.

## Brainstorming

Brainstorming is probably the best known of the specialized methods presented in this section. Elements of brainstorming, such as suspending judgment, have long been recognized as effective techniques. Alex Osborn (1963), however, was the first to develop a systematic set of rules for generating creative ideas, which he called brainstorming.

During brainstorming, total effort is directed toward creative thinking rather than analytical or evaluative thinking. Analytical and evaluative thinking can reduce ability to generate creative ideas. Members are concerned about their status in a group, and if they expect critical judgments about their thoughts and ideas they are not likely to express them. Analytical and evaluative thinking can also serve as a social control mechanism. Members who continue to present ideas that are viewed critically are likely to be sanctioned. Members may also screen out potentially creative, but controversial, ideas before they are ever expressed. By attempting to reduce analytical and evaluative thinking, brainstorming encourages a "free" disclosure of ideas.

Four rules are used to manage the group's interaction during brainstorming:

1. "Freewheeling" is welcomed. Members are encouraged to express all their ideas no matter what they might be. Members should not hold back on ideas that might be considered wild, far-out, crazy, repetitious, or obvious.
2. Criticism is ruled out. Members are asked to withhold analyses, judgments, and evaluations about any of the ideas presented during the idea-generating process. Members should not try to defend or explain their ideas.
3. Quantity is wanted. According to Osborn (1963) and Clark (1958), the more ideas suggested by members in the allotted time, the better. The greater number of ideas generated, the greater the quality of ideas. Quality will occur by itself if enough ideas are generated.
4. Combining, rearranging, and improving ideas are encouraged. Often called "hitchhiking," this technique calls upon group members to build upon ideas that have already been expressed. Members can combine or modify ideas and suggest how other members' ideas can be improved.

*Procedures.*   Although large groups may tend to inhibit idea generation and reduce a member's ability to participate in the allotted time, brainstorming can be conducted in large or small groups. Because brainstorming encourages the generation of creative and unique ideas, a heterogeneous membership representing many points of view will help to facilitate the process. The procedure can be conducted in a short period of time (fifteen minutes) but longer meetings may produce more quality ideas. This occurs because ideas presented in the last third of a group's meeting are often of a higher quality than ideas produced during the first two thirds of the meeting (Sattler and Miller, 1968).

At the beginning of the meeting, the worker explains the problem to be brainstormed and the four basic rules of brainstorming. A warm-up period of ten to fifteen minutes can then be used to familiarize members with the procedure and to help them learn to express and to hear ideas without criticizing them. During this time, the worker can model appropriate behavior and can make some suggestions about procedures, such as lateral thinking, that may help to increase creativity. Even when some members of the group have used brainstorming procedures previously, such as lateral thinking gives all members an opportunity to prepare to change routine patterns of analyzing and evaluating ideas. It also allows them to become acclimated to "freewheeling" idea generation.

During the brainstorming procedure, a leader or a co-leader writes the members' ideas on a flip chart or a blackboard. Having a co-leader record ideas is particularly helpful during warm-up sessions, because it is difficult for the leader to train members, record ideas, and model appropriate behavior all at the same time. Ideas should be recorded, using the words of the speaker as much as possible. Key words should be abstracted in order to reduce suggestions sufficiently so that they can be easily written on newsprint or a blackboard.

The interaction pattern in the group should encourage the free flow of ideas. Members are asked to present one idea at a time and to allow everyone to have a turn presenting ideas. Occasionally, it is necessary to limit talkative members by encouraging those who have not contributed extensively to express their ideas. In large groups (more than fifteen), it has been recommended that members raise their hands before they begin to speak (Scheidel and Crowell, 1979). This procedure also makes it easier to record, because ideas can be clarified more quickly when the recorder's attention is focused on the speaker.

Sometimes groups run out of ideas or repeat similar ideas without pursuing new or alternative thinking patterns. Instead of closing a session, the worker should read ideas from the list to stimulate thinking, focus the group's attention on unexplored areas of the problem, or pick out one or two ideas around which the group may want to generate additional ideas. Throughout the process, the worker should (1) express interest in the ideas as they are presented, (2) urge members to continue to produce creative ideas, and (3) help the group to elaborate on ideas that have already been presented.

The worker should not try to have the group evaluate ideas immediately after the brainstorming procedure. Waiting one or more days allows members to think of new ideas to add to the list and allows time for them to return to an analytical way of evaluating ideas. Once the meeting has ended, the worker should ensure that members are not blamed or sanctioned for the ideas they have expressed. If they are, brainstorming will not succeed in future meetings.

*Uses.*   Brainstorming procedures are very useful under certain conditions. Brainstorming should be done in groups that have already defined a problem. In many respects, brainstorming can be used as a substitute for the methods described in the "developing plans" portion of the problem-solving model described previously. Brainstorming procedures are particularly appropriate if the problem the group is working on is specific and limited in range (Scheidel and Crowell, 1979). It has been shown that the quality of solutions improves in brainstorming groups that have been instructed to focus on specifically defined problems rather than on broadly defined problems (Davis, Manske, and Train, 1966). Parnes (1967) suggests using "limited critical thinking" rather than "free associating" as recommended by Osborn (1963). This ensures that group members focus their ideas, making them relevant to a specific situation being examined by the group.

Brainstorming methods are useful when the group is particularly interested in generating as many ideas as possible. Brainstorming, therefore, should not be used when the group faces a technical problem that requires systematic, organized thinking. Implicit in the brainstorming approach is the notion that the problem is capable of having many solutions (Scheidel and Crowell, 1979). In many situations, groups confront problems that can be solved in a number of ways, but sometimes problems have only one right answer. In these situations, brainstorming is not an appropriate technique, and other rational, structured problem-solving methods such as social judgment analysis and the nominal group technique are more likely to help a group produce the best solution (Toseland and Rivas, in press).

*Effectiveness.*    Most of the evidence for the effectiveness of brainstorming is based on anecdotal accounts of its use in business meetings (see, for example, Clark, 1958; Osborn, 1963), but the method has been investigated through empirical research (see, for example, Maltzman, Simon, Raskin, and Licht, 1960; Bayless, 1967; Taylor and others, 1958). Although the Taylor study is often cited to disclaim the effectiveness of brainstorming, this study did not compare brainstorming and nonbrainstorming conditions. Taylor and colleagues (1958) found that brainstorming produced better results when it was done by individuals working alone than by individuals in a group. Findings from the study suggest that nominal group brainstorming is better than interacting group brainstorming but do not suggest whether group brainstorming is better than a group meeting without brainstorming. Other studies show that when brainstorming is used in a group context, the results are positive (Maltzman and others, 1960; Bayless, 1967). Groups that use brainstorming produce more ideas of a higher quality than groups that do not use this approach (D'Zurilla and Goldfried, 1971). Nominal brainstorming in which members generate as many ideas as possible without interacting may be even more effective than brainstorming in interactive groups.

Brainstorming generates ideas from a wide base because it encourages all group members to fully participate. The method also tends to establish members' commitment to the idea that is ultimately decided upon because members have had a chance to shape the idea that is selected. Napier and Gershenfeld (1981) have listed other benefits of brainstorming in groups, including:

1. Reducing dependency on a single authority figure.
2. Encouraging open sharing of ideas.

3. Increasing safety in highly competitive groups.
4. Providing for a maximum output of ideas in a short period of time.
5. Providing for immediate visibility of members' ideas as they are posted.
6. Developing accountability because ideas are generated internally rather than imposed from outside of the group.
7. Being enjoyable and self-stimulating.

Despite its benefits, brainstorming is not without its drawbacks. It is not easy to achieve an atmosphere in which ideas are generated freely. Brainstorming can initially cause discomfort to those who are not used to freely sharing their ideas (Hammond and Goldman, 1961; Collaros and Anderson, 1969; Broom, Grant, and Cotton, 1969). The brainstorming procedure breaks norms that ordinarily protect members from making suggestions that may result in overt or covert sanctions (Bouchard, 1972b).

There are also factors that may reduce the efficacy of brainstorming procedures. For example, although the warm-up period is essential for optimum performance during brainstorming, warm-ups require time, which may not be available. Inertia may also interfere with brainstorming because brainstorming requires a change from ordinary group procedures. The worker may not feel justified in imposing the procedure on reluctant or skeptical members who are unaware of its benefits. Although brainstorming has many potentially beneficial effects, if it is to be used effectively, members must be made aware of its usefulness and workers must apply it correctly.

## Variations on Brainstorming

*Reverse Brainstorming.* First proposed by Richards (1974), reverse brainstorming is a procedure that can be used to list the negative consequences of actions quickly and thoroughly. Group members are asked "what might go wrong with this idea?" Reverse brainstorming is useful after a variety of ideas have been generated. Members should first use a scanning procedure such as the one suggested by Etzioni (1968, Chapter 12) to reduce a long list of ideas to several alternatives. Members are then asked to brainstorm about the consequences of carrying out each alternative. In addition, when the group is aware of potential obstacles to solving the problem, the worker can ask members to suggest ideas for how the potential solution might be improved to overcome these obstacles.

*Trigger Groups.* The trigger group procedure attempts to utilize the findings of Taylor and colleagues (1958), and Dunnette and others (1963), who discovered that brainstorming is more effective when it is done by individuals working alone than by individuals in interacting groups. In a trigger group, each individual works alone for five to ten minutes, developing a list of ideas and suggestions (Richards, 1974). One member at a time then reads the whole list of ideas to the group. After a member reads his or her ideas, the group takes about ten minutes to clarify, add to, or combine ideas that a member has presented. As in brainstorming, these suggestions are made without criticism. In this manner, all members, in turn, present their ideas to the entire group. After all members have presented their ideas, the group then decides together about criteria for evaluating ideas. Ideas are then screened by the group, one at a time, to arrive at a single solution to a problem.

Among the benefits of this approach is that it allows members to work on their own, developing their ideas without verbal or nonverbal evaluative comments from other group members. This avoids some of the difficulties that group members have when attempting to present their ideas freely in brainstorming groups. At the same time, it focuses the attention of the entire group on the ideas of one individual. This gives members a feeling that their ideas are heard, understood, and carefully examined and it also gives each member an opportunity to receive constructive comments from all group members. Trigger groups are best when conducted with five to eight members, because the time necessary to develop ideas, to brainstorm, and to critically evaluate each individual's ideas can be prohibitive in larger groups.

*Synectics.*    Synectics is a method for generating creative ideas during problem solving. *Synectics* is a Greek word which means the joining together of different and seemingly irrelevant elements. Gordon (1961) developed synectics after years of exploring methods to increase creativity. Prince (1970) added to Gordon's ideas and expanded the method for use in group problem solving.

A synectics meeting lasts about three hours and takes place with from five to eight members who have diverse interests and experiences. Much of the meeting follows an ordinary problem-solving sequence. A problem is introduced by the worker and members are encouraged to present their ideas about it. To avoid coercion and intimidation, the worker should not be someone with influence or power over other group members. The worker should have a neutral view of the problem. A major goal of synectics is to develop a climate of trust in which all ideas are valued. During the preliminary discussion the problem is clarified and specified. The worker's job is to help members to reframe the problem by separating it from its usual context, to help members present unique ideas without criticism, and to help the group refrain from making premature decisions.

As the problem-solving process continues, the worker may notice that members are making predictable noncreative responses to a problem. At a timely point during this discussion, the worker can suggest that the group go on an "excursion" (Napier and Gershenfeld, 1981). An "excursion" is a method of using analogies to stimulate new ideas. For members who have not participated in synectics meetings before, the worker should begin with a direct analogy that is easy to develop.

A direct analogy is an analogy to something in the environment, such as "what is there about this problem that's like what is often found in nature?" Other types of analogies include a personal analogy, such as "how would you feel if you were this problem?", a symbolic analogy, such as "what object or thing do you associate with this problem?", or a fantasy analogy, such as "imagine that you could control time—how would you use time to help resolve this problem?" These can be used to help members develop creative ideas about a problem (Gordon, 1961).

Synectics is an interesting alternative to rational problem-solving approaches such as social judgment analysis. Although there have been a number of anecdotal accounts of the effectiveness of synectics (see, for example, Prince, 1970), there is only one study which confirms assertions that groups using this method develop more creative ideas than they would if they had used ordinary problem-solving or brainstorming approaches (Bouchard, 1972a).

Others, (see, for example, Parnes and Harding, 1962) have attempted to discover the processes that encourage creative thinking. They have found that reducing criticism and encouraging the free expression of ideas are useful methods in generating creative ideas. It is unclear, however, whether using analogies during "excursions" further increases the problem-solving ability of task groups. More research should be conducted on synectics and other creative problem-solving methods, such as lateral thinking, to ascertain whether they are viable alternatives for generating creative ideas and effective solutions to problems.

## Nominal Group Technique

The nominal group technique (NGT) represents a change from traditional interacting approaches to solving problems in task groups. The technique was developed by Andre Delbecq and Andrew Van de Ven as they studied program planning groups in social service agencies and the operation of committees and other idea-aggregating and decision-making groups in business and industry (Delbecq, Van de Ven, and Gustafson, 1975). The technique has been used extensively since its development in the late 1960s in health, social service, industrial, educational, and governmental agencies as an aid in planning and managing programs.

*Procedures.* An NGT meeting should be held with between six and nine group members. Larger groups should be separated into two or more smaller groups. Because participants are required to write and because ideas are presented on a flip chart, group members should be seated around a table in the shape of a "U." A flip chart with newsprint should be placed at the open end of the "U" shape. Supplies that are needed include a flip chart, a felt tip pen, a roll of tape, index cards, work sheets, and pencils.

An opening statement is made about the purpose of the meeting. Before an NGT meeting, the worker should have already developed a clear statement of the problem. According to Delbecq, Van de Ven, and Gustafson (1975), it is the responsibility of the agency to decide on the group's purpose and the problem to be addressed before the meeting. The worker hands out work sheets (lined paper) with the problem statement written at the top of the page, reads the problem statement and asks that all members take five minutes to list their ideas or responses to the problem. Ideas and responses should be written in brief phrases, without verbal or nonverbal communications to other group members. To give the members some notion of what type of responses are being asked for, workers may want to prepare some sample ideas or responses as models. While group members are working, the leader writes his or her ideas in silence and ensures that members of the group do not interact with one another.

The next step is a round-robin recording of ideas generated by each group member. The ideas are listed on a flip chart that is visible to all group members. The worker asks one member for an idea and writes it on the flip chart. The worker then proceeds to the next member, going around the group asking each member in turn for one idea. Members are encouraged to "hitchhike," that is, they can use ideas already on the chart to stimulate their thinking, writing ideas on their work sheet that they did not think of during the silent period. When a member has no new ideas, he or she passes and allows the next group member to present an idea until all members have presented all their ideas.

The ideas should be recorded as rapidly as possible in the words members have used. During the round robin, members should not critique, elaborate on, or defend ideas. Completed sheets from a flip-chart should be taped to a flat surface in view of all group members.

The third step is a serial discussion in order to clarify the ideas that have been presented. The worker explains that the purpose of this step is to clarify each idea. Items from the flip chart are taken in order and discussed for two or three minutes. Members who expressed each idea are encouraged to explain briefly the evidence and the logic used in arriving at the idea. At this point, members are free to express their agreement or their disagreement with the idea and to discuss its relative importance. Although evaluative comments are welcome, the group should not be allowed to focus on any one idea for a long period of time or to get into a debate over the merits of a particular idea.

The fourth step is a preliminary ordering of the importance of the ideas that have been listed. Each member is asked to work independently in selecting a predetermined number of highest priority ideas from the list. The number of items selected varies, depending on the length of the list, but should include about one quarter to one half of the original ideas on the list. Each member writes his or her choice of high-priority ideas on index cards and hands them to the worker. The number of votes that each idea receives from all members is recorded next to that item. This process helps individual members obtain feedback about ideas that are highly regarded by their fellow members.

Each member is then asked to choose five highest priority ideas from the list. The members rank order these ideas from 5 = highest priority to 1 = lowest priority. The idea and its rank order are then placed on an index card. One index card is used for each idea. The cards are collected and the rank orders are tallied by writing them next to their corresponding idea on the flip chart. After all ranks have been tallied, the mean rank for each idea is determined by adding the numbers (ranks) next to each item and dividing by the number of group members.

Delbecq, Van de Ven, and Gustafson (1975) suggest that the group may want to discuss the ranks when (1) there are large discrepancies among members' rating patterns, or (2) items that are obviously rated too high or low (in the worker's opinion) appear when the items are tallied. Delbecq, Van de Ven, and Gustafson (1975) claim the the resulting discussion and second vote often serve to increase the judgmental accuracy of the group. It is usually the worker or a powerful group member who calls aspects of preliminary votes into question. This may be viewed by less powerful group members as a way to manipulate the group process. Therefore, it is recommended that before beginning NGT, the group as a whole should decide under what circumstances a second vote should be taken.

*Uses.* NGT was created to "increase rationality, creativity, and participation in problem-solving meetings associated with program planning" (Delbecq, Van de Ven, and Gustafson, 1975, p. 1). In a brief review of the small group literature, Van de Ven and Delbecq (1971) identified eight inhibiting influences on the performance of interacting groups including:

1. A focus effect in which interacting groups pursue a single thought pattern for long periods.
2. Members participate only to the extent that they feel equally competent with other members.
3. Covert judgments are made but not expressed as overt criticism.
4. The inhibiting effect of status differentials within a group.
5. Group pressure for conformity resulting from sanctions by "expert" group members.
6. Influence of dominant personalities upon the group.
7. The amount of time and energy spent by interacting groups to maintain themselves rather than to work on the task.
8. Members' tendencies to reach quick decisions without fully exploring the problem.

By combining the positive aspects of noninteracting nominal groups and interacting problem-solving groups, Delbecq, Van de Ven, and Gustafson (1975) developed NGT. According to Van de Ven and Delbecq (1971), NGT:

1. Stimulates activity by the presence of others and by everyone working in silence.
2. Avoids evaluative comments when the problem dimensions are being formed.
3. Provides each member an opportunity to search his or her own thought processes.
4. Avoids dominance by strong personalities.
5. Prevents premature decision making.
6. Encourages all members to participate.
7. Allows minority opinions to be expressed.
8. Tolerates conflicting and incompatible ideas that are written in silence before they are presented to the entire group.
9. Alleviates hidden agendas.
10. Gains members' cooperation in achieving a solution.
11. Structures the process so that members feel obligated to work on the problem.

NGT can be used to create a long list of ideas or alternative solutions to a problem. Scheidel and Crowell (1979) suggest that it produces more ideas than any of the other idea-generating and problem-solving techniques that they reviewed. NGT can also be used as a consensus-binding technique. Each group member is given an equal opportunity to express ideas and to participate in reaching a decision. By structuring the interaction, NGT reduces the domination of a few members and makes full use of the creative capabilities and pooled wisdom of all group members. This, in turn, helps to ensure a broad base of support for any decision made by the group.

*Effectiveness.* The NGT procedure is based on social science findings about task groups that have been accumulated over decades of research. Each step is designed to make use of these findings. Delbecq, Van de Ven, and Gustafson (1975) report that research findings indicate that the following procedures increase judgmental accuracy in decision making:

1. Having members make independent judgments.
2. Expressing judgments mathematically by rank ordering or by rating items.
3. Using the arithmetic mean of independent judgments to form the group's decision.
4. Having members make decisions anonymously.
5. Using feedback about preliminary judgments for final voting.

NGT utilizes these research findings in its decision making step by taking the mean rating of independent rank order judgments that have been placed on anonymous index cards. In a similar manner, scientific evidence is presented as the basis for each step in the NGT procedure. Reliance on scientific evidence in developing NGT has apparently worked. Overall, the empirical evidence supports contentions that NGT is more effective than interacting group methods for idea generation, problem solving and for consensus building (see, for example, Van de Ven, 1974, Toseland, Rivas, and Chapman, in press). Some recent evidence indicates that social judgment analysis may be as good as NGT in problem resolution and better than NGT in producing group consensus (Rohrbaugh, 1981), but other evidence (Toseland, Rivas, and Chapman, in press) does not confirm these findings.

Despite its benefits, NGT has some drawbacks. The method is cumbersome. It takes a considerable amount of time (at least one and one half hours), which may not be available to a task group that must complete its work in a short time. This is especially true for routine decisions that may not require the precision afforded by this method. The worker has to be trained in the method and equipped with the necessary supplies to conduct an NGT meeting.

A seemingly inconsequential, though often important, drawback of NGT is that the group process is highly structured, which members may find unpleasant. A recent study found that members of NGT groups were less satisfied than members of less structured discussion groups or members of SJA groups (Toseland, Rivas, and Chapman, in press). Initially members may be suspicious that they are being manipulated by the use of NGT. Aspects of NGT tend to exacerbate rather than to quell these fears. For example, having the worker rather than group members define the problem, and having the worker or a powerful group member influence voting procedures by calling for a second vote, both tend to undermine members' feeling of freedom in solving a problem. Despite these drawbacks, NGT can be a useful procedure in helping task groups to generate ideas and to solve difficult problems effectively. Some evidence, however, suggests that no approach to problem solving in task groups produces a clearly superior solution under all problem circumstances (Fischer, 1981; Hackman and Morris, 1975). If this finding is correct, then the shorter and more familiar generic problem-solving model may be preferred over NGT in some situations.

## Social Judgment Analysis

Whereas NGT is concerned about structuring the method used in problem-solving groups to maximize beneficial group dynamics, social judgment analysis (SJA) focuses on the content of the interactions in a group. SJA structures the group only to the extent that participants are given a method for using information about a problem. SJA uses decision rules to specify the relationship between attributes of a problem. These decision rules, often called multiattribute utility models, are used to maximize the utility of decisions made by task groups.

SJA is based on the cognitive social judgment theory of Tolman (1932) and Brunswick (1943). Tolman and Brunswick (1935) suggest that to integrate information and come up with a decision individuals will (1) place a certain amount of importance on each piece of information (a weight), (2) develop a specific functional relationship (functional form) for each piece of information, and (3) use an organizing principle to interpret all the pieces of information about a problem. A similar process for making judgments has been pointed out more recently by Hammond, McClelland, and Mumpower (1980). They suggest that group members (1) obtain whatever pieces of information they can find, (2) weight each piece of information in terms of its importance or value, and (3) organize the weighted information in some way so as to arrive at a decision. SJA utilizes these findings in its approach to decision making in task groups.

*Procedures.* SJA begins by having each member work alone. This can be done either in separate individual meetings between each member and the worker or in a nominal group meeting where all members work separately on the instructions given by the worker. During this time, the problem and its alternative solutions are explained to members. For example, members might be informed that a group has been appointed to decide among applicants for the position of assistant program director. The worker helps group members to clarify their thinking about the problem. Specifically, the worker helps each member to determine the attributes that are thought to be relevant to making a decision, the "levels" of each attribute and how attributes are weighted in relationship to one another. A member decides that the attributes she considers important for the position of assistant program director include (1) amount of supervisory experience, (2) amount of clinical experience, (3) level of management skills and (4) extent that the candidate likes to develop new and innovative service programs.

The worker also helps each member to specify the levels of each attribute that members have identified as important to the problem situation. This is done by specifying minimal criteria for the solution, any constraints on the solution, and the functional form of each attribute. For example, members decide that minimal criteria for the assistant program director's position include three years of supervisory experience and five years of clinical experience. The members also decide that one constraint on choosing a candidate is that he or she must have an MSW or an MPA degree.

The functional form of an attribute specifies the attributes' relationship to the overall solution, that is, how levels of an attribute are related to the choice of a particular alternative solution. Figure 9–3 gives one member's functional forms for the four attributes mentioned previously. The functional forms indicate that as the amount of clinical experience increases, satisfaction with the candidate (the utility of choosing a particular candidate) increases until the candidate has more than ten years of experience, at which time the member's satisfaction with the candidate declines. This occurs because after ten years the member feels that a candidate may have "too much supervisory experience for the position." For the attribute, clinical experience, a similar functional form occurs except that satisfaction with a candidate increases until the candidate has more than fifteen years of clinical experience. For the attribute "level of management skill" a straight linear relationship exists, suggesting that the higher the score on a management skills test and interview, the higher the satisfaction with the candidate. In the case of developing new and innovative programs, a curvilinear relationship is present, that is, candidates who are either low or high on this attribute are less preferred than candidates who have a moderate inclination to develop new programs.

Figure 9–3 also shows the weight that a group member gave to each attribute. Weights can be assigned by dividing 100 points among all attributes in a manner that reflects the relative importance of each in relation to the others. In Figure 9–3 the attribute, management skills, is assigned a weight of 40, making it four times as important as clinical experience, which has been assigned a weight of 10.

The procedure of establishing minimal criteria, constraints, and attributes with their weight and functional forms is the basis of a member's decision rule, that is, how a group member will use information about a problem to make a judgment. Each member develops his or her own decision rules. When all members have completed this task, they share their decision rules with each other. It is helpful for the worker to post each member's decision rules side by side on a flip chart or a blackboard so that all members can see how their decision rules compare with their fellow member's.

The next step in SJA is to have members discuss the logic behind their decision rules. During this unstructured discussion, the only rule is to focus on the reasoning behind members' choice of attributes, weights, and functional forms (Huber, 1980; Rohrbaugh, 1979, 1981; Edwards, 1977). For example, members would not be allowed to discuss individual candidates for assistant program director but would be encouraged to discuss why a member gave management skills four times the weight of clinical experience when considering candidates for this particular job.

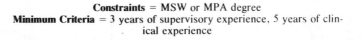

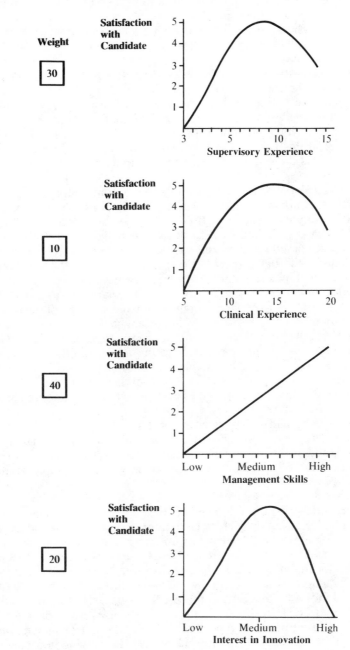

Figure 9–3 A Group Member's Decision Rules for Deciding Between Applicants for Assistant Program Director

Members discuss the decision rules until they reach consensus about a common group rule that satisfies all members. Consensus is usually not difficult to reach because members find it easier to agree on how information will be used than about specific alternatives. Once a group decision rule has been decided upon, it is a routine procedure to see how each alternative is ranked on the basis of the decision rule. First, alternatives which do not meet the criteria or the constraints set up by the decision rule are eliminated. The next step is to calculate each alternative's score on the decision rule. Each score is multiplied by that attribute's weight, and the total score is summed across each attribute. A total score on each alternative is calculated. The alternative (in this case, a candidate) that is rated the highest based on the decision rule is the one selected by the group as its final decision.

*Uses.*   SJA has been used in a variety of different settings including business, industry, urban planning, health, and mental health (see, for example, Rohrbaugh, in press, Edwards, 1977, Rohrbaugh and Harmon, 1981, Huber, 1980). SJA is used primarily as a decision-making technique for choosing between distinct alternatives and should not be used for generating ideas.

Although Rohrbaugh (1979, 1981) has shown that SJA is better than other group methods in helping to achieve consensus, other evidence does not confirm his findings (see, for example, Toseland, Rivas, and Chapman, in press). SJA tends to enhance commitment and support for decisions made by the group. This is particularly important in groups that face difficult choices between alternatives. By providing for a thorough discussion of each individual's decision rules, rather than the more traditional discussion of alternative choices, the group achieves consensus about how information will be used to make a decision. This type of discussion also helps to eliminate the polarization that often takes place when members try to defend their choices of alternative solutions. Once the group decides on a common decision rule, all alternatives are rated according to that rule. Because members have had a chance to influence the decision rule, the choice that is made by the group reflects the input of all members and therefore, is likely to have the cooperation and commitment of all members when it is implemented.

*Effectiveness.*   SJA is the most rational and technical method for leading task groups described in this chapter. It attempts to order and systematize information by assigning each piece of information a weight and a functional relationship to the overall decision. Empirical evidence about this approach (Rohrbaugh, 1979, 1981; Edwards, 1977; Huber, 1980) suggests that it can be helpful as an analytical tool in making decisions that are based on the information available in a problematic situation. Rohrbaugh's research (1979, 1981) also indicates that SJA is more effective than both interacting group methods and NGT in developing group consensus and commitment to a decision. Recent research by Toseland, Rivas, and Chapman (in press) suggests that SJA is better than NGT or problem solving in producing consistent high-quality decisions.

The primary drawback to SJA is that it is a complicated method that is limited to making decisions between clearly delineated and already established alternatives. When decisions between clearly delineated alternatives are crucial and consensus is important, SJA should be considered as the method of choice for problem-solving groups. SJA should be used only by a trained worker who has some conceptual as well as practical experiences in developing decision rules. SJA is not as useful as brainstorming or NGT to generate ideas or alternative solutions, but it can be used once alternatives have been developed by other methods (see, for example, Rohrbaugh, in press). For further information about this relatively recent approach to decision making in problem-solving groups, see Huber (1980, especially, Chapter 5).

## PROBLEM-SOLVING METHODS
## FOR LARGE TASK GROUPS

### Parliamentary Procedure

Parliamentary procedure is a framework for guiding decision making and problem solving in large task groups. Parliamentary procedure has been developed over time in many different settings to meet the needs of a variety of different task groups. Although there are some commonly accepted rules, there is no single body of laws that is universally accepted as parliamentary procedure.

Parliamentary procedure had its origins in 1321 in the English Parliament as a set of rules called "modus tenedia Parlia-mentarium" (Gray, 1964). From these roots, Thomas Jefferson developed a *Manual of Parliamentary Practice* in 1801 for use in Congress, and Luther Cushing formulated a manual for use in lay, as well as legislative, assemblies in 1845 (Robert, 1970). *Robert's Rules of Order* was initially published in 1876 and has had many subsequent revisions and printings. Today, Robert's rules are still the set of parliamentary procedures most frequently followed by task groups.

*Procedures.*   In parliamentary meetings, the activity of the group is determined by motions brought by group members. Motions fall into one of four classes:

1. Privileged motions are those which deal with the agenda of the group meeting as a whole. They do not have a relationship with the business before the group and include motions such as adjournment and recess.
2. Incidental motions are concerned with procedural questions relating to issues presently being dealt with. Some examples include a point of order or a point of information.
3. Subsidiary motions assist in the handling and disposal of motions currently "on the floor." Motions to table, postpone, or amend are subsidiary motions.
4. Main motions introduce the central, substantive issues for group consideration. There can be no pending motions when a main motion is proposed. Examples of main motions include reconsideration of an issue previously disposed of and resuming consideration of a tabled motion.

All motions made from the floor follow procedures governing the introduction of that type of motion. It is the chairperson's job to ensure that these rules and procedures are followed. Although the chairperson is supposed to remain neutral during group deliberations, he or she can influence the group's work in a variety of ways. Group members must be recognized by the chair before they can make a motion. The chairperson rules on questions of procedure that arise during a meeting. The chairperson also organizes the meeting by specifying the order of agenda items and the amount of time available to discuss each item.

Although the rules of parliamentary procedure are not universally standardized, that is, groups often modify a set of procedures such as *Robert's Rules of Order*, there is a method of prioritizing motions that is adhered to by most groups conducting parliamentary meetings. Table 9–1 (pages 296–297) shows the priority that each motion takes during a meeting. Although main motions contain the essential business of the parliamentary meeting, they receive the lowest priority. This is because privileged motions govern how all agenda items are considered, and incidental and subsidiary motions are always made in reference to a main motion. Therefore, these motions are given a higher priority than main motions. For further information about parliamentary meetings, see *Robert's Rules of Order* (1970).

*Uses.*   Parliamentary procedure is often used in large groups because they provide a well-defined structure to guide group process. The rules of parliamentary procedure help to ensure a high level of order and efficiency in task group meetings when many agenda items are discussed. Order and efficiency are achieved through rules that demand consideration of only one issue at a time. They prescribe the way in which issues are brought before the group, processed by the group, and disposed of by the group.

Parliamentary procedure is especially useful for considering well-developed agenda items that need some discussion and debate and a relatively speedy decision by an entire task group (Gulley, 1968). Parliamentary procedure is designed for reaching a decision regarding an alternative currently "on the floor." Parliamentary procedure is of limited value when a problem or issue facing the group has not been clearly defined, when sufficient data have not been gathered about the problem, or when alternative solutions have not been explored and developed for consideration during decision making. Thus, these procedures should not be used as a substitute for problem solving done by subcommittees of the larger task group.

*Effectiveness.*   The long history of using parliamentary procedure in important decision-making bodies throughout the Western world testifies to its usefulness in providing a structure for task group meetings. By limiting and focusing the deliberations of a task group to one solution at a time, discussion and debate are facilitated and motions are dealt with in an expeditious manner. Clearly specified rules lead to an orderly and systematic consideration of each agenda item. Rules that remain consistent throughout the life of a group assure members that there is an established order, which they can rely on for fair and equitable treatment when sensitive or controversial issues are presented during a group meeting.

Parliamentary procedure also protects the rights of the minority. For example, it takes only two members to introduce a main motion, one to make the motion and another to second the motion. Some motions can be made by a single member. Every group member is given an equal opportunity to participate. Majority rights are also protected because a quorum is needed to conduct a meeting and majority rule is relied upon for all decisions.

Despite these advantages, there are several potential disadvantages to parliamentary meetings. Meetings are subject to manipulation by those who are familiar with parliamentary procedures. Members who are less familiar with the procedures may be reluctant to speak, unsure of when to speak, or how to raise an objection to a motion. Another limitation is that private deals may be made outside of a meeting to gain a member's support for an agenda item in a forthcoming meeting. Private deals circumvent the intent of parliamentary procedure, which is based on debating the merits of a proposal being considered by the group. Private deals also tend to enforce the will of powerful members who offer attractive incentives for members who support their position on particular agenda items.

There are other limitations of parliamentary meetings. The procedure encourages debate. This often leads to polarization of members' opinions. Members try to defend their position rather than to understand the logic behind opposing viewpoints. Perhaps the most important limitation of parliamentary procedure is that it is not well suited for problem solving, especially when the problem is complex, muddled, or not fully understood. A large task group using parliamentary procedure does not usually attain the level of interaction, the depth of communication, or the flexibility necessary to explore alternative solutions that may be necessary to resolve difficult problems. Large task groups should conduct most of their problem-solving efforts in subcommittees which report back to the larger group. The larger group can then debate the merits of a proposed solution and reach a decision based on majority rule.

## Phillip's 66

Phillip's 66, or "buzz groups," as the method is often called, was developed as a way to facilitate discussion in large groups (Phillip, 1948). Originally, Phillip's 66 referred to a technique of dividing a large group or audience into groups of six and having each group spend six minutes formulating one question for the speaker. The method has been expanded since 1948 to include many different ways to facilitate communication in large groups. For example, Maier and Zerfoss (1952) suggest using multiple role playing strategies for training staff in large groups. Members of the larger group are asked to form smaller groups and role play the same or similar situations. Each group designates a recorder who reports a summary of group members' experiences when the large group reconvenes.

Other variations have also been developed. For example, Bradford and Corey (1951) have suggested organizing audience listening teams in which each team is asked to listen to, discuss, and report back to the larger group about an aspect of the speaker's presentation. They have also suggested

Table 9–1

## PROCEDURES FOR ACTING ON MOTIONS DURING A PARLIAMENTARY MEETING

| Type of Motion | Priority of the Motion | Can the Speaker be Interrupted? | Does the Motion Need a Second? | Is the Motion Debatable? | Can the Motion be Amended? | Vote Needed to Adopt the Motion |
|---|---|---|---|---|---|---|
| *Privileged Motions* | | | | | | |
| Set the time of adjournment | 1 | N | Y | N | Y | Majority |
| Call for adjournment | 2 | N | Y | N | N | Majority |
| Call for recess | 3 | N | Y | N | Y | Majority |
| Question of privilege | 4 | Y | N | N | N | Chair's Decision |
| Call for pre-scheduled items of business | 5 | Y | N | N | N | No Vote |
| *Incidental Motions* | | | | | | |
| Point of order | 6 | Y | N | N | N | Chair's Decision |
| Request for Information | 6 | Y | N | N | N | No Vote |
| Call for a re-vote | 6 | N | N | N | N | No Vote |
| Appeal the Chair's Decision | 6 | Y | Y | N | N | Majority |
| Object to consideration of a motion | 6 | Y | N | N | N | 2/3 |
| Call to suspend the rules | 6 | N | Y | N | N | 2/3 |
| Request to withdraw a motion | 6 | Y | Y | N | N | Majority |

| Type of Motion | Priority of the Motion | Can the Speaker be Interrupted? | Does the Motion Need a Second? | Is the Motion Debatable? | Can the Motion be Amended? | Vote Needed to Adopt the Motion |
|---|---|---|---|---|---|---|
| *Subsidiary Motions* | | | | | | |
| Table a motion | 7 | N | Y | N | N | Majority |
| Call for immediate vote | 8 | N | Y | N | N | 2/3 |
| Limit/Extend Debate | 9 | N | Y | N | Y | 2/3 |
| Postpone the motion to another time | 10 | N | Y | Y | Y | Majority |
| Refer the motion to a sub-committee | 11 | N | Y | Y | Y | Majority |
| Amend the motion | 12 | N | Y | Y | N | Majority |
| Postpone the motion indefinitely | 13 | N | Y | Y | N | Majority |
| *Main Motions* | | | | | | |
| General main motion | 14 | N | Y | Y | Y | Majority |
| Reconsider a motion already voted on | 14 | Y | Y | Y | N | Majority |
| Rescind a motion under consideration | 14 | N | Y | Y | Y | 2/3 |
| Resume consideration of a tabled motion | 14 | N | Y | N | N | Majority |
| Set a special order of business | 14 | N | Y | Y | Y | 2/3 |

selecting individuals from the audience to serve on an "audience repre-
sentational panel" to react to the speaker. All of these techniques are modifications and expansions of the basic principles of Phillip's 66.

*Procedures.*   In our experiences in facilitating large group meetings, we have
found that Phillip's 66 should only be used after clear instructions are given
to members about what they will be doing during the procedure. This is
especially important because once the large group has broken down into
smaller groups, the sudden change from the structure and control of a large
group meeting can cause confusion. If the groups are not clear about their
direction, they may flounder or begin to work on something other than what
was assigned by the leader.

To reduce the chances for confusion, the worker should ensure that each
group is clear about the problem or task they are facing. Problem statements,
tasks, and goals should be specific. When they are broad and nonspecific, it
will take the small groups some time to refine them. Further, this refinement
may lead to work that is quite different from what the worker had intended.
Members should also be clear about their assignments. They should understand what subgroup they belong to, what the group is supposed to do, what
should be contained in the recorder's report, how much time they have, and
where and when they are supposed to form their small group.

The size of the subgroups and the amount of time each subgroup spends
together depends on the situation. The original design for Phillip's 66, six
member groups each meeting for six minutes, may be appropriate in some
situations but not in others. Generally, at least twenty to thirty minutes are
required for a large group to break down into smaller groups and accomplish
any meaningful work. Subgroups should be separated so members can hear
each other and conduct their work. However, in a large meeting room it is
not necessary to ask members to talk quietly. The noise and activity of other
groups can be contagious, causing all groups to work harder (Maier, 1963).

In very large meetings, having each subgroup report back to the larger
group may be monotonous and time consuming. Alternatives include limiting the reporting time to a few minutes for each subgroup, having each
subgroup report on a portion of the discussion, or developing a brief written
report prepared by each subgroup that can be shared after the meeting.

*Uses.*   Although most problem-solving activities take place in small task
groups, occasionally there is a need for large groups such as members of a
social agency or a delegate assembly to engage in problem-solving discussions. Parliamentary procedure, in which the chair must recognize individual
speakers from the floor, is not designed for large problem-solving discussions. It is designed for debating the merits of proposals and voting on
alternatives that are already well developed. Phillip's 66 can be used as an
alternative method for problem solving in large task groups.

Although Maier (1963) suggests that a skillful worker who is self-
confident can conduct large problem-solving discussions by using techniques such as summarizing and posting alternatives, obstacles to large
group interaction tend to make it difficult to conduct these discussions. For

example, it may be difficult for the worker to maintain order and to encourage participation while helping the larger group work on a problem. It is also difficult to encourage shy members to express themselves particularly as to minority opinions during a large meeting. Using Phillip's 66, the worker can involve all members in a group discussion. The small size of individual "buzz groups" makes it easier for shy members to express themselves. Reporting ideas generated by individual "buzz groups" back to the larger assembly ensures that input from all members is considered in the problem-solving process. Overall, Phillip's 66 is a useful method that overcomes the limitations of parliamentary procedures when large groups are called upon to solve problems.

*Effectiveness.* Phillip's 66 is a practical, commonsense procedure for facilitating discussion and problem solving in large groups. Its effective use has been reported in a variety of sources (see, for example, Maier, 1963; Sattler and Miller, 1968; Gulley, 1968). When it is applied correctly, it can be a valuable technique in a wide variety of situations. However, with poor planning, confused, or nonspecific instructions, or a muddled explanation of the goals of the procedure, it can turn a large task group meeting into disorganization and chaos.

## SUMMARY

This chapter focused on the skills that are needed in order to work effectively with task groups. Task groups have an important place in all human service organizations. Each day, meetings take place that have an important impact on what services are provided and how they are delivered. Social workers and other helping professionals are frequently called upon to chair or to staff committees, teams, and other task groups. When meetings are well run, members become a satisfied and cohesive team that is committed to achieving its objectives. Poorly run meetings, however, can, and often do, lead to boredom and frustration.

Task groups can be distinguished from treatment groups in terms of their functions. The functions of task groups include (1) sharing information, (2) getting members involved, (3) developing information, (4) making effective decisions, (5) monitoring and evaluating, and (6) problem solving. Although some of the functions of task groups and treatment groups overlap, they can be distinguished by their primary focus. Task groups are concerned with the results produced by the group as a whole, whereas treatment groups are concerned with the functioning of individual group members.

Problem solving is probably the single most important function of task groups. Six major steps in problem solving include (1) identifying a problem, (2) developing goals, (3) collecting data, (4) developing plans, (5) selecting the best plan, and (6) implementing the plan. In practice, these steps overlap and they are interconnected by feedback channels. Task groups repeat variations of problem-solving processes as they perform their functions and work on the tasks that confront them.

A variety of other methods have been developed in industry, business administration, and human service organizations to aid task groups in developing effective solutions to problems. This chapter has examined some of the most widely used methods so that workers may choose among them when helping task groups accomplish their objectives. Brainstorming procedures, for example, can be used to help generate new and creative ideas, alternative plans, and problem solutions. Brainstorming is designed to help groups break out of routine patterns and overcome the inhibiting effect that evaluative judgments have on creative thinking. Variations such as reverse brainstorming, trigger groups, and synectics are other methods used for creative problem solving.

Another important method for solving problems is called the nominal group technique. Developed in business, industry, and human service organizations and from social science findings about effective problem solving in task groups, NGT breaks with the tradition of problem solving in interacting groups. By combining nominal group and interacting group procedures in a highly structured format, NGT has proven to be successful in generating ideas and solving problems.

Social judgment analysis is a rational decision-making method. It provides a way to use information to make decisions. SJA helps members to specify the relationships between attributes of a problem and the problem's solution. The resulting decision rule is used to sort through alternative solutions. SJA has proven to be especially effective in encouraging group consensus when members must choose between distinct alternatives.

The final portion of this chapter focuses on methods that group workers can use in large task group meetings. By far, most large task group meetings are run by parliamentary procedure. Although task groups often use modified and streamlined versions, *Robert's Rules of Order* is still the major source for the conduct of parliamentary meetings. Phillip's 66 was presented as a method that can be used to reduce the inhibiting effects of size on communication and interaction in large problem-solving groups. The worker who is able to use the skills and methods presented in this chapter should be able to lead or to staff any task group that may be convened in a human service organization.

PART **V**
# The Ending Phase

# 10
# Evaluation

All workers who are curious about the effects of their interventions gather information about the groups with which they work. Evaluation is the process of obtaining information about the effects of a single intervention or the effect of the total group experience. Workers can use either informal or formal measures to obtain evaluative information. In conducting an informal evaluation, a worker might ask several members of a group how they thought the group was progressing. To complete a formal evaluation, a worker might collect information systematically using preplanned measurement devices before, during, or after the group has met. In either case, the worker obtains information that can be used to evaluate the group. The purposes of this chapter are to explore the many ways to obtain information about a group and to guide the worker in deciding what evaluation methods will be most useful in various situations.

## The Practitioner's Dilemma

Increasingly in social work and allied disciplines, there has been a push toward accountability and empirically validated practice. Workers have been urged to become practitioner-researchers to improve their work as they practice (Browning and Stover, 1971; Thomas, 1975; Jayaratne and Levy, 1979). The push for evaluating practice has occurred even though group workers sometimes fail to keep adequate records, let alone perform systematic evaluations of their practice (Garvin, 1981).

The dilemma for many practicing group workers is that although they are urged to perform evaluations, other demands of practice seem to be more pressing and important than evaluations that require valuable time and energy. Further, many practitioners find it difficult to understand the logic of evaluation methods or their day-to-day usefulness. It has been proposed that practitioners (1) leave most research to the researcher, (2) become consumers of research, and (3) concentrate on developing experience and expertise as group leaders (Trotzer, 1977). However, Trotzer (1977) and most others urge group workers to evaluate their own practice whenever possible.

## Why Evaluate?—The Group Worker's View

When considering whether or not to evaluate their work with a particular group, workers will need to (1) determine their reasons for conducting an evaluation, (2) assess the ability of their agencies to provide the encouragement and the resources necessary for evaluating their own practice, (3) determine the time they have available for an evaluation, and (4) match their information needs and available time with an appropriate method for evaluating their practice.

*Reasons for Conducting Evaluations.*   Workers' reasons for wanting information about a group depend on how they believe the information obtained will be useful to them. Some of the benefits of evaluation for group workers include the following:

1. Evaluations can satisfy workers' curiosity and professional concerns about the effects of specific interventions they perform while working with a group.
2. Information from evaluations can help workers improve their leadership skills.
3. Evaluations can demonstrate the usefulness of a specific group or a specific group work method to an agency, a funding source, or society.
4. Evaluation can help workers assess the progress of group members and the group as a whole in accomplishing agreed upon purposes.
5. Evaluations allow group members and others who may be affected to express their satisfactions and dissatisfactions with the group.
6. Evaluations give workers the opportunity to develop knowledge that can be shared with others who are using group methods for similar purposes and in similar situations.

*Agency Encouragement and Support.*   To evaluate their practice with a group, workers should begin by assessing the willingness of their agency to provide the resources they need to conduct an evaluation. Some agencies do little or nothing to encourage evaluations and may even penalize the worker for attempting an evaluation. Agency norms, peer pressure, or administrative directions may suggest to workers that other tasks are more important than evaluating their practice. In other cases, requirements to serve many clients inhibit workers' abilities to evaluate their practice.

Without active encouragement by agency administrators and the agency's professional staff, workers are left to rely on their own motivations for evaluating their work with a group. Agencies can increase workers' motivation by including evaluation tasks as a part of group workers' practice responsibilities, by providing the time for practice evaluations, and by encouraging workers to discuss evaluations during regularly scheduled staff meetings. Rather than requiring workers to fill out forms and records that they do not use and often do not see again after being processed for administrative purposes, agencies can encourage the development of information systems that can be used for evaluation. A well-designed information and evaluation system can provide feedback for group work practitioners as well as for agency administrators.

*Time Considerations.*   Workers should also consider how much time is available to conduct an evaluation. Most workers collect some information about the groups they lead, and this information can often serve as the basis for an evaluation if it is collected in an appropriate manner. Little additional time is needed for evaluation beyond the time necessary to make modifications in the original data collection system. In other instances, workers may want information that is not routinely collected. They should estimate the amount of time it will take them to collect, process, and analyze the additional information. They can then compare the time needed for the evaluation with the time they have available and decide whether or not the evaluation is feasible. When workers have valid reasons for evaluating their practice, they may be able to persuade the agency to allow them sufficient time to conduct the evaluation. This is particularly true when workers are developing new, innovative programs to achieve goals that the agency has set as priority areas for service delivery.

*Selecting an Evaluation Method.*   Another factor workers should consider is how to match their information needs and available time to an appropriate evaluation method. This chapter will review the major types of evaluations. Each evaluation method will be discussed in terms of its strengths and weaknesses, time requirements, and flexibility.

Workers must also decide on what data collection instruments they will use in conjunction with a particular evaluation method. Some of the major types of data collection instruments used by group workers include:

1. Progress notes.
2. Self-reports of workers, members, and observers.
3. Questionnaires.
4. Analysis of reports or other group products.
5. Review of audio and video tapes of group meetings.
6. Observational coding schemes.
7. Role play or in-vivo performance tests.
8. Reliable and valid scales.

These data collection instruments can be used with any of the major types of evaluation methods. Some measures, however, are frequently associated with one type of evaluation. For example, progress notes are often used in monitoring evaluation methods, and reliable and valid scales are often used in effectiveness and efficiency evaluations. As each type of evaluation method is reviewed, the association between particular methods and particular measures should become clearer.

# EVALUATION METHODS

Workers can use four broad types of evaluation methods to obtain the data they decide to collect. These include evaluations for (1) planning a group, (2) monitoring a group, (3) developing a group, and (4) testing the effectiveness and efficiency of a group method. Workers can use any of these types of evaluation methods to obtain information about the process or the outcome of a group. Process evaluations are those that focus on how a group is conducted, properties of a group such as cohesion, norms, roles, and communication patterns, or other aspects of the functioning of a group. Outcome evaluations focus on the products or tasks achieved by individual members or the group as a whole.

Regardless of the type of evaluation employed, or whether the evaluation focuses on processes or outcomes, workers should be able to use evaluations as opportunities to receive feedback about their practice. Instead of viewing practice evaluations as administrative requirements that are not useful for practitioners, they should be viewed as a way to help workers to become more effective. Evaluations can be used to test new interventions that may prove to be more effective in helping clients achieve their objectives. They can also be useful as a means for workers to begin to understand what interventions work under what conditions.

# EVALUATIONS FOR PLANNING THE GROUP

Evaluations used for planning a group are seldom mentioned in the group work literature. This chapter will discuss two important evaluation methods for planning. These include (1) obtaining program information, technical data, and materials for specific groups that the worker is planning to lead, and (2) conducting needs assessments to determine the feasibility of organizing a proposed group.

## Obtaining Program Information

The worker can often benefit from information about previous methods used in working with similar groups. Workers can often obtain this information from colleagues or from workers in other agencies where similar groups have been conducted. Workers may also (1) examine records from previous groups that focused on similar concerns, (2) review relevant journals[1] or

---

[1]Some of the most important journals that focus on specific groups and specific group work methods include *Group and Organization Studies, Group Psychotherapy, Psychodrama and Sociometry, International Journal of Group Psychotherapy, Small Group Behavior,* and *Social Work with Groups.*

texts, and (3) attend conferences where group workers share recent developments in the field.

For planning task groups, helpful information often includes (1) the minutes of previous group meetings, (2) the operating procedures of previous groups, (3) the charges and responsibilities of previous groups, and (4) information about how similar tasks have been accomplished previously. In treatment groups, program information needs may include the methods used by previous workers in conducting similar groups, the success of previous groups in attaining treatment goals, and members' satisfaction with the treatment process.

## Needs Assessments

Workers might also find it useful to have some information about potential members of a proposed group. This information might include (1) potential members' willingness to attend the group, (2) their motivations for attending, and (3) their capabilities for helping the group achieve its purposes. In treatment groups, workers may want to conduct a needs assessment by asking other workers if clients with whom they work might be appropriate for the group or if workers have received requests for a particular group service they have been unable to meet. Data from community needs assessments designed for multiple purposes can be useful in obtaining information about potential group members. Contacting persons or organizations in the community may also provide access to clients the worker wants to include in a group. When workers have identified potential members they can contact them directly by a personal interview, a telephone call, or a letter. Toseland (1981a) has described these methods of reaching out to clients in more detail.

In some task groups, membership may result from elections, appointments, or because of a potential member's position in an organization. A planning evaluation can familiarize a worker with rules and regulations governing a task group's composition and operation. Planning evaluations can also help a worker collect information and assess the potential contributions that members can make in helping the group achieve its objectives (Rothman, 1974). For further information about conducting planning evaluations, see Rossi, Freeman, and Wright (1979), or Polansky (1960).

## EVALUATIONS FOR MONITORING A GROUP

Monitoring refers to collecting information about group members and about group processes. Monitoring has already been discussed in Chapter 7 as an assessment device, but it can also be used as a method of evaluating group work practice. Monitoring is the least demanding and most flexible of the evaluation procedures described in this chapter. It can be useful for obtaining information for process or outcome evaluations.

## Monitoring Methods

The first step in the monitoring process is to decide what information to collect. For example, those who work with remedial groups designed for clients with psychological disorders may be interested in monitoring changes in individual members over the course of the group on the five axes of the DSM-III. A worker asked to lead an interdepartmental committee of a large public welfare agency may be interested in monitoring the extent to which individual committee members complete assigned tasks.

Whatever information group workers decide to collect by monitoring, they must be clear about how they define it, so that it can be monitored using appropriate measures. Concepts that are ambiguous, obscure, or unspecified can not be measured accurately.

The next step in monitoring is to decide on how the needed information will be collected. Data can be collected by administering questionnaires, asking for verbal feedback about the group, or by recording information about the group through written records, tape recordings, or video recordings of group sessions. In treatment groups, members may be asked to record information about their own behavior or the behavior of other group members. Both Rose (1977) and Garvin (1981) described a variety of procedures group members can use to monitor their own behavior. These include (1) counting discrete behaviors, (2) keeping a checklist, a log, or a journal of events that occur before, during, and after a behavior or a task that is being monitored, and (3) recording ratings of feeling states on self-anchored rating scales. Monitoring methods such as these have been described in Chapter 7 because they are often used for assessment. As illustrated in the following sections, in the monitoring process, collecting data can be the task of either the worker or the group members.

## Monitoring by the Group Worker

One of the easiest methods of monitoring a group's progress is to record activities that occur during or after each meeting. This form of record keeping involves writing or dictating notes after a meeting (Wilson, 1980). The worker may use a process recording method of monitoring or a summary recording method. Process recordings are narrative, step-by-step descriptions of a group's development. Wilson and Ryland (1949) note that process recordings can help a worker analyze the interactions that occur during a group meeting. However, because process recordings are detailed accounts of a group session, they are time-consuming to complete. For this reason, process recordings are rarely used by experienced group workers. They are, however, useful in the training and supervision of beginning group workers because they provide rich detail and give trainees an opportunity to reflect on what occurs during group meetings.

A method of recording that is less time-consuming, more selective, and more focused than processed recording is called summary recording. Summary recording focuses on critical incidents that occur in a group. Summary recording devices consist of a series of open-ended questions. They are most frequently used for monitoring a group's progress after each group session, although they may be used at less frequent intervals during a group's development. Figure 10–1 is an example of a summary recording form used to record a meeting of a family life education group for foster parents.

When using either summary or process recordings, it is important for the worker to record the information as soon as possible after the meeting so that events are remembered as accurately as possible. The meaning of the open-ended summary recording questions should be as clear as possible so that workers' recordings of each group meeting are as consistent as possible with one another. Ambiguous questions open to a variety of interpretations should be avoided. The amount of time that summary recordings require depends on the amount of questions to which the worker responds and the amount of analysis each question requires.

In using open-ended questions, summary recording devices sometimes fail to focus or define the recorded information sufficiently, especially when the worker wants similar information about all clients. Summary recording devices are usually not designed to connect the group worker's activities to specific goals and specific outcomes. Some recent recording systems, such as the problem-oriented record (Kane, 1974), have been designed to overcome problems in summary recording systems. In the problem-oriented record keeping system (Weed, 1969), problems to be worked on by the group are clearly defined, goals are established, and data are collected and recorded in relation to each problem that is specified. Interventions that are made for each problem are also entered in the record under each specific problem. The problem-oriented record keeping system enables workers to show how group work interventions designed to accomplish a certain goal are connected to a specific assessment of a particular problem. Periodic entries are made in the problem-oriented record, assessing progress toward established goals. A final entry is made when the goals for a particular problem have been reached.

In task groups, the minutes of a meeting serve as the record of the group's business. They are often the official record of the proceedings of a group. Minutes are prepared from notes taken during the meeting by a person designated by the worker or elected by the group's membership. A staff person, the secretary of the group, or some other person may take notes on a regular basis. Sometimes, minutes are taken on a rotating basis by each member of a group. The minutes of each meeting are usually distributed to members before the next meeting and are approved by members, with any revisions, during the first part of the next meeting.

Workers may also want to use automated monitoring devices such as audio and video tape recorders to obtain information about a group. Such recordings have the advantage of providing an accurate, unedited record of the meeting. In remedial groups, audio tapes provide immediate feedback about members' verbal behavior. Members may want to replay a segment of the tape if there is a discrepancy about what was said during some portion of the meeting.

In educational groups, video taping can be used in demonstrating appropriate behavior and in critiquing inappropriate behavior. Videotaping is es-

Group name: _____     Beginning date: _____

Worker's name: _____     Termination date: _____

Session number: _____     Date of session: _____

*Members present:* _____

_____

_____

_____

*Members absent:* _____

_____

_____

*Purpose of the group:* _____

_____

*Goals for this meeting:* _____

_____

*Activities to meet these goals:* _____

_____

_____

_____

*Worker's analysis of the meeting:* _____

_____

_____

_____

_____

_____

_____

*Plan for future meetings:* _____

_____

_____

**Figure 10–1** Group Recording Form

pecially useful during program activities, such as role playing, that are designed to increase skills or change behavior patterns. Video feedback helps members to review their behavior during role play practices in order to discuss alternative ways of behaving. For example, members of an assertion training group observe video tapes of their responses to a situation requiring an assertive response. They may analyze voice tone, facial expressions, and body posture, as well as the verbal interactions that occurred. Audio tapes and video tapes provide the worker with a permanent record that can be shared with the group, with supervisors, or in educational workshops.

Although there are many advantages to having an accurate, unedited version of a group available through audio and video tape recordings, there are also some disadvantages to this method of monitoring. Because of its absolute quality, it is not possible for group members to make confidential statements "off the record." This may inhibit the development of trust in the group. The worker may not find it necessary or desirable to have the level of detail provided by this form of recording. The worker may have to spend too much time reviewing irrelevant portions of a tape in order to gain access to information that could have been obtained quickly if brief, summary recordings had been used instead of audio or video tape recordings. However, if a worker is interested in monitoring the group's interaction patterns in a thorough and precise fashion or if an entire transcript of the group session is needed, then audio tape or video tape recordings may be preferable to other methods of collecting data.

Sometimes, it is desirable to use specialized coding systems to obtain reliable and valid data from tape recorded group sessions. This is particularly true when the worker wishes to obtain a detailed and accurate picture of group processes for research. Coding systems can be used by one or more raters of the tapes to determine the frequency and the content of a group's interactions. Coding systems described by Rose (1977), Hill (1977), Bales (1950), and Bales, Cohen, and Williamson (1979) are examples of methods that can be used to analyze specific group interactions.

## Monitoring by Group Members

Members, as well as the group worker, can monitor their own behavior or the behavior of the group. When members monitor their own behavior, they provide an important source of information about the effects of the group and the effects of the worker's interventions. At the same time, members may not be as accurate or as consistent as the group worker in collecting information. Workers should ensure that members understand and are able to carry out data collection procedures when monitoring their own behavior or the behavior of the group. Training in the procedures to be used is often necessary for accurate monitoring.

The most common use of monitoring by group members occurs in treatment groups where individual members keep a record of their behavior between group meetings and report back on these behaviors during the next meeting. An illustration of the steps in the self-monitoring procedure appears in Figure 10–2. During the self-monitoring procedure, the worker and the group members together decide about (1) what data to collect, (2) when to collèct the data, (3) how much data to collect, (4) how to collect the data, and (5) when the information collected by members should be analyzed by the group. As these questions are discussed and answered, the worker reviews each member's monitoring plan.

Members can also monitor a group's progress at the end of each meeting or at intervals in the life of the group. Members may use a short questionnaire devised for such purposes or they can discuss the group's performance orally with the worker. Monitoring allows members to share their feelings with one another and with the worker as the group progresses. Workers benefit from this process because they can use the data to modify their leadership to reflect members' concerns. Shulman (1979) has called the process of using feedback to change the way the worker interacts with members "tuning in." It is most noticeable in the early phases of a group's development but the effective worker constantly solicits feedback from members throughout the development of a group.

Group members also benefit from self-monitoring procedures. Members can share ideas about the group's performance and how it could be improved. This helps to give them a sense of control and influence over the

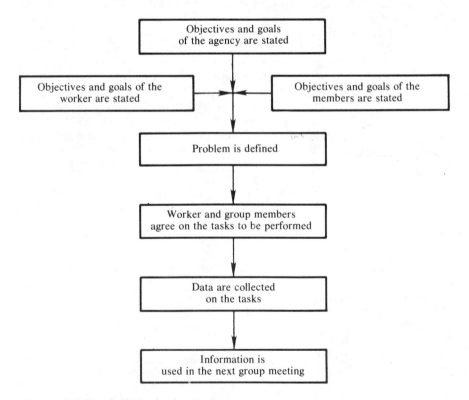

**Figure 10–2** The Self-Monitoring Process

group's progress and increases their identification with the group's purposes. Also, members who feel that their ideas are valued, respected, and listened to are more likely to feel satisfied with their participation in the group.

Verbal evaluations of a group's performance do not provide a permanent record. An evaluation form, consisting of close-ended, fixed category responses and open-ended items, can be used if the worker, group members, or the agency wants written feedback about the group. Figure 10–3 shows a session evaluation form developed by a worker leading a group for single parents. As can be seen, the form contains several easily understood close-ended and open-ended questions. The close-ended questions are Likert-type scales that require respondents to rate their opinions on an ordered scale. Because the same scale values are used for all group members, responses made by each member can be compared to one another. Open-ended items are designed to allow each member to reply in a unique manner with responses that may vary considerably from member to member.

In task groups, members often make oral reports of their progress. Although they are often not considered as evaluation devices, oral reports of progress are an important means by which the worker and the members monitor the group's work. At the completion of a task group, products, or final reports that result from the group's efforts can also be used to evaluate the success of the group.

In treatment groups, an important indicator of the group's performance is the completion of contracts, which individual members make with the group or the worker about tasks to be done during the week to resolve a problem or change a particular behavior. Rose (1977) calls the completion of tasks or assignments the "products of group interaction." He suggests that the rate of completion of assigned tasks is an important indicator of the success of the group.

Monitoring methods have received more attention in the group work literature than other types of evaluation methods. Process recordings, summary recordings, automated recording devices, oral evaluations, written evaluation forms, and products of group interaction can all be used for monitoring a group's progress. Information collected from monitoring a group can serve a variety of purposes in helping workers improve their practice methods and their skills in working with groups. For additional information about evaluation methods used for monitoring a group, refer to Epstein and Tripodi (1977), or Rossi, Freeman, and Wright (1979).

## EVALUATIONS FOR DEVELOPING A GROUP

A third method of evaluating group work practice, developmental evaluation, is useful for the worker who is interested in preparing new group work programs, developing new group work methods, or improving existing group programs. Developmental research, as it has been called by Thomas (1978), is similar to research and development in business and industry. It allows practicing group workers to create and to test new group work programs.

Was the information presented about child development helpful to you in understanding your child's behavior?

| 4 | 3 | 2 | 1 |
|---|---|---|---|
| Very Helpful | Somewhat Helpful | A Little Helpful | Not at All Helpful |

What information did you find most helpful? _____

_____

_____

Rate the effectiveness of the leader in this group session.

| 4 | 3 | 2 | 1 |
|---|---|---|---|
| Very Helpful | Somewhat Helpful | A Little Helpful | Not at All Helpful |

What did you find most helpful about the group during this session?

_____

_____

_____

What did you find least helpful about the group? _____

_____

_____

Overall, rate your satisfaction with today's group meeting.

| 5 | 4 | 3 | 2 | 1 |
|---|---|---|---|---|
| Very Satisfied | Satisfied | Neutral | Dissatisfied | Very Dissatisfied |

Additional comments: _____

_____

_____

_____

**Figure 10–3** Session Evaluation Form

The process of developmental evaluation includes developing, testing, evaluating, modifying, and reevaluating intervention methods as new groups are offered. Developmental evaluations are especially appealing for workers who offer the same or similar group programs repeatedly, because they require workers to evaluate group programs in a sequential manner. A developmental evaluation occurs as successive group programs are offered.

Unlike monitoring evaluations, that are relatively easy for group workers to conduct, developmental evaluations are more complex. They require careful thought, planning, and design by the worker. The process of conducting a developmental evaluation consists of (1) identifying a need or problem, (2) gathering and analyzing relevant data, (3) developing a new group program or method, (4) evaluating the newly developed program or method, and (5) modifying the program or method on the basis of the data obtained. As shown in Figure 10–4, this process may be conducted several times as new group programs are offered and evaluated by the worker. Although developmental research requires careful thought as well as the worker's time and energy, it yields improvements in programs and methods that can make group work practice more effective and more satisfying.

In developing and evaluating a new group program or a new group method, the worker can select from a large variety of research designs, depending on the type of program or method being developed and the context in which the evaluation will occur. Single system methods and case study methods are particularly useful for developmental evaluations. Although quasi-experimental design methods are also frequently used in developmental research, these methods will be described in relation to effec-

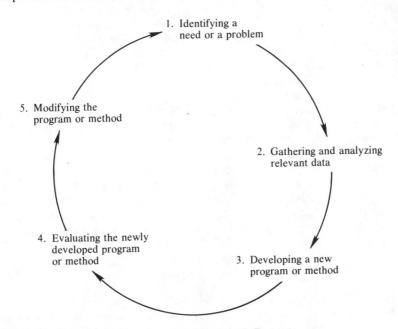

**Figure 10–4** Steps in the Developmental Research Process

tiveness and efficiency evaluations, because they are also frequently used in evaluations of group outcomes. For a more thorough discussion of the issues involved in choosing an appropriate method for developmental research, see Thomas, (1978), Fairweather (1967), Toseland (1981b), or Rothman (1974).

## Single System Methods

Single system methods (often called single subject designs) have been developed to evaluate data that are collected over time from a single system such as a group. The data obtained by using single system designs may include information about a single group member or the group as a whole. Single system methods compare baseline data to data collected when an intervention is made in the group. The baseline period occurs before the intervention period. Data collected during the preintervention or baseline period are intended to represent the functioning of the group as a whole or a group member on a particular variable. After the baseline period, an intervention occurs that may cause a change in the data collected during the baseline period.

As shown in Figure 10–5, there may be a change in level or in slope of the data collected after the intervention. Observations before and after the intervention are compared to see how the change has affected what the group worker is measuring. For example, after collecting baseline data and finding that members of a group were talking almost exclusively to the worker rather than to each other, the worker intervenes by discussing the issue with the group, prompting members to talk with one another more frequently, and praising them when they initiate conversation with one another. After the intervention, communications between members and the worker decrease and communications between members increase. Figure 10–6 is a graph of the results of such an intervention. The single system method illustrated in Figure 10–6 (page 318) is often called an AB design, in which A is the baseline period before intervention and B is the postintervention data collection period.

Various single system designs include multiple baseline, withdrawal, reversal, and changing criterion designs. These single system designs are more complicated to apply for the practicing group worker than the AB, baseline-intervention design, but they are also more effective than the AB design in evaluating practice outcomes. They are especially useful when workers have the time, energy, interest, and resources to test the efficacy of a new or an alternative intervention to improve practice with future groups working on similar problems. For additional information about single system methods, see Rose (1977), Bloom and Fisher (1982), Jayaratne and Levy (1979), and Toseland, Krebs, and Vahsen (1978).

## Case Study Methods

For the practicing group worker, case study methods can be useful in developing new group programs or in improving current programs. Case study methods are generally qualitative rather than quantitative (Toseland, 1981b).

Case studies rely on precise descriptions, accurate observations, and detailed analyses of a single example or case. Because they are based on a single case, the data collected may not be as internally or externally valid as data collected using classical control group designs. Despite this, the strengths of case studies are that they can provide a clear, detailed, vivid description of the processes and procedures of a group in action and they are

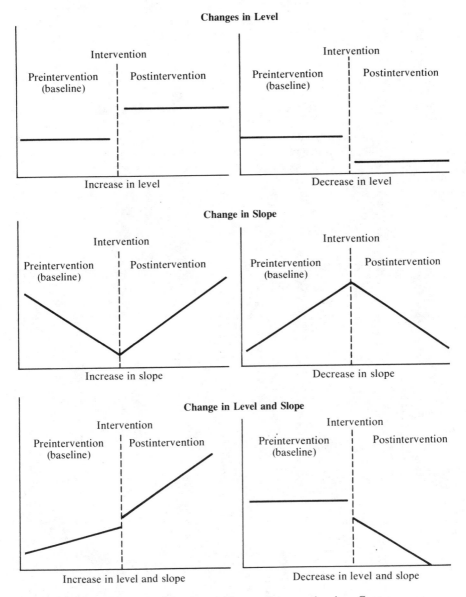

Figure 10-5 Changes in Baseline Data After an Intervention in a Group

often more feasible to apply in practice settings than control group designs.

Case study methods include participant and nonparticipant observation (Johnson, 1975), case comparison methods (Butler, Davis, and Kukkonen, 1979), and ethnographic methods (Watts, 1981). For example, a group worker who is considering leading a preventive health group for cardiac patients may find it useful to observe a group being conducted at another hospital or to have the group tape recorded for playback and analysis. The worker could use case study methods to analyze the content of the tape recordings or notes made from observing the group and use the information obtained to change group work methods or develop new group programs in the worker's own setting.

Using a case comparison method, a worker who has developed a group program for alcoholics may want to compare his or her program with similar programs offered by Alcoholics Anonymous and a county alcoholism program. A comparison of the three programs along prespecified dimensions created by the worker to answer his or her specific information needs could lead to innovations in the program developed by the worker. These innovations could then be evaluated for their efficacy, as described in the process shown in Figure 10–4.

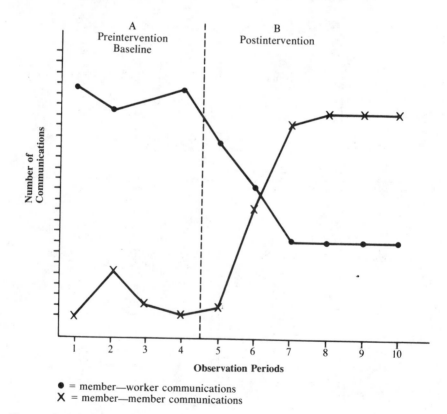

● = member—worker communications
X = member—member communications

**Figure 10–6** Graphed Data from a Single System Evaluation

Group workers might also want to use case study methods in working with task groups. For example, a worker may want to use non-participant observation to compare the methods that other day treatment mental health agencies use when reviewing clients in treatment team meetings.

Taken together, both single system methods and case study methods offer workers the opportunity to develop and improve their practice on a continuing basis. Rigorous application of developmental research methods requires that workers spend time in designing and implementing evaluation methods and collecting data that are not routinely available. The worker must decide whether or not the extra effort spent in organizing and carrying out a developmental evaluation is worth the new or improved programs that can result.

## EVALUATIONS FOR DETERMINING EFFECTIVENESS AND EFFICIENCY

Group workers may also want to assess the effectiveness or the efficiency of their practice using evaluation methods. Effectiveness evaluations focus on the extent to which a group accomplishes its objectives. They give workers the opportunity to gain objective feedback about the helpfulness of the methods being used. Efficiency evaluations compare the benefits of a group program to its cost. They attempt to place a monetary value on the outcomes of a group and to compare this to the costs incurred by conducting a group.

Effectiveness and efficiency evaluations rely on experimental and quasi-experimental designs, reliable and valid measures, and statistical procedures to determine the significance of an intervention on the outcome of task or treatment groups. As compared to the other types of evaluations mentioned in this chapter, effectiveness and efficiency evaluations are less flexible, more technically complex, and more difficult to conduct. Because of the nature of the methods employed and the precision and rigor necessary to apply them, a flexible and cooperative setting is needed to conduct effectiveness and efficiency evaluations. The sponsoring agency must be willing to supply the needed resources and the technical assistance necessary for conducting such evaluations.

One method for evaluating outcomes, which is less difficult to apply than many other effectiveness evaluation methods, is called goal attainment scaling (Kiresuk and Sherman, 1968). Using this method, the worker can obtain information about the achievement of goals by individual group members or the group as a whole. An example of goal attainment scaling is shown in Figure 10–7 (page 320), where each of several problem areas is listed on a five-point scale from most unfavorable outcome to most favorable outcome. The third scale point represents the expected outcome. Members and the group leader can work together to develop outcome measures for each scale level. For example, the group decided that the most unfavorable outcome for the problem of depression is suicide. Similarly, the group decided that the most favorable outcome for loss of appetite is to eat three meals a day and to snack between meals. After work on the problem areas is completed, goal

| Scale Levels | Problem Areas | | |
|---|---|---|---|
| | Anxiety | Depression | Loss of Appetite |
| 1. Most unfavorable expected outcome | Four or more self-rated occurrences of feeling anxious each day. | Suicide. | Refuses to eat any daily meals. |
| 2. Less than expected outcome | Three self-rated occurrences of feeling anxious each day. | One or more attempts at suicide. | Eats one meal each day. |
| 3. Expected outcome | Two self-rated occurrences of feeling anxious each day. | No attempts at suicide, discusses feelings of depression. | Eats two meals each day. |
| 4. More than expected outcome | One self-rated occurrence of feeling anxious each day. | No attempts at suicide, discusses possible causes of depression. | Eats three meals each day. |
| 5. Most favorable expected outcome | No self-rated occurrence of feeling anxious each day. | No attempts at suicide, identifies two causes for depression. | Eats three meals a day and snacks between meals. |
| Weight | 5 | 25 | 5 |
| Goal Attainment Score | 4 | 3 | 3 |
| Weighted Goal Attainment Score | 20 | 75 | 15 |

**Figure 10–7** Example of Goal Attainment Scaling

attainment can be measured by using the scales that have been developed for each problem area. In the example in Figure 10–7, goal attainment is indicated by a box around the actual outcome. For the problem of anxiety, the outcome was one self-rated occurrence of feeling anxious each day. This outcome was given a score of 4.

As shown in Figure 10–7, it is possible to weight each scale differentially so that attaining more important goals receives greater emphasis in the overall evaluation than attaining less important goals, Thus, the goal attainment score of 4 obtained for the problem of anxiety is multiplied by its weight of 5, yielding a goal attainment score of 20. Even though the goal attainment score on the problem area of depression is a 3, after it is multiplied by its weight

(25), the weighted goal attainment score for the problem of depression (75) is much greater than that obtained on the problem of anxiety (20). Goal attainment scores on each scale can be added together to form a composite score for individual or group goal attainment. Statistical procedures have been developed to compare goal attainment scores across individual group members and across groups (Garwick, 1974). Although goal attainment scaling procedures have received some methodological criticism (Seaberg and Gillespie, 1977), the procedure remains an important tool for group workers to consider when conducting effectiveness evaluations.

Effectiveness evaluations rely on experimental and quasi-experimental designs to determine whether or not a group accomplishes its objectives. A true experimental design employs random assignment of participants to treatment and control groups. It compares the treatment and control groups on specific outcome variables to measure differences between treatment and control group subjects. Quasi-experimental designs are those in which participants cannot be randomly assigned to treatment and control groups. It is often difficult to randomly assign subjects to treatment and control groups in practice settings. Therefore, quasi-experimental designs are often used in effectiveness evaluations even though they are subject to possible biases because non-randomly assigned subjects may not be equivalent on important variables that may affect the outcome variables being measured (see, for example, Toseland, Kobat, and Kemp, 1983).

It is especially difficult to conduct adequate effectiveness evaluations in group research projects. In order to do valid statistical analyses of data from experimental designs, observations or measures on each unit of analysis must be independent. Researchers testing the effectiveness of group treatment sometimes assume that individual group members are the unit of analysis. However, individual members are not independent of one another in a group setting because they are affected by other members of the group. Members are also affected in similar ways by interventions in the group as a whole. For example, while members are taking a questionnaire, a lawn mower goes past the window and disturbs all members of the group. Members' scores are not totally independent of one another; that is, the lawn mower has affected all members in a similar manner. For this reason, the unit of analysis in group research should be the entire group rather than an individual group member.

The requirement for independent observations is sometimes violated by group researchers, and statistical procedures such as ANOVA are not robust to this violation. This can lead to serious overestimations of the effectiveness of group procedures (Eisenhart, 1972). Because there must be a relatively large number of units of analysis in order to obtain valid statistical comparisons, effectiveness evaluations of group work practice require that a relatively large number of groups must be conducted in both treatment and control conditions. This is often difficult to do in practice settings because of the limitations on resources, group participants, and competent group leaders,

Efficiency evaluations can also be complex and time-consuming to conduct, but they can be useful to those who want to assess whether or not their programs are cost-effective. For example, a nonprofit health agency employs a group worker as a consultant to conduct a smoking cessation group program. The worker conducts an effectiveness evaluation and finds that 60 percent of the group members become nonsmokers after the group program. The worker also collects data about the costs of the program and the costs to employers who have employees who smoke. This provides the basis for the worker's efficiency evaluation.

Figure 10–8 shows the worker's calculations and illustrates that at a 50 percent success rate the smoking cessation group program saves the employer $220.00 each year, beginning one year after the program ends. Savings to the employer last for as long as the employee remains with the company as a nonsmoker. Because the smoking cessation program has a success rate of 50 percent, employers who have long-term employees are likely to save more than $220.00 each year for each employee who participates in the smoking cessation program. This information is helpful to the nonprofit health agency in motivating a number of large employers, whose workers' average length of employment exceeds one year, to offer smoking cessation group programs to their employees.

| *Costs of Smoking to the Employer per Employee Per Year** | |
|---|---:|
| *Insurance:* | |
| Health | $220.00 |
| Fire | 10.00 |
| Workmen's Compensation and Other Accidents | 40.00 |
| Life and Early Disability | 30.00 |
| *Other:* | |
| Productivity | 166.00 |
| Absenteeism | 100.00 |
| Smoking Effects on Nonsmokers | 110.00 |
| Total Cost of Smoking | $660.00 |
| *Per Employee Cost of the Smoking Cessation Program* | |
| Smoking Cessation Program | $120.00 |
| Employee Time to Take the Program | 100.00 |
| Total Cost for Each Employee | $220.00 |
| Total cost of achieving one nonsmoker based on a projected success rate of 50% | $440.00 |
| *Savings to Employers* | |
| Total Cost of Smoking | $660.00 |
| Total Cost of the Smoking Cessation Program | − 440.00 |
| Total Cost Savings | $220.00 |

*Cost figures taken from Marvin Kristein, "How Much Can Business Expect to Earn from Smoking Cessation," presented at a Conference of the National Interagency Council on Smoking and Health, Chicago, Illinois, January 9, 1980, 1–11.

**Figure 10–8** An Efficiency Evaluation of a Group Program for Smoking Cessation.

A complete description of the methodology necessary for conducting effectiveness and efficiency evaluations is given in Rossi, Freeman, and Wright (1979) and Campbell and Cook (1979). Group workers should have a basic understanding of these methods in order to be able to assess the efficacy of their own practice and to be able to critically evaluate methodologies used in published reports about the effectiveness and efficiency of group methods and group programs.

## EVALUATION MEASURES

The four broad types of evaluation methods described previously provide a framework that workers can use to collect information for planning, monitoring, developing, or assessing the efficacy or efficiency of their practice with a group. In applying these methods, workers can choose from a variety of measures to collect the necessary information for an effective evaluation. Numerous measures have been developed for evaluating group work practice. These include some that specifically focus on properties of the group as a whole and others that may be useful to the worker in evaluating changes in members of specific groups. Decisions about which measures to use depend on (1) the objectives of the evaluation, (2) properties of the measures being considered for use, (3) the form in which the data will be collected, and (4) what constructs will be measured.

### Choosing Measures

The first and most essential step in choosing appropriate measures is to decide on the objectives of the evaluation. Clarifying the information that is needed, what the information collected will be used for, and who will use the information can help the worker to decide on the appropriate measures to select for the evaluation. For example, if the worker is interested in obtaining feedback from members about their satisfaction with a particular group, the worker may be less concerned about the reliability and validity of a measure than about the difficulties group members might experience in responding to the measure. The worker may also be concerned about members' reactions to the measures that are used and the time it will take to administer them. This is particularly true if the worker has a limited amount of group time available for conducting an evaluation.

The worker should be familiar with two properties of measures that govern the quality of the data to be collected. Reliability refers to the extent to which an instrument measures the same phenomenon the same way each time it is used. A reliable measure is consistent. When measuring the same variable, it yields the same score each time it is administered. Validity refers to the extent to which a data collection instrument measures what it purports to be measuring. A valid measure is one that yields a true or actual representation of the variable being measured. The ideal situation is for a group worker to use a reliable and valid measure that has already been constructed. When such measures exist, they are generally superior to measures that are made quickly by the worker without regard to reliability or validity. Reliable and valid measures that can be quickly and easily administered are becoming more widely available (Levitt and Reid, 1981), but there are a number of variables for which no reliable and valid measures exist.

Constructing reliable and valid measures takes a considerable amount of time. Workers should decide what level of measurement precision and objectivity is needed when deciding on how much time to spend in constructing and validating measures. For additional information about constructing reliable and valid measures, see Wodarski (1981) or Stanley and Hopkins (1972).

Another consideration in choosing appropriate measures for an evaluation is to decide on what form of data collection would be most useful to the group worker and most convenient for group members. Data can be collected orally by interviewing members, by written response to a questionnaire, or by audio tape or video tape recordings. The data collection form that will be most helpful to the worker depends on how the data will be used and the extent to which group members are willing and able to cooperate with the data collection procedures used. In evaluating group work with children, older people, and handicapped persons, for example, audio taped responses can often help to overcome the difficulties these group members have in making written responses.

A final consideration when choosing evaluation measures is deciding on how a particular property or concept will be measured. For example, after a worker decides that the objective of an evaluation is to test the effectiveness of a particular group, the worker must decide whether information is sought about changes in the behavior, cognitions, or the affect of individual group members. In task groups, the worker may want to measure the extent to which a group completes its tasks, as well as the quality and the quantity of the products or tasks achieved. In conducting evaluations, it is often helpful to have multiple measures of the property being measured. When measuring the effectiveness of a group program for drug abusers, for example, the worker might want to measure reductions in drug intake, changes in self-concept, and changes in beliefs about the effects of drug abuse. Multiple measures including a blood test, an attitude scale, and a questionnaire concerning information about drug use might all be useful in assessing the group's effectiveness in helping members become drug free.

## Types of Measures

A wide array of reliable and valid measures is available for group workers to use when they are evaluating interventions with specific groups (see, for example, Buros, 1966, and Robinson and Shaver, 1973). These include self-report measures, observational measures, and measures of the products of group interaction. In describing each of these types of measures we will mention particular ones that have often been used in evaluations of group work.

*Self-Report Measures.*   Perhaps the most widely used evaluation measures are written and oral self-reports, in which group members are asked to respond to a series of questions about a particular phenomenon. Although they may focus on any phenomenon, self-report measures are particularly useful in measuring intrapersonal phenomena such as beliefs or attitudes that cannot be measured directly using observational measures. There are a wide variety of published self-report measures available including measures of anxiety, depression, assertiveness, self-concept, and locus of control. Group workers can also construct their own self-report measures for specialized situations in which no published self-report measures exist. Three published self-report measures that may be of particular interest to group workers include Hemphill's Index of Group Dimensions (Hemphill, 1956), the Hill Interaction Matrix (HIM-A, HIM-B, HIM-G) (Hill, 1977), and Seashore's Group Cohesiveness Index (Seashore, 1954). Hemphill's Index of Group Dimensions measures thirteen properties of groups: autonomy, control, flexibility, hedonic tone, homogeneity, intimacy, participation, permeability, polarization, potency, stability, stratification, and visicidity. The measure consists of 150 items to which group members respond on a five-point scale from definitely true to mostly false.

The Hill Interaction Matrix is a self-report measure in which a group leader, a group member, or an observer responds to seventy-two items about group process. The measure is designed to discriminate between different types of group interactions on two dimensions, the content discussed and the level and type of work occurring in the group. Seashore's Group Cohesiveness Index is a measure of group cohesiveness, defined as members' attraction to the group. It is especially designed for task groups and has been used with industrial work groups. Hemphill's Index of Group Dimensions, Hill's Interaction Matrix, and Seashore's Group Cohesiveness Index have all proven to be reliable and valid measures in a number of evaluations of group work.

*Observational Measures.*   Unlike self-report measures that rely on the accuracy of a respondent's memory, observational measures use independent, objective observers to collect data that are recorded while they occur or as they are replayed using video-taped or audio-taped recordings. Although observational measures are less susceptible to biases and distortions than self-report measures, they are used less frequently than self-report measures because they require the availability and training of one or more observers to collect the data. The observers code discrete group interactions into categories that are mutually exclusive and exhaustive; that is, during each observation period, one observation is recorded and it can be recorded in one, and only one, category.

The most well-known observational measure for groups is called Bale's Interaction Process Analysis (Bales, 1950). This observational index consists of twelve categories. Interactions are coded by assigning each person a number and, for example, marking a 1–4 or a 3–1 in the appropriate category when an interaction occurs from member one to member four or member three to member one. With well-trained observers, Bales Interaction Process Analysis can be a useful tool for the evaluation of group interactions.

Recently, Bales, Cohen, and Williamson (1979) and Bales (1980) have developed a new measure that is called SYMLOG (Systematic Multiple Level Observation of Groups). As explained in Chapter 7, SYMLOG is a method for analyzing the overt and covert behaviors of group members. With SYMLOG, a three-dimensional graphic presentation or field diagram of the interaction of group members is made. Through the field diagram, group members can analyze the way they interact with one another and improve the ability of the group to accomplish its tasks. An example of the use of SYMLOG for assessing group functioning has been given in Chapter 7. As an evaluation tool, SYMLOG can be used to measure a number of variables affecting both the socioemotional and the task aspects of members' behavior in groups.

Other observational measures have also been used for evaluating changes in a group over time. For example, Moreno's (1934) scales of sociometric choice and sociometric preference, described more fully in Chapter 7, assess relationships between members of a group. This is done by having each member rank order other members on certain dimensions such as their preference for working with other group members or their liking for other group members.

*Products of Group Interaction.*   A worker may be able to measure the products of group interaction directly in a simple and straightforward manner. In task groups, products of the group's work are often tangible. For example, a team may develop a written document that governs how services will be delivered to clients. The work of a delegate council may be evaluated by the number of agenda items it acts on during its monthly meeting. In both instances, group products can be used for purposes of evaluation. In treatment groups, products of group interaction may also be useful measures. Rose (1977) suggests that measurable products of group interaction include behavior change, the number of between-meeting tasks generated at a group meeting, and the number of tasks actually completed.

Evaluation measures from which workers can choose when evaluating their practice with a group range from those consisting of a few open-ended questions made by a worker who wants to get some feedback from group members to sophisticated observational measures requiring highly trained observers. Workers develop or select measures in relation to the evaluation design they are going to use and ultimately to the information they hope to obtain. While selecting appropriate measures and implementing effective evaluations is time-consuming for the practicing group worker, it is often well worth the effort because it may result in improved service and in new and innovative group programs.

## SUMMARY

Evaluation is the method by which practitioners obtain information and feedback about their work with a group. In the current age of accountability and fiscal constraints where difficult decisions between program choices will have to be made, evaluation methodologies are useful tools for practitioners. This chapter has discussed some of the reasons why group workers may choose to use evaluation methods in their practice.

Practitioners are often faced with a dilemma when considering whether or not to evaluate their practice. They must decide whether the demands of serving clients are compatible with developing and conducting evaluations. This chapter has described the strengths and weaknesses of a number of evaluation methods that may be used in differing practice situations and settings.

Four broad types of evaluation methods include evaluations for (1) planning a group, (2) monitoring a group, (3) developing a group, and (4) testing the effectiveness and efficiency of a group. These methods are used with a variety of evaluation measures to help practitioners develop, test, and implement more effective group work methods. Evaluation methods can also be combined with knowledge accumulated from practice experiences, sometimes referred to as "practice wisdom," to improve the methods used by group workers to meet a variety of needs in diverse practice settings.

# 11
# Ending the Group's Work

Although it has not received as much attention in the practice literature as the beginning or middle phase of group work, the ending phase is an important part of group work practice (Fox, Nelson, and Bolman, 1969). The skills that workers use in the ending phase determine the success of the entire group experience. In the ending phase, workers and members alike form their lasting impressions of the group. An otherwise satisfying and effective group can be ruined by a worker who is not skillful in the ending phase.

During the ending phase, the group's work is consolidated. In task groups, the decisions, reports, recommendations, and other products of the group as a whole are completed, and consideration is given to the ways in which the results of a group's work can best be implemented. In treatment groups, the changes made by individual group members are stabilized, and plans are made for maintaining these gains after the group ends. In groups where member self-disclosure has been at a high level, it is necessary to help members work through their feelings about terminating their relationships with the worker and with each other. It is also a time when workers confront their own feelings regarding ending their work with a particular group.

## Planned and Unplanned Termination

At the beginning of closed, time-limited groups, workers and members plan the number of times the group will meet. As Northen (1969, p. 223) points out, "ideally, termination occurs when a person or a group no longer needs the professional services." Sometimes members stop attending before the planned ending date. Unplanned termination of membership is a relatively common experience. Yalom (1975), for example, reports unplanned termination rates ranging from a high of 51 percent to a low of 25 percent. In treatment groups in which participation is voluntary, a reduction in membership sometimes occurs after the first and second meeting of a group. After this initial drop in membership, groups generally develop a stable core of members who continue to participate until the group ends.

Unplanned termination occurs in many forms of service. For example, in a study of family service agencies, Beck and Jones (1973) report that only 57 percent of the closings were planned in advance. In 43 percent of the cases, clients decided not to continue treatment even though service had not been completed.

In leading groups, workers sometimes find themselves asking rhetorically, "what is it that I have done to cause members to fail to return to the group?" In follow-up contacts with members who terminated prematurely, many workers find that there is nothing that they have done to cause premature termination. For example, in a group for separated and divorced persons, three people did not return to the second group meeting. When these persons were contacted, it was found that one person lived forty miles from where the group met and decided not to return after driving home on foggy rural roads following the first group meeting. Another member's job had unexpectedly changed, requiring the person to be at work during the group's meeting. It was learned from the third person's employer that one of his children had a serious accident. The member called two weeks later to explain that "I have been running between the hospital and my responsibilities to the other two (children)."

Similarly, in evaluating a smoking cessation group treatment program (Toseland, Kabat, and Kemp, 1983), it was found that members left treatment prematurely for a variety of reasons. Several were dissatisfied with their group or their group's leader, but others left for personal reasons unrelated to their treatment experience. Although it is commonly assumed that dropouts are treatment failures, in evaluating eight smoking cessation groups, it was found that one of seven dropouts left treatment prematurely because he had stopped smoking and believed he no longer needed treatment. Another dropout quit smoking before a follow-up evaluation. Thus, it is important to realize that unplanned termination of members may be the result of their lack of interest or motivation, particular life circumstances, or other factors beyond the control of the worker that have little or nothing to do with a worker's leadership skills.

Yalom (1975) lists nine factors that may cause group members to drop out of treatment prematurely. According to Yalom (1975), some of these arise out of faulty selection of members for the group. They include (1) external factors, such as scheduling conflicts and changes in geographic location, (2) group deviancy, such as being the richest group member, the only unmarried member, and the like, (3) problems in developing intimate relationships, and (4) fear of emotional contagion. Others arise out of "faulty therapeutic technique" (Yalom, 1975, p. 235). These include such factors as (5) inability to share the worker, (6) complications of concurrent individual and group therapy, (7) early provocateurs, (8) inadequate orientation to therapy, and (9) complications arising from subgrouping.

Workers should not, however, automatically assume that members' decisions to terminate prematurely have nothing to do with the group's process or its leadership. Some members drop out as a result of their dissatisfaction with the group or its leader. In remedial and growth-oriented groups where confrontation is used as a therapeutic technique, members occasionally become so angry when confronted with an emotionally charged issue that they threaten to terminate. To prevent premature termination resulting from anger, some workers specify in the initial contract that members must give two weeks' notice before leaving the group. This gives members a chance to rethink decisions about terminating prematurely.

When workers are willing to explore members' reasons for terminating, the data they gather can help them to improve their practice skills. Sometimes, simply arranging babysitting while the group is in session helps to reduce the number of dropouts. Arranging transportation to and from the group may also help members remain in the group. At other times, workers may find that there are particular ways that they can improve their own skills and prevent members from dropping out of the group. For example, they may learn to be more gentle or tentative when they use confrontation as a leadership skill.

Occasionally, an entire group may end prematurely. Just as there are many reasons for the premature termination of individuals, there are also many reasons for the premature termination of groups. A group that begins with a small number of members may lose several of them and may no longer be able to continue functioning effectively (Hartford, 1971). Groups may not receive sufficient support from their sponsoring agency to continue functioning, or they may be unable or unwilling to respond to external pressure to change their functioning.

Groups may also end prematurely as a result of internal dysfunction. For example, communication and interaction patterns may be maldistributed, causing subgroupings, scapegoating, or domination by a few members. The group may lack sufficient attraction for its members and, therefore, may fail to coalesce or to function as a cohesive unit (Northen, 1969). Social controls such as norms, roles, status hierarchies, and power may cause severe tension and conflict as some members revolt against the control of the worker or other members. A lack of appropriate social controls may cause chaos or an aimless drift that eventually leads to dissolution of the group as a whole. Members may also have great difficulty deciding on common values, preferences, ways of working together, or other aspects of the group's culture. This may also eventually lead to the group's demise.

Whenever workers confront the prospects of a group ending prematurely, they should carefully examine what factors are contributing to the problem. It is often possible to trace a group's dysfunction back to the planning phase. A careful examination of the factors that contributed to a group's demise can help workers avoid pitfalls when leading future groups.

## Variations in Endings

The process of ending varies considerably from group to group (Lewis, 1978). In some treatment groups, particularly those that are growth-oriented or remedial, termination may be accompanied by a strong emotional reaction. In other treatment groups, such as educationally oriented ones, termination may not result in strong expressions of emotion.

What are some of the factors that influence group endings? Endings vary depending on whether a group has an open or closed membership policy. In closed groups, unless there are unplanned terminations, all members end at the same time. In these groups, the worker can help all members to deal with common issues and feelings that arise as the group draws to a close. Open groups present a more difficult challenge for the worker. Some members may be experiencing reactions to termination at the same time that others are experiencing reactions common to the beginning or middle phases of group work. In open groups, the worker should individualize his or her work with each member. However, because each member will eventually experience disengagement from the group, the worker can utilize the reactions of members who are terminating to help those who will be experiencing similar reactions in the future.

Endings vary depending on the attraction of the group for its members. In groups that members find attractive, ending may not be viewed as a positive event. Conversely, if group meetings are viewed as something to be endured, news of the last meeting may be received with welcome relief.

Endings also vary considerably depending on whether the worker is leading a treatment group or a task group. In many treatment groups, members reveal intimate details of their personal lives. They let down their defenses and become vulnerable as they share concerns and issues that are of particular importance to them. In effective treatment groups, mutual aid and support develop as members deepen relationships with one another and the worker. They come to trust each other and to rely on the therapeutic advice and suggestions given by the worker and fellow group members.

Terminating the relationships that may have influenced the members of treatment groups is quite different than terminating the relationships formed in task groups. In task groups, members' self-disclosure is generally at a relatively low level. Because the focus of these groups is on a product, such as a report or the development of a plan of action, members often look forward to the end of a group with a sense of accomplishment or with relief that their work is finished. Because they have not let down their defenses or shared their personal concerns to any great extent, there is rarely an intense emotional reaction to ending. Members of task groups may work together again on other committees, teams, or councils. Therefore, the endings of task groups do not have the same sense of finality as is often the case with treatment groups.

In the task group literature, the focus is on what skills the leader can use to end individual group meetings rather than on how a leader ends the entire group experience (see, for example, Tropman, 1980; Scheidel and Crowell, 1979). This contrasts sharply to the treatment group literature, which generally focuses on ending work with the group rather than ending work in a particular meeting (see, for example, Northen, 1969; Shulman, 1979; Hartford, 1971; Johnson, 1974). This chapter will examine the tasks and skills involved in ending individual group meetings and will then consider the tasks and skills involved in effectively closing the work of the group as a whole.

## ENDING GROUP MEETINGS

According to Scheidel and Crowell (1979), there are four generic worker tasks in ending group meetings. These include (1) closing the group's work, (2) arranging another meeting, (3) preparing a summary or a report of the group's work, and (4) planning future group actions. In preparing to close, the worker should help the group keep to its agenda. The worker should assure that all items of business and all members' concerns are given sufficient attention, but the worker should not allow the group to spend too much time discussing one item of business or one member's concerns. To move the group along the worker can:

1. Keep members focused on the topic of discussion.
2. Limit the time that each member has to discuss an issue.
3. Summarize what has been said.
4. Obtain closure on each issue or concern as it is discussed.

In order to close the group's work, the worker should not bring up new issues, concerns, or items of business. Despite efforts to use structure to reduce discussion of important issues at the end of a meeting, Shulman (1979) points out that members will occasionally raise "door knob issues" just before ending. If consideration of these issues can be postponed, they are best handled during the next meeting when they can be given fuller consideration. When discussion of an important issue can not be postponed, the worker should ask group members if they would like to continue the discussion for a brief period. If not, the issue may be taken up outside of the group by the worker and any interested members.

In closing the group's work, the worker should also help members to resolve any remaining conflicts. Resolving conflicts will help members to work in harmony for the decisions reached by the group as a whole. In addition, the worker may want to discuss the strengths and weaknesses of the working relationship that has developed among members during the group meeting, particularly if the group will work together in the future.

During the ending minutes, the worker should help the group to plan for future meetings. When considering whether or not to meet again, it is helpful to review and summarize the group's work. A summary of the group's activities during the meeting clarifies issues that have been resolved and points out other issues that remain unresolved. A clear summary of the group's progress is a prerequisite for arranging another meeting. Summaries also remind members of the activities or tasks that they have agreed to work on between meetings, and they help the worker become aware of items that should be included in the agenda for the next meeting.

If a group has completed action on a particular task, the final minutes can also be used to ensure that all members understand and agree to the oral or written information that will be presented at the conclusion of a group's work. Some task forces may prepare extensive written reports of their findings and conclusions. In these groups, it is not productive to prepare the report during the group meeting. The closing minutes can be used to formulate and highlight the major conclusions to be enumerated in the report, to assign members responsibility for preparing major sections of the report, and to develop a mechanism for obtaining approval from members before disseminating the report.

Scheidel and Crowell (1979) also suggest that the endings of group meetings should be used to plan future group actions. However, because planning for action is a time-consuming process, plans are usually developed during the middle of a group meeting. At the ending of a meeting, plans are summarized and members select, or are assigned, roles to carry out.

The worker should help members to maintain their motivation, their commitment, and their responsibility to implement plans and carry out tasks they have agreed to complete between meetings. To help members maintain their motivation, the worker should praise them for their work in the group and for their willingness to commit themselves to tasks outside of the meeting. The worker may also want to mention any benefits that will accrue to members for maintaining their commitment to the plans and activities they have agreed to complete.

## ENDING THE GROUP

There are a variety of tasks associated with ending a group including:

1. Maintaining and generalizing change efforts.
2. Reducing group attraction and promoting the independent functioning of individual members.
3. Helping members with their feelings about ending.
4. Planning for the future.
5. Making referrals.
6. Evaluating the work of a group.

With the exception of evaluating the work of a group, which has been discussed in Chapter 10, the remaining portion of this chapter will examine each of these tasks and indicate the skills and techniques the worker can use to facilitate the effective ending of a group. Many of these tasks may be carried out simultaneously. The specific order in which each task is completed depends on the specific group the worker is leading.

### Maintaining and Generalizing Change Efforts

After treatment plans have been developed and carried out, workers should ensure that the changes that have been achieved are maintained and generalized to other important aspects of members' lives. Why the concern about maintenance and generalization? Evaluations of the results of therapeutic interventions suggest that positive changes are often difficult to maintain over time. For example, in an evaluation of a group treatment program for smokers (Toseland, Kabat, and Kemp, 1983), it was found that although more than 60 percent of those who attended the program initially stopped smoking, after three months the cessation rate had dropped to 36 percent. Results obtained for a variety of other treatment programs for addictive disorders, such as narcotics use, alcohol use, and overeating (see, for example, Hunt, Barnett, and Branch, 1971) show similar relapse rates. Maintenance is also difficult to achieve when working with antisocial group members such as juvenile delinquents and when working with group members who have severe psychological disorders.

Both novice and experienced workers often mistakenly believe that changes in specific behaviors can be taken as a sign of generalized improvement in a member's level of functioning. These workers do little to ensure that specific behavior changes generalize to related, but untreated, behaviors. Results of a variety of different treatment programs have shown, however, that therapeutic changes occurring in specific behaviors do not always generalize to similar behaviors performed by a member in other contexts (Stokes and Baer, 1977; Goldstein, Keller, and Sechrest, 1966). For example, an unassertive group member may learn to be assertive in a particular situation but may continue to be nonassertive in other situations. Similarly, a parent may learn how to reduce a child's temper tantrums, but this success may not affect the parent's ability to help the child play cooperatively with other children.

Although some people seek group treatment only for changes in specific behaviors, most people enter group treatment with the expectation that there will be a generalized improvement in their life situation. For example, educational, growth, and program-oriented groups often provide benefits in a number of areas of a member's life. Therefore, it is important for workers to help members generalize changes achieved in specific behaviors and performed in particular situations to related behaviors performed in other contexts.

Despite the importance of maintaining and generalizing change efforts, with the notable exception of Rose (1974, 1977), little has been written about these topics in group work. Almost all the theoretical and clinical work on maintenance and generalization of change has come from the literature on behavior modification and learning theory (Stokes and Baer, 1977). This literature suggests a number of things that workers can do to help members maintain and generalize the changes they have achieved, including:

1. Helping members to work on relevant situations.
2. Helping members to develop confidence in their abilities.
3. Using a variety of different situations and settings when helping members learn new behaviors.
4. Utilizing a variety of different, naturally occurring consequences.
5. Extending treatment by utilizing follow-up sessions.
6. Preventing setbacks in an unsympathetic environment.

7. Helping members to solve problems independently by providing a framework for organizing data and solving problems that can be used in many different situations.

*Relevant Situations.* In order to achieve long lasting changes that will generalize to similar situations in members' lives, the concerns and issues worked on in the group should be a relevant and realistic sample of those experienced by members in their daily lives. Sometimes members become distracted by issues that are not central to their concerns. This may be a sign that they are avoiding difficult issues and the changes they necessitate. The worker can help by drawing members' attention back to the central concerns that brought them together as a group.

In other cases, the situations discussed may be highly specific and individual. Although it is important to be as specific and concrete as possible when developing treatment plans, it is also important to ensure that situations that are relevant to all group members, are included in the group's work. This helps to ensure that members are prepared for situations they are likely to encounter in the future.

Although group meetings should provide a protected environment where members receive support, encouragement, and understanding, the group should also be a place where members can get honest feedback about how their behavior is likely to be seen outside the group. Members should be encouraged to try out new behaviors in the group, but they should not be misled into thinking that they will receive the same level of support and encouragement for trying new behaviors outside the group. In short, although the group should provide a supportive and caring atmosphere in which to work, the group should help members to understand, cope with, and prepare for reactions likely to be experienced outside the group.

*Helping Members Develop Confidence.* Many treatment groups spend much of their time discussing members' problems and concerns as well as their inappropriate ways of handling situations. Although ventilating thoughts and feelings may be therapeutic, as Goldstein, Keller, and Sechrest (1966) point out, perhaps too much time in treatment is spent on the negative aspects of members' concerns, issues, and problems. They suggest that the emphasis on negative thoughts, feelings, and experiences only serves to reinforce the members' tendency to continue to express them outside the group.

As the group progresses, workers should encourage members to focus on adaptive alternatives to the problematic situations they are experiencing. If members dwell on poor performances and inhibiting thoughts throughout the group experience, they are less likely to feel confident about their abilities to cope with or resolve the problems they experience in their daily lives. Although it is not possible or desirable to avoid discussions of problems in treatment groups, workers should help members become more aware of their abilities. Members should be encouraged to use their abilities and their resources to resolve the problematic situations that they encounter as they prepare for leaving the group. Program activities, role plays and exercises are particularly useful in helping members to become more aware of their strengths and to build confidence in their ability to problem solve. This, in turn, will help members to gain confidence in their ability to continue to function adaptively after they leave the group.

*Using a Variety of Different Situations and Settings.*   Another aspect of maintaining and generalizing change that should not be limited to the last few meetings but should be emphasized during this time is preparing members for a variety of different situations that may interfere with their ability to maintain the changes they have made. Issues and concerns brought to group treatment are rarely, if ever, confined to only one specific situation or setting in a member's life. A member who experiences communication difficulties, for example, often experiences them in many different situations with many different people. Therefore, in treatment groups it is often helpful to have members practice responses with different members in a variety of different situations. Because of the availability of group members who will respond differently from one another, group treatment is ideally suited for this purpose. Bandura's research (1969) confirms that the use of multiple models (group members) promotes generalization of treatment effects.

As mentioned in Chapter 8, it is helpful to structure practice so that easier situations are practiced before more difficult ones. What constitutes an easy or a difficult situation varies from person to person, so the worker should assess each person's unique needs when developing a hierarchy of situations to work on in the group. Once a member demonstrates ability to handle a variety of different situations in the group, he or she should be encouraged to get additional practice by trying new ways of behaving between meetings.

Program activities can also be used to simulate situations that may be encountered outside the group. For example, children who are referred to a group because they have difficulty in playing cooperatively with classmates can be encouraged to participate in a team sport where cooperative play is essential. Long-term chronic psychiatric patients may be encouraged to prepare and participate in a group dinner as a way of practicing skills that will help them when they are deinstitutionalized and placed in a community residence.

*Utilizing Naturally Occurring Consequences.*   Although it is often difficult to make changes initially, changes are maintained and generalized by the positive consequences that result from them. For example, although losing weight is initially uncomfortable, it soon results in positive compliments from peers and feeling better about oneself. In order to maintain and generalize behavior changes, the worker should help group members to experience the positive consequences of changes as soon as possible and to maintain the positive consequences for as long as possible after changes are made.

One method for doing this is to help members focus on positive consequences while reducing their attention to negative consequences. For example, a member who decided to stop smoking should be encouraged to seek out the reactions of family members, friends, and group members who no longer have to put up with the smell of stale cigarettes and smoke-filled rooms. At the same time, the member should be encouraged to replace urges to smoke with thoughts about the soon to be experienced positive effects of not smoking, such as increased lung capacity and greater vitality and endurance. The worker can also contact significant others in the member's life and ask that they continue to reinforce the ex-smoker's resolve for not smoking after the treatment program has ended.

Another way to enhance naturally occurring contingencies is to help members modify environmental consequences so that behavior change is more readily maintained and generalized. For example, a buddy system may be established so that group members receive positive feedback for changes between group sessions. Group members may be asked to modify friendship patterns, social activities, or their home environment so as to provide them with positive consequences for changes they have made through their efforts in the group. By enhancing and highlighting naturally occurring positive consequences and by reducing negative consequences, initial changes can be maintained and generalized.

*Follow-up Sessions.*   Another way to help ensure that treatment results are maintained and generalized is to provide members the opportunity to meet together for follow-up sessions after the completion of a formal group treatment program. A follow-up session is a meeting designed to maintain treatment gains that occur after a time-limited treatment group has ended. For example, a time-limited outpatient psychotherapy group meets for twelve weekly sessions and then meets for six follow-up sessions at one-month intervals. After this time, two quarterly meetings during the rest of the year complete the treatment offered to members.

Although follow-up sessions are infrequently used by professionals, they make self-help groups appealing to participants. The popularity of self-help groups can, in part, be attributed to the flexible, open-ended, long-term membership that is encouraged in many of these groups. Self-help groups often have a small group of members who regularly attend meetings, along with many other members who attend occasionally on an "as needed" basis (Toseland and Hacker, 1982). For self-help group participants who have attended sessions on a regular basis in the past, sporadic attendance at regularly scheduled meetings acts to maintain treatment gains and gradually reduce members' dependency on the group.

There are several advantages to providing follow-up sessions for members (Toseland, Kabat, and Kemp, 1983). They review members' commitment to maintaining changes. They remind members of the changes that have taken place in their lives since they began treatment. Members can share similar experiences about the difficulties they have encountered trying to maintain changes and trying to generalize changes to new situations and new life experiences.

Follow-up sessions are generally not used to introduce members to new material. Instead, they are used as an opportunity for members to share their experiences since last meeting together. Members are encouraged to discuss any new problem situations they have encountered and to describe how they have handled them. The emphasis is on helping members to identify the coping skills they have used to maintain changes achieved during treatment.

Follow-up sessions are particularly helpful for members who have difficulty maintaining treatment gains. Members can discuss the circumstances surrounding particular relapses, consulting the group's worker and the other members about how to best handle these occurrences. The additional support provided by follow-up sessions is often sufficient to help members overcome brief relapses that might otherwise turn into treatment failures.

*Preventing Setbacks in Unsympathetic Environments.*   Even when careful attention has been given to the environment that a member faces outside the group, the support, trust, and sharing found in well-functioning treatment groups is rarely duplicated in the members' home or community environments. Members should be prepared to face possible setbacks in the unsympathetic environment they are likely to experience outside the group. Rose (1977) suggests that the experiences of the worker in leading previous groups, as well as the experiences of former group members, are useful in developing vignettes that describe realistic and typical situations group members are likely to encounter as they attempt to maintain the changes they have made during group treatment. During the last few group sessions, members discuss how to respond to these situations and practice responses with one another, using modeling, role play, rehearsal, and coaching.

Because members are likely to experience situations that threaten their treatment gains soon after changes are initiated, members should be encouraged to describe these situations in the group. In this way, all group members become exposed to a variety of different situations and different reactions to changes that they can learn to handle before they occur in their own life situations. Meichenbaum (1977), for example, reports that a stress inoculation treatment program in which members are taught to anticipate negative reactions and ways to cope with them can be effective in helping to maintain treatment gains.

Members may encounter difficult situations that threaten their treatment gains at any time of day or night. During many of these situations, the group worker may not be available to members. To help members prevent setbacks, workers should inform them about how to contact on-call workers, emergency hotlines, and other services that are available on a twenty-four-hour basis.

Some problems affect many aspects of a person's life. The pervasive nature of these problems suggests that they may respond best to intensive and extensive treatment. For such problems, group treatment with a professional worker may be supplemented by linkages with self-help organizations. Alcoholics Anonymous groups, for example, often meet each evening, or at least several times each week, providing members with an alternative to spending their evenings in a neighborhood bar or drinking alone at home. They also encourage recovered alcoholics to form close relationships with new members. This provides new members with others who act as models of sobriety and encourages the development of a network of supportive relationships. Similarly, organizations such as Recovery, Inc., Parents Without

Partners, Parents Anonymous, and Gamblers Anonymous help members with all types of problems and concerns to become involved with a network of people to whom they can turn at particularly difficult times of the day or evening.

Members of task groups can also benefit from preparing for an unsympathetic environment. Plans, reports, and other products of a task group's work may encounter resistance as they are considered by others outside the group. Resistance is especially likely when the products of a task group are controversial or have negative implications for a particular program, an entire organization or a social service delivery system. Also, resistance is more likely to be encountered when proposals must go through several levels of review before they are approved (Brager and Holloway, 1978). Therefore, it is important for task group members to anticipate resistance to implementing the group's work and to plan strategies to counteract this resistance.

***Helping Members to Solve Problems Independently.*** No matter how many different situations are discussed and practiced within a group, it is not possible to cover the full range of situations that members may experience outside a group. Group members' unique situations and needs make it impossible to predict the situations they may encounter in real life. Therefore, before contact with the group ends, it is important to help members learn how to solve their own problems independently, gradually lessening the need for continued treatment. This process should begin as early as possible in the group experience and be given particular emphasis in the last few meetings of the group.

Workers can support independent functioning by building members' confidence in their existing coping skills and by having them develop and rely on new coping skills throughout the group treatment process. Workers should also teach members the principles underlying the interventive methods used in the group. Workers sometimes fail to teach members the underlying therapeutic principles of an intervention because they think professional knowledge should not be shared with clients. Others fear that group members may not be able to understand these principles or may misuse the information they receive.

Most group members who enter treatment voluntarily are eager to learn more about ways to cope with their concerns. For example, having members of an assertion training group read *Your Perfect Right* (Alberti and Emmons, 1974), having members of a parent training group read *Parents Are Teachers* (Becker, 1971), or having members of a weight loss group read *Slim Chance In a Fat World* (Stuart and Davis, 1972) helps them to learn some basic principles that can be useful to them as they encounter new situations not discussed in the group.

Some treatment approaches, such as Eric Berne's *Transactional Analysis* (see Berne, 1961) and Albert Ellis's *Rational-Emotive Therapy* (see Ellis, 1962), encourage workers to help members understand the basic principles underlying their treatment approaches. Workers using other treatment approaches should spend more time teaching members the basic principles underlying therapeutic interventions. When teaching members, it is important to make sure that their language abilities do not interfere with their learning and that technical terms are translated into jargon-free explanations. This is an especially important consideration when English is a second language for members.

Having members summarize what they have learned in the group and deducing general principles from these summaries is also effective in helping them understand basic principles that can be applied in other situations. For example, in summarizing what they have learned, members of a couples group became aware of some general principles regarding communication. These included maintaining eye contact to show that they are listening, summarizing core content of messages to ensure correct understanding of their partner's messages, and using "I" messages to communicate their feelings and thoughts.

### Reducing Group Attraction

In addition to helping members maintain, and generalize the changes they have made in a group, the ending phase of group work should help members to become less dependent on the group. This can be done by helping them to rely on their own skills and resources as well as on sources of support outside the group.

Just as program activities can be useful in simulating situations that may be encountered outside the group, they can also be useful in helping to reduce the group's attraction for its members (Henry, 1981; Wayne and Avery, 1979; Johnson, 1974). Appropriate program activities for ending a group include those that (1) demonstrate or encourage reflection about the skills members have learned in the group, (2) allow members to express their feelings about the group and its members, (3) focus on future activities, and (4) encourage individual as well as group participation. For example, getting together for a dinner is a program activity that is commonly used at the ending of a group. Planning for a dinner encourages individual as well as group-oriented participation. During the dinner, members often discuss the things they have learned in the group, their feelings about ending, and their plans for the future.

As Garvin (1981) points out, endings are often marked by ceremonies. Program activities, such as having a party, a potluck dinner, giving out certificates of merit, or having each member say or write something special about other members, can be viewed as ceremonies that signify the end of the group. When they are used creatively, ceremonies can also help to maintain and generalize changes made by members. For example, in the next to last session of a weight loss group, members were asked to write themselves two letters containing (1) their feelings about being overweight, (2) how good it felt to be losing weight, and (3) reiterating their commitment to continue losing weight. These self-addressed letters were mailed by the worker at three-week intervals after the group ended as a reminder to members of their commitment to losing weight and maintaining weight losses.

Group attraction can also be reduced in other ways. Having members summarize their accomplishments and discuss why they no longer need the group can be an effective exercise. Scheduling group meetings less frequently or for shorter periods of time can help to reduce the importance of the group for a member. Encouraging members to become involved in activities outside the group that will compete with the group for members' time and energy is another way to reduce members' attraction to the group. In addition to competing with the group, these activities can serve to support members and maintain changes.

## Feelings About Ending

The feelings that members and workers have about ending are related to the relationships which have developed in the group. As Germain and Gitterman (1980, p. 258) point out, "the intensity of feeling associated with a relationship and with its ending depends upon its duration and its quality of mutual regard, respect, and reciprocity." Although the group work literature often suggests that the endings of groups are a painful time during which members experience a variety of feelings such as denial, anger, sadness, rejection, and hostility, the ending of a group can also be a positive, growth-promoting experience. Endings are most frequently characterized by members' ambivalence as they vacillate between positive and negative feelings about terminating their relationship with the worker and with others in the group (Fortune, in press; Lewis, 1978).

What are some of the positive feelings that can result when the worker is skillful in facilitating the ending of a group? One of the most important is a feeling of potency as members realize they are capable of accomplishing goals. A closely related feeling results from being in control of their own lives rather than feeling their lives are controlled by their environment. A third important feeling is a sense of satisfaction, pride, and usefulness in being able to help others by providing feedback, support, suggestions, information, and alternative frames of reference (Lieberman and Borman, 1979). A fourth feeling is that of accomplishment when members realize that they have been able to take part in and successfully complete the group experience. Another is that of growth, as members learn how to cope with termination, an experience they will encounter in other aspects of their lives.

At the same time, members may experience negative feelings about the ending of a group. A common reaction is denial (Levine, 1979). Not wanting to show that they will miss the worker or others in the group, members sometimes ignore workers' attempts to prepare them for ending by changing the topic of discussion or by indicating that they are looking forward to ending. Another common reaction is feeling abandoned or rejected. Members may express the rejection they are feeling by becoming angry or hostile. In other cases, they may engage in regressive behavior that exhibits the symptoms or problems they had when first entering the group. Other reactions to feeling rejected can include clinging to the worker, acting out, and devaluing the group experience or the skill of the worker (Levinson, 1977).

Reactions that are less extreme than denial, feeling abandoned, or feeling rejected are members' feelings of sadness and loss. Members may feel that they would like to continue with the warm, supportive relationships they have found in the group. Therefore, they may experience a sense of loss and accompanying sadness at the ending of the group. Members may also question their ability to maintain changes without the help of the group.

Workers are not immune to reactions to ending a group. According to Levine (1979), workers should be aware of their own reactions to ending in order to fully appreciate the difficulties that members may be experiencing regarding ending. If workers are not aware of their own feelings, they may withdraw emotionally or they may encourage the dependence of members and prolong treatment beyond what is needed.

Workers may want to share their own reactions to endings as a way of helping members identify their own feelings and reactions. Members may have some difficulty expressing their feelings about ending. Therefore, in order to help members prepare for ending, it is helpful to begin the process several meetings prior to ending. As members begin to react to ending, the worker can point out that conflicting or ambivalent feelings during this phase are common. Members should be encouraged to discuss their ambivalent and conflicting feelings.

Workers can reduce members negative emotional reactions to ending by helping them to realize their strengths and the gains they have made as a result of being in the group (Lacoursiere, 1980; Northen, 1969). The worker can prepare members for ending by clarifying what the role of the worker and the sponsoring agency will be in helping members to maintain gains after the group ends. The worker should plan for the future with each member. Plans should include the support systems and resources that will be available after the group ends. Workers should also encourage members to use their own skills, resources, and strengths to meet their needs. This can be done by expressing confidence in members' abilities, encouraging them to try out new skills outside the group (Feldman and Wodaski, 1975), and by repeating successful skill building activities and role plays so that members develop a feeling of mastery and self-confidence.

## Planning for the Future

In time-limited groups, some members may wish to recontract for additional services. When considering new services, the worker should help members to clarify (1) their continuing needs, (2) the goals they hope to achieve, (3) the duration of the new service period, and (4) any modifications in the original contract that are appropriate.

Recontracting should occur when there is a clear need for additional services and when members are highly motivated to achieve additional goals or to continue work on original goals that they have only partially achieved.

Occasionally, all members of a group may express interest in continuing to meet. In such cases, the worker may recontract for additional meetings with all members or may encourage members to meet on their own without the worker. When workers encourage members to continue to meet on their own, they are participating in the development of a self-help group. The worker helps groups continue to meet by developing natural leadership, and by helping with any resources that may be needed (Toseland and Coppola, 1984). Rather than total independence, many new self-help groups prefer continuing contact, guidance, and leadership from the worker until the new group has been firmly established. Many existing self-help groups have been started by professional workers in this manner (Toseland and Hacker, 1982). The worker can continue to assist self-help groups after they have developed by (1) providing material support to maintain a group, (2) referring clients to a group, and (3) acting as a consultant to a group.

In some instances the members of a group may wish to continue meeting because they are unable to terminate the group in a positive and responsible fashion. The group may develop a culture that supports members' dependency rather than preparing them for independent functioning in the environment outside the group. When this occurs, the worker should explore this with the group and, in a supportive manner, assist the members in ending the group experience by utilizing the activities previously mentioned in this chapter. Klein (1972) has referred to this process as "a worker's skill in letting go of the group."

Sometimes the ending of a group may result in no further contact with members. However, workers are rarely sure that members will not need services in the future. Changing life situations, new crises, or relapses may cause members to seek additional services. The worker should discuss how members can seek additional services if they are needed. In some agencies, the worker may explain that he or she has an open-door policy, so that members who need additional services can contact the worker directly. In other agencies, the policy may be for former clients to apply for services in the same manner that other clients apply. This clarifies the position of the worker and the agency with regard to how members can obtain any additional services that may be needed.

In some situations, preparations for the future may involve planning with others for continuing treatment for members. For example, in preparing for the ending of the children's group, the worker should contact the children's parents to review each child's progress and to plan for additional services. In groups where members are participating in other agency services such as individual counseling, the worker should contact the member's case manager or primary worker to evaluate the member's progress in the group and to plan for additional services. Similarly, in residential and inpatient settings, the ending of a group may not signify the end of service. The worker should meet with other staff, perhaps in a case conference or team meeting, to report progress and to plan for the future needs of members.

Those who prematurely terminate from groups should not be forgotten when planning for future service needs. Without follow-up contact, dropouts may feel abandoned. Their failure to continue with a particular group may signify to them that their situation is hopeless. Therefore, dropouts from treatment should be contacted whenever possible. One of the primary objectives of a follow-up contact is to motivate those who terminate prematurely to seek further treatment if it is needed. The worker can inquire about difficulties that former members may be having in continuing to attend group meetings, and may suggest ways to overcome these impediments. During this process, the worker should identify any needs that former group members have for continuing service and refer them to appropriate resources and services whenever possible.

## Making Referrals

During the ending phase of group work, workers frequently connect members to other services or resources. In some cases, members may be transferred to workers in the same agency. In other cases, referrals may be made to workers in other agencies.

A referral should be made only after the worker and the member have made a joint appraisal of the member's need for additional services or resources. If the member is motivated to seek additional services, the referral can proceed. If the member is not motivated to seek additional services but the worker's assessment suggests that they may be beneficial, the worker should proceed by helping the member explore his or her resistance.

Whenever possible, the member should be helped to use informal, natural helping systems. If these are unavailable, or are judged to be inadequate, then the member should be referred to a professional agency. Before making a referral, the member and his or her family or significant others should be prepared by discussing the reasons for the referral. It is often helpful to find out if the member has had any prior contact with the referral source or has heard anything about it. Members' impressions and previous experiences with particular referral sources can be influential in determining whether or not they follow through and utilize the resources to which they are referred.

In preparing themselves for making effective referrals, workers should become familiar with available community resources. If possible, workers should get to know a particular contact person in frequently used referral sources. It is also helpful to be familiar with some basic information about referral sources to share with members who are being referred. This includes information about eligibility requirements, the waiting time for service, the business hours of the agency, and the type of service provided. Such information will help to prepare the member for what to expect when contacting the referral source and will avoid members' developing expectations that will not be met. Because it may be difficult for workers to be familiar with all of the community resources that are available in an area, it is helpful for agencies to maintain up-to-date files with basic information about such resources and services.

When making a referral, the worker should write the name of the agency, the contact person, and the agency's address on a card to give to the member. In some cases, referral sources may have particular forms that have to be filled out before a member can be seen. Often, release forms need to be signed by the member so that information in a member's file can be sent to the referral source. Because many persons never reach the resources or services to which they were referred (see, for example, Weissman, 1976; Craig, Huffine and Brooks, 1974), it is helpful for the worker to call the contact person while the member is with the worker to emphasize that the member is expected at the referral source for a particular appointment. The worker should also ensure that the member (1) knows how to get to the agency to which he or she was referred, (2) has an available means of transportation, and (3) is capable of getting to the referral source independently. Members who are severely impaired may need help in getting to referral sources. The worker, a volunteer, or a case aide may have to accompany the member during the first visit.

The worker should check to ensure that members have reached the referral resource and have received the needed service. In addition, members should be instructed to contact the worker if they fail to get what they need from the referral source. A referral may fail for a number of reasons including (1) the referral source has had a change in policy; for example, eligibility requirements have become more stringent; (2) the member lacks motivation; (3) the member lacks the skill necessary to obtain the needed resources; or (4) the worker has given the member incorrect information or insufficient help to contact the referral resource. Follow-up contacts allow workers to assess why members did not obtain needed services or resources. They also allow workers to plan with members about how to obtain needed resources and services in the future.

## SUMMARY

The ending phase is a critical time in the life of a group. During the ending phase, the work of the group is consolidated and lasting impressions are made about the efficacy of the entire group experience. Endings can either be planned or unplanned. Unfortunately, in many voluntary groups, unplanned terminations are fairly common. This chapter made suggestions about how to facilitate planned endings and what to do when members terminate before the planned ending of a group.

Procedures for facilitating endings vary, depending on the type of group being led. In task groups and treatment groups where members have not been encouraged to self-disclose or form supportive relationships, endings are less emotionally charged than in groups where a great deal of self-disclosure has taken place and where members depend on one another for help with their personal concerns and problems. Other variations in group endings depend on whether the group has an open or closed membership policy, whether the group is short-term or long-term, and whether a group is attractive or unattractive to its members. This chapter examined how these factors influence the use of worker skills during the ending phase.

This chapter also examined the tasks that workers are often called upon to perform in ending meetings and in ending the group as a whole. Major tasks in ending a meeting of a group include (1) closing the work, (2) arranging another meeting, (3) preparing a summary or a report of the group's work, and (4) planning for future group actions. Major tasks in ending the group as a whole include (1) maintaining and generalizing change efforts, (2) evaluating the work of the group, (3) reducing group attraction and promoting independent member functioning, (4) helping members with their feelings about ending, (5) planning for the future, and (6) making effective referrals.

# Appendixes

## APPENDIX A
### Suggested Readings on Task Groups

**Committees**

Bradford, L. P. *Making meetings work: A guide for leaders and group members.* LaJolla, CA: University Associates, 1976.

Carnes, W. T. *Effective meetings for busy people.* New York: McGraw-Hill Book Company, 1981.

Edson, J. B. How to survive on a committee. *Social Work*, 1977, *22*(3), 224–226.

Gouran, D. S. *Making decisions in groups: Choices and consequences.* Glenview, IL: Scott, Foresman and Company, 1982.

Jay, A. How to run a meeting. *Harvard Business Review*, 1976, *54*, 43–57.

Napier, R., and Gershenfeld, M. *Groups: Theory and practice* (2nd ed.). Boston: Houghton Mifflin Company, 1981.

Scheidel, T. M., and Crowell, L. *Discussing and deciding: A deskbook for group leaders and group members.* New York: Macmillan Publishing Co., Inc., 1979.

Tropman, J. *Effective meetings.* Beverly Hills, CA: Sage Publishing Co., 1980.

Tropman, J., Johnson, H., and Tropman, E. *The essentials of committee management.* Chicago: Nelson-Hall, 1979.

**Administrative Groups**

Baker, J. C. *Directors and their functions: A preliminary study*, Cambridge, MA: Harvard University Press, 1945.

Brown, C., and Smith, E. (Eds.). *The director looks at his job*, New York: Columbia University Press, 1957.

Child Welfare League of America. *The board member of a social agency: Responsibilities and functions.* New York: Child Welfare League of America, Inc., 1965.

Conrad, W. R., and Glenn, W. R. *The effective voluntary board of directors: what it is and how it works.* Chicago: The Swallow Press, Inc., 1976.

Fisher, J. *How to manage a non-profit organization.* Toronto: Management and Fund Raising, Centre Pub. Div., 1978.

Hagenback, B. R. *Getting local agencies to cooperate.* Baltimore: University Park Press, 1982.

Hartogs, N., and Weber, J. (Eds.). *Board of directors.* New York: Oceana Publications, Inc., 1974.

Houle, C. *The effective board.* New York: Association Press, 1966.

Huber, G. *Managerial decision making.* Glenview, IL: Scott, Foresman and Company, 1980.

Koontz, H. *The board of directors and effective management.* New York: McGraw-Hill Book Company, 1967.

Lewis, J. Management team development, will it work for you? *Personnel*, 1975, *52*(4), 11–25,

Louden, J. K. *The effective director in action.* New York: Amacon Books, 1975.

Mueller, R. K. *Board life: Realities of being a corporate director.* New York: Amacom Books, 1974.

Mueller, R. K. *New directions for directors; Behind the by-laws.* Lexington, MA: Lexington Books, 1978.

Oleck, H. L. *Non-profit corporations, organizations and associations* (4th ed.). Englewood Cliffs, NJ: Prentice-Hall, Inc., 1980.

Payne, R., and Cooper, C. (Eds.). *Groups at work.* New York: John Wiley & Sons, Inc., 1981.

Puckey, W. *The board room: A guide to the role and function of directors.* London: Hutchinson Publishing Group, 1969.

Swanson, A. *The determinative team: A handbook for board members of voluntary organizations.* New York: Exposition Press, 1978.

Trecker, H. B. *Citizen boards at work: new challenges to effective action.* New York: Association Press, 1970.

Vandervelde, M., The semantics of participation. *Administration in Social Work*, 1979, *3*(1).

### Delegate Councils and Delegate Assemblies

Gulley, H. *Discussion, conference and group process* (2nd ed.). New York: Holt, Rinehart and Winston, 1968.

Maier, N. R. F. *Problem solving discussion and conferences: Leadership methods and skills.* New York: McGraw-Hill Book Company, 1963.

Sattler, W. M., and Miller, N. E. *Discussion and conference* (2nd ed.). Englewood Cliffs, NJ: Prentice-Hall, Inc., 1968, 423–455.

### Teams

Brill, N. *Teamwork: Working together in the human services.* Philadelphia: J. B. Lippincott Company, 1976.

Browning, L. D. Diagnosing teams in organizational settings. *Group and Organizational Studies*, 1971, *2*(2), 187–197.

Compton, B. R. and Galaway, B. *Social work process* (revised edition). Homewood, IL: Dorsey Press, 1979, Chapter 14.

Connaway, R. S. Teamwork and social work advocacy: Conflicts and possibilities. *Community Mental Health Journal*, 1975, *11*(4), 387–388.

Horwitz, J. J. Dimension of rehabilitative teamwork. *Rehabilitation Record*, 1969, *10*, 37–40.

Horwitz, J. *Team practice and the specialist: An introduction to interdisciplinary teamwork.* Springfield, IL: Charles C. Thomas, Publisher, 1970.

Kane, R. A. The interprofessional team as a small group. *Social Work In Health Care*, 1975, *1*(1) 19–32.

Kane, R. A. *Interprofessional teamwork.* Syracuse: Syracuse Vocational School of Social Work, 1975.

Kramer, R. M. Dynamics of teamwork in the agency, community and neighborhood. *Social Work*, 1956, *1*(3), 56–62.

Lonsdale, S., Webb, A., and Briggs, T. *Teamwork in the personal social services and health care.* London: Croom Helm, 1980.

Lowe, J. Understanding teamwork: Another look at the concepts. *Social Work In Health Care*, 1981, 7(2), 1–11.

Lowe, J., and Herranen, M. Conflict in teamwork: Understanding roles and relationships. *Social Work In Health Care*, 1973, *3*, 323–330.
Naji, S. Z. Teamwork in health care in the U.S.: A sociological perspective. *The Millbank Memorial Fund Quarterly*, 1975, *53*, 79–91.
New, K. M. An analysis of the concept of teamwork. *Community Mental Health Journal*, 1968, *4*(4), 326–333.
Odhner, F. Group dynamics of the interdisciplinary team. *The American Journal of Occupational Therapy*, September 1970, *24*, 484–487.
Rae-Grant, Q. A., and Marcuse, D. F. The Hazards of teamwork. *American Journal of Orthopsychiatry*, 1968, *38*(1), 4–9.
Regenburg, J. A venture in interprofessional discussion. In H. Rehr (Ed.), *Medicine and Social Work*. New York: Prodist, 1974.
Rothberg, J. S. The rehabilitation team: Future direction. *Archives of Physical and Medical Rehabilitation*, 1981, *62*, 407–410.
Rubin, I. and Beckhard, R. Factors influencing the effectiveness of health teams. In I. Rubin et al. (Eds.), *Managing human resources in health care organizations*. Reston, VA: Reston Publishing Co., Inc., 1978.
Stevenson, O. *Specialization in social service teams*. London: George Allen and Unwin, Ltd., 1981.
Toseland, R., Palmer-Ganeles, J., and Chapman, D. Teamwork in psychiatric settings. Albany, N.Y.: School of Social Welfare, 1983.
Whitehouse, F. A. *Professional teamwork, the social welfare forum*. New York: Columbia University Press, 1957, 148–157.
Wise, H. *Making health teams work*. Cambridge, MA: Ballinger Publishing Co., 1974.

**Treatment Conferences**

Carter, R. M. It is respectfully recommended. *Federal Probation*, 1966, *30*(2), 28–42.
Overs, R. P. The staffing conference. *Rehabilitation Literature*, 1967, *28*(4), 110–112.
Weinstein, B. The parent counseling conference. *Rehabilitation Literature*, 1968, *29*, 233–236.

**Social Action Groups**

Abels, P. Instructed advocacy and community group work. In A. Alissi (Ed.), *Perspective in social group work practice*. New York: The Free Press, 1980.
Cox, F., Erlich, J., Rothman, J., and Tropman, J. *Tactics and techniques of community practice*. Illinois: F. E. Peacock Publishers, 1977.
Cox, F., Erlich, J., Rothman, J., and Tropman, J. *Strategies of community organization*. Illinois: F. E. Peacock Publishers, 1979.
Pearlman, M., and Edwards, M. Enabling in the eighties: The recent advocacy group. *Social Casework*, 1982, *63*(9), 532–534.
Pincus, A. and Minahan, A. *Social work practice: Model and method*. Itasca, Ill.: F. E. Peacock, 1973.
Smith, U. How interest groups influence legislators. *Social Work*, 1979, *24*(3), 234–240.
Thursz, D. The arsenal of social action strategies: Options for social workers. *Social Work*, 1971, *16*(1), 27–34.

## APPENDIX B
### Group Announcements

**Support Group for New Parents**

You are invited to join a support group of parents who have children between 6 months and 2 years. The group will discuss concerns identified by its members including such possible issues as infant care, sharing household responsibilities, disciplining your child, toilet training, and child care resources.

| | |
|---|---|
| *Sponsor* | Greenwich Community Mental Health Center<br>49 Cambridge Avenue<br>Greenwich, NY<br>(212) 246-2468 |
| *Group Leaders* | George Oxley, ACSW, Clinic Director<br>Marybeth Carol, BSW, Clinic Social Worker |
| *Membership* | Open to all parents with children between the ages of 6 months and 2 years |
| *Dates and Times* | March–April–May, Thursday evenings from 7:30–9:30 P.M. |
| *Child Care* | Parents are encouraged to bring their children to the center. Child care will be available from Human Service interns of Hudson Center Community College. |
| *Cost* | Enrollment fee for the 3-month group, total $90.00 per couple, payable on a monthly basis. |

For further information: Call Mr. Oxley or Ms. Carol at 211-246-2468.

**Youth Center Interest Meeting**

The residents of the Johnsonville, Pittstown, and Valley Falls area are invited to discuss the proposed establishment of a youth center for these communities. Issues to be discussed include cost of service, fund raising, need for service, and support for such a service.

| | |
|---|---|
| *Sponsor* | Rensselaer Council of Community Services |
| *Meeting Place* | Johnsonville Firehouse |
| *Date and Time* | Thursday, March 25 from 7 to 9 P.M. |
| *Further Information* | Call Jim Kesser, ACSW<br>241-2412 |

Refreshments will be served.

## APPENDIX C
### Outline for a Group Proposal
### (Treatment/Task)

| | |
|---|---|
| *Abstract* | Short statement summarizing major points of group. |
| *Purpose* | Brief statement of purpose.<br>How the group will conduct its work.<br>Job description of the worker. |

| | |
|---|---|
| *Agency Sponsorship* | Agency name and mission. |
| | Agency resources (physical facilities, financial staff). |
| | Geographic, demographic data on agency. |
| *Membership* | Specific population for the group. |
| | Why population was chosen. |
| *Recruitment* | Methods to be used. |
| *Composition* | Criteria for member inclusion/exclusion. |
| | Size, open or closed group, demographic characteristics. |
| *Orientation* | Specific procedures to be used. |
| *Contract* | Number, frequency, length, and time of meeting. |
| *Environment* | Physical arrangements (room, space, materials). |
| | Financial arrangements (budget, expense, income). |
| | Special arrangements (child care, transportation). |

# APPENDIX D
## Treatment Group Proposal

**Adolescent Discharge Group**
**(The Children's Refuge Home)**

*Abstract* — This is a proposal for a social skills training group for adolescents who are about to be released into the community from the children's refuge home.

*Purpose* — The group will discuss what each member will expect to be doing upon release to the community. The group will reinforce social learning that has taken place during the residential placement and will help members learn new social skills that will be needed to successfully relate to parents, siblings, teachers, and employers. Role playing, behavior rehearsal, modeling, and reinforcement will be employed as methods of teaching social skills.

*Agency Sponsorship* — The Children's Refuge Home, a residential treatment facility for delinquent youth, serves teenage boys who cannot live at home because of law-breaking activities. About 200 boys reside here in fifteen cottages. The agency has a 200-acre campus with an on-campus school. Staff ratio is about one staff per four boys, and direct care staff include child care workers, social workers, nursing staff, psychologists, psychiatrists, and clergy.

*Membership* — Approximately 10 boys are released to the community each month. The discharge group will be composed from a population of boys for whom discharge is planned within the next 3 months.

*Recruitment* — Because this group represents a new service for the institution, members will be recruited by asking cottage parents for volunteers from their respective cottages. An announcement will be printed and delivered to the senior cottage parents for all cottages. Additionally, teachers and social workers will be contacted to suggest possible candidates for the group.

*Composition*     The group will be composed of 6 to 8 boys between 12 and 14 years old who anticipate discharge from CRH within the next three months. Additionally, this first group will include only those children who will be returning to natural parents or relatives rather than to foster care or group homes. The group will be closed and will not add new members because it is important that social skills be learned in a gradual and cumulative fashion.

*Orientation*     Each member will be interviewed by the leaders. During this interview, the members will view a tape on group treatment for children, and the details of the tape will be discussed to demonstrate how group meetings will be conducted.

*Environment*     The ideal location for this group is the diagnostic classroom within the campus school. Proximity to video taping equipment is necessary so group members can tape and view role plays. A small budget is required ($120) for proposed field trips, charts, and materials for listing skills and posting individual and group progress, and for refreshments after meetings. Additional expenses include two color video tapes ($60). Special arrangements will have to be made so that each member's after-school recreation schedule is free for Monday afternoon meeting times.

## APPENDIX E
## Task Group Proposal

**Task Force on Research Utilization in Probation**

*Abstract*     This is a proposal for establishing an interagency task force to study how research and research procedures are utilized in three county probation offices. The group will issue a report with recommendations for increasing research utilization in probation settings.

*Purpose*     This group will be formed to study the use of research in county probation offices. The group will meet to discuss the results of surveys taken on each probation office regarding the extent to which probation workers use published research to inform their practice and the extent to which they conduct research in conjunction with their practice. The group will be convened by Robert Rivas, ACSW, at Siena College.

*Agency Sponsorship*     The task force will be sponsored by the tri-county consortium of probation agencies. The Rockwell County agency will provide physical facilities for meetings. Financial costs will be shared by all county agencies.

| | |
|---|---|
| *Membership* | Each county agency will nominate three representatives to attend meetings to ensure equal representation among agencies. |
| *Recruitment* | Mailings will be sent to all agency directors. Members of the tri-county association will be informed by an announcement in the newsletter. Each agency director will be requested by letter to appoint three representatives to the task force. |
| *Composition* | The task force will require that each agency appoint one representative from each of the following categories: probation administrator, probation supervisor (or senior officer), and probation officer. The task force will include nine representatives from agencies and two research consultants from local colleges. All members of the task force should have some knowledge about research methods. This will be a closed group, although interested people may attend specific meetings after obtaining permission from the group's leader. |
| *Orientation* | The group will be given several research reports to read in order to prepare them for discussions. The group leader will contact each member individually to get ideas for composing an agenda. |
| *Contact* | The task force will meet for six sessions, on a once-a-month basis. Meetings will last for three hours and will be held every fourth Monday of the month from 9 A.M. to 12 noon. The group will be required to compose and issue a preliminary report on research utilization within one month after the final meeting. |
| *Environment* | The Rockwell County agency will provide the use of its staff meeting room, which is equipped with tables and blackboards for the group's work. Copying facilities will be provided by Rockwell County, and each county will be billed for one third of these expenses (limit $30.00 per county). Approximately $100.00 will be required to prepare and distribute the task force's final report and recommendations (contributed by the county association). Agency directors for each county have been requested to provide travel allowance (25¢/mile) for all travel in conjunction with the work of the task force. |

# APPENDIX F

## Suggested Readings on Program Activities

**Program Activities for Groups of Children and Adolescents**

Borba, M., and Borba, C. *Self-esteem: A classroom affair*. Minnesota: Winston Press, 1978.

Cartledge, G., and Milbrun, J. F. (Eds.). *Teaching social skills to children*. Elmsford, NY: Pergamon Press Inc., 1980.

Dinkmeyer, D. C., and Muro, J. J. *Group counseling* (2nd ed.). Itasca, IL: Peacock Press, 1979.

Duncan, T., and Gumaer, J. *Developmental group for children*. Springfield, IL: Charles C. Thomas, Publisher, 1980.

Hazel, J. S. et al. *Asset: A social skills program for adolescents*. Chicago, IL: Research Press, 1981.

Middleman, R. *The non-verbal method in working with groups*. New York: Association Press, 1968.

Norem-Hebeisen, A. A. *Exploring self-esteem*. New York: National Humanities Education Center, 1976.

Pfeiffer, J. W., and Jones, J. E. *The annual handbook for group facilitators*. CA: University Associates, 1969–1982.

Rathjen, D. P., and Foreyt, J. P. (Eds.) *Social competence: Interventions for children and adults*. Elmsford, NY: Pergamon Press, Inc., 1980.

Smith, M. *A practical guide to value clarification*. CA: University Associates, 1977.

Wells, H. C., and Canfield, J. *One hundred ways to enhance self-concept in the classroom*. Englewood Cliffs, NJ: Prentice-Hall, Inc., 1976.

## Program Activities for Groups of Older Persons

Burnside, I. *Working With the Elderly: Group Process and Techniques*. MA: Durbury Press, 1978.

Harbert, A., and Ginsberg, L. *Human Services for Older Adults: Concepts and Skills*, New York: Wadsworth Publishing Co., Inc., 1979.

Stabler, N. The Use of Groups In Day Centers For Older Adults. *Social Work With Groups*, Vol. 4(3/4), Fall 1981, 49–58.

Toseland, Ron, and Coppola, Mary. *A Task-Centered Approach to Group Work with the Elderly*, in A. Fortune, *Task-Centered Practice with Families and Groups*. New York: Springer Publishing Co., Inc., 1984.

Toseland, R. Group problem solving with the elderly. In Sheldon Rose (Ed.) *A casebook in group therapy*. Englewood Cliffs, NJ: Prentice-Hall, Inc., 1978, 66–82.

Weiner, M., Brok, A., and Snadowsky, A. *Working with the Aged: Practical Approaches in the Institution and Community*. Englewood Cliffs, NJ: Prentice-Hall, Inc., 1978.

# Bibliography

Abels, P. Instructed advocacy and community group work. In A. Alissi (Ed.). *Prospectives on social group work practice*. New York: The Free Press, 1980, 326–331.

Addams, J. *The spirit of youth and the city streets*. New York: Macmillan Publishing Co., Inc., 1909.

Addams, J. *Twenty years at Hull House*, New York: Macmillan Publishing Co., Inc., 1926.

Alberti, R., and Emmons, M. *Your perfect right* (2nd ed.). San Luis Obispo, CA: Impact Press, 1974.

Alissi, A. Social Group work: Commitments and perspectives. In A. Alissi (Ed.). *Perspectives on social group work practice*. New York: The Free Press, 1980, 5–35.

Allport, F. *Social psychology*. Boston: Houghton Mifflin Company, 1924.

American Association of Group Workers. *Toward professional standards*. New York: Association Press, 1947.

Anderson, J. Social work practice with groups in the generic base of social work practice. *Social Work with Groups*, 1979, *2*(4), 281–293.

Anderson, J. *Social work methods and processes*. New York: Wadsworth Publishing Co., Inc., 1981.

Argyris, C. Organizational learning and management information systems. *Accounting, Organizations and Society*, 1977, *2*, 113–123.

Aronson, H., and Overall, B. Therapeutic expectations of patients in two social classes. *Social Work*, 1966, *11*, 35–41.

Asch, P. An experimental investigation of group influences. *Preventive and Social Psychiatry*. Symposium presented at Walter Reed Army Institute of Research, Washington, DC, 1957.

Bachman, J., Bowers, D., and Marcus, P. Bases of supervisory power: A comparative study in five organizational settings. In S. Tannenbaum (Ed.). *Control In organization*. New York: McGraw-Hill Book Company, 1968.

Back, K. Influence through social communication. *Journal of Abnormal and Social Psychology*, 1951, *46*, 9–23.

Bales, R. *Interaction process analysis: A method for the study of small groups.* Reading, MA: Addison-Wesley Publishing Co., Inc., 1950.

Bales, R. In conference. *Harvard Business Review*, 1954, *32*, 44–50.

Bales, R. How people interact in conference. *Scientific American*, 1955, *192*, 31–35.

Bales, R. *SYMLOG case study kit.* New York: The Free Press, 1980.

Bales, R., Cohen, S., and Williamson, S. *SYMLOG: A system for the multiple level observation of groups.* New York: The Free Press, 1979.

Balgopal, P. and Vassil, T. *Groups in social work: An ecological perspective.* New York: Macmillan Publishing Co., Inc., 1983.

Bandura, A. *Principles of behavior modification.* New York: Holt, Rinehart and Winston, 1969.

Bandura, A. Self-efficacy: Toward a unifying theory of behavioral change. *Psychological Review*, 1977(a), *84*(2), 191–215.

Bandura, A. *Social learning theory.* Englewood Cliffs, NJ: Prentice-Hall, Inc., 1977(b).

Barker, L. *Groups in process: An introduction to small group communication.* Englewood Cliffs, NJ: Prentice-Hall, Inc., 1979.

Bates, P. *The effects of interpersonal skills training on the acquisition and generalization of interpersonal communication behaviors by moderately mildly retarded adults.* Unpublished doctoral dissertation, Madison, WI: University of Wisconsin, 1978.

Bavelas, A. Communications patterns in task-oriented groups. *Journal of the Acoustical Society of America*, 1950, *22*, 725–730.

Bayless, O. An alternative pattern for problem solving discussion. *Journal of Communication*, 1967, *17*, 188–197.

Beck, A. *Cognitive therapy on emotional disorders.* New York: International Universities Press, 1976.

Beck, A., Rush, A., Shaw, B., and Emery, G. *Cognitive therapy of depression.* New York: Guilford Press, 1979.

Beck, D., and Jones, M. *Progress on family problems.* New York: Family Service Association of America, 1973.

Becker, G. and McClintock, G. Value: Behavioral decision theory. *Annual Review of Psychology*, 1967, *18*, 239–286.

Becker, W. *Parents are teachers.* Champaign, IL: Research Press, 1971.

Bednar, K., and Kaul, T. Experimental group research: Current perspectives. In A. Garfield and A. Bergen (Eds.). *Handbook of psychotherapy and behavior change* (2nd ed.). New York: John Wiley & Sons, Inc., 1978, 769–816.

Bell, J. *Family therapy.* New York: Jason Aronson, 1975.

Bell, J. The small group perspective: Family group-therapy. In E. Tolson and W. Reid (Eds.). *Models of family treatment.* New York: Columbia University Press, 1981, 33–51.

Benne, K., and Sheats, P. Functional roles of group members. *Journal of Social Issues*, 1948, *4*(2).

Bennis, W., Benne, K., and Chin, R. (Eds.). *The planning of change.* New York: Holt, Rinehart and Winston, 1969.

Berger, R. *Interpersonal skill training with institutionalized elderly patients.* Unpublished doctoral dissertation, Madison, WI: University of Wisconsin, 1976.

Berne, E. *Transactional analysis in psychotherapy.* New York: Ballantine Books, 1961.

Berne, E. *The structure and dynamics of organization and groups.* Philadelphia: J. B. Lippincott Company, 1963.

Bernstein, D., and Borkovec, T. *Progressive relaxation training: A manual for the helping professions.* Champaign, IL: Research Press, 1973.

Bernstein, S. Conflict in group work. In S. Bernstein (Ed.). *Explanations in group work.* Boston: Charles River Books, 1976, 72–106.

Bertcher, H., and Maple, F. *Creating groups.* Beverly Hills, CA: Sage Publications, 1977.

Bertcher, H., and Maple, F. Elements and issues in group composition. In P. Glasser, R. Sarri, and R. Vinter (Eds.), *Individual change through small groups.* New York: The Free Press, 1974, 186–208.

Bertcher, H. *Group participation: Techniques for leaders and members.* Beverly Hills, CA: Sage Publications, 1979.

Bieri, J. Analyzing stimulus information in social judgments. In S. Messick and J. Ross (Eds.). *Measurement in personality and cognition.* New York: John Wiley & Sons, Inc., 1962.

Bieri, J., Atkins, A., Briar, S., Leanan, R., Miller, H., and Tripodi, T. *Clinical and social judgment.* New York: John Wiley & Sons, Inc., 1966.

Bion, W. *Experiences in groups and other papers.* New York: Basic Books, Inc., Publishers, 1959.

Blatner, H. *Acting-In.* New York: Springer Publishing Co., Inc., 1973.

Blau, P. *Exchange and power in social life.* New York: John Wiley & Sons, Inc., 1964.

Blazer, D. Techniques for communicating with your elderly patient. *Geriatrics*, 1978, *33*(11), 79–84.

Bloom, B., and Broder, L. *Problem-solving processes of college students.* Chicago: University of Chicago Press, 1950.

Bloom, M., and Fisher, J. *Evaluating practice: Guidelines for the accountable professional.* Englewood, NJ: Prentice-Hall, Inc., 1982.

Boatman, F. *Caseworkers' judgments of clients' hope: Some correlates among client-situation characteristics and among workers' communication patterns.* Unpublished doctoral dissertation. New York: Columbia University, 1975.

Bouchard, T. A comparison of two group brainstorming procedures. *Journal of Applied Psycholooy*, 1972(a), *56*, 418–421.

Bouchard, T. Training, motivation and personality as determinants of the effectiveness of brainstorming groups and individuals. *Journal of Applied Psychology*, 1972(b), *56*, 324–331.

Bowers, D., and Franklin, J. *Survey-guided development: Data-based organizational change.* Ann Arbor, MI: Institute for Social Research, 1976.

Bowman, L. Dictatorship, democracy, and group work in America. *Proceedings of the National Conference of Social Work.* Chicago: University of Chicago Press, 1935.

Boyd, N. Group work experiments in state institutions in Illinois. In *Proceedings of the National Conference of Social Work*, 1935. Chicago: University of Chicago Press, 1935, 344.

Boyd, N. Play as a means of social adjustment. In J. Lieberman (Ed.). *New trends in group work.* New York: Association Press, 1938, 210–220.

Brackett, J. *The charity organization movement: Its tendency and its duty.* New Haven, CT: Proceedings of the 22nd National Conference of Charities and Corrections, 1895.

Bradford, L., and Corey, S. Improving large group meetings. *Adult Education*, 1951, *1*, 122–137.

Bradford, L. *Making meetings work: A guide for leaders and group members.* La Jolla, CA: University Associates, 1976.

Bradford, L., Stock, D., and Horowitz, M. How to diagnose group problems. *Adult Leadership*, 1953, *2*(7), 12–19.

Brager, G., and Holloway, A. *Changing human service organizations: Politics and practice.* New York: The Free Press, 1978.

Brammer, L. *The helping relationship: Process and skills.* Englewood Cliffs, NJ: Prentice-Hall, Inc., 1979.

Brieland, D. *An experimental study of the selection of adoptive parents at intake.* New York: Child Welfare League of America, 1959.

Brilhart, J. *Effective group discussion* (2nd ed.) Dubuque, IA: William C. Brown Company, Publishers, 1974.

Brill, N. *Working with people: The helping process.* Philadelphia: J. B. Lippincott Company, 1973.

Brill, N. *Team-work: Working together in the human services.* Philadelphia: J. B. Lippincott Company, 1976.

Brown, I. Working towards goals. *Adult Leadership*, 1952, *1*(4), 13–20.

Browning, L. Diagnosing teams in organizational settings. *Group and Organization Studies*, 1977, *2*(2), 187–197.

Browning, R., and Stover, D. *Behavior modification in child treatment.* Chicago: Aldine Publishing Company, 1971.

Brunswick, E. Organismic achievement and environmental probability. *Psychological Review*, 1943, *50*, 255–272.

Bunker, D., and Dalton, G. The comparative effectiveness of groups and individuals in solving problems. In J. Lorsch and P. Lawrence (Eds.). *Managing group and intergroup relations.* Homewood, Dorsey Press, 1972.

Burke, R. Methods of resolving superior-subordinate conflict: The constructive use of subordinate differences and disagreements. *Organizational Behavior and Human Performance*, 1970, *5*, 393–411.

Buros, O. *Mental measurements yearbook* (Vol. 7). Highland Park, NJ: The Gryphon Press, 1966.

Butler, H., Davis, I., and Kukkonen, R. The logic of case comparison. *Social Work Research and Abstracts*, 1979, *15*(3), 3–11.

Cabral, R., Beso, J., and Paton, A. Patients and observer's assessments of process and outcome in group therapy: A follow-up study. *The American Journal of Psychiatry*, 1975, *132*, 1052–1054.

Campbell, D., and Cook, T. *Quasi-experimentation: Design and analysis for field settings.* Skokie, IL: Rand McNally & Company, 1979.

Campbell, J. Individual versus group problem solving in an industrial sample. *Journal of Applied Psychology*, 1968, *52*, 205–210.

Carlock, C., and Martin, P. Sex composition and the intensive group experience. *Social Work*, 1977, *22*(1), 27–32.

Carnes, W. *Effective meetings for busy people.* New York: McGraw-Hill Book Company, 1980.

Cartwright, D. Achieving change in people. *Human relations*, 1951, *4*, 381–392.

Cartwright, D. The nature of group cohesiveness. In D. Cartwright and A. Zander (Eds.). *Group dynamics: Research and theory* (3rd ed.). New York: Harper & Row, Publishers, 1968, 91–109.

Cartwright, D., and Lippitt, R. Group dynamics and the individual. In W. Bennis and R. Chin (Eds.). *The Planning of Change.* New York: Holt, Rinehart and Winston, 1961.

Cartwright, D., and Zander, A. (Eds.). *Group dynamics: Research and theory* (3rd ed.). New York: Harper & Row, Publishers, 1968.

Chung, K., and Ferris, M. An inquiry of the nominal group process. *Academy of Management Journal*, 1971, *14*, 520–524.

Clark, C. H. *Brainstorming*. New York: Doubleday & Company, Inc., 1958.

Clark, K. *Evaluation of a group social skills training program with psychiatric inpatients: Training Vietnam era veterans in assertion, heterosexual dating, and job interview skills*. Unpublished doctoral dissertation, University of Wisconsin-Madison, 1971.

Collaros, R., and Anderson, L. Effects of perceived expertness upon creativity of members of brainstorming groups. *Journal of Applied Psychology*, 1969, *53*(2), part 1, 159–164.

Collins, A., and Pancoast, D. C. *Natural helping networks: A strategy for prevention*. Washington, DC: National Association of Social Workers, 1970.

Collins, B., and Guetzkow, H. *A social psychology of group processes for decision making*. New York: John Wiley & Sons, Inc., 1964.

Collins, B., and Raven, B. Group structure: Attraction, coalition, communication and power. In G. Lindzey and E. Aronson (Eds.). *The handbook of social psychology* (2nd ed., Vol. 4). Reading, MA: Addison Wesley Publishing Co., Inc., 1969.

Compton, B., and Galaway, B. *Social work processes*. Homewood, IL: Dorsey Press, 1979.

Cooley, C. *Social organization*. New York: Charles Scribner's Sons, 1909.

Cone, J., and Hawkins, R. (Eds.). *Behavioral assessment: New directions in clinical psychology*. New York: Brunner/Mazel, 1977.

Coons, W. Interaction and insight in group psychotherapy. *Canadian Journal of Psychology*, 1957, *11*, 1–8.

Cooper, L. Co-therapy relationships in groups. *Small Group Behavior*, 1976, 473–498.

Corey, G., and Corey, M. *Groups: process and practice*. Monterey, CA: Brooks/Cole Publishing Company, 1977.

Corsini, R. *Roleplaying in psychotherapy*. Chicago: Aldine Publishing Company, 1966.

Cowger, C. Social group work educators: Factors associated with literature preferences. *Social Work with Groups*, 1980, *3*, 87–94.

Cox, F., Erlich, J., Rothman, J., and Tropman, J. (Eds.). *Strategies of community organization*. Itaska, IL: F. E. Peacock Publishers, 1974.

Cox, F., Erlich, J., Rothman, J., and Tropman, J. (Eds.). *Tactics and techniques of community practice*. Itaska, IL: F. E. Peacock Publishers, Inc., 1977.

Coyle, G. *Social process in organized groups*. New York: Richard Smith, Inc., 1930.

Coyle, G. Group work and social change. In *Proceedings of the National Conference of Social Work, 1935*. Chicago: University of Chicago Press, 1935, 393.

Coyle, G. *Studies in group behavior*. New York: Harper & Row, Publishers, 1937.

Craig, T., Huffine, C., and Brooks, M. Completion of referral to psychiatric services by inner-city residents. *Archives of General Psychiatry*, *31*(3) 1974, 353–357.

Crano, W., and Brewer, M. *Principles of research in social psychology*. New York: McGraw-Hill Book Company, 1973.

Croxton, T. The therapeutic contract in social treatment. In P. Glasser, R. Sarri, and R. Vinter (Eds.). *Individual change through small groups*. New York: The Free Press, 1974.

Davis, F., and Lohr, N. Special problems with the use of co-therapists in group psychotherapy. *International Journal of Group Psychotherapy*, 1971, *21*, 143–158.

Davis, G., Manske, M., and Train, A. An instructional method of increasing originality. *Psychonomic Science*, 1966, *6*, 73–74.

Davis, I. Advice-giving in parent counseling. *Social Casework*, 1975, *56*, 343–347.

Davis, J., Laughlin, P., and Komorita, S. The social psychology of small groups:

Cooperative and mixed-motive interaction. *Annual Review of Psychology*, 1976, *27*, 501–541.

DeBono, E. *New think: The use of lateral thinking in the generation of new ideas.* New York: Basic Books, Inc., Publishers, 1968.

DeBono, E. *Lateral thinking for management.* New York: American Management Associations, Inc., 1971.

DeBono, E. *Lateral thinking: Productivity step by step.* New York: Harper & Row, Publishers, 1972.

DeLange, J. *Effectiveness of systematic desensitization and assertive training with women.* Doctoral dissertation, Madison, WI: University of Wisconsin, 1977.

Delbecq, A. The management of decision making within the firm: Three strategies for three types of decision making. *Academy of Management Journal*, 1967, *10*, 329–339.

Delbecq, A., Van de Ven, A., and Gustafson, D. *Group techniques for program planning: A guide to nominal group and delphi processes.* Glenview, IL: Scott, Foresman and Company, 1975.

Deutsch, M. *The resolution of conflict.* New Haven, CT: Yale University Press, 1973.

Dinkmeyer, D., and McKay, G. *Systematic Training for effective parenting.* Circle Pine, MN: American Guidance Service, 1982.

Dinkmeyer, D., and Muro, J. *Group counseling: Theory and practice* (2nd ed.). Itaska, IL: F. E. Peacock Publishers, 1979.

Dion, K., Miller, N., and Magnan, M. Cohesiveness and social responsibility as determinants of risk taking. *Proceedings of the American Psychological Association*, 1970, *5*(1), 335–336.

Dollard, J., and Miller, N. *Personality and psychotherapy.* New York: McGraw-Hill Book Company, 1950.

Douglas, T. *Group processes in social work: A theoretical synthesis.* New York: John Wiley & Sons, Inc., 1979.

Draper, B. Black language as an adaptive response to the hostile environment. In C. Germain (Ed.). *Social work practice.* New York: Columbia University Press, 1979, 267–281.

Drum, D., and Knott, J. *Structured groups for facilitating development: Acquiring life skills, resolving life themes and making life transitions.* New York: Human Science Press, 1977.

DuCarnes, A., and Gobin, A. *The interdisciplinary health care team: A handbook.* Rockville, MD: Aspin Publishers, 1974.

Dunnette, M., Campbell, J., and Joastad, K. The effect of group participation on brainstorming effectiveness for two industrial samples. *Journal of Applied Psychology*, 1963, *47*, 30–37.

D'Zurilla, T., and Goldfried, M. Problem solving and behavior modification. *Journal of Abnormal Psychology*, 1971, *78*, 107–126.

Ebbesen, E., and Bowers, R. Proportion of risky to conservative arguments in a group discussion and choice shift. *Journal of Personality and Social Psychology*, 1974, *29*, 316–327.

Edleson, J. Teaching children to resolve conflict: A group approach. *Social Work*, 1981, *26*(6), 488–494.

Edelson, J., Miller, D., and Stone, G. *Counselling men who batter: Group leader's handbook.* Albany, NY: School of Social Welfare, 1983.

Edson, J. How to survive on a committee. *Social Work*, 1977, *22*, 224–226.

Edwards, W. Behavioral decision theory. *Annual Review of Psychology*, 1961, *1*, 473–498.

Edwards, W. How to use multiattribute utility measurement for social decision making. *IEEE Transactions on Systems, Man and Cybernetics*, 1977, *7*, 326–340.

Edwards, W., Lindman, H., and Phillips, L. Emerging technologies for decision making. In T. Newcomb (Ed.). *New directions in psychology*. New York: Holt, Rinehart and Winston, 1965.

Egan, G. *The skilled helper*. Monterey, CA: Brooks/Cole Publishing Company, 1975.

Egan, G. *Interpersonal living*. New York: Wadsworth Publishing Co., Inc., 1976.

Eisenhart, C. The Assumptions Underlying the Analysis of Variance. In R. Kirk (Ed.) *Statististical issues*. Monterey, CA: Brooks/Cole Publishing Company, 1972, 226–240.

Elliott, H. *Process of group thinking*. New York: Association Press, 1928.

Ellis, A. *Reason and emotion in psychotherapy*. Secaucus, NJ: Lyle Stuart Publishers, 1962.

Epstein, I., and Tripodi, T. *Research techniques for program planning, monitoring, and evaluation*. New York: Columbia University Press, 1977.

Etcheverry, R., Siporin, M., and Toseland, R. The uses and abuses of role playing. In P. Glasser and N. Mayadas (Eds.), *Group workers at work: Theory and practice in the 1980's*. Littlefield, Adams, and Company, in press.

Etzioni, A. *A comparative analysis of complex organizations on power, involvement and their correlates*. New York: The Free Press, 1961.

Etzioni, A. *The active society: A theory of societal and political processes*. New York: The Free Press, 1968.

Ewalt, P., and Kutz, J. An examination of advice giving as a therapeutic intervention. *Smith College Studies in Social Work*, 1976, *47*, 3–19.

Fairweather, R. *Methods for experimental social intervention*. New York: John Wiley & Sons, Inc., 1967.

Feldman, R., and Caplinger, T. Social work experience and client behavior change: A multivariate analysis of process and outcome. *Journal of Social Service Research*, 1977, *1*(1), 5–33.

Feldman, R., Caplinger, T., and Wodarski, J. *The St. Louis conundrum: The effective treatment of antisocial youth*. Englewood Cliffs, NJ: Prentice-Hall, Inc., 1983.

Feldman, R., and Wodarski, J. *Contemporary approaches to group treatment: Traditional, behavior modification and group-centered*. San Francisco, CA: Jossey-Bass, 1975.

Festinger, L. Informal social communication. *Psychological Review*, 1950, *57*, 271–282.

Fiedler, R. *A theory of leadership effectiveness*. New York: McGraw-Hill Book Company, 1967.

Filley, A. *Interpersonal conflict resolution*. Glenview, IL: Scott, Foresman and Company, 1974.

Fischer, G. When oracles fail—A comparison of four procedures for aggregating subjective probability forecasts. *Organizational Behavior and Human Performance*, 1981, *28*, 94–110.

Fish, J. *Placebo therapy*. San Francisco, CA: Jossey-Bass, 1973.

Fisher, J. *Effective casework practice: An eclectic approach*. New York: McGraw-Hill Book Company, 1978.

Fisher, J., and Gochros, H. L. *Planned behavior change: Behavior modification for social work*. New York: The Free Press, 1975.

Flowers, J. Behavior analysis of group therapy and a model for behavioral group therapy. In D. Upper and S. Ross (Eds.). *Behavioral group therapy, 1979: An annual review*. Champaign, IL: Research Press, 1979, 5–37.

Fortune, A. Communication in task-centered treatment. *Social Work*, 1979, *24*, 390–397.

Fortune, A. (Ed.). *Task-centered practice with families and groups*. New York: Springer Publishing Co., Inc., in press.

Fox, E., Nelson, M., and Bolman, W. The termination process: A neglected dimension in social work. *Social Work*, 1969, *14*(4), 53–63.

Frank, J. *Persuasion and healing: A comparative study of psychotherapy*. New York: Schocken Books, Inc., 1961.

Freedman, B. *An analysis of social behavioral skill deficits in delinquent and undelinquent adolescent boys*. Doctoral dissertation, Madison, WI: University of Wisconsin, 1974.

French, J., and Raven, B. The bases of social power. In D. Cartwright (Ed.). *Studies in social power*. Ann Arbor, MI: Institute for Research, University of Michigan, 1959.

Freud, S. *Group psychology and the analysis of the ego*. London: The International Psychoanalytic Press, 1922.

Galinsky, M., and Schopler, J. Warning: Groups may be dangerous. *Social Work*, 1977, *22*(2), 89–94.

Galinsky, M., and Schopler, J. Structuring co-leadership in social work training. *Social Work with Groups*. 1980, *3*(4), 51–63.

Garfield, S. Research on client variables in psychotherapy. In A. Garfield and A. Bergin (Eds.). *Handbook of psychotherapy and behavior change*. New York: John Wiley & Sons, Inc., 1978.

Garland, J., and Kolodny, R. Characteristics and resolution of scapegoating. *Social Work Practice*. New York: Columbia University Press, 1967.

Garland, J., Jones, H., and Kolodny, R. A model of stages of group development in social work groups. In S. Bernstein (Ed.). *Explorations in Group Work*. Boston: Charles River Books, 1976, 17–71.

Garvin, C. *Contemporary group work*. Englewood Cliffs, NJ: Prentice-Hall, Inc., 1981.

Garvin, C. D., and Glasser, P. H. Social group work: The preventive and rehabilitative approach. *The Encyclopedia of Social Work*. New York: National Association of Social Workers, 1971, 1263–1272.

Garvin, C., Reid, W., and Epstein, L. A task-centered approach. In R. Roberts and H. Northen (Eds.). *Theories of social work with groups*. New York: Columbia University Press, 1976, 238–267.

Garwick, G. *Guideline for goal attainment scaling*. Minneapolis: Program Evaluation Project, 1974.

Gazda, G., and Mobley, J. INDS-CAL multidimensional scaling. *Journal of Group Psychotherapy, Psychodrama and Sociometry*, 1981, *34*, 54–72.

Germain, C., and Gitterman, A. *The life model of social work practice*. New York: Columbia University Press, 1980.

Gibb, J. Defensive communication. *The Journal of Communication*, 1961, *11*, 141–148.

Gibb, C. Leadership. In G. Lindzey and E. Aronson (Eds.). *The handbook of social psychology* (Vol. 4). Reading, MA: Addison-Wesley Publishing Co., Inc., 1969.

Gilbert, N., Miller, H., and Specht, H. *An introduction to social work practice*. Englewood Cliffs, NJ: Prentice-Hall, Inc., 1980.

Giordano, J. *Ethnicity and mental health*. New York: Institute of Human Relations, 1973.

Gitterman, A., and Schaeffer, A. The white professional and the black client. *Social Casework*, 1972, *53*(5), 280–291.

Glasser, P., Sarri, R., and Vinter, R. (Eds.). *Individual change through small groups*. New York: The Free Press, 1974.

Goldfried, M., and D'Zurilla, T. A behavioral-analytic model for assessing competence. In C. D. Spielberger (Ed.). *Current topics in clinical and community psychology* (Vol. 1). New York: Academic Press, Inc., 1969, 151–196.

Goldsmith, J., and McFall, R. Development and evaluation of an interpersonal skill training program for psychiatric inpatients. *Journal of Abnormal Psychology*, 1975, *84*, 51–58.

Goldstein, A. *Structured learning therapy.* Elmsford, NY: Pergamon Press, Inc., 1973.

Goldstein, A., Keller, K., and Sechrest, L. *Psychotherapy and the psychology of behavior change.* New York: John Wiley & Sons, Inc., 1966.

Goodman, G. An experiment with companionship therapy: College students and troubled boys—assumptions, selections and design. In B. G. Guerney (Ed.). *Psychotherapeutic agents: New roles for non-professionals, parents and teachers.* New York: Holt, Rinehart and Winston, 1969, 121–128.

Gordon, T. P.E.T. New York: Plume Books, 1975.

Gordon, W. *Synectics: The development of creative capacity.* New York: Harper & Row, Publishers, 1961.

Gottman, J., and Leiblum, S. *How to do psychotherapy and how to evaluate it.* New York: Holt, Rinehart and Winston, 1974.

Gouran, D. *Making decisions in groups: Consequences & choices.* Glenview, IL: Scott, Foresman and Company, 1982.

Gray, G. Points of emphasis in teaching parliamentary procedure. *The Speech Teacher*, 1964, *13*, 10–15.

Grinnell, R. Environmental modification: Casework's concern or casework's neglect. *Social Service Review*, 1973, *47*(2), 208–220.

Guetzkow, H., and Gyr, J. An analysis of conflict in decision-making groups. *Human Relations*, 1954, 7, 368–381.

Gulley, H. *Discussion, conference and group process* (2nd ed.). New York: Holt, Rinehart and Winston, 1968.

Hackman, J., and Morris, C. Group tasks, group interaction process and group performance effectiveness: A review and proposed integration. In L. Berkowitz (Ed.). *Advances in experimental and social psychology* (Vol. 8). New York: Academic Press, Inc., 1975.

Haley, J. *Uncommon therapy: The psychiatric techniques of Milton H. Erickson, M.D.* New York: W. W. Norton & Company, Inc., 1973.

Halpin, A. *Theory and research in administration.* New York: Macmillan Publishing Co., Inc., 1961.

Hammond, K., McClelland, G., and Mumpower, J. *Human judgment and decision making: Theories, methods and procedures.* New York: Praeger Publishers, Inc., 1980.

Hammond, L., and Goldman, M. Competition and non-competition and its relationship to individuals' non-productivity. *Sociometry*, 1961, *24*, 46–60.

Hare, A. *Handbook of small group research* (2nd ed.). New York: The Free Press, 1976.

Harnack, R., and Fest, T. *Group discussion: Theory and technique.* New York: Appleton-Century-Crofts, 1964.

Hartford, M. (Ed.). *Working papers toward a frame of reference for social group work.* New York: National Association of Social Workers, 1962(a).

Hartford, M. *The social group worker and group formation.* Unpublished doctoral dissertation, University of Chicago, School of Social Service Administration, 1962(b).

Hartford, M. Frame of reference for social group work. *Papers toward a frame of reference for social group work.* New York: National Association of Social Workers, 1964.

Hartford, M. *Groups in Social Work*. New York: Columbia University Press, 1971.

Hartford, M. Groups in the human services: Some facts and fancies. *Social Work with Groups*, 1978, *1*(1), 7–13.

Hasenfeld, Y. Organizational factors in services to groups. In P. Glasser, R. Sarri, and R. Vinter (Eds.). *Individual change through small groups*. New York: The Free Press, 1974, 307–322.

Health Services Research Group. Development of an index of medical underservedness. *Health Service Research*, 1975, *10*, 168–180.

Heap, K. *Process and action in work with groups*. Elmsford, NY: Pergamon Press, Inc., 1979.

Hemphill, J. *Group dimensions: A manual for their measurement*. Columbus, Ohio: Monographs of the Bureau of Business Research, Ohio State University, 1956, *87*.

Henley, N. *Body politics*. Englewood Cliffs, NJ: Prentice-Hall, Inc., 1977.

Henry, S. *Group skills in social work: A four-dimensional approach*. Itaska, IL: F. E. Peacock, 1981.

Hersen, M., and Bellack, A. *Behavioral assessment: A practical handbook*. Elmsford, NY: Pergamon Press, Inc., 1976.

Hersey, R., and Blanchard, K. *Management of organizational behavior: Utilizing human resources* (3rd ed.). Englewood Cliffs, NJ: Prentice-Hall, Inc., 1977.

Hersey, R., Blanchard, K., and Natemeyer, W. Situational leadership, perception and the impact of power. *Group and Organization Studies*, 1979, *4*(4), 418–428.

Herzog, J. Communication between co-leaders: Fact or Myth. *Social Work with Groups*, 1980, *3*(4), 19–29.

Hill, W. Hill interaction matrix (HIM): The conceptual framework, derived rating scales, and an updated bibliography. *Small Group Behavior*, 1977, *8*(3), 251–268.

Hirschowitz, R. Small-group methods in the promotion of change within interagency networks: Leadership models. In A. Jacobs and W. Spradlin (Eds.). *The group as agent of change*. New York: Behavioral Publications, 1974, 228–251,

Homans, G. *The human group*. New York: Harcourt Brace Jovanovich, Inc., 1950.

Homans, G. *Social behavior: Its elementary forms*. New York: Harcourt Brace Jovanovich, Inc., 1961.

Houle, C. *The effective board*. New York: Association Press, 1960.

Howard, J. *Please touch*. New York: McGraw-Hill Book Company, 1970.

Huber, G. *Managerial decision making*. Glenview, IL: Scott, Foresman and Company, 1980.

Hudson, W. *The clinical measurement package*. Homewood, IL: Dorsey Press, 1982.

Huff, F., and Prantianida, T. The effect of group size on information transmitted. *Psychodynamic Science*, 1968, *11*(10), 365–366.

Hunt, W., Barnett, L., and Branch, L. Relapse rates in addiction programs. *Journal of Clinical Psychology*, 1971, *27*(4), 455–456.

Ivancevich, J., and Donnelly, G. Leader influence and performance. *Personnel Psychology*, 1970, *23*(4), 539–549.

Jamieson, D., and Thomas, K. Power and conflict in the student-teacher relationship. *Journal of Applied Behavioral Science*, 1974, *10*(3), 321–336.

Janis, I. *Victims of group think*. Boston: Houghton Mifflin Company, 1972.

Janis, I., and Mann, L. *Decision making: A psychological analysis of conflict, choice and commitment*. New York: The Free Press, 1977.

Jay, A. How to run a meeting. In F. Cox, J. Erlich, J. Rothman, and J. Tropman (Eds.). *Tactics and techniques of community practice*. Itaska, IL: F. E. Peacock, 1977, 255–269.

Jayaratne, S., and Levy, R. *Empirical clinical practice*. New York: Columbia University Press, 1979.

Jennings, H. Leadership and sociometric choice. *Sociometry* (10), 1947, 32–49.

Jennings, H. *Leadership and isolation* (2nd ed.). New York: Longman, Inc., 1950.

Johnson, C. Planning for termination of the group. In P. Glasser, R. Sarri, and R. Vinter (Eds.). *Individual change through small groups*. New York: The Free Press, 1974.

Johnson, J. *Doing field research*. New York: The Free Press, 1975.

Kadushin, A. *The social work interview*. New York: Columbia University Press, 1972.

Kane, R. Look to the record. *Social Work*, 1974, *19*, 412–419.

Kane, R. The interprofessional team as a small group. *Social Work in Health Care*, 1975, *1*(1), 19–32.

Kane, R. Teams: Thoughts from the bleachers. *Health and Social Work*, 1976, *18*, 52–59.

Kanfer, F. and Goldstein, A. (Eds.). *Helping people change*. Elmsford, NY: Pergamon Press, Inc., 1975.

Kart, G., Metress, E., and Metress, J. *Aging and health*. Reading, MA: Addison-Wesley Publishing Co., Inc., 1978.

Kelley, H. Communication in experimentally created hierarchies. *Human Relations*, 1951, *4*, 39–56.

Kelley, H., and Stakelski, A. Errors in perception of intentions in a mixed-motive game. *Journal of Experimental Social Psychology*, 1970, *6*, 379–400.

Kelley, H., and Thibaut, J. Group problem solving. In G. Lindzey and E. Aronim (Eds.). *Handbook of social psychology* (2nd ed., Vol. 10). Reading, MA: Addison Wesley Publishing Co., Inc., 1969.

Kelly, G. *The psychology of personal constructs*. New York: W. W. Norton & Company, Inc., 1955.

Kephart, M. A quantitative analysis of intragroup relationships. *American Journal of Sociology*, 1951, *60*, 544–549.

Kiesler, S. *Interpersonal processes in groups and organizations*. Arlington Heights, IL: AHM Publishing Co., 1978.

Kiresuk, T., and Sherman, R. Goal attainment scaling: A general method for evaluating comprehensive community mental health programs. *Community Mental Health Journal*, 1968, *4*(6), 443–453.

Klein, A. *Society, democracy and the group*. New York: Whiteside, Inc., 1953.

Klein, A. *Role Playing*. New York: Association Press, 1956.

Klein, A. *Social work through group process*. Albany, NY: School of Social Welfare, State University of New York at Albany, 1970.

Klein, A. *Effective group work*. New York: Association Press, 1972.

Kolodny, R. The dilemma of co-leadership. *Social Work with Groups*, 1980, *3*(4), 31–34.

Konopka, G. *Therapeutic group work with children*. Minneapolis: University of Minnesota Press, 1949.

Konopka, G. *Group work in the institution*. New York: Association Press, 1954.

Konopka, G. *Social group work: A helping process*. Englewood Cliffs, NJ: Prentice-Hall, Inc., 1963.

Kristein, M. "How much can business expect to earn from smoking cessation?" Paper presented at the Conference of the National Interagency Council on Smoking and Health, Chicago, IL, January 9, 1980, 1–11.

Kurland, R. Planning: The neglected component of group development. *Social Work with Groups*, 1978, 1, 173–178.

Kurland, R. Group formulation: A guide to the development of successful groups.

Albany, NY: Social Welfare Continuing Education Program, Monograph No. 3, 1982.

Lang, N. A broad range model of practice in the social work group. *Social Service Review*, 1972, *46*(1), 76–84.

Lang, N. A comparative examination of therapeutic uses of groups in social work and in adjacent human service professions: Part I—The literature from 1955–1968. *Social Work with Groups*, *2*(2), 1979(a), 101–116.

Lang, N. A comparative examination of the therapeutic uses of groups in social work and in adjacent human service professions: Part II—The literature from 1967–1978. *Social Work with Groups*, *2*(3), 1979(b), 197–220.

Lacoursiere, R. B. *The life cycle of groups: Group developmental stage theory*. New York: Human Sciences Press, 1980.

Larsen, J., and Mitchell, C. Task-centered, strength-oriented group work with delinquents. *Social Casework*, 1980, *61*(3), 154–163.

Lauffer, A. *Grantsmanship*. Beverly Hills, CA: Sage Publications, 1977.

Lauffer, A. *Social planning at the community level*. Englewood Cliffs, NJ: Prentice-Hall, Inc., 1978.

Lazarus, A. *Behavior therapy and beyond*. New York: McGraw-Hill Book Company, 1971.

League of Women Voters Educational Fund. How to plan an environmental conference. In F. Cox, J. Erlich, J. Rothman, and J. Tropman (Eds.). *Tactics and techniques of community practice*. Itaska, IL: F. E. Peacock Publishers, Inc., 1977, 111–152.

Leavitt, H. Some effects of certain communication patterns on group performance. *Journal of Abnormal and Social Psychology*, 1951, *46*, 39–56.

LeBon, G. *The crowd: A study of the popular mind*. London: George Allen & Unwin Ltd., 1910.

Levine, B. *Group psychotherapy: Practice and development*. Englewood Cliffs, NJ: Prentice-Hall, Inc., 1979.

Levine, B. Co-leadership approach to learning group work. *Social Work with Groups*, 1980, *3*(4), 35–38.

Levinson, H. Termination of psychotherapy: Some salient issues. *Social Casework*, 1977, *58*(8), 480–489.

Levitt, J., and Reid, W. Rapid assessment instruments for social work practice. *Social Work Research and Abstracts*, 1981, *17*(1), 13–20.

Lewin, K. Behavior as a function of the total situation. In L. Carmichael (Ed.). *Manual of Child Psychology*. New York: John Wiley & Sons, Inc., 1946, 791–844.

Lewin, K. Frontiers in group dynamics. *Human Relations*, 1947, *1*, 2–38.

Lewin, K. *Resolving social conflict*. New York: Harper & Row, Publishers, 1948.

Lewin, K. *Field theory in social science*. New York: Harper & Row, Publishers, 1951.

Lewin, K., and Lippitt, R. An experimental approach to the study of autocracy and democracy: A preliminary note. *Sociometry*, 1938, *1*, 292–300.

Lewin, K., Lippitt, R., and White, R. Patterns of aggressive behavior in experimentally created "social climates." *Journal of Social Psychology*, 1939, *10*, 271–299.

Lewis, B. An examination of the final phase of a group development theory. *Small Group Behavior*, 1978, *9*, 507–517.

Lewis, R., and Ho, M. Social work with native Americans. In A. Morales and B. Sheafor (Eds.). *Social Work: A practice of many faces*. Boston: Allyn & Bacon, Inc., 1977, 193–204.

Lieberman, M. Reinforcement of cohesiveness in group therapy. *Archives of General Psychiatry*, 1971, *25*, 168–177.

Lieberman, M. Groups for personal change: New and not-so-new forms. In D. Freedman and J. Dyrad (Eds.). *American handbook of psychiatry*. New York: Basic Books, Inc., Publishers, 1975.

Lieberman, M. Change induction in small groups. *Annual Review of Psychology*, 1976, *27*, 217–250.

Lieberman, M., and Borman, L. (Eds.). *Self-help groups for coping with crisis*. San Francisco, CA: Jossey-Bass, 1979.

Lieberman, M., Yalom, I., and Miles, M. *Encounter groups: First facts*. New York: Basic Books, Inc., Publishers, 1973.

Likert, R. *New patterns of management*. New York: McGraw-Hill Book Company, 1961.

Likert, R. *The human organization*. New York: McGraw-Hill Book Company, 1967.

Lippitt, R. Group dynamics and the individual. *International Journal of Psychotherapy*, 1957, 7(10), 86–102.

Lowe, J., and Herranen, M. Conflict in teamwork: Understanding roles and relationships. *Social Work in Health Care*, 1978, *3*, 323–330.

MacLennon, B. Co-therapy. *International Journal of Group Psychotherapy*, 1965, *15*, 154–166.

Mahler, C. *Group counseling in the schools*. Boston: Houghton Mifflin Company, 1969.

Mahoney, M. *Cognition and behavior modification*. Cambridge, MA: Ballinger Publishing Co., 1974.

Maier, N. *Problem-solving discussions and conferences: Leadership methods and skills*. New York: McGraw-Hill Book Company, 1963.

Maier, N., and Hoffman, L. Quality of first and second solutions in group problem solving. *Journal of Applied Psychology*, 1960, *44*, 278–283.

Maier, N., Solem, A., and Maier, A. *The role-play technique*. LaJolla, CA: University Associates, 1975.

Maier, N., and Zerfoss, L. MRP: A technique for training large groups of supervisors and its potential use in social research. *Human Relations*, 1952, *5*, 177–186.

Maloney, S. *Development of group work education in social work schools in U.S.*, Ph.D. dissertation, School of Applied Social Science, Case Western Reserve University, 1963.

Maltzman, I., Simon, S., Raskin, D., and Licht, L. Experimental studies in the training of originality. *Psychological Monographs*, 1960, *7*, Whole No. 493.

Maluccio, A. *Learning from clients*. New York: The Free Press, 1979.

Maple, F. *Shared decision making*. Beverly Hills, CA: Sage Publications, 1977.

Maultsby, M. *Help yourself to happiness*. New York: Rational Living, 1975.

Maultsby, M., and Carpenter, L. *The rational self-counseling coursebook: The ABC's of more personal happiness*. Lexington, KY: University of Kentucky Press, 1980.

Mayer, J., and Timms, N. *The client speaks: Working class impressions of casework*. New York: Atherton Press, 1970.

McCaskill, J. *Theory and practice of group work*. New York: Association Press, 1930.

McDougall, W. *The group mind*. New York: G. P. Putnam's Sons, 1920.

McGee, T., and Schuman, B. The nature of the co-therapy relationship. *International Journal of Group Psychotherapy*, 1970, *20*, 25–36.

McLaughlin, R., White, E., and Byfield, B. Modes of interpersonal feedback and leadership structure in six small groups. *Nursing Research*, 1974, *23*(4), 207–318.

Meichenbaum, D. *Cognitive-behavior modification: An integrative approach*. New York: Plenum Publishing Corporation, 1977.

Melnick, J. *Risk, responsibility, and structure: A conceptual framework for initiating group work*. Paper presented at the American Psychological Association Convention, New Orleans, 1974.

Meltzoff, J., and Kornreich, M. *Research in psychotherapy*. New York: Atherton Press, 1970.

Middleman, R. *The non-verbal method in working with groups*. New York: Association Press, 1968.

Middleman, R. Returning group process to group work. *Social Work with Groups*, 1978, *1*(1), 15–26.

Middleman, R. The use of program: Review and update. *Social Work with Groups*, 1980, *3*(3), 5–23.

Miller, H., and Tripodi, T. Information accrual and clinical judgment. *Social Work*, 1967, *12*(3), 63–69.

Miller, S., Nunnally, E., and Wackman, D. *The Minnesota couples communication program couples handbook*. Minneapolis, MN: Minnesota Couple Communication Program, 1972.

Mills, T. *The sociology of small groups*. Englewood Cliffs, NJ: Prentice-Hall, Inc., 1967.

Miner, F. A comparative analysis of three diverse group decision making approaches. *Academy of Management Journal*, 1979, *22*, 81–93.

Morales, A., and Sheafor, B. *Social work: A profession of many faces*. Boston: Allyn & Bacon, Inc., 1977.

Moreno, J. *Who shall survive?* Washington, D.C.: Nervous and Mental Diseases Publishing Co., 1934.

Moreno, J. *Psychodrama* (Vol. 1). Boston: Beacon Press, 1946.

Mullen, E. The relationship between diagnosis and treatment in casework. *Social Casework*, 1969, *50*, 218–226.

Mullen, E. *Evaluating social work effectiveness in a turbulent world*. Paper presented at the Seventh NASW Symposium, Philadelphia, November 18–21, 1981, 1–27.

Munzer, J., and Greenwald, H. Interaction process analysis of a therapy group. *International Journal of Group Psychotherapy*, 1957, *7*, 175–190.

Murphy, M. The social group work method in social work education. In W. Boehm (Ed.). *Project report of the curriculum study*. New York: Council of Social Work Education, 1959.

Myers, D., and Arenson, S. Enhancement of the dominant risk in group discussion. *Psychological Reports*, 1972, *30*, 615–623.

Nadler, D. *Feedback and organizational development: Using data base methods*. Reading, MA: Addison-Wesley Publishing Co., Inc., 1977.

Nadler, D. The effects of feedback on task group behavior: A review of the experimental research. *Organizational Behavior and Human Performance*, 1979, *23*, 309–338.

Napier, H. Individual versus group learning: Note on task variable. *Psychological Reports*, 1967, *23*, 757–758.

Napier, R., and Gershenfeld, M. *Groups: theory and experience* (2nd ed.). Boston: Houghton Mifflin Company, 1981.

Newcomb, T. The prediction of interpersonal attraction. *American Psychologist*, 1956, *2*, 575–586.

Nixon, H. *The small group*. Englewood Cliffs, NJ: Prentice-Hall, Inc., 1979.

Northen, H. *Social work with groups*. New York: Columbia University Press, 1969.

Northen, H. *Clinical social work*. New York: Columbia University Press, 1982.

Northen, H., and Roberts, R. The status of theory. In R. Roberts and H. Northen (Eds.). *Theories of social work with groups*. New York: Columbia University Press, 1976, 386–387.

Novaco, R. *Anger control: The development and evaluation of an experimental treatment.* Massachusetts: Lexington Books, 1975.

Olmsted, M. *The small group.* New York: Random House, Inc., 1959.

Olsen, M. *The process of social organization.* New York: Holt, Rinehart and Winston, 1968.

Orlinsky, D., and Howard, K. The relation of process to outcome in psychotherapy. In S. Garfield and A. Bergin (Eds.). *Handbook of psychotherapy and behavior change.* New York: John Wiley & Sons, Inc., 1978.

Osborn, A. *Applied imagination: Principles and procedures of creative problem solving* (3rd ed.). New York: Charles Scribner's Sons, 1963.

Osgood, C., Suci, C., and Tannenbaum, P. *The measurement of meaning.* Urbana, IL: University of Illinois Press, 1957.

Oxley, G., Wilson, S., Anderson, J., and Wong, G. Peer-led groups in graduate education. *Social Work with Groups,* 1979, *1*, 67–75.

Papell, C., and Rothman, B. Social group work models: Possession and heritage. In A. Alissi (ed.). *Perspectives on social group work practice.* New York: The Free Press, 1980(a).

Papell, C., and Rothman, B. Relating the mainstream model of social work with groups to group psychotherapy and the structured group approach. *Social Work with Groups,* 1980(b), *3*(2), 5–22.

Parloff, M. Therapist-patient relationships and outcome of psychotherapy. *Journal of Consulting Psychology,* 1961, *25*, 29–38.

Parloff, M. Waskow, I., and Wolfe, B. Research on therapist variables in relation to process and outcome. In S. Garfield and A. Bergin (Eds.). *Handbook of psychotherapy and behavior change.* New York: John Wiley & Sons, Inc., 1978.

Parnes, S. *Creative behavior guidebook.* New York: Charles Scribner's Sons, 1967.

Parnes, S., and Harding, H. (Eds.). *A sourcebook for creative thinking.* New York: Charles Scribner's Sons, 1962.

Parsons, T. *The social system.* New York: The Free Press, 1951.

Parsons, T., Bales, R., and Shils, E. (Eds.). *Working papers in the theory of action.* New York: The Free Press, 1953.

Parsons, T., and Shils, E. (Eds.). *Toward a general theory of action.* Cambridge, MA: Harvard University Press, 1951.

Patti, R. Organizational resistance and change: The view from below. *Social Service Review,* 1974, *48*(3), 367–383.

Pepitone, A., and Reichling, G. Group cohesiveness and the expression of hostility. *Human Relations,* 1955, *8*, 327–337.

Perlman, H. The problem-solving method in social casework. In R. Roberts and R. Nee (Eds.). *Theories of social casework.* University of Chicago Press, 1970, 129–180.

Peterson, J. The interface of institution and group process. In A. Jacobs and W. Spradlin (Eds.). *The group as agent of change.* New York: Behavioral Publications, 1974, 5–17.

Pfeiffer, J., and Jones, J. *The annual handbook for group facilitators.* La Jolla, CA: University Associates, 1962–1982.

Phillips, H. *The essentials of group work skills.* New York: Association Press, 1951.

Phillips, J. Report on discussion 66. *Adult Education Journal,* 1948, *7*, 181–182.

Pincus, A., and Minahan, A. *Social work practice: Model and method.* Itaska, IL: F. E. Peacock Publishers, Inc., 1973.

Pinkus, H. *Casework techniques related to selected characteristics of clients and workers.* Unpublished doctoral dissertation, Columbia University Press, 1968.

Piper, W., Montvila, R., and McGihon, A. Process analysis in therapy groups: A behavior sampling technique with many potential uses. In D. Upper & S. Ross

(Eds.). *Behavior group therapy, 1979: An annual review.* Champaign, IL: Research Press, 1979, 55–70.

Polansky, N. (Ed.). *Social work research.* Chicago: University of Chicago Press, 1960.

Polansky, N. *Integrated ego psychology.* Chicago: Aldine Publishing Company, 1982, Chapter 13.

Prince, G. *The practice of creativity.* New York: Harper & Row, Publishers, 1970.

Rahaim, S., Lefebvre, C., and Jenkins, T. The effects of social skills training on behavioral and cognitive components of anger management. *Journal of Behavior Therapy and Experimental Psychiatry*, 1980, *5*, 3–8.

Redl, F. Group emotion and leadership. *Psychiatry*, 1942, *5*, 573–596.

Redl, F. Diagnostic group work. *American Journal of Orthopsychiatry*, 1944, *14*(1), 53–67.

Reid, K. *From character building to social treatment: The history of the use of groups in social work.* Westport, CT: Greenwood Press, 1981.

Reid, W. J. *The task-centered system.* New York: Columbia University Press, 1978.

Reid, W., and Epstein, L. *Task-centered casework.* New York: Columbia University Press, 1972.

Reid, W., and Hanrahan, P. Recent evaluations of social work: Grounds for optimism. *Social Work*, 1982, *27*(4), 328–340.

Reid, W., and Shapiro, B. Client reactions to advice. *Social Service Review*, 1969, *43*, 165–173.

Reid, W., and Shyne, A. *Brief and extended casework.* New York: Columbia University Press, 1969.

Resnick, H., and Patti, R. (Eds.). *Change from within: Humanizing social welfare organizations.* Philadelphia: Temple University Press, 1980.

Richards, T. *Problem solving through creative analysis.* New York: John Wiley & Sons, Inc., 1974.

Richmond, M. *Social diagnosis.* New York: Russell Sage Foundation, 1917.

Rimm, D., and Masters, J. *Behavior Therapy.* New York: Academic Press, Inc., 1974.

Rivas, R., and Toseland, R. The student group leadership evaluation project: A study of group leadership skills. *Social Work with Groups*, 1981, *4*(3/4), pp. 159–175.

Robert, H. *Robert's rules of order.* Glenview, IL: Scott, Foresman and Company, 1970.

Roberts, R., and Northen, H. (Eds.). *Theories of social work with groups.* New York: Columbia University Press, 1976.

Robinson, J., and Shaver, P. (Eds.). *Measures of social psychological attitude* (2nd ed.). Ann Arbor, MI: Institute for Social Research, University of Michigan Press, 1973.

Roethlisberger, F. *Management and morale.* Cambridge, MA: Harvard University Press, 1941.

Roethlisberger, F., and Dickson, W. *Management and the worker.* Cambridge, MA: Harvard University Press, 1939.

Roethlisberger, F., and Dickson, W. A fair day's work. In P. V. Crosbie (Ed.). *Interaction in small groups.* New York: Macmillan Publishing Co., Inc., 1975, 85–94.

Rohrbaugh, J. Improving the quality of group judgment: Social judgment analysis and the delphi technique. *Organizational Behavior and Human Performance*, 1979, *24*, 73–92.

Rohrbaugh, J. Improving the quality of group judgment: Social judgment analysis and the nominal group technique. *Organizational Behavior and Human Performance*, 1981, *26*, 272–288.

Rohrbaugh, J. Making decisions about staffing standards: An analytical approach to human resource planning in health administration. In L. Nigro (Ed.). *Decision making for public administration.* New York: Marcel Dekker, Inc., in press.

Rohrbaugh, J., and Harmon, J. *Social judgment analysis: Methodology for improving interpersonal communication and understanding.* Paper presented at the 89th Annual Convention of the American Psychological Association, Los Angeles, August 1981.

Rokeach, M. *Beliefs, attitudes and values: A theory of organization and change.* San Francisco, CA: Jossey Bass, 1968.

Rose, S. *Treating children in groups.* San Francisco, CA: Jossey-Bass, 1974.

Rose, S. *Group therapy: A behavioral approach.* Englewood Cliffs, NJ: Prentice-Hall, Inc., 1977.

Rose, S. (Ed.). *A casebook in group therapy.* Englewood Cliffs, NJ: Prentice-Hall, Inc., 1980.

Rose, S. Assessment in groups. *Social Work Research and Abstracts*, 1981, *17*(1), 29–37.

Rose, S., Cayner, J., and Edleson, J. Measuring interpersonal competence. *Social Work*, 1977, *22*(2), 125–129.

Rose, S., and Hanusa, D. *Parenting skill role play test.* Interpersonal skill training and research project, Madison, WI: University of Wisconsin, 1980.

Rosenblatt, A. The application of role concepts to the intake process. *Social Casework*, 1962, *43*(1), 8–14.

Rosenthal, L. *Behavioral analysis of social skills in adolescent girls.* Unpublished doctoral dissertation, Madison, WI: University of Wisconsin, 1978.

Rossi, P., Freeman, H., and Wright, S. *Evaluation: A systematic approach.* Beverly Hills, CA: Sage Publishers, 1979.

Rothman, J. *Planning and organizing for social change: Action principles for social science research.* New York: Columbia University Press, 1974.

Rotter, G., and Portugal, S. Group and individual effects in problem solving. *Journal of Applied Psychology*, 1969, *53*, 338–341.

Ryder, E. A functional approach. In R. Roberts and H. Northen (Eds.). *Theories of social work with groups.* New York: Columbia University Press, 1976, 153–170.

Sage, P., Olmsted, D., and Atlesk, F. Predicting maintenance of membership in small groups. *Journal of Abnormal and Social Psychology*, 1955, *51*, 308–331.

Sarri, R. Behavioral theory and group work. In P. Glasser, R. Sarri, and R. Vinter (Eds.). *Individual change through small groups.* New York: The Free Press, 1974.

Sarri, R., and Galinsky, M. A conceptual framework for group development. In P. Glasser, R. Sarri, and R. Vinter (Eds.). *Individual change through small groups.* New York: Macmillan Publishing Co., Inc., 1974.

Sarri, R., Galinsky, M., Glasser, P., Siegel, S., and Vinter, R. Diagnosis in group work. In R. D. Vinter (Ed.). *Readings in group work practice.* Ann Arbor, MI: Campus Publishing, 1967.

Stattler, W., and Miller, N. *Discussion and conference* (2nd ed.). Englewood Cliffs, NJ: Prentice-Hall, Inc., 1968.

Schachter, S. *The psychology of affiliation.* Stanford, CA: Stanford University Press, 1959.

Scheidel, T., and Crowell, L. *Discussing and deciding: A deskbook for group leaders and members.* New York: Macmillan Publishing Co., Inc., 1979.

Schinke, S., Blythe, B., Gilchrist, L., and Smith, T. Developing intake-interviewing skills. *Social Work Research and Abstracts*, 1980, *16*(4), 29–34.

Schinke, S., and Rose, S. Interpersonal skill training in groups. *Journal of Counseling Psychology*, 1976, *23*, 442–448.

Schlenoff, M., and Busa, S. Student and field instructor as group co-therapists: Equalizing an unequal relationship. *Journal of Education for Social Work*, 1981, *17*, 29–35.

Schopler, J., and Galinsky, M. Goals in social group work practice: Formulation, implementation and evaluation. In P. Glasser, R. Sarri, and R. Vinter (Eds.). *Individual change through small groups*. New York: The Free Press, 1974, 126–148.

Schopler, J., and Galinsky, M. When groups go wrong. *Social Work*, 1981, *26*(5), 424–429.

Schutz, W. *Joy: Expanding human awareness*. New York: Grove Press, Inc., 1967.

Schwartz, W. The social worker in the group. *The Social Welfare Forum*. New York: Columbia University Press, 1961.

Schwartz, W. Discussion of three papers on the group method with clients, foster families, and adoptive families. *Child Welfare*, 1966, *45*(10), 571–575.

Schwartz, W. On the use of groups in social work practice. In W. Schwartz and S. Zalba (Eds.). *The practice of group work*. New York: Columbia University Press, 1971, 3–24.

Schwartz, W. The social worker in the group. In R. W. Klenk and R. M. Ryan (Eds.). *The practice of social work*. New York: Wadsworth Publishing Co., Inc., 1974.

Schwartz, W. Between client and system: The mediating function. In R. Roberts and H. Northen (Eds.). *Theories of social work with groups*. New York: Columbia University Press, 1976, 171–197.

Schwartz, W. *The group work tradition and social work practice*. Paper presented at Rutgers University, School of Social Work, New Brunswick, NJ, April 1981, 1–33.

Schwartz, W., and Zalba, S. *The practice of group work*. New York: Columbia University Press, 1971.

Seaberg, J., and Gillespie, D. Goal attainment scaling: A critique. *Social Work Research and Abstracts*, 1977, *13*(2), 4–9.

Seashore, S. *Group cohesiveness in the industrial work group*. Ann Arbor, MI: Survey Research Center, Institute for Social Research, University of Michigan, 1954.

Seligman, M. *Helplessness: On depression, development, and death*. San Francisco: W. H. Freeman and Company, Publishers, 1975.

Selltiz, C., Wrightsman, L., and Cook, S. *Research methods in social relations* (3rd ed.). New York: Holt, Rinehart and Winston, 1976.

Shaw, C. *The jack roller*. Chicago: University of Chicago Press, 1930.

Shaw, M. Communication networks. In L. Berkowitz (Ed.). *Advances in experimental social psychology* (Vol. 1). New York: Academic Press, Inc., 1964.

Shaw, M. *Group dynamics: The psychology of small group behavior*. New York: McGraw-Hill Book Company, 1976.

Shaw, M. and others. *Role-playing*. LaJolla, CA: University Associates, 1980.

Shelly, M., and Bryan, G. (Eds.). *Human judgment and optimality*. New York: John Wiley & Sons, Inc., 1964.

Shepard, C. *Small groups: Some sociological perspectives*. San Francisco, CA: Chandler Publishing Co., 1964.

Sherif, M. *The psychology of social norms*. New York: Harper & Row, Publishers, 1936.

Sherif, M. Experiments in group conflict. *Scientific American, 1956, 5*, (195), 54–58.

Sherif, M., and Sherif, C. *Groups in harmony and tension: An introduction of studies in group relations.* New York: Harper & Row, Publishers, 1953.

Sherif, M., and Sherif, C. *Social Psychology.* New York: Harper & Row, Publishers, 1969.

Sherif, M. White, J., and Harvey, O. Status in experimentally produced groups. *American Journal of Sociology*, 1955, *60*, 370–379.

Shils, E. Primary groups in the American army. In R. Merton and P. Lazarsfeld (Eds.). *Continuities in social research.* New York: The Free Press, 1950.

Shipley, R., and Boudewyns, P. Flooding and implosive therapy: Are they harmful? *Behavior Therapy*, 1980, *11*(4), 503–508.

Shulman, L. A study of practice skills. *Social Work*, 1978, *23*(4), 274–280.

Shulman, L. *The skills of helping individuals and groups.* Itaska, IL: F. E. Peacock Publishers, 1979.

Shulman, L. *Identifying, measuring and teaching helping skills.* New York: C.S.W.E. and C.A.S.S.W., 1981.

Siporin, M. Situational assessment and intervention. *Social Casework*, 1972, *53*(2), 91–109.

Siporin, M. *Introduction to social work practice.* New York: Macmillan Publishing Co., Inc., 1975.

Siporin, M. Ecological system theory in social work. *Journal of Sociology and Social Work*, 1980(a), *7*, 507–532.

Siporin, M. *Group membership and experience: Older insights and current needs.* Paper presented at the Second Symposium of Social Work with Groups, Arlington, Texas, November 1980(b), 1–24.

Slavson, S. R. *Creative group education.* New York: Association Press, 1945.

Slavson, S. R. *Recreation and the total personality.* New York: Association Press, 1946.

Smith, A. Group play in a hospital environment. In *Proceedings of the National Conference of Social Work*, 1935. Chicago: University of Chicago Press, 1935, 372–373.

Smith, M. *Value clarification.* LaJolla, CA: University Associates, 1977.

Smith, P. Group work as a process of social influence. In N. McCaughan (Ed.). *Group work: Learning and practice.* London: George Allen and Unwin Ltd., 1978, 36–57.

Somers, M. Problem-solving in small groups. In R. Roberts and H. Northen (Eds.). *Theories of social work with groups.* New York: Columbia University Press, 1976.

Spergel, I. *Street gang work.* Reading, MA: Addison-Wesley Publishing Co., Inc., 1966.

Spergel, I. *Community problem solving.* Chicago: University of Chicago Press, 1969.

Spivak, G., and Spotts, J. *Devereaux behavior rating scale.* Devon, PA: Devereaux Foundation, 1966.

Stanley, J., and Hopkins, K. *Educational and psychological measurement and evaluation.* Englewood Cliffs, NJ: Prentice-Hall, Inc., 1972.

Starak, Y. Co-leadership: A new look at sharing group work. *Social Work with Groups*, 1981, *4*(3/4), 145–157.

Steiner, C. (Ed.). *Readings in radical psychiatry.* New York: Grove Press, Inc., 1975.

Steiner, I. *Group process and productivity.* New York: Academic Press, Inc., 1972.

Stogdill, R. *Handbook of leadership.* New York: The Free Press, 1974.

Stokes, T., and Baer, D. An implicit technology of generalization. *Journal of Applied Behavior Analysis*, 1977, *10*(2), 349–367.

Stoner, J. *A comparison of individual and group decision including risk.* Masters Thesis, School of Industrial Management, MIT, Cambridge, Mass., 1961.

Stoner, J. Risky and cautious shifts in group decisions: The influence of widely held values. *Journal of Experimental Social Psychology*, 1968, *4*, 442–459.

Stotland, E. *The psychology of hope.* San Francisco, CA: Jossey-Bass, 1969.

Stouffer, S. *The American soldier, combat and its aftermath.* Princeton, NJ: Princeton University Press, 1949.

Strauss, B., and Strauss, F. *New ways to better meetings.* New York: The Viking Press, Inc., 1952.

Stuart, R. *Trick or treatment: Who and when psychotherapy facts.* Champaign, IL: Research Press, 1970.

Stuart, R. (Ed.). *Behavioral self-management: Strategies, techniques, and outcomes.* New York: Brunner Mazel Publications, 1977.

Stuart, R., and Davis, B. *Slim chance in a fat world.* Champaign, IL: Research Press, 1972.

Sundel, M., Radin, N., and Churchill, S. Diagnosis in group work. In P. Glasser, R. Sarri, and R. Vinter (Eds.). *Individual change through small groups.* New York: The Free Press, 1974.

Swanson, A. *The determinative team: A handbook for board members of voluntary organizations.* New York: Exposition Press, 1978.

Tannenbaum, R., and Schmidt, W. How to choose a leadership pattern. In Lorsch, J., and Lawrence, P. (Eds.). *Managing groups and intergroup relations.* Homewood, IL: Dorsey Press, 1972.

Taylor, D., Berry, P., and Block, C. Does group participation when using brainstorming facilitate or inhibit creative thinking? *Administrative Science Quarterly*, 1958, *3*, 23–47.

Taylor, R. Group management. *Transactions of the American Society of Mechanical Engineers*, *24*, 1903, 1337–1480.

Teger, A. and Pruitt, D. Components of group risk-taking. *Journal of Experimental Psychology*, 1967, *3*, 189–205.

Thelen, H. *Dynamics of groups at work.* Chicago: University of Chicago Press, 1954.

Thibaut, J., and Kelley, H. Experimental studies of group problem-solving process. In G. Kindzey (Ed.). *Handbook of social psychology* (Vol. 2). Reading, MA: Addison-Wesley Publishing Co., Inc., 1954, 735–785.

Thibaut, J. and Kelley, H. *The social psychology of groups.* New York: John Wiley & Sons, Inc., 1959.

Thomas, E. Uses of research methods in interpersonal practice. In N. Polansky (Ed.). *Social work research.* Chicago: University of Chicago Press, 1975.

Thomas, E. Generating innovation in social work: the paradigm of developmental research. *Journal of Social Services Research*, 1978, *2*(1), 95–115.

Thoresen, C., and Mahoney, M. *Behavioral self-control.* New York: Holt, Rinehart and Winston, 1974.

Thorndike, R. On what type of task will a group do well? *Journal of Abnormal and Social Psychology*, 1938, *33*, 409–413.

Thrasher, F. *The gang.* Chicago: University of Chicago Press, 1927.

Tolman, E. *Purposive behavior in animals and men.* New York: Appleton-Century-Crofts, 1932.

Tolman, E., and Brunswick, E. The organism and the causal texture of the environment. *Psychological Review*, 1935, *42*, 43–77.

Tompkins, R., and Gallo, R. Social group work: A model for goal formulation. *Small Group Behavior*, 1978, *9*(3), 307–317.

Torrance, E. Group decision making and disagreement. *Social Forces*, 1957, *35*, 314–318.

Toseland, R. Group versus individual decision-making: An experimental analysis. Paper presented at the Group Work Symposium, October 1983, 1–17.

Toseland, R. Increasing access: Outreach methods in social work practice. *Social Casework*, 1981(a), *62*(4), 227–234.

Toseland, R. Choosing an appropriate research method. In R. Grinnell. *Social Work Research and Evaluation*. Itaska, IL: Peacock Publishers, 1981(b).

Toseland, R. Group problem solving with the elderly. In S. Rose (Ed.). *A casebook in group therapy, a behavioral-cognitive approach*. Englewood Cliffs, NJ: Prentice-Hall, Inc., 1980, 66–84.

Toseland, R. A problem-solving workshop for older persons. *Social Work*, 1977, *22*(4), 325–327.

Toseland, R., and Coppola, M. A task-centered approach to group work with the elderly. In A. Fortune. *Task-Centered Practice with Families and Groups*. New York: Springer Publishing Co., Inc., 1984.

Toseland, R., Decker, J., and Bliesner, J. A community program for socially isolated older persons. *Journal of Gerontological Social Work*, 1979, *1*(3), 211–224.

Toseland, R., and Hacker, L. Self-help and professional social work. *Social Work*, 1982, *27*(4), 341–347.

Toseland, R., and Hacker, L. Professionals and self-help groups. *Social Work*, in press.

Toseland, R., Kabat, D., and Kemp, K. An evaluation of a smoking cessation group program. *Social Work Research and Abstracts*, 1983, 19(1), 12–19.

Toseland, R., Krebs, A., and Vahsen, J. Changing group interaction patterns. *Social Service Research*, 1978, *2*(2), 219–232.

Toseland, R., Palmer-Ganeles, J., and Chapman, D. Teamwork in psychiatric settings. Albany, NY: School of Social Welfare, 1983.

Toseland, R., and Rivas, R. Techniques for working with task groups. *Administration in Social Work*, in press.

Toseland, R., Rivas, R., and Chapman, D. An evaluation of decision making in groups. *Social Work*, in press.

Toseland, R., and Rose, S. Evaluating social skills training for older adults in groups. *Social Work Research and Abstracts*, 1978, *14*(1), 25–33.

Toseland, R., Sherman, E., and Bliven, S. The comparative effectiveness of two group work approaches for the evaluation of mutual support groups among the elderly. *Social Work with Groups*, 1981, *4*(1/2), 137–153.

Toseland, R., and Spielberg, G. The development of helping skills in undergraduate social work education: Model and evaluation. *Journal of Education for Social Work*, 1982, *18*(1), 66–73.

Trecker, H. *Group process in administration*. New York: Women's Press, 1946.

Trecker, H. (Ed.) *Group work in the psychiatric setting*. New York: William Morrow & Co., Inc., 1956.

Trecker, H. *Social group work: Principles and practices*. New York: Association Press, 1972.

Trecker, H. Administration as a group process: Philosophy and concepts. In A. Alissi (Ed.), *Perspectives on social group work practice*. New York: The Free Press, 1980, 332–337.

Triplett, N. The dynamogenic factors in pacemaking and competition. *American Journal of Psychology*, *65*(1), 1898, 93–102.

Tripodi, T., and Miller, H. The clinical judgment process: A review of the literature. *Social Work*, 1966, *11*, 63–69.

Tropman, E. Staffing committees and studies. In F. Cox, J. Erlich, J. Rothmann, and J. Tropman (Eds.). *Tactics and techniques of community practice*. Itaska, IL: F. E. Peacock Publishers, Inc., 1977, 105–111.

Tropman, J. *Effective meetings: Improving group decision-making.* Beverly Hills, CA: Sage Publishing Company, 1980.

Tropman, J., Johnson, H., and Tropman, E. *The essentials of committee management.* Chicago, IL: Nelson-Hall, 1979.

Tropp, E. The group in life and in social work. *Social Casework*, 1968, *49*, 267–274.

Tropp, E. A developmental theory. In R. Roberts and H. Northen (Eds.). *Theories of social work with groups.* New York: Columbia University Press, 1976, 198–237.

Trotzer, J. *The counselor and the group: Integrating theory, training and practice.* Monterey, CA: Brooks/Cole Publishing Company, 1977.

Tuckman, B. Developmental sequence in small groups. *Psychological Bulletin*, 1963, *63*, 384–399.

Upper, D., and Cautela, J. (Eds.). *Covert conditioning.* Elmsford, NY: Pergamon Press, Inc., 1982.

Van De Ven, A. *Group decision making and effectiveness: An experimental study.* Ohio: Kent State University Press, 1974.

Van De Ven, A., and Delbecq, A. Nominal versus interacting group processes for committee decision-making effectiveness. *Academy of Management Journal*, 1971, *9*, 203–212.

Vinter, R. (Ed.). *Readings in group work practice.* Ann Arbor, MI: Campus Pub., 1967.

Vinter, R. The essential components of social group work practice. In P. Glasser, R. Sarri, and R. Vinter (Eds.). *Individual change through small groups.* New York: The Free Press, 1974(a), 9–33.

Vinter, R. Program activities: An analysis of their effects on participant behavior. In P. Glasser, R. Sarri, and R. Vinter (Eds.). *Individual change through small groups.* New York: The Free Press, 1974(b), 233–243.

Vinter, R., and Galinsky, M. Extra group relations and approaches. In P. Glasser, R. Sarri, and R. Vinter (Eds.). *Individual change through small groups.* New York: The Free Press, 1974, 281–291.

Vroom, V. H. Industrial social psychology. In G. Lindsey and E. Aronson (Eds.). *Handbook of social psychology* (Vol. 5). Reading, MA: Addison-Wesley Publishing Co., Inc., 1969.

Vroom, V. Grant, L., and Cotton, T. The consequence of social interaction in group problem solving. *Journal of Organizational Behavior and Human Performance*, 1969, *4*, 79–95.

Vroom, V., and Yetton, P. *Leadership and decision making.* Pittsburgh: University of Pittsburgh Press, 1973.

Walker, J. *Walker problem behavior identification checklist.* Los Angeles, CA: Western Psychological Services, 1970.

Wallach, M., and Wing, C. Is risk a value? *Journal of Personality and Social Psychology*, 1968, *9*, 101–106.

Walls, R., Werner, T., Bacon, A., and Zane, T. *Behavior checklists in behavioral assessment: New directions in clinical psychology.* New York: Brunner/Mazel, 1977.

Warren, R. *Social change and human purpose: Toward understanding and action.* Skokie, IL: Rand McNally & Company, 1977.

Watts, T. Ethnomethodology. In R. Grinnell (Ed.). *Social work research and evaluation.* Itaska, IL: F. E. Peacock, 1981.

Watzlawick, P., Weakland, J., and Fisch, R. *Change: Principles of problem formation and problem resolution.* New York: W. W. Norton & Company, Inc., 1974.

Wayne, J., and Avery, N. Activities for group termination. *Social Work*, 1979, *24*(1), 58–62.

Weed, L. *Medical records, medical education and patient care: The problem-*

*oriented record as a basic tool.* Ohio: Case Western Reserve University Press, 1969.

Weissman, A. Industrial social services: Linkage technology. *Social Casework* 1976, *57*(1), 50–54.

Weissman, H. (Ed.), *Individual and group services in the mobilization for youth experiment.* New York: Association Press, 1969.

Wells, R. *Planned short-term treatment.* New York: The Free Press, 1982.

Whitaker, D. Some conditions for effective work with groups. *British Journal of Social Work*, 1975, *5*, 423–439.

Whitaker, D., and Lieberman, M. *Psychotherapy through the group process.* New York: Atherton Press, 1964.

Whittaker, J. Models of group development. *Social Service Review*, 1976, *44*, 308–322.

Whittaker, J. Program activities: Their selection and use in a therapeutic milieu. In P. Glasser, R. Sarri, and R. Vinter (Eds.). *Individual change through small groups.* New York: The Free Press, 1974.

Whyte, W. *Street corner society.* Chicago: University of Chicago Press, 1943.

Wilson, G. *The practice of social group work.* New York: Report of the committee on practice, group work section, National Association of Social Workers, 1956.

Wilson, G. From practice to theory: A personalized history. In R. W. Roberts and H. Northen (Eds.). *Theories of social work with groups.* New York: Columbia University Press, 1976.

Wilson, G., and Ryland, G. *Social group work practice.* Boston: Houghton Mifflin Company, 1949.

Wilson, G., and Ryland, G. The social group work method. In A. Alissi (Ed.). *Perspectives on social group work practice.* New York: The Free Press, 1980, 169–182.

Wilson, S. *Informal groups: An intruduction.* Englewood Cliffs, NJ: Prentice-Hall, Inc., 1978.

Wilson, S. *Recording: Working guidelines for social workers.* New York: The Free Press, 1980.

Wise, H. *Making health teams work.* Cambridge, MA: Ballinger Pub. Co., 1974.

Wodarski, J. *The role of research in clinical practice: A practical approach for the human services.* Maryland: University Park Press, 1981.

Wolfe, M., and Proshansky, H. The physical setting as a factor in group function and process. In A. Jacobs and W. Spradlin (Eds.). *The group as agent of change.* New York: Behavioral Publications, 1974.

Wolins, M. The problem of choice in foster home finding. *Social Work*, 1959, *4*(4), 40–48.

Wolpe, J. *The practice of behavior therapy* (2nd ed.). Elmsford, NY: Pergamon Press, I,c., 1973.

Wyss, D. *Psychoanalytic schools: From the beginning to the present.* New York: Jason Aronson, 1973.

Yalom, I. *The theory and practice of group psychotherapy* (2nd ed.). New York: Basic Books, Inc., Publishers, 1975.

Zajonc, R., Wolosin, R., and Wolosin, W. Group risk-taking under various group decision schema. *Journal of Experimental and Social Psychology*, 1972, *8*, 16–30.

Zander, A. *Groups at work.* San Francisco: Jossey-Bass, 1977.

Ziller, R. Four techniques of group decision making under uncertainty. *Journal of Applied Psychology*, 1957, *41*, 384–388.

Zimet, C., and Schneider, C. Effects of group size on interaction in small groups. *Journal of Social Psychology*, 1969, *77*(2), 177–187.

# Name Index

Abels, P., 36
Addams, J., 40, 41
Alberti, R., 339
Alissi, A., 12, 43
Allport, G., 45
American Association of
   Group Workers, 39
Anderson, J., 10, 51, 56, 95
Anderson, L., 259*t*., 283
Arenson, S., 261
Argyris, C., 259
Aronson, H., 103
Asch, P., 45
Atkins, A., 166
Atlesk, F., 66
Avery, N., 340

Bachman, J., 84
Back, K., 65, 66
Bacon, A., 173
Baer, D., 334
Bales, R., 38, 51, 52, 73,
   72*t*., 74, 149, 180, 181,
   182, 311, 325, 326
Balgopal, P., 51
Bandura, A., 48, 49, 205,
   212, 223, 225, 336
Barker, L., 271
Barnett, L., 334
Bates, P., 171
Bavelas, A., 60, 62

Bayless, O., 282
Beck, A., 216, 217
Beck, D., 329
Becker, G., 277
Becker, W., 339
Bednar, K., 56, 78, 86, 92,
   236
Bell, J., 14
Bellack, A., 165, 173
Benne, K., 10, 175
Bennis, W., 10
Berger, R., 171
Berne, E., 47, 141, 339
Bernstein, D., 221
Bernstein, S., 102
Berry, P., 282, 283
Bertcher, H., 114, 115*t*., 125,
   126, 127, 134, 158
Beso, J., 96
Bieri, J., 166
Bion, W., 47
Blanchard, K., 82, 85, 92
Blatner, H., 205, 226, 227,
   230
Blau, P., 50
Blazer, D., 59
Bliesner, J., 14, 65, 153, 232
Bliven, S., 14, 153, 199
Block, C., 282, 283
Bloom, D., 272
Bloom, M., 169, 170, 316
Blythe, B., 95
Boatman, F., 103

Bolman, W., 328
Borman, L., 8, 203, 341
Bouchard, T., 283, 285
Boudewyns, P., 219
Bowers, D., 84, 259
Bowers, R., 261
Bowman, L., 40
Boyd, N., 24, 25, 39, 40
Brackett, J., 39
Bradford, L., 163, 173, 253,
   258, 295
Brager, G., 244, 339
Brammer, L., 95
Branch, L., 334
Brewer, M., 179
Briar, S., 166
Brieland, D., 164
Brilhart, J., 116*t*., 126, 127
Brill, N., 5, 248, 254
Broder, L., 272
Brokovec, T., 221
Brooks, M., 334
Brown, I., 116*t*.
Browning, L., 88, 92
Browning, R., 303
Brunswick, E., 289
Bryan, G., 277
Bunker, D., 79, 89
Burke, R., 262
Buros, O., 173, 324
Busa, S., 107
Butler, H., 318
Byfield, B., 86

377

# Subject Index

Action system, 36–37
Administrative groups, 30–31
Advocate role, 211–12
Agency sponsorship, 119–20, 243–44
Assessment, 11, 162–87
  definition, 162–63
  environment, 183–87
  group as a whole, 173–83, 178n., 179n.,
    181n., 182n.
  group attraction, 179–80
  group communication, 177–79
  group environment, 183–87
  group members, 166–73, 170n.
  link to intervention, 186, 188n.
  membership, 120–21, 168–73
    charting, 169
    logs, diaries, problem cards, 169–70
    reporting by others, 172–73
    self anchored ratings scales, 170
    self observation, 168–69
    standardized instruments, 173
    worker observation, 170, 170n., 171–72
  planning phase, 119–21
  process, 163–66
  sponsorship, 119–20
Attraction to the group, 65–67
  assessment, 179–80
  changing, 239–40
  reducing, 340–41

Beginning phase of group work, 11–12, 141–
  61

objectives, 143
  variations, 146–47
Bond, 60–61
Brainstorming, 280–85
Broker role, 210–11

Closed groups, 128–29
Cognitive imagery, 219–20
Cognitive self-instruction, 218–19
Cohesion, 50, 65–67
Co-leadership, 107–110
Committees, 26–27, 30
Communication, 57–59
  assessment, 177–79
  changing, 237–39
  patterns, 58n.
Composition, 124–30
  demographic characteristics, 129–30
  heterogeneity, 125
  homogeneity, 124
  open vs. closed membership, 128–29
  size, 126–28
Consensus, 50
Contingency management, 232–35
Contracting, 132–34, 157–58
  group procedures, 133, 133n., 134
  member goals, 134–35, 201–202
Cues, 60

Decision making, 260–64
Definition of group work, 12–13, 42
Delegate councils, 31–33